365 Ultimate Broiling Recipes

(365 Ultimate Broiling Recipes - Volume 1)

Linda Crawford

Copyright: Published in the United States by Linda Crawford/ © LINDA CRAWFORD

Published on December, 11 2020

All rights reserved. No part of this publication may be reproduced, stored in retrieval system, copied in any form or by any means, electronic, mechanical, photocopying, recording or otherwise transmitted without written permission from the publisher. Please do not participate in or encourage piracy of this material in any way. You must not circulate this book in any format. LINDA CRAWFORD does not control or direct users' actions and is not responsible for the information or content shared, harm and/or actions of the book readers.

In accordance with the U.S. Copyright Act of 1976, the scanning, uploading and electronic sharing of any part of this book without the permission of the publisher constitute unlawful piracy and theft of the author's intellectual property. If you would like to use material from the book (other than just simply for reviewing the book), prior permission must be obtained by contacting the author at author@thymerecipes.com

Thank you for your support of the author's rights.

Content

365 AWESOME BROILING RECIPES 9

1. "21" Club Burger 9
2. A Smooth And Creamy Pâté 9
3. Alain Ducasse's Gratin Of Blueberries With Vanilla 10
4. Artichoke Heart Frittata 11
5. Asparagus With Red Pepper Sauce 12
6. Baingan Bharta 12
7. Baked Codfish With Spinach And Cheese Sauce 13
8. Baked Endives With Parmesan Cheese (Endives Au Parmesan) 14
9. Baked Mashed Potatoes With Parmesan .. 14
10. Baked Ricotta With Spring Vegetables 15
11. Baked Salmon Fillets With Goat Cheese And Cilantro 15
12. Baked Tapioca Pudding With Cinnamon Sugar Brûlée 16
13. Barbecued Chicken 16
14. Barbecued Pork 17
15. Barbecued Shrimp 18
16. Bass Fillets Broiled With Mustard Mayonnaise 18
17. Bass Steaks In Rosemary Sherry Vinaigrette 19
18. Bass With Truffle Vinaigrette 19
19. Beef Brochettes With Red Peppers And Coriander 19
20. Black Cod Broiled With Miso 20
21. Bombay Leg Of Lamb With Yogurt And Lime 21
22. Boudin Aux Pommes Les Halles 21
23. Braised Melange Of Vegetables Glazed With Parmesan 22
24. Bratwurst With Sauerkraut And Potatoes . 23
25. Broccoli Salad With Hazelnut Romesco 23
26. Broiled Calf's Liver 24
27. Broiled Chicken Breast Salad With Curry Dressing 24
28. Broiled Chicken Breasts With Cayenne And Ginger 25
29. Broiled Chicken With Piquillo Tomato Sauce 26
30. Broiled Cornish Hens With Lemon And Balsamic Vinegar 26
31. Broiled Cornish Hens With Spicy Salt 27
32. Broiled Duck With Orange Glazed Turnips 27
33. Broiled Fennel With Parmesan Cheese 28
34. Broiled Fiery Bluefish 28
35. Broiled Fish Cakes With Ginger And Cilantro 29
36. Broiled Fish Tacos 29
37. Broiled Lamb Chops With Apricots 30
38. Broiled Lobsters With Sichuan Peppercorns 31
39. Broiled Mackerel Fillets With Tomato Caper Sauce 32
40. Broiled Melon With Balsamic 32
41. Broiled Or Grilled Chicken With Coconut And Lime 33
42. Broiled Oysters With Salsa 33
43. Broiled Portobello Mushrooms 34
44. Broiled Sardines With Lemon And Thyme 34
45. Broiled Sea Scallops With Orange Butter Sauce 35
46. Broiled Shrimp With Dried Lime 35
47. Broiled Steak With Pineapple And Onion Salsa 36
48. Broiled Tomatoes 36
49. Broiled Tuna Couscous Salad 37
50. Broiled Veal Chops With Anchovy Butter 38
51. Bruschetta Dinner Salad 38
52. Brussels Sprouts And Potato Gratin With Taleggio 39
53. Buffalo Chicken Dip 39
54. Burnt Passion Fruit Curd 40
55. California Sandwiches 41
56. Canard Grille (Broiled Duck) 41
57. Cannelloni With Bitter Greens And Artichoke Saute 42
58. Caribbean Jerked Pork Tenderloins 43
59. Caribbean Sweet Potato Soup With Gingered Shrimp 44
60. Carrot And Leek Frittata With Tarragon .. 44
61. Celery Root Au Gratin 45
62. Charred Asparagus With Green Garlic Chimichurri 46
63. Charred Lamb And Eggplant With Date

3

Yogurt Chutney 46
63. Cheddar Cheese Crostini 47
64. Cheese Croutons 47
65. Cherry Bread Pudding 48
66. Chick Pea And Pesto Canapes 48
67. Chicken Paved With Tomatoes 49
68. Chicken Roulades With Shrimp 49
69. Chicken Skewers With Peanut Sauce 50
70. Chicken Teriyaki 51
71. Chicken Wings Stuffed With Chevre 52
72. Chicken Wing Salad With Toasted Garlic Vinaigrette 52
73. Chimichurri Hanger Steak 53
74. Chinese Glazed Chicken 53
75. Chipotle Chicken Sausage 54
76. Clam Frittata 54
77. Cleopatra's Caesar Salad 55
78. Colombian Corn And Cheese Arepas 56
79. Composed Salad With Green Olive And Garlic Vinaigrette 57
80. Cool Ziti With Eggplant And Tomatoes .. 57
81. Coquilles St. Jacques Portugaise (Scallops With Peppers And Capers) 58
82. Corn Con Cotija (Courtesy Of Martine Garcia) 59
83. Corn And Green Bean Salad With Tomatillo Dressing 59
84. Corn Seafood Stew With Avocado And Chiles 60
85. Country Omelet 61
86. Crab Meat Au Gratin 61
87. Crab And Spinach Mornay 62
88. Creamy Gruyere Potatoes 63
89. Creamy Mussel Stew With Peas, Fennel And Lemon 63
90. Croque Monsieur With Gruyere Cheese ... 64
91. Crostini With Porcini Butter And Summer Truffles 65
92. Croutons With Parmesan 65
93. Crusty Broiled Cod With Littlenecks And Chouriço 65
94. Cumin Chicken With Black Bean Sauce ... 66
95. Cumin Lamb Meatballs With Tahini Yogurt Dipping Sauce 67
96. Curried Grilled Jumbo Shrimp 67
97. Curried Beef Skewers 68
98. Curry Spiced Lamb Burgers 68

100. Cyrus's Express Bread And Butter Pudding 69
101. Deviled Chicken Thighs 70
102. Easy Party Paella 70
103. Eggplant Parmagiano 72
104. Eggplant And Beef Creole 73
105. Eggplant And Feta With Fusilli 73
106. Eggplant And Tomatoes Au Gratin 74
107. Eggplant, Tomato And Onion Pasta 75
108. Eggs Florentine 75
109. Eggs Kejriwal 76
110. Endives Au Gratin 77
111. Fig Brochettes With Tapioca Cream 77
112. Fillets Of Scrod 78
113. Fillets Of Shad Stuffed With Swiss Chard 78
114. Fish With Cilantro And Garlic 79
115. Flounder In Orange Sauce With Pine Nuts 79
116. Four Seasons Oysters In Champagne Veloute 80
117. Fragrant Citrus Couscous With Pork 81
118. French Crepes 81
119. Frisee Salad With Fish And Chips (Salmon And Seaweed) 82
120. Frittata With Sorrel, Potatoes And Prosciutto 83
121. Frittata With Turnips And Olives 83
122. Frittata With Zucchini, Goat Cheese And Dill 84
123. Gabriella Marriotti's Egg And Eggplant Appetizer 85
124. Garlic Croutons 86
125. Garlicky Steak With Carrot, Walnut And Dill Salad 86
126. Ginger Glazed Loin Lamb Chops 87
127. Glazed Pork 87
128. Gordon Hamersley's Boned Stuffed Leg Of Lamb 88
129. Gratin Of Brussels Sprouts With Parmesan 89
130. Gratin Of Zucchini And Yellow Squash ... 90
131. Green Garlic Toast 90
132. Green Papaya Salad With Shrimp 91
133. Green Pea Guacamole 91
134. Grilled Bread Salad 92
135. Grilled California Goat Cheese On Toast 93
136. Grilled Chicken And Pineapple Salad 93

137. Grilled Chicken Breasts With Turmeric And Lime 94
138. Grilled Chicken Thighs With Sauce Au Chien 95
139. Grilled Chicken Topped With Mixed Melon Salsa 95
140. Grilled Cornish Hens With Pecan Crust ... 96
141. Grilled Duck Legs With Frisee Salad 96
142. Grilled Fish Setubal Style 97
143. Grilled Flank Steak With Worcestershire Butter 98
144. Grilled Goat's Cheese And Eggplant, From Chris Cox 98
145. Grilled Lamb 99
146. Grilled Lamb Fillet 99
147. Grilled Leeks With Romesco Sauce 100
148. Grilled Leg Of Lamb With Mustard Seeds 101
149. Grilled Maple Chicken With Corn Relish 102
150. Grilled Marinated Lamb Brochettes 102
151. Grilled Marinated Quail 103
152. Grilled Moroccan Lamb Sausage 103
153. Grilled Polenta With Chanterelles 104
154. Grilled Pork Satay 105
155. Grilled Quail 105
156. Grilled Quail With Oyster Sauce 106
157. Grilled Quail Wrapped In Grape Leaves On White Bean Salad 107
158. Grilled Salmon With Sage 107
159. Grilled Salmon With Shrimp 108
160. Grilled Sea Scallops (Sign Of The Dove) 109
161. Grilled Seasoned Lamb With Greek Potato Salad 109
162. Grilled Shrimp With Coriander Salsa 110
163. Grilled Shrimp With Oil And Basil Sauce 111
164. Grilled Skewered Sausages 111
165. Grilled Striped Bass With Mango Salsa ... 112
166. Grilled Swordfish With Tomatillo Sauce 112
167. Grilled Tuna With Herbs 113
168. Grilled Tuna With Red Peppers 113
169. Grilled Tuna With Salad 114
170. Grilled Veal Chop Sicilian Style 114
171. Grilled Veal Chops With Morels 115
172. Halibut Steaks With Pesto Sauce 116
173. Halloumi Tzaganaki 116
174. Hamburgers (With Goat Cheese) 117
175. Hamburgers With Garlic And Shallot Butter 117
176. Hard Shell Clams With Parsley Pesto 118
177. Harissa 118
178. Herb Polenta With Red Bell Pepper Sauce 119
179. Herb Crumbed Broiled Tomatoes 120
180. Herb Marinated Chicken Wings Stuffed With Scallion Goat Cheese 120
181. Homemade Merguez 121
182. Huevos Rancheros 121
183. Indoor S'mores 122
184. Iranian Herb And Walnut Frittata 123
185. Italian Wedding Soup With Turkey Meatballs 124
186. Jeremiah Tower's Duck With Endive Salad 124
187. Jerusalem Artichokes Or Sun Chokes Au Gratin (Topinambours Au Gratin) 125
188. Kasu Cod 126
189. Kosher Pot Roast (Brisket) 126
190. Lamb Chops 127
191. Lamb Chops With Red Leicester Potato Cake 127
192. Lamb Chops, Yellow Pepper Tarragon Sauce 128
193. Lamb Medallions With Curry Sauce 128
194. Lamb With Red Wine And Dried Cherries 129
195. Lamb And Red Pepper Fajitas 130
196. Loin Of Pork With Peaches And Apricots 130
197. Macaroni With Cheese 131
198. Macaroni And Beef Casserole 132
199. Maine Coast Lobster Rolls 132
200. Maple Mustard Salmon With Mango 133
201. Marinated Broiled Tuna Steaks With Sauce Nicoise 133
202. Marinated Hamburgers 134
203. Marinated Pork 135
204. Marinated Pork Tenderloin 135
205. Maureen Abood's Eggplant With Lamb, Tomato And Pine Nuts 136
206. Mesclun Salad With Roasted Peppers 137
207. Mexican White Shrimp In Champagne Sauce 137

208. Middle Eastern Inspired Herb And Garlic Chicken 138
209. Miso Broiled Scallops 139
210. Miso Glazed Eggplant 139
211. Miso Glazed Fish 140
212. Mock Eggs Benedict 140
213. Monkfish Rolls 141
214. More Vegetable Than Egg Frittata 142
215. Moroccan Lamb 142
216. Mousse De Poivrons Doux (Red Pepper Mousse) 143
217. Mrs. Sebastiani's Malfatti 143
218. Mushroom Soup Gratinée 144
219. Mussel And Spinach Gratin 145
220. Mustard Marinated Breaded Chicken 146
221. My Pain Catalan With Extra Tomatoes And Goat Cheese 146
222. Naan (Indian Flatbread) 147
223. Napoleon Of Tuna With A Mosaic Salad 148
224. New Potato, Red Pepper And Chive Salad 149
225. Nina Simonds's Broiled Halibut With Miso Glaze 149
226. Ninh Hoah (Skewered Vietnamese Meatballs) 150
227. Oatmeal Crème Brûlée With Almond And Orange 150
228. Olivada 151
229. One Pot French Onion Soup With Garlic Gruyère Croutons 151
230. Orange Glazed Pork 152
231. Oven Baked Tomatoes 153
232. Oven Dried Tomato And Zucchini Salad 153
233. Oysters With Bacon And Horseradish 154
234. Oysters With Miso Glaze 154
235. Paillard Of Portobello Mushroom Glazed With Balsamic Vinegar 155
236. Pan Fried Pizza 156
237. Panqueque 156
238. Panzanella With Grilled Eggplant 157
239. Parmesan Cheese Croutons 157
240. Parmesan Cheese Hard Rolls 158
241. Parsleyed Rack Of Lamb (Carre D'Agneau Persille) 158
242. Pear Gratin With Mascarpone Custard ... 159
243. Pears With Raspberries And Meringue ... 160
244. Penne With Peppers And Cream 161
245. Pepper Pasta With Crab (Fearrington House) 161
246. Pepper Shrimp 162
247. Pepper And Snow Pea Salad 163
248. Pickled Green Beans 163
249. Pineapple Avocado Salsa 164
250. Pineapple Rhubarb Salsa And Shad 164
251. Poached Eggs With Sorrel Sauce 165
252. Poireaux Au Gratin (Leeks Au Gratin) ... 166
253. Polenta With Broccoli Rabe 166
254. Polenta With Vegetables And Tomato Sauce 167
255. Pomegranate Glazed Lamb Meatballs 168
256. Pork Tenderloin With Sweet And Hot Mustard 168
257. Pork With Orange Sauce 169
258. Pork In Sweet Mustard Marinade 169
259. Potato And Onion Frittata 170
260. Potato Onion Frittata 170
261. Potatoes Country Style 171
262. Pressure Cooker Spicy Pork Shoulder 171
263. Pumpkin Creme Brulee 172
264. Pumpkin And Onion Soup 173
265. Puree Of Green Beans Au Gratin 174
266. Quail Roasted In Vine Leaves 174
267. Red Beans And Rice, Louisiana Style 175
268. Red Pepper Puree 176
269. Red Snapper With Sweet And Hot Pepper Sauce 176
270. Restaurant Style Pork Chops 177
271. Rib Steaks With Parsley And Crouton Salad 178
272. Rich Red Wine Vegetable Stew 178
273. Ricotta And Spinach Frittata With Mint 179
274. Rio's Spicy Chicken Wings 180
275. Roast Lamb 181
276. Roasted Asparagus Frittata 181
277. Roasted Asparagus With Crunchy Parmesan Topping 182
278. Roasted Fillet Of Beef With Black Pepper 183
279. Rosh Ha Shanah Pot Roast 183
280. Rum And Chile Roasted Chicken Thighs With Pineapple 184
281. Saffron Sweet Potato And Red Pepper Soup

281. ... 185
282. Salad With Herbs And Warm Goat Cheese 185
283. Salad Of Spiced Lamb, Rice Vermicelli, Coriander And Holy Basil ... 186
284. Salmon Fillet With Thyme And Roasted Tomatoes ... 187
285. Salmon Fillets With Sorrel Sauce ... 187
286. Salmon Fillets With Horseradish Crust, Cucumbers And Salmon Caviar ... 188
287. Salmon Steaks With Orange And Tarragon Sauce ... 188
288. Salmon With Lemon Herb Marinade ... 189
289. Salmon And Olives With Linguine ... 189
290. Salsa Fresca With Kohlrabi ... 190
291. Sausages With Ginger, Star Anise And Soy Sauce ... 190
292. Sausages With Peppers ... 191
293. Savory Bread Pudding ... 191
294. Serious Potato Skins ... 192
295. Sesame Chicken Kebabs With Orange Hoisin Sauce ... 193
296. Sheet Pan Chicken With Apple, Fennel And Onion ... 193
297. Sheet Pan Chicken With Shallots And Grapes ... 194
298. Sheet Pan Gochujang Shrimp And Green Beans ... 195
299. Sheet Pan Shrimp With Tomatoes, Feta And Oregano ... 195
300. Shiitake Crusted Chicken With Spinach Sauce ... 196
301. Shirley Savis's Amendoa Cake ... 197
302. Shortcut Tortilla Soup ... 197
303. Shredded Potato Cake With Egg And Cheese And Bacon ... 198
304. Shu Mai Style Burgers ... 199
305. Skillet Macaroni And Broccoli And Mushrooms And Cheese ... 199
306. Smoky Eggplant Spread ... 200
307. Soft Tacos With Roasted Or Grilled Tomatoes And Squash ... 201
308. Soft Shell Crab Crostini With Arugula Butter ... 202
309. Souffléed Horseradish Oysters ... 202
310. Spanish Tortilla With Mushrooms And Kale 203
311. Spice Rubbed Lamb Skewers With Herb Yogurt Sauce ... 203
312. Spiced Pasta, Avocado And Onion Feta Salad 204
313. Spicy Ecuadorean Shrimp ... 205
314. Spicy Marinated Chicken ... 205
315. Spicy Shrimp Salad With Mint ... 206
316. Spinach And Red Pepper Frittata ... 206
317. Spring Quiche ... 207
318. Squid And Arugula Salad With Sesame Seeds 208
319. Steven Raichlen's Romesco Sauce ... 209
320. Stuffed Clams ... 209
321. Stuffed Peppers (Chiles Rellenos) ... 210
322. Sugar Glazed Duck And Exotic Fruit ... 210
323. Suzanne Hart's Bluefish With Garlic Mayonnaise ... 211
324. Sweet Peppers Conserved In Oil ... 212
325. Sweet Potato Tian With Spiced Shrimp And Prosciutto ... 212
326. Swordfish Nicoise ... 213
327. Swordfish Roll Ups As Prepared In Messina 214
328. Swordfish With Bread Crumb Salsa ... 215
329. Swordfish With Scallions And Cracked Peppercorns ... 215
330. Swordfish On Black Bean And Pineapple Salsa 216
331. Tabbouleh Salad With Grilled Eggplant 217
332. Tagliata With Radicchio And Parmesan. 217
333. Tamarind Glazed Pork Chops ... 218
334. Tandoori Mushrooms ... 218
335. Tandoori Steak ... 219
336. Thai Beef Salad ... 219
337. Thai Beef Salad With Mint ... 220
338. Thai Style Broiled Shrimp ... 220
339. The Four Seasons Chopped Lamb Steak With Pine Nuts ... 221
340. Tiger Shrimp With Pineapple And Smoked Bacon ... 221
341. Toasted Rhubarb Pudding (Hambleton Hall) 222
342. Tomates Grillees (Broiled Tomatoes) ... 223
343. Tomatillo Guacamole ... 223
344. Tomato Bread Salad With Chorizo And Herbs ... 224
345. Tomatoes And Gorgonzola ... 224

346. Troisgros Potatoes Gratin 225
347. Tuna Steaks Moroccan Style 225
348. Turkey Cutlets With Prosciutto And Cheese 226
349. Turkey Hash With Lemon Chili Mayonnaise 226
350. Turkey Scaloppine With Prosciutto And Cheese...227
351. Vegetables Au Gratin 228
352. Warm Barley And Mushroom Salad Over Portobellos..229
353. Warm Bread Salad...................................... 229
354. Warm Passion Fruit Gratin With Raspberries 230
355. Warm Plums With Cinnamon Toast And Red Plum Sorbet...231
356. Warm White Bean And Shrimp Salad With Lime Vinaigrette 232
357. Watermelon & Tomato Salsa 233
358. Welsh Rabbit 233
359. Whole Baked Fish, Moroccan Style 234
360. Whole Roasted Cauliflower With Romesco 234
361. Wolfgang Puck's Salmon With Celery Root Puree 235
362. Yakitori Chicken With Ginger, Garlic And Soy Sauce 236
363. Yellow Fruited Rice With Fish.................. 236
364. Yellow Tomato Gazpacho With Goat Cheese Croutons... 237
365. Zucchini With Parmesan Cheese............. 238

INDEX.. 239

CONCLUSION... 244

365 Awesome Broiling Recipes

***

1. "21" Club Burger

Serving: 8 hamburgers | Prep: | Cook: | Ready in: 45mins

Ingredients

- Herb butter:
- ½ cup butter (1 stick) at room temperature
- 2 tablespoons finely chopped fresh basil
- 1 tablespoon finely chopped fresh thyme
- 1 tablespoon finely chopped fresh parsley
- Salt and freshly ground black pepper to taste
- Salad garnish:
- 24 slices ripe red tomato
- 16 thin slices red onion
- 1 ½ cups olive oil
- 1 cup freshly squeezed lemon juice
- Hamburgers:
- 6 pounds fresh chuck
- Salt and freshly ground black pepper to taste
- 16 1/2-inch-thick slices Italian country-style bread, toasted
- ½ cup olive oil

Direction

- For the herb butter, place the butter, basil, thyme, parsley, salt and pepper in a food processor and pulse until smooth. Place it on plastic wrap, and loosely fold the wrap over. Roll it into a log and freeze.
- For the salad, combine the tomatoes, onion, olive oil and lemon juice in a nonreactive bowl.
- For the hamburgers, remove the butter from the plastic wrap and cut into 8 cylinders. Divide the meat into 8 equal balls.
- With each ball, make an indentation with your thumb, press a butter cylinder in and close the meat over the butter. Shape each ball into a 1-inch-thick patty, and sprinkle with salt and pepper on both sides.
- Grill, broil or fry the patties in a preheated cast-iron skillet for 4 minutes per side over medium-low heat for medium rare.
- Brush the toast with the olive oil and grill under a broiler until both sides are golden. Center each hamburger on 2 slices of the toast, top with the salad garnish and eat with a knife and fork.

Nutrition Information

- 1260: calories;
- 48 grams: carbohydrates;
- 14 grams: sugars;
- 8 grams: polyunsaturated fat;
- 1 gram: trans fat;
- 51 grams: monounsaturated fat;
- 11 grams: dietary fiber;
- 84 grams: protein;
- 2032 milligrams: sodium;
- 85 grams: fat;
- 22 grams: saturated fat;

2. A Smooth And Creamy Pâté

Serving: 6 servings, about 2 cups | Prep: | Cook: | Ready in: 1hours30mins

Ingredients

- 16 ounces chicken livers
- ½ cup milk, approximately
- ½ cup (8 tablespoons) unsalted butter, softened

- 6 tablespoons heavy cream
- Salt and freshly ground black pepper to taste
- 2 to 3 tablespoons brandy
- 2 to 3 tablespoons green peppercorns, optional
- ¼ cup (4 tablespoons) cold unsalted butter, cubed

Direction

- Trim livers of little sinews or dark spots. Place in a bowl and add milk to cover. Set aside 30 minutes.
- Melt one-third of the softened butter, about 2 1/2 tablespoons, in a shallow skillet over medium-high heat. Drain livers. When butter starts to foam, slip livers into pan (they will spit) and sauté quickly, turning once, until lightly crusted and golden outside and cooked but still pink in the center.
- Place contents of pan, remaining softened butter, cream and salt and pepper into a blender or food processor and purée.
- Bring brandy to a boil in the skillet, add to the blender or food processor and briefly process again. Taste and add salt and pepper as needed, remembering that the pâté will be served chilled so the seasoning will not be as strong.
- Pass pâté through a fine sieve into a bowl, fold in green peppercorns if desired, then transfer to a ceramic terrine or serving bowl. Smooth top and refrigerate for 30 minutes, uncovered. Meanwhile, melt remaining butter and skim off solids.
- Pour clarified butter over pâté to seal top, cover with plastic wrap, and return to refrigerator at least 3 hours or overnight.

Nutrition Information

- 370: calories;
- 14 grams: protein;
- 33 grams: fat;
- 2 grams: carbohydrates;
- 0 grams: dietary fiber;
- 9 grams: monounsaturated fat;
- 337 milligrams: sodium;
- 20 grams: saturated fat;
- 1 gram: sugars;

3. Alain Ducasse's Gratin Of Blueberries With Vanilla

Serving: 4 to 6 servings | Prep: | Cook: | Ready in: 20mins

Ingredients

- For the compote:
- 2 pints (4 cups) blueberries
- 2 tablespoons unsalted butter
- 1 teaspoon sugar
- Half a vanilla bean
- 3 mint leaves
- 1 tablespoon creme de cassis
- For the sabayon:
- 4 large egg yolks
- 2 tablespoons vermouth
- 1 teaspoon sugar
- Seeds from 1 vanilla bean
- ¼ cup heavy cream
- Confectioners' sugar

Direction

- To make the compote, rinse the berries in cold water. In a medium saucepan on medium-low heat, melt the butter. Add the sugar, vanilla bean, mint, creme de cassis and blueberries. Cook slowly until the berries are softened, about 7 minutes. Transfer to an ovenproof gratin or baking dish and let cool.
- To make the sabayon, begin whisking the yolks in the top of a double boiler set over barely simmering water. Whisk in the vermouth, sugar and seeds from the vanilla bean. Continue whisking until the mixture doubles in volume. Remove from the heat and let cool slightly.
- When ready to serve, preheat the broiler or have a small culinary blowtorch ready. Whip the cream until it holds soft peaks. Fold it into

the cooled sabayon. Pour the mixture over the berries and sprinkle the top with the confectioners' sugar. Place under the broiler or cook with the blowtorch until the top is lightly browned. (The sabayon will melt slightly.) Serve immediately.

Nutrition Information

- 188: calories;
- 3 grams: protein;
- 1 gram: polyunsaturated fat;
- 0 grams: trans fat;
- 20 grams: carbohydrates;
- 2 grams: dietary fiber;
- 14 grams: sugars;
- 11 milligrams: sodium;
- 11 grams: fat;
- 6 grams: saturated fat;

4. Artichoke Heart Frittata

Serving: Serves four to six | Prep: | Cook: | Ready in: 30mins

Ingredients

- 1 pound baby artichokes, trimmed, or one 12-ounce package frozen artichoke hearts
- 8 eggs
- 2 tablespoons low-fat milk
- Salt, preferably kosher salt
- freshly ground pepper
- 2 tablespoons extra virgin olive oil
- 2 garlic cloves, minced
- 3 tablespoons minced Italian parsley, dill, fennel fronds or wild fennel
- 1 tablespoon freshly grated Parmesan or pecorino

Direction

- If using fresh artichokes, steam until tender or boil gently in a pot of generously salted water, 10 to 15 minutes. Drain, refresh with cold water and quarter the artichokes. Thaw frozen artichokes as directed, and drain off any liquid in the bowl.
- Beat the eggs in a medium bowl. Whisk in the milk, about 1/2 teaspoon salt and freshly ground pepper to taste.
- Heat the oil over medium-high heat in a 10-inch, heavy nonstick skillet, and add the artichokes. Cook, stirring often, until golden brown, about five to eight minutes. Add the garlic, and cook for another 30 seconds to a minute until fragrant. Stir in the herbs, and season with salt and pepper. Pour in the egg mixture. Swirl the pan to distribute the eggs and filling evenly over the surface. Shake the pan gently, tilting it slightly with one hand while lifting up the edges of the omelet with a spatula in your other hand, so that the eggs run underneath during the few minutes of cooking.
- Turn the heat down to low, cover (use a pizza pan if you don't have a lid that will fit your skillet) and cook 10 minutes, shaking the pan gently every once in a while. From time to time, remove the lid and loosen the bottom of the omelet with a wooden spatula, tilting the pan so that the bottom doesn't burn. Instead it should turn a deep golden brown. Meanwhile, heat the broiler.
- Finish the omelet under the broiler for one to two minutes, watching very carefully to make sure the top doesn't burn. (It should brown slightly, and it will puff under the broiler.) Remove from the heat and immediately sprinkle on the Parmesan or pecorino. Serve hot, warm or room temperature.

Nutrition Information

- 172: calories;
- 9 grams: carbohydrates;
- 4 grams: dietary fiber;
- 1 gram: sugars;
- 345 milligrams: sodium;
- 11 grams: protein;

- 0 grams: trans fat;
- 6 grams: monounsaturated fat;
- 3 grams: saturated fat;
- 2 grams: polyunsaturated fat;

5. Asparagus With Red Pepper Sauce

Serving: 4 servings | Prep: | Cook: |Ready in: 35mins

Ingredients

- 2 red bell peppers
- ½ cup olive oil
- Balsamic vinegar to taste
- Course salt and freshly ground pepper to taste
- 1 ½ pounds asparagus
- Fresh tarragon leaves to garnish

Direction

- Preheat broiler.
- Cut the peppers into quarters and remove the stems and seeds. Place the quarters skin side up on foil placed on a broiling rack. Broil until the skins are charred. Place the pepper strips in a sealed paper or plastic bag for a few minutes, then slip off the skins.
- Combine the pepper strips in a blender or food processor with the olive oil and puree. Add vinegar, salt and pepper to taste. Set aside.
- Cut the tough stems from the asparagus. With a vegetable peeler, pare away any tough skin from the lower half of the stalk. Rinse the asparagus in cold water.
- Either cook the asparagus in a steamer or tie in bundle standing in two inches of water. Cook, covered, until tender but firm. Drain and place on individual plates. Cool to room temperature before serving.
- Pour a pool of sauce on each plate and garnish with tarragon leaves.

6. Baingan Bharta

Serving: 4 servings | Prep: | Cook: |Ready in: 45mins

Ingredients

- 2 pounds eggplant
- 2 tablespoons lime juice
- 2 to 3 tablespoons vegetable oil
- 1 medium onion, peeled and chopped
- 3 cloves garlic, peeled and finely chopped
- 1 fresh hot green chile like a jalapeño, or more to taste, thinly sliced (discard seeds for less heat)
- 1 pound fresh tomatoes, chopped
- ½ teaspoon turmeric
- 1 teaspoon kosher salt or to taste
- ½ cup chopped cilantro, thin stems included
- 2 teaspoons garam masala

Direction

- Prick the eggplant with a thin-blade knife. Grill over or next to very high heat, turning as necessary until the skin is blackened and the eggplant collapses. Or broil, or roast on a heated cast-iron pan in the hottest possible oven. It will take about 20 minutes.
- When the eggplant is cool enough to handle, peel (this will be easy) and trim away the hard stem. Chop or mash in a bowl, with lime juice.
- Heat the oil in a skillet over medium-high heat; add the onion. Cook, stirring often, until the onion is golden brown, about 10 minutes. Add the garlic and chiles and cook for another minute. Add the tomato, turmeric and salt. Cook until the tomato is soft, 5 minutes or so.
- Stir in the eggplant purée and cook, stirring, 3 to 5 minutes. Stir in the cilantro and garam masala and turn off the heat. Serve hot with warm chapati bread or pita, or over rice.

Nutrition Information

- 176: calories;
- 1 gram: saturated fat;
- 0 grams: trans fat;

- 2 grams: polyunsaturated fat;
- 9 grams: dietary fiber;
- 12 grams: sugars;
- 4 grams: protein;
- 10 grams: fat;
- 484 milligrams: sodium;
- 6 grams: monounsaturated fat;
- 23 grams: carbohydrates;

7. Baked Codfish With Spinach And Cheese Sauce

Serving: 4 servings | Prep: | Cook: | Ready in: 30mins

Ingredients

- 3 tablespoons butter
- 2 tablespoons flour
- 1 ½ cups milk
- ¼ cup heavy cream
- 1 cup Gruyere or Swiss cheese cut in small cubes
- 1 egg yolk
- Salt and freshly ground pepper to taste
- ⅛ teaspoon freshly grated nutmeg
- 1 pinch cayenne pepper
- 1 pound fresh spinach
- 2 tablespoons finely chopped shallots
- 4 boneless, skinless codfish steaks, about 6 ounces each
- ½ cup white wine
- 2 tablespoons grated Parmesan cheese

Direction

- Melt 1 tablespoon of the butter in a saucepan. Add the flour and stir with a wire whisk until blended.
- Add the milk and cream all at once. Stir rapidly with the whisk. Bring to a boil and add the Gruyere cheese. Stir until the cheese has melted. Add the egg yolk, stirring rapidly with the whisk. Add salt, pepper, nutmeg and cayenne. Simmer, stirring, for 1 minute. Set aside, cover and keep warm.
- Pick over spinach and discard any tough stems. Wash spinach thoroughly to remove any sand. Put spinach in a large saucepan, add salt and cook over high heat, stirring, until wilted, about 2 minutes. Drain well and squeeze out excess moisture. Set aside and keep warm.
- Preheat the oven to 450 degrees.
- Grease a metal baking dish with 1 tablespoon of the butter. Scatter the shallots over the dish. Neatly arrange the pieces of codfish over the shallots. Season with salt and pepper. Add the wine, cover with foil and bring to a boil on top of the stove. Put the dish in the oven and bake 5 minutes.
- Select a baking dish large enough to hold the fish in one layer. Spread the remaining 1 tablespoon butter over the bottom of the dish. Spoon the spinach over the bottom and carefully transfer the cooked codfish over the spinach, reserving the wine liquid in the first dish.
- Reduce by half the wine liquid in the metal baking dish and add it to the cheese sauce. Bring to a boil, stirring with a wire whisk.
- Spoon the hot sauce over the fish, smoothing it over to cover the fish. Sprinkle with Parmesan cheese. Turn on the broiler unit and put the dish under the broiler with the door open until nicely browned and bubbling.

Nutrition Information

- 536: calories;
- 0 grams: trans fat;
- 8 grams: monounsaturated fat;
- 2 grams: polyunsaturated fat;
- 3 grams: dietary fiber;
- 7 grams: sugars;
- 48 grams: protein;
- 29 grams: fat;
- 17 grams: saturated fat;
- 16 grams: carbohydrates;
- 1109 milligrams: sodium;

8. Baked Endives With Parmesan Cheese (Endives Au Parmesan)

Serving: 4 servings | Prep: | Cook: | Ready in: 25mins

Ingredients

- 8 cooked, well-drained endives (see recipe)
- 2 tablespoons butter
- ¼ cup freshly grated Parmesan cheese

Direction

- Preheat oven to 425 degrees.
- Drain the endives well on absorbent paper towels.
- Using one tablespoon of the butter, lightly butter the bottom and sides of a baking dish large enough to hold the endives close together in one layer. Add the endives. Sprinkle with the cheese and dot with the remaining butter.
- Place in the oven and bake 15 minutes. Run briefly under the broiler until browned and nicely glazed.

Nutrition Information

- 97: calories;
- 100 milligrams: sodium;
- 8 grams: fat;
- 5 grams: saturated fat;
- 0 grams: sugars;
- 2 grams: monounsaturated fat;
- 4 grams: protein;
- 3 grams: dietary fiber;

9. Baked Mashed Potatoes With Parmesan

Serving: 4 servings | Prep: | Cook: | Ready in: 40mins

Ingredients

- 4 large Idaho potatoes, about 1 1/2 pounds
- 4 garlic cloves, peeled
- Salt to taste
- 1 cup milk
- 2 tablespoons butter
- ½ teaspoon nutmeg, freshly grated
- Freshly ground black pepper to taste
- 3 tablespoons grated Parmesan or other cheese

Direction

- Peel potatoes and rinse well.
- Place potatoes and garlic in a saucepan with water to cover. Add salt and bring to a boil. Simmer 15 to 20 minutes or until potatoes are tender. Drain and mash and place in a saucepan.
- Preheat broiler.
- Heat milk in a saucepan.
- Add butter and nutmeg to milk. Stir with a wooden spatula until butter melts. Add milk gradually to the potatoes, stirring with a spatula. Add salt, if desired, and pepper.
- Spoon potatoes into a heatproof serving dish measuring 1 1/2 by 6 1/2 by 10 1/2 inches.
- Smooth top with a spatula and sprinkle with cheese. Place potatoes under broiler until nicely browned.

Nutrition Information

- 236: calories;
- 7 grams: saturated fat;
- 27 grams: carbohydrates;
- 4 grams: sugars;
- 11 grams: fat;
- 0 grams: polyunsaturated fat;
- 3 grams: dietary fiber;
- 9 grams: protein;
- 588 milligrams: sodium;

10. Baked Ricotta With Spring Vegetables

Serving: 2 to 4 servings | Prep: | Cook: | Ready in: 40mins

Ingredients

- 4 medium-thick asparagus, ends snapped, slant-cut in 1-inch pieces
- 1 ounce fresh mushrooms, preferably morels or oyster mushrooms, separated in pieces
- 1 ½ tablespoons extra-virgin olive oil
- 12 ounces whole-milk ricotta cheese
- ½ ounce grated Parmigiano-Reggiano (about 1/3 cup)
- 3 tablespoons shredded mozzarella
- ½ tablespoon fresh oregano leaves
- 1 large egg plus 1 yolk
- Salt and ground black pepper
- 2 tablespoons pesto
- 4 freshly cooked, canned or frozen baby artichoke hearts, quartered
- 2 scallions, trimmed and minced
- 1 teaspoon fresh mint leaves, in chiffonade
- 4 slices sourdough or multigrain bread
- 1 clove garlic

Direction

- Bring a small saucepan of water to a boil, add the asparagus and blanch 5 minutes. Drain and set aside. Toss mushrooms with 2 teaspoons of the oil and sear in a small skillet over medium heat until softened, about 5 minutes. Set aside.
- Grease a 9-inch cast iron skillet with 1 teaspoon oil. Place ricotta in a bowl. Fold in the Parmesan, mozzarella, oregano, egg and egg yolk. Season with salt and pepper. Spread in the cast-iron skillet. Gently swirl in the pesto, leaving streaks of it.
- Heat a broiler. Place the cast-iron skillet on a burner turned to low and let cook about 10 minutes, until heated through and showing signs of browning along the edges. Remove from heat. Scatter the asparagus, mushrooms and artichokes on top. Sprinkle with scallions and mint. Place under the broiler close to the source of heat until it starts to become lightly dappled, about 6 minutes.
- Meanwhile grill or toast the bread. Brush with the remaining 1 1/2 teaspoon olive oil and rub with garlic. Serve the cheese and vegetables directly from the skillet, with grilled bread alongside.

11. Baked Salmon Fillets With Goat Cheese And Cilantro

Serving: 4 servings | Prep: | Cook: | Ready in: 25mins

Ingredients

- 4 tablespoons olive oil
- ½ cup chopped onion
- 1 tablespoon finely chopped garlic
- ½ cup dry red wine
- 4 tablespoons capers
- 1 tablespoon chopped fresh rosemary or 1 teaspoon dried
- 1 teaspoon chopped fresh oregano or 1/2 teaspoon dried
- ⅛ teaspoon hot red pepper flakes
- ½ cup canned crushed tomatoes
- Salt and freshly ground pepper to taste
- 12 pitted black olives
- 4 boneless salmon fillets, about 6 ounces each
- ⅓ pound goat cheese, crumbled
- 2 tablespoons anise-flavored liquor, like Ricard
- 4 tablespoons chopped fresh cilantro

Direction

- Heat 2 tablespoons of the olive oil in a saucepan. Add the onion and garlic, and cook briefly while stirring. Add the wine, capers, rosemary, oregano, pepper flakes, tomatoes,

salt, pepper and olives. Bring to a boil and simmer 5 minutes.
- Preheat the oven to 475 degrees.
- Pour 1 tablespoon of the oil in a baking dish large enough to hold the fish in one layer. Arrange the fish skin-side down, sprinkle with salt and pepper. Pour the tomato sauce around the fish fillets, brush the top of the fillets with the remaining 1 tablespoon oil and the cheese.
- Bake for 5 minutes and sprinkle with Ricard. Switch to the broiler and broil for 5 minutes. Do not overcook the fish. Sprinkle with the cilantro and serve immediately

Nutrition Information

- 662: calories;
- 19 grams: monounsaturated fat;
- 8 grams: polyunsaturated fat;
- 2 grams: dietary fiber;
- 5 grams: sugars;
- 43 grams: protein;
- 46 grams: fat;
- 776 milligrams: sodium;
- 13 grams: saturated fat;
- 10 grams: carbohydrates;

12. Baked Tapioca Pudding With Cinnamon Sugar Brûlée

Serving: 6 to 8 servings. | Prep: | Cook: | Ready in: 1hours10mins

Ingredients

- 3 cups whole milk
- 1 cup heavy cream
- 1 cinnamon stick
- ⅓ cup small pearl tapioca
- 4 large egg yolks
- 85 grams granulated sugar (about 1/3 cup)
- ¼ teaspoon fine sea salt
- 45 grams Demerara sugar (about 3 tablespoons)
- ¼ teaspoon ground cinnamon.

Direction

- Heat oven to 300 degrees
- In a medium saucepan, bring the milk, cream and cinnamon stick to a simmer. Whisk in the tapioca. Simmer until the pearls are completely tender, about 20 minutes.
- In a large bowl, whisk together the egg yolks, granulated sugar and salt. Whisking constantly, pour in a third of the tapioca mixture. Whisk yolk mixture into the pot of tapioca; simmer over medium-low heat, stirring constantly with a heat-proof spatula, until thick enough to coat the back of a spoon, about 5 minutes.
- Transfer pudding to a buttered 1.5-quart gratin dish. Sprinkle the top with Demerara sugar and cinnamon. Bake, uncovered, until the pudding is firm around the edges and jiggly in the center, about 30 minutes. Put under the broiler until top is bubbling and golden, 3 to 5 minutes. (Watch carefully to make sure it doesn't burn.) Eat warm, or chill and serve cold, removing the cinnamon stick while serving.

Nutrition Information

- 249: calories;
- 16 grams: fat;
- 9 grams: saturated fat;
- 5 grams: protein;
- 17 grams: sugars;
- 1 gram: polyunsaturated fat;
- 22 grams: carbohydrates;
- 0 grams: dietary fiber;
- 129 milligrams: sodium;

13. Barbecued Chicken

Serving: Twenty servings | Prep: | Cook: | Ready in: 1hours45mins

Ingredients

- 5 cups white vinegar
- 1 tablespoon whole cloves
- 2 teaspoons ground Salt and freshly ground pepper to taste
- 15 pounds chicken pieces
- ¼ cup vegetable oil
- 3 cloves garlic, minced
- 3 cups ketchup
- 1 cup dark brown sugar
- ½ cup mustard
- ¼ cup Worcestershire sauce
- Juice of 1 lemon
- 1 small onion, grated
- 1 tablespoon Tabasco sauce
- 3 teaspoons chili powder
- 1 teaspoon celery seeds

Direction

- The night before serving, combine the vinegar with 10 cups water, the whole cloves, salt and pepper. Add the chicken and marinate, refrigerated, overnight.
- To make the sauce, heat the oil in a large pan and saute the garlic until golden. Add all the remaining ingredients and a dash of salt, and bring to a simmer, stirring constantly. Cook over medium-low heat for 45 minutes, stirring occasionally. Remove and cool.
- Forty-five minutes before cooking, light the charcoal fire.
- Remove the chicken and discard the marinade. Cook the chicken over low heat for about 30 minutes, turning to cook evenly on each side. Brush the pieces with the sauce and cook 30 minutes more, basting and turning occasionally. Serve the chicken hot or at room temperature, with the remaining sauce on the side.

Nutrition Information

- 843: calories;
- 12 grams: polyunsaturated fat;
- 64 grams: protein;
- 920 milligrams: sodium;
- 54 grams: fat;
- 0 grams: trans fat;
- 23 grams: monounsaturated fat;
- 1 gram: dietary fiber;
- 15 grams: sugars;
- 19 grams: carbohydrates;

14. Barbecued Pork

Serving: 2 servings | Prep: | Cook: | Ready in: 35mins

Ingredients

- 1 tablespoon coarsely grated fresh or frozen ginger
- 1 tablespoon sherry vinegar
- 1 teaspoon reduced-sodium soy sauce
- 8 ounces pork tenderloin
- 1 teaspoon canola oil

Direction

- If using a broiler, turn it on.
- Place the ginger, the vinegar and the soy sauce in a dish large enough to hold the meat.
- Wash and trim the fat from the pork; cut into three pieces, making the thin end longer than the middle and other end. Coat with the soy sauce marinade and allow to marinate until it is time to cook.
- If using a stove-top grill, prepare. With a brush, lightly coat the grill with canola oil. (No oil is needed if broiler is used.) Cook the meat, allowing about 10 minutes for the thin tail end and 15 minutes for the rest of the meat, which should still be slightly pink when done.

Nutrition Information

- 161: calories;
- 24 grams: protein;
- 140 milligrams: sodium;
- 6 grams: fat;

- 2 grams: saturated fat;
- 0 grams: sugars;
- 3 grams: monounsaturated fat;
- 1 gram: carbohydrates;

15. Barbecued Shrimp

Serving: Four servings | Prep: | Cook: | Ready in: 15mins

Ingredients

- 1 tablespoon coarsely ground black pepper
- ½ teaspoon crushed chili pepper flakes
- ¼ teaspoon cayenne pepper
- Dash of Tabasco
- ½ teaspoon salt
- 1 tablespoon olive oil
- ¼ cup freshly squeezed lemon juice
- 2 pounds medium-size shrimp, in the shell

Direction

- In a bowl, combine the peppers, Tabasco and salt; whisk in the olive oil and lemon juice. Add the shrimp and toss to cover. Cover the bowl and refrigerate for at least 3 and up to 24 hours before cooking.
- Heat a charcoal grill or a broiler. Cook the shrimp in their shells until pink, about 3 to 4 minutes on each side. Serve in the shell, or allow to cool and shell before serving.

Nutrition Information

- 199: calories;
- 6 grams: fat;
- 1 gram: dietary fiber;
- 0 grams: sugars;
- 3 grams: monounsaturated fat;
- 4 grams: carbohydrates;
- 31 grams: protein;
- 1286 milligrams: sodium;

16. Bass Fillets Broiled With Mustard Mayonnaise

Serving: Four servings | Prep: | Cook: | Ready in: 10mins

Ingredients

- ¼ cup mayonnaise
- 1 tablespoon Dijon mustard
- Pinch of cayenne
- ¼ teaspoon salt
- 4 bass fillets (about 4 ounces each), all bones removed
- 1 lemon, cut into wedges

Direction

- Preheat broiler. Stir the mayonnaise and mustard together until well combined. Season with the cayenne and salt. Coat the flesh side of the fillets with the mayonnaise mixture and place on a baking sheet, skin side down. Broil until the fish is just cooked through and the top browns, about 5 minutes. Place 1 fillet on each of 4 plates and serve immediately with lemon wedges.

Nutrition Information

- 217: calories;
- 2 grams: carbohydrates;
- 0 grams: sugars;
- 8 grams: polyunsaturated fat;
- 1 gram: dietary fiber;
- 20 grams: protein;
- 14 grams: fat;
- 4 grams: monounsaturated fat;
- 340 milligrams: sodium;

17. Bass Steaks In Rosemary Sherry Vinaigrette

Serving: Four serving | Prep: | Cook: | Ready in: 30mins

Ingredients

- 1 teaspoon Dijon mustard
- 2 tablespoons sherry vinegar
- 2 teaspoons chopped fresh rosemary
- 1 clove garlic, peeled and minced
- ¼ teaspoon salt
- Freshly ground pepper to taste
- 1 teaspoon olive oil
- 8 1-inch-thick bass steaks (about 2 ounces each)

Direction

- Preheat broiler. In a medium-size bowl, combine the mustard, vinegar, rosemary, garlic, salt and pepper. Whisk in the oil. Coat the bass in the marinade. Let stand for 20 minutes, turning the steaks once.
- Place the bass on a broiler pan and spoon some marinade over each one. Broil until just cooked through, about 4 minutes per side. Place 2 steaks on each of 4 plates, sprinkle with pepper and serve immediately.

Nutrition Information

- 208: calories;
- 15 grams: fat;
- 6 grams: saturated fat;
- 1 gram: carbohydrates;
- 7 grams: monounsaturated fat;
- 0 grams: sugars;
- 17 grams: protein;
- 189 milligrams: sodium;

18. Bass With Truffle Vinaigrette

Serving: 6 servings | Prep: | Cook: | Ready in: 30mins

Ingredients

- For the vinaigrette:
- 1 cup chicken stock
- ½ cup finely diced shallots
- ½ cup sherry vinegar
- Salt and pepper to taste
- ½ cup truffle oil
- ½ cup grapeseed oil
- ½ cup extra virgin olive oil
- For the bass:
- 6 (6-ounce) fillets sea bass or striped bass, with skin on
- Salt and pepper
- 2 tablespoons Wondra flour if using striped bass
- 4 to 8 tablespoons unsalted butter
- 2 teaspoons corn oil if using sea bass

Direction

-
-
-
-

Nutrition Information

- 797: calories;
- 32 grams: monounsaturated fat;
- 22 grams: polyunsaturated fat;
- 34 grams: protein;
- 14 grams: saturated fat;
- 71 grams: fat;
- 1 gram: dietary fiber;
- 5 grams: carbohydrates;
- 2 grams: sugars;
- 742 milligrams: sodium;

19. Beef Brochettes With Red Peppers And Coriander

Serving: 4 servings | Prep: | Cook: | Ready in: 40mins

Ingredients

- 1 ½ pounds lean beef, like fillet or sirloin
- 2 red onions, about 1/2 pound
- 2 medium-size red peppers
- 2 tablespoons fresh lemon juice
- 2 tablespoons coriander seeds
- 1 teaspoon chopped garlic
- ¼ teaspoon red pepper flakes
- ½ teaspoon cumin
- 4 sprigs fresh thyme, or 1 teaspoon dried
- ¼ cup dry red wine
- 2 tablespoons honey
- 2 tablespoons olive oil
- 4 tablespoons coarsely chopped fresh coriander
- Salt and freshly ground pepper to taste

Direction

- Preheat a charcoal grill to high or an oven broiler to 500 degrees. If wooden skewers are used, soak them in cold water until ready to use.
- Cut the beef into 1-inch cubes. There should be 24 cubes.
- Peel and cut the onions into 24 1-inch cubes. Reserve the remaining onion for another use. Set the cubes aside until ready to cook.
- Cut away and discard the pepper cores, veins and seeds. Cut the peppers into 24 equal-size pieces and set aside until ready to cook.
- Combine the meat and remaining ingredients in a mixing bowl. Blend well and marinate 15 minutes.
- Drain the meat and arrange equal portions of meat, onions and peppers on skewers. Reserve the marinade for basting.
- If the brochettes are to be cooked under the broiler, arrange them on a rack about 4 inches from the source of heat, leaving the door slightly ajar. Cook about 4 minutes for rare, basting with the reserved marinade and turning often. If the brochettes are to be cooked on a grill, place them on the grill and cook 4 minutes for rare, basting often with the reserved marinade while turning.

Nutrition Information

- 524: calories;
- 32 grams: fat;
- 11 grams: saturated fat;
- 14 grams: sugars;
- 36 grams: protein;
- 779 milligrams: sodium;
- 16 grams: monounsaturated fat;
- 2 grams: polyunsaturated fat;
- 21 grams: carbohydrates;
- 4 grams: dietary fiber;

20. Black Cod Broiled With Miso

Serving: 4 servings | Prep: | Cook: | Ready in: 20mins

Ingredients

- ½ cup sugar
- 1 cup miso, preferably dark
- ½ cup mirin, sake or white wine
- 1 ½ to 2 pounds black cod fillets (skin may be on or off)

Direction

- Heat broiler; set rack 3 to 4 inches from heat source. Combine first three ingredients in a small saucepan and, over low heat, bring almost to a boil, stirring occasionally just until blended; mixture will be fairly thin. Turn off heat.
- Put fillets in an ovenproof baking dish or skillet, preferably nonstick, and spoon half the sauce on top. Broil until sauce bubbles and begins to brown, then spoon remaining amount over fish. Continue to broil, adjusting heat or rack position if sauce or fish is browning too quickly, until fish is just cooked through. Serve immediately.

Nutrition Information

- 419: calories;
- 1 gram: monounsaturated fat;
- 44 grams: carbohydrates;
- 29 grams: sugars;
- 5 grams: fat;
- 43 grams: protein;
- 2672 milligrams: sodium;
- 3 grams: polyunsaturated fat;
- 4 grams: dietary fiber;

21. Bombay Leg Of Lamb With Yogurt And Lime

Serving: 4 servings | Prep: | Cook: | Ready in: 25mins

Ingredients

- 1 2-pound boned leg of lamb, butterflied
- 1 cup plain low-fat yogurt
- 2 large limes
- Freshly ground black pepper, to taste
- ¼ teaspoon kosher salt

Direction

- In a large nonreactive bowl, combine lamb and yogurt. Grate zest of 1 lime, and squeeze the juice of 2 limes (you will have approximately 1/4 cup). Add to bowl with freshly ground black pepper and the salt. Mix well so that lamb is thoroughly coated with yogurt marinade. Cover, and refrigerate for 6 to 8 hours. Turn once or twice during the marinating period.
- Preheat the broiler. Remove lamb from the marinade. Place lamb in a heavy baking pan. Place marinade in a small pot.
- Broil lamb on each side for 6 to 8 minutes. It should be 150 degrees on a meat thermometer for rare; 160 degrees for medium-rare. Meanwhile, warm marinade over low heat, whisking constantly; do not let boil. Remove lamb from oven. Let rest 5 minutes. Slice thinly, and serve with marinade (if curdled, pour through a fine strainer).

Nutrition Information

- 423: calories;
- 262 milligrams: sodium;
- 27 grams: fat;
- 11 grams: monounsaturated fat;
- 2 grams: polyunsaturated fat;
- 5 grams: sugars;
- 36 grams: protein;
- 12 grams: saturated fat;
- 9 grams: carbohydrates;
- 1 gram: dietary fiber;

22. Boudin Aux Pommes Les Halles

Serving: Four servings | Prep: | Cook: | Ready in: 45mins

Ingredients

- 4 Idaho potatoes
- 1 cup cream
- 8 ounces butter
- Salt and pepper to taste
- ½ cup sugar
- 2 Granny Smith apples, peeled and cut into 1-inch wedges
- 1 teaspoon cumin seeds
- 1 teaspoon chopped fresh parsley, plus additional for garnish
- 4 blood sausages

Direction

- Place the potatoes in a saucepan, cover with cold, salted water and bring to a boil. Let simmer about 20 minutes, or until just cooked through. Let cool slightly, then peel and pass through a food mill. Set aside in a mixing bowl.
- In a small saucepan, bring the cream to a boil and remove from heat. Add half the butter to the potatoes and pour in the hot cream. Mix gently but well. Add salt and pepper to taste.

- While the potatoes are still simmering, caramelize the apples. Place the remaining butter and the sugar in a skillet and cook over high heat until the sugar turns golden brown, about 2 to 3 minutes. Add the apples, and cook, stirring gently, 4 to 5 minutes or until golden brown on both sides and well coated with the caramel. Add the cumin seeds and the chopped parsley. Set aside in a warm place until ready to serve.
- Preheat the grill or broiler.
- Prick the sausages all over with a fork or the point of a knife. Grill 5 minutes on each side. To serve, arrange the mashed potatoes in the center of a serving platter. Surround with the caramelized apples and top with the grilled, whole sausage. Sprinkle with chopped parsley.

Nutrition Information

- 1274: calories;
- 2 grams: trans fat;
- 33 grams: monounsaturated fat;
- 6 grams: polyunsaturated fat;
- 38 grams: sugars;
- 20 grams: protein;
- 55 grams: saturated fat;
- 8 grams: dietary fiber;
- 1243 milligrams: sodium;
- 100 grams: fat;
- 78 grams: carbohydrates;

23. Braised Melange Of Vegetables Glazed With Parmesan

Serving: Four servings | Prep: | Cook: | Ready in: 2hours10mins

Ingredients

- ½ pound peeled baby carrots
- 1 pound small red potatoes, halved or quartered, depending on size
- ½ pound sugar snap peas or 1/4 pound snow peas, trimmed
- ½ pound fresh or frozen green peas
- 15 scallions, trimmed to 6 inches, then halved crosswise
- 1 pint cherry tomatoes
- 10 cloves garlic, unpeeled
- 2 ½ teaspoons kosher salt
- Freshly ground pepper to taste
- 2 tablespoons extra virgin olive oil
- 2 cups chicken broth, homemade or low-sodium canned
- ½ cup freshly grated Parmesan cheese

Direction

- Preheat the oven to 350 degrees. Combine the carrots, potatoes, sugar snap or snow peas, green peas, scallions, tomatoes and garlic in a large, shallow casserole. Toss with the salt and pepper. Drizzle the olive oil over the top and pour in the chicken broth. Bake until all of the vegetables are soft, about 2 hours.
- Sprinkle the cheese over the top and place under the broiler until lightly browned, about 3 minutes. Serve with grilled veal chops or roast chicken, if desired.

Nutrition Information

- 376: calories;
- 7 grams: monounsaturated fat;
- 18 grams: protein;
- 15 grams: sugars;
- 1343 milligrams: sodium;
- 13 grams: fat;
- 4 grams: saturated fat;
- 1 gram: polyunsaturated fat;
- 51 grams: carbohydrates;
- 11 grams: dietary fiber;

24. Bratwurst With Sauerkraut And Potatoes

Serving: 4 servings | Prep: | Cook: | Ready in: 1hours

Ingredients

- 1 pound sauerkraut (1 can), drained
- 1 onion, sliced thin
- 1 tablespoon butter
- ½ cup dry white wine
- 1 cup chicken stock
- 1 tablespoon brown sugar
- 1 tablespoon white wine vinegar
- Coarse salt and freshly ground pepper to taste
- 8 bratwurst sausages
- 12 small red-skinned potatoes

Direction

- Simmer the sauerkraut for 10 minutes in boiling salted water. Drain.
- Meanwhile, in a large skillet, soften the onions in the butter, browning lightly. Add the sauerkraut, wine, stock, sugar, vinegar, salt and pepper. Bring to boil, turn down, cover and simmer, stirring occasionally, for 30 minutes.
- Meanwhile, simmer the bratwurst in water to cover for 20 minutes.
- Add the potatoes to the sauerkraut in the skillet and cook, covered, for 15 to 20 minutes or until tender.
- While the potatoes are cooking, drain the bratwurst and brown lightly on all sides under a hot broiler.
- To serve, put the sauerkraut and potatoes on a heated platter and arrange the bratwurst over the top.

Nutrition Information

- 740: calories;
- 17 grams: dietary fiber;
- 0 grams: trans fat;
- 3 grams: polyunsaturated fat;
- 123 grams: carbohydrates;
- 23 grams: protein;
- 2027 milligrams: sodium;
- 6 grams: monounsaturated fat;
- 11 grams: sugars;

25. Broccoli Salad With Hazelnut Romesco

Serving: 4 to 6 servings | Prep: | Cook: | Ready in: 30mins

Ingredients

- 2 medium red bell peppers, halved and cored
- 1 plum tomato, halved
- 3 garlic cloves, peeled
- ½ cup toasted, peeled hazelnuts, more for garnish
- ½ cup dried breadcrumbs
- ¼ cup extra-virgin olive oil
- 1 tablespoon sherry vinegar, more as needed
- 1 tablespoon pomegranate molasses or 1 teaspoon honey, more as needed
- 1 ½ teaspoons hot smoked paprika
- 1 teaspoon kosher salt, more as needed
- 2 pounds broccoli, cut into bite-sized florets

Direction

- Heat the broiler. Arrange an oven rack in the position closest to flame. Place peppers (cut side down), tomato halves (cut-side up) and garlic on a rimmed baking sheet. Broil until peppers and garlic are slightly charred, 3 to 5 minutes. Turn garlic (but do not turn peppers or tomato); broil 1 to 2 minutes longer until garlic is well browned but not burned. Transfer garlic to a large bowl. Continue broiling peppers and tomatoes until both are well charred, 4 to 5 minutes longer. Transfer tomato and peppers to the bowl with the garlic. Cover bowl with plastic wrap. Let stand until vegetables are cool enough to handle but still warm, then peel peppers and tomatoes.

- In the bowl of a food processor fitted with the blade attachment, pulse hazelnuts until coarsely ground. Add peppers, tomato, garlic, breadcrumbs, oil, vinegar, pomegranate molasses, paprika and salt. Purée until smooth. Taste and adjust seasonings. Scrape romesco into a bowl.
- Bring a large pot of salted water to a boil. Have ready a large bowl of ice water. Boil broccoli until just tender, 2 to 3 minutes. Use a slotted spoon to transfer to ice water; drain.
- In a large bowl, toss broccoli with enough romesco to coat vegetables well. (Reserve any remaining romesco for dipping or for another use.) Garnish with hazelnuts and serve warm or at room temperature.

Nutrition Information

- 195: calories;
- 1 gram: polyunsaturated fat;
- 7 grams: monounsaturated fat;
- 23 grams: carbohydrates;
- 6 grams: protein;
- 8 grams: sugars;
- 434 milligrams: sodium;
- 10 grams: fat;

26. Broiled Calf's Liver

Serving: 2 servings | Prep: | Cook: |Ready in: 30mins

Ingredients

- 8 ounces sliced bacon
- 2 tablespoons olive oil
- 4 medium sweet onions, halved root-to-stem and thinly sliced
- ½ teaspoon paprika
- 1 pound calf's liver, sliced in half horizontally
- Salt
- freshly ground black pepper

Direction

- Preheat a broiler. In a large skillet over medium heat, sauté bacon, turning as needed, until crispy. Transfer to paper towels to drain. Discard excess bacon fat but do not wash pan.
- Return pan to medium heat. Add oil, onions and paprika. Sauté until onions are very soft and beginning to brown, 15 to 20 minutes. Toward the end of cooking, season liver with salt and pepper to taste, and broil as desired, 1 1/2 to 2 minutes a side for a medium (lightly pink) center.
- To serve, remove onions from heat and season with salt to taste. Place a slice of liver on each of two serving plates. Smother with onions and top with bacon. Serve hot.

27. Broiled Chicken Breast Salad With Curry Dressing

Serving: 4 servings | Prep: | Cook: |Ready in: 30mins

Ingredients

- 4 skinless boneless chicken breast halves, about 1 1/4 pounds
- 2 teaspoons olive oil
- 2 tablespoons fresh lemon juice
- 2 tablespoons chopped fresh rosemary or 1 teaspoon dried
- 2 teaspoons finely chopped garlic
- Salt and freshly ground pepper to taste
- 1 head radicchio, about 1/4 pound, core removed, rinsed and dried
- 2 heads bibb lettuce, core removed, rinsed and dried
- ¼ pound arugula, cut into manageable pieces, rinsed and dried
- Warm curry dressing (see recipe)
- ¼ cup coarsely chopped fresh basil or chervil

Direction

- If chicken breasts are connected, separate halves and cut away membrane or fat. Place oil in mixing bowl with lemon juice, rosemary,

garlic, salt and pepper. Stir well. Add chicken pieces and turn them in the marinade to coat well. Cover and set aside until ready to cook. (If marinating for a long period, refrigerate them.)
- Preheat a charcoal grill or broiler.
- Put the chicken pieces on the grill or the broiler rack. Cover grill or close broiler. Cook 2 to 3 minutes, turning pieces. Continue cooking till done, about 3 to 5 minutes on the grill, possibly longer under the broiler.
- Remove pieces. Slice each breast on the bias about 1/4 inch thick.
- In a large mixing bowl add the radicchio, bibb lettuce and arugula. Toss well. Add half the warm dressing, and toss again. Place the sliced chicken over the salad and sprinkle with the remaining dressing and basil.

Nutrition Information

- 222: calories;
- 6 grams: carbohydrates;
- 2 grams: sugars;
- 34 grams: protein;
- 7 grams: fat;
- 1 gram: polyunsaturated fat;
- 0 grams: trans fat;
- 3 grams: monounsaturated fat;
- 687 milligrams: sodium;

28. Broiled Chicken Breasts With Cayenne And Ginger

Serving: 4 servings | Prep: | Cook: | Ready in: 35mins

Ingredients

- 4 skinless, boneless chicken breasts, about 6 ounces each
- 2 tablespoons olive oil
- 3 tablespoons fresh lemon juice
- 2 teaspoons freshly grated ginger
- 1 teaspoon ground cumin
- 2 teaspoons ground turmeric
- 1 pinch cayenne pepper to taste
- 1 teaspoon ground coriander
- Salt to taste
- 2 tablespoons melted butter
- 2 tablespoons freshly chopped cilantro

Direction

- Place in a small mixing bowl the olive oil, lemon juice, ginger, cumin, turmeric, cayenne pepper, ground coriander and salt. Using a wire whisk, blend well.
- Place the chicken breasts in a shallow baking dish large enough to hold them in one layer. With a pastry brush, coat each piece on both sides with all the marinade. Cover the dish with plastic wrap, and let stand for 10 to 15 minutes.
- Meanwhile, preheat the broiler to high. Remove the chicken from the marinade, and broil in a broiling pan 3 to 4 inches from the source for 4 minutes on the first side.
- Turn the chicken over, and broil it for 3 to 4 minutes more or until done. Do not overcook.
- Reduce temperature to 400 degrees. Return the chicken to the baking dish, and add the melted butter to the sauce in the pan. Return to the oven, and bake for 3 minutes.
- Sprinkle with the fresh coriander, and serve.

Nutrition Information

- 356: calories;
- 8 grams: saturated fat;
- 4 grams: polyunsaturated fat;
- 29 grams: protein;
- 464 milligrams: sodium;
- 25 grams: fat;
- 0 grams: sugars;
- 12 grams: monounsaturated fat;
- 3 grams: carbohydrates;
- 1 gram: dietary fiber;

29. Broiled Chicken With Piquillo Tomato Sauce

Serving: 4 servings | Prep: | Cook: | Ready in: 30mins

Ingredients

- 8 chicken thighs, or an equivalent amount of other parts
- Salt and pepper
- 3 cloves garlic
- 3 tablespoons extra virgin olive oil
- 3 anchovies, or more to taste
- 6 ounces piquillo peppers
- 2 medium tomatoes, cored and chopped
- Chopped parsley for garnish, optional

Direction

- Heat broiler: fire should be moderately hot and rack about 6 inches from heat source. (Alternatively, grill chicken.) Sprinkle chicken with salt and pepper, then broil, beginning with skin side down. Make sure skin crisps and browns and interior cooks through; this will take about 20 minutes.
- Meanwhile mince about half the garlic. Put it in a saucepan with 2 tablespoons oil and about half the anchovies, and turn heat to medium-high. Cook until mixture sizzles, then add piquillos and tomatoes. Bring to a boil and cook, stirring occasionally and adding salt and pepper as necessary, until mixture breaks up. Cool a bit, then transfer to a blender. Purée with remaining garlic and anchovies, then taste and adjust seasoning. Add remaining olive oil.
- Serve chicken and sauce hot or warm, garnished if you like with parsley.

Nutrition Information

- 780: calories;
- 28 grams: monounsaturated fat;
- 12 grams: polyunsaturated fat;
- 3 grams: sugars;
- 51 grams: protein;
- 60 grams: fat;
- 0 grams: trans fat;
- 7 grams: carbohydrates;
- 2 grams: dietary fiber;
- 974 milligrams: sodium;
- 15 grams: saturated fat;

30. Broiled Cornish Hens With Lemon And Balsamic Vinegar

Serving: 4 servings | Prep: | Cook: | Ready in: 30mins

Ingredients

- 2 Cornish hens
- 1 to 2 tablespoons extra virgin olive oil
- Salt and freshly ground black pepper
- 2 lemons
- 2 teaspoons balsamic vinegar, or to taste
- Chopped parsley for garnish, optional

Direction

- Preheat the broiler, and adjust the rack to about 4 inches from the heat source. Use a sharp, sturdy knife to split the hens through their backbones; it will cut through without too much effort. Rub the skin side with olive oil. Flatten the hens in a broiling or roasting pan, skin side down, and liberally sprinkle the exposed surfaces with salt and pepper. Slice one lemon as thinly as you can (a mandoline is best for this) and lay the slices on the birds.
- Broil for about 10 minutes, or until the lemon is browned and the birds appear cooked on top; rotate the pan if necessary. Turn the birds over, sprinkle with salt and pepper, and return to the heat. Cook another 10 minutes, or until the skin is nicely browned. Meanwhile, slice the remaining lemon as thinly as possible.
- Lay the lemon slices on the skin, and broil 5 minutes. The lemons should be slightly browned and the birds cooked through; if not, cook a couple of minutes more. Drizzle with

the balsamic vinegar, garnish with parsley and serve.

Nutrition Information

- 393: calories;
- 29 grams: protein;
- 7 grams: saturated fat;
- 14 grams: monounsaturated fat;
- 5 grams: polyunsaturated fat;
- 4 grams: carbohydrates;
- 1 gram: sugars;
- 477 milligrams: sodium;

31. Broiled Cornish Hens With Spicy Salt

Serving: 4 servings | Prep: | Cook: | Ready in: 30mins

Ingredients

- 1 tablespoon Sichuan peppercorns
- 2 Cornish hens, split in half
- Salt
- Juice of a lime

Direction

- Adjust broiler rack of oven so that it is about 6 inches from heating element. Preheat oven on broil setting. Place a large skillet or broiling pan into oven, and heat for 10 or 15 minutes.
- Meanwhile, toast peppercorns in another dry skillet over medium heat, shaking occasionally, until fragrant, about 5 minutes. Grind to a powder in a spice mill or a coffee grinder or with mortar and pestle. Sprinkle about one teaspoon of ground peppercorns over skin side of hens; sprinkle with a bit of salt as well. Combine remaining powder with an equal amount of salt, and set aside.
- Carefully remove skillet from oven, and put hens in it, skin side up. Broil without turning, moving pieces as necessary to brown evenly, about 20 minutes, or until nicely browned and cooked through.
- Remove birds to a plate, and drizzle with a little of their pan juices and lime juice. Serve, passing spicy salt at the table.

Nutrition Information

- 345: calories;
- 7 grams: saturated fat;
- 3 grams: carbohydrates;
- 0 grams: sugars;
- 1 gram: dietary fiber;
- 29 grams: protein;
- 434 milligrams: sodium;
- 24 grams: fat;
- 10 grams: monounsaturated fat;
- 5 grams: polyunsaturated fat;

32. Broiled Duck With Orange Glazed Turnips

Serving: 2 servings | Prep: | Cook: | Ready in: 45mins

Ingredients

- 1 4 to 4 1/2 pound duck
- 1 orange
- ½ teaspoon rosemary
- Coarse salt and freshly ground black pepper to taste
- 1 large turnip, cut into walnut-sized pieces
- 2 teaspoons sugar
- ½ stick butter
- 1 tablespoon fresh chopped parsley

Direction

- Cut the duck in half lengthwise with poultry shears, working up from the tail and down the center (or have it cut in half by the butcher). Remove as much fat as possible from the carcass. Prick the skin lightly all over with a fork so the fat will pour off as the duck cooks.

- Pare the orange thinly and set the peel aside. Squeeze the juice from the orange and pour it over the duck on the bone side. Sprinkle that side with rosemary, salt and pepper.
- Heat broiler to medium-hot. Place the duck halves on a broiler rack, bone side up, and broil four inches from the heat for 15 minutes. Drain off the fat and turn the duck pieces so the skin side is up. Season with salt and pepper. Broil for 20 minutes or until the skin is browned and crisp. Be careful not to burn the skin. If it cooks too fast, move the broiling rack to a lower rung. The duck is done when the juices are pink.
- While the duck is cooking, bring the turnip pieces to a boil in enough water to cover. After five minutes add the orange peel. When the turnips are almost tender - after about 10 minutes - drain off all but half a cup of water. Add the sugar and butter and cook until glazed, turning occasionally with a wooden spoon. Meanwhile, cut the orange peel into julienne strips and add to the turnips. Correct seasoning.
- Serve the turnips in a heated dish and the duck halves on heated individual plates. Garnish with parsley and serve.

33. Broiled Fennel With Parmesan Cheese

Serving: 4 servings | Prep: | Cook: | Ready in: 25mins

Ingredients

- 3 large unblemished fennel bulbs, about 1/2 pound each
- Salt and freshly ground pepper to taste
- ½ teaspoon ground cumin
- 2 tablespoons olive oil
- 4 tablespoons freshly grated Parmesan cheese or Romano

Direction

- Preheat broiler.
- Trim the fennel, leaving the bulb intact. Cut each fennel lengthwise into 1/2-inch slices. Arrange the slices in one layer in a baking dish or pan.
- Sprinkle the fennel evenly with salt, pepper and cumin. Brush the top of the slices with 1 tablespoon of the olive oil.
- Place the fennel slices under the broiler about 6 inches from the heat, leaving the door partly open. Broil 5 minutes. Turn the fennel and brush with remaining oil. Cook 5 minutes.
- Sprinkle the fennel with the cheese, return it to the broiler and broil until it is lightly browned.

Nutrition Information

- 170: calories;
- 11 grams: fat;
- 5 grams: dietary fiber;
- 7 grams: protein;
- 446 milligrams: sodium;
- 13 grams: carbohydrates;
- 3 grams: saturated fat;
- 6 grams: monounsaturated fat;
- 1 gram: polyunsaturated fat;

34. Broiled Fiery Bluefish

Serving: 6 servings | Prep: | Cook: | Ready in: 11mins

Ingredients

- 3 medium-size bluefish fillets (14 ounces to 1 pound each, about an inch thick)
- ½ teaspoon salt
- 1 ½ teaspoons Italian seasoning
- 1 teaspoon Tabasco sauce
- 1 tablespoon olive oil

Direction

- Cut each fillet into two steaks (7 to 8 ounces each). Cut 2 crosswise slits through the skin

and into the flesh of each fillet to a depth of about 1/4 inch. Sprinkle the steaks with the salt, Italian seasoning, Tabasco and olive oil and arrange them on a broiler pan. Set aside, covered and refrigerated, until cooking time.
- Preheat broiler.
- When ready to cook, place the pan under a hot broiler, about 3 inches from the source of heat, and broil for 5 to 6 minutes without turning, until the skin begins to blister and brown and the flesh is cooked through. If the fillets are thicker than 1 inch, add 1 to 2 minutes to the cooking time. Slide a fillet, skin-side up, onto each serving plate.

Nutrition Information

- 114: calories;
- 1 gram: polyunsaturated fat;
- 3 grams: monounsaturated fat;
- 0 grams: sugars;
- 15 grams: protein;
- 182 milligrams: sodium;
- 5 grams: fat;

35. Broiled Fish Cakes With Ginger And Cilantro

Serving: 4 servings | Prep: | Cook: | Ready in: 1hours

Ingredients

- 1 baking potato weighing about 1/2 pound
- Salt to taste
- 1 ½ pounds fillet of cod or other mild, delicate white fish
- 1 tablespoon peeled and minced ginger
- ½ cup minced cilantro leaves, plus more for garnish
- 1 fresh or dried hot red chile, minced, or 1/4 teaspoon cayenne, or to taste
- Freshly ground black pepper to taste
- 2 tablespoons peanut or other oil
- Lime wedges

Direction

- Boil potato in salted water to cover until it is tender but not mushy, 30 to 40 minutes.
- Meanwhile, place fish in a skillet that can later be covered. Add water to cover, salt the water, and bring to a boil over high heat. Cover, turn off heat, and set a timer for 10 minutes. After that time, use a slotted spoon to remove fish to a bowl.
- When potato is done, peel it and mash it with the fish. Add seasonings, along with some salt and pepper, and work the mixture with your hands until it is well blended. Shape into 8 equal burger-shaped patties.
- Preheat broiler, and set rack about 4 inches from heat source. Brush patties on both sides with oil, then place on a non-stick baking sheet. Broil carefully, until nicely browned on top, then turn and brown on the other side. Sprinkle with more cilantro, and serve hot, with lime wedges.

Nutrition Information

- 242: calories;
- 559 milligrams: sodium;
- 5 grams: fat;
- 1 gram: sugars;
- 2 grams: monounsaturated fat;
- 13 grams: carbohydrates;
- 37 grams: protein;

36. Broiled Fish Tacos

Serving: 4 servings | Prep: | Cook: | Ready in: 20mins

Ingredients

- 3 limes
- ¼ cup grapeseed or canola oil
- 1 packed cup cilantro leaves, chopped (from about half a bunch)

- 1 packed cup fresh mint, parsley or basil leaves, or a combination, chopped
- ½ teaspoon kosher salt, plus more for seasoning
- ½ teaspoon paprika
- ½ teaspoon ground coriander
- 4 boneless mahi-mahi or halibut fillets, about 6 ounces each
- 8 corn tortillas
- Mexican crema or crème fraîche, for serving

Direction

- Finely zest the limes into a medium bowl. Remove the peel and pith from each lime. Discard the peel and pith, and cut the flesh into rounds. Chop into small pieces and add to the bowl. Set aside, along with 1 tablespoon vegetable or grapeseed oil and the chopped herbs. (You'll add them right before serving.)
- Move the broiler rack to less than 6 inches from the flame or coil, and heat broiler to high. Place the fish fillets in a flat, ovenproof dish. Combine the remaining 3 tablespoons of oil, salt, paprika and coriander in a small bowl. Drizzle all over the fish, rubbing to make sure all surfaces are coated. Broil until fish is crispy golden brown around the edges and just cooked through, about 5 to 6 minutes (do not overcook).
- Meanwhile, lay out the tortillas in an even layer (overlapping slightly) on a baking sheet. Remove from the fish from the oven, and immediately toast the tortillas under the broiler until golden around the edges, about 2 minutes. Flip and toast 30 seconds to 1 minute more. (These are warm and pliable right out the oven, but crisp up as they cool. Wrap in a clean kitchen towel to keep soft.)
- Toss together the lime zest, lime flesh, herbs and oil and season with salt. Break each fish fillet in half with a fork or spoon to make 8 portions, and fill each tortilla with fish and herb salad. Drizzle or serve with crema.

Nutrition Information

- 397: calories;
- 2 grams: saturated fat;
- 0 grams: trans fat;
- 9 grams: monounsaturated fat;
- 35 grams: protein;
- 416 milligrams: sodium;
- 5 grams: polyunsaturated fat;
- 29 grams: carbohydrates;
- 6 grams: dietary fiber;
- 1 gram: sugars;
- 17 grams: fat;

37. Broiled Lamb Chops With Apricots

Serving: 2 servings | Prep: | Cook: | Ready in: 20mins

Ingredients

- 1 tablespoon onion chopped fine
- 8 small dried apricot halves
- 2 double rib (or loin) lamb chops with a pocket cut between the bones, completely trimmed of fat
- ½ teaspoon dried rosemary
- ½ teaspoon dried thyme
- ½ teaspoon grated lemon peel
- Freshly ground black pepper to taste

Direction

- Cover the broiler pan with aluminum foil. Preheat the broiler.
- Combine the chopped onion with the apricots. Divide in half, and stuff each chop with mixture.
- Place the chops on the broiler pan, and press the herbs, grated lemon peel and pepper on both sides of each chop.
- Place the broiler pan 2 or 3 inches from the source of heat, and broil the chops for about 7 minutes per side until crusty but still pink.

Nutrition Information

- 454: calories;
- 8 grams: carbohydrates;
- 1 gram: dietary fiber;
- 6 grams: sugars;
- 39 grams: fat;
- 17 grams: protein;
- 16 grams: monounsaturated fat;
- 3 grams: polyunsaturated fat;
- 65 milligrams: sodium;

38. Broiled Lobsters With Sichuan Peppercorns

Serving: 4 first-course or 2 entree servings | Prep: | Cook: | Ready in: 1hours

Ingredients

- ¼ cup Sichuan peppercorns
- 1 shallot, finely chopped
- ¾ cup white wine
- 4 tablespoons cold, unsalted butter, diced
- Fine sea salt, to taste
- 2 1-pound lobsters
- Chopped chervil for garnish

Direction

- Place a small, heavy skillet over medium heat. Add the peppercorns and cook, shaking the pan, until they are fragrant and lightly toasted, about 3 minutes. Transfer them to a mortar and crush coarsely, or place on a cutting board and crush with the side of a knife. Set aside.
- Place the shallot and wine in a small saucepan and simmer until the mixture is almost dry, 5 to 6 minutes. Reduce the heat as low as possible and whisk in the diced butter a chunk at a time. Season with sea salt. Set aside.
- Place a small-enough cutting board in a sheet pan. (This will catch the lobster juices.) Lay a lobster on the cutting board. Place the tip of a large, heavy knife at the indentation where the carapace meets the lobster head, insuring that the cutting blade is facing toward the lobster's eyes. Swiftly and forcefully, plunge the knife through the lobster until the knife point hits the cutting board. Immediately force the blade down, splitting the lobster's head. (Although it's dead, it may still move.) Continue splitting the lobster so that the head and tail are split. Repeat with the remaining lobster.
- Remove and discard the intestine from the tail as well as the spongy green parts from the body. Twist off the claws, and using the flat of the knife, crack each claw and remove some of the shell to expose as much of the meat as possible.
- Preheat the broiler. In a roasting pan just large enough to hold the lobster pieces in a single layer, scatter all but 1 1/2 teaspoons of the cracked peppercorns. Lay the lobster pieces, flesh side up, in the pan and baste the shells and meat generously with some of the butter sauce and sprinkle them with the reserved peppercorns. Season the meat lightly with sea salt.
- Broil the lobsters about 8 inches from the heat for 5 minutes. Remove from the oven, brush again with butter sauce and broil until the meat is just opaque, 4 to 5 more minutes. Transfer the pieces to plates, surround with some of the peppercorns from the pan, garnish with chervil and serve.

Nutrition Information

- 339: calories;
- 13 grams: fat;
- 4 grams: monounsaturated fat;
- 1 gram: polyunsaturated fat;
- 2 grams: sugars;
- 8 grams: carbohydrates;
- 0 grams: trans fat;
- 39 grams: protein;
- 966 milligrams: sodium;

39. Broiled Mackerel Fillets With Tomato Caper Sauce

Serving: 4 servings | Prep: | Cook: | Ready in: 15mins

Ingredients

- 8 boneless mackerel fillets, about 1 1/2 pounds
- Salt and freshly ground pepper to taste
- 4 tablespoons olive oil
- 3 tablespoons chopped fresh thyme or 1 teaspoon dried
- 4 ripe plum tomatoes, about 1/2 pound
- ½ cup chopped onion
- 1 tablespoon finely chopped garlic
- ½ teaspoon turmeric
- ½ cup drained capers
- 1 tablespoon lemon juice
- ½ teaspoon grated lemon rind
- Pinch cayenne pepper
- 4 tablespoons chopped parsley

Direction

- Preheat the broiler to high.
- Place the mackerel fillets on a flat dish and sprinkle them with salt and pepper. Brush the fillets with 2 tablespoons of the olive oil and sprinkle the thyme evenly over the fillets. Set aside.
- Place the tomatoes in boiling water for about 10 seconds. Drain and pull away the skin. Cut away the core and discard. Cut the tomatoes crosswise and then cut into small cubes. Set aside.
- Heat the remaining oil in a saucepan over medium-high heat. Add the onion and cook, stirring, until wilted. Add the garlic, turmeric, capers, lemon juice and rind, tomatoes, cayenne, salt and pepper. Cook, stirring, 3 minutes. Set aside and keep warm.
- Place the mackerel fillets skin side up under the broiler and cook about 3 minutes. Carefully flip the fillets and cook another 3 to 4 minutes until the fish is cooked through.
- Transfer the fillets to a warm serving plate and spoon equal portions of the tomato-caper sauce over them. Sprinkle with parsley and serve immediately.

Nutrition Information

- 503: calories;
- 0 grams: trans fat;
- 7 grams: polyunsaturated fat;
- 3 grams: dietary fiber;
- 33 grams: protein;
- 677 milligrams: sodium;
- 38 grams: fat;
- 8 grams: carbohydrates;
- 19 grams: monounsaturated fat;
- 2 grams: sugars;

40. Broiled Melon With Balsamic

Serving: 4 servings | Prep: | Cook: | Ready in: 30mins

Ingredients

- 1 cantaloupe or honeydew melon, cut into 1-inch-thick slices, rinds and seeds removed
- 4 teaspoons vegetable oil
- ½ teaspoon salt
- ½ cup chopped pine nuts
- Black pepper
- 2 tablespoons balsamic vinegar

Direction

- Turn on broiler; heat should be medium-high and rack no closer than 4 inches from heat source.
- Brush melon all over with oil and put on a rimmed baking sheet. Broil until beginning to color, 3 to 8 minutes depending on your broiler.
- Turn melon carefully (or skip it if the melon seems too tender to turn), sprinkle with salt. Broil until melon is fully tender, another 2 or 3 minutes; sprinkle with nuts and pass under broiler again until pieces just begin to toast, no

more than 1 minute. Sprinkle with lots of black pepper and drizzle with balsamic. Serve warm or at room temperature.

Nutrition Information

- 254: calories;
- 17 grams: fat;
- 1 gram: saturated fat;
- 27 grams: carbohydrates;
- 3 grams: dietary fiber;
- 22 grams: sugars;
- 338 milligrams: sodium;
- 0 grams: trans fat;
- 7 grams: polyunsaturated fat;
- 4 grams: protein;

41. Broiled Or Grilled Chicken With Coconut And Lime

Serving: 4 servings | Prep: | Cook: | Ready in: 20mins

Ingredients

- 2 limes
- 1 to 1 ½ pounds boneless, skinless chicken breasts in 4 pieces
- ½ cup canned or fresh coconut milk
- Salt and ground cayenne pepper
- 1 teaspoon nam pla, fish sauce (optional)
- 4 minced scallions
- ¼ cup minced cilantro

Direction

- Remove the zest from the limes, with either a zester or a vegetable peeler (if you use a peeler, scrape off the white inside of the zest with a paring knife). Mince the zest, and juice the limes. Marinate chicken in half the lime juice while heating broiler; adjust rack to about 4 inches from heat source. (Or grill the chicken if you prefer.)
- Warm the coconut milk over low heat; season it with salt (hold off on this if you are using nam pla) and a pinch of cayenne. Add the lime zest.
- Put chicken, smooth side up, on ungreased baking sheet lined with foil, and place the sheet in broiler. Add about half the remaining lime juice to coconut milk mixture.
- When the chicken is nicely browned on top, in about 6 minutes or more, it is done (to be sure, make a small cut in the thickest part and peek inside). Transfer chicken to a warm platter. Add the nam pla, if you are using it, to the coconut milk; taste, and adjust seasoning as necessary. Spoon a little of the sauce over and around the breasts; then, garnish with the scallions and cilantro, and sprinkle with the remaining lime juice. Serve with white rice, passing the remaining sauce.

Nutrition Information

- 254: calories;
- 11 grams: fat;
- 7 grams: saturated fat;
- 0 grams: trans fat;
- 33 grams: protein;
- 515 milligrams: sodium;
- 1 gram: polyunsaturated fat;
- 6 grams: carbohydrates;
- 2 grams: sugars;

42. Broiled Oysters With Salsa

Serving: 6 - 8 servings | Prep: | Cook: | Ready in: 25mins

Ingredients

- 2 medium tomatoes
- Rock salt
- ¾ cup finely diced fresh Anaheim chilies
- 1 ½ tablespoons minced white onion
- ½ teaspoon minced garlic

- 2 tablespoons finely chopped cilantro, plus extra for garnish
- Salt
- 24 oysters, opened and on the half shell
- ⅓ cup sour cream

Direction

- Bring medium pot of water to a boil, and blanch tomatoes for 8 seconds. Rinse under cool water, and remove skins. Halve tomatoes, discarding pulp and seeds, and cut into 1/8-inch dice; there should be about 3/4 cup.
- Line a serving platter with a layer of rock salt, and set aside.
- In medium bowl, combine tomato, chilies, onion, garlic and 2 tablespoons cilantro. Season with salt to taste.
- Preheat broiler with rack 6 inches under heating element. Place oysters in broiling pan, and broil 1 minute. Transfer to prepared platter. Top each oyster with small spoonful of salsa, and dab of sour cream. Garnish platter with sprinkling of cilantro, and serve immediately.

Nutrition Information

- 150: calories;
- 470 milligrams: sodium;
- 5 grams: fat;
- 2 grams: sugars;
- 1 gram: dietary fiber;
- 10 grams: carbohydrates;
- 15 grams: protein;

43. Broiled Portobello Mushrooms

Serving: 2 servings | Prep: | Cook: | Ready in: 15mins

Ingredients

- 2 portobello mushrooms
- Few shakes of salt

Direction

- Turn on broiler in toaster oven or oven.
- Wash and stem mushrooms; dry.
- Arrange under broiler close to source of heat, top side up. Broil mushrooms 5 to 7 minutes, until they soften a little, turning once.
- Sprinkle lightly with salt, and serve.

Nutrition Information

- 18: calories;
- 1 gram: dietary fiber;
- 2 grams: protein;
- 195 milligrams: sodium;
- 0 grams: polyunsaturated fat;
- 3 grams: carbohydrates;

44. Broiled Sardines With Lemon And Thyme

Serving: 4 servings | Prep: | Cook: | Ready in: 20mins

Ingredients

- 1 lemon, thinly sliced, plus lemon wedges for serving
- 12 or more fresh thyme sprigs, plus chopped fresh thyme for garnish
- 1 ½ pounds sardines 8 to 12 large, gutted, with heads on
- Salt
- Black pepper
- 3 tablespoons extra virgin olive oil

Direction

- Heat the broiler until hot. Move the oven rack as close to the heat source as possible (four to two inches away). Heat a sturdy pan for about 5 minutes.
- Wrap a lemon slice around each thyme sprig and stuff inside the sardines; sprinkle with salt and pepper. When the pan is hot, remove it

from the oven and pour in half of the olive oil, then put the sardines in the pan and drizzle with the remaining oil. Broil for 4 to 5 minutes, then check the sardines; they're ready when they're opaque, the tip of a knife flakes the thickest part easily, and the outside is nicely browned.
- To serve, carefully remove the sardines with a spatula, sprinkle with more herbs if you like, and pour the pan juices over all. Serve with lemon wedges.

Nutrition Information

- 314: calories;
- 35 grams: protein;
- 420 milligrams: sodium;
- 18 grams: fat;
- 4 grams: polyunsaturated fat;
- 9 grams: monounsaturated fat;
- 0 grams: sugars;

45. Broiled Sea Scallops With Orange Butter Sauce

Serving: 4 servings | Prep: | Cook: | Ready in: 1hours25mins

Ingredients

- 1 ½ pounds sea scallops
- Salt and freshly ground white pepper to taste
- 2 tablespoons olive oil
- 4 sprigs fresh thyme or 1 teaspoon dried
- 1 tablespoon chopped fresh rosemary or 2 teaspoons dried
- 2 teaspoons finely chopped garlic
- ⅛ teaspoon red pepper flakes
- 2 tablespoons lemon juice
- ½ cup freshly squeezed orange juice, pulp included
- 4 tablespoons butter at room temperature
- ¾ cup diced and seeded ripe tomatoes
- ¼ cup chopped fresh coriander or parsley

Direction

- Place the scallops in a mixing bowl with the salt, pepper, olive oil, thyme, rosemary, garlic, pepper flakes and lemon juice. Blend well, and refrigerate for 1 hour.
- If using wooden skewers, soak the skewers in water for at least 1/2 hour.
- Meanwhile, place the orange juice in a saucepan, and cook over high heat until it is reduced by half.
- Add the butter, tomatoes and coriander, and cook briefly until the combination is well blended. Season with salt and pepper. Keep warm.
- Heat a broiler or a grill until it is quite hot.
- Divide the scallops into four equal batches, and place them on 4 skewers. Brush with the marinade.
- Place the skewers on the grill or under the broiler, and cook about 4 minutes. Turn the skewers, and cook for 4 more minutes on the other side.
- Serve immediately with the orange-butter sauce.

Nutrition Information

- 305: calories;
- 671 milligrams: sodium;
- 12 grams: carbohydrates;
- 4 grams: sugars;
- 21 grams: protein;
- 19 grams: fat;
- 8 grams: monounsaturated fat;
- 0 grams: trans fat;
- 1 gram: dietary fiber;

46. Broiled Shrimp With Dried Lime

Serving: 4 servings | Prep: | Cook: | Ready in: 15mins

Ingredients

- 16 jumbo shrimp (about 1 pound)
- 2 teaspoons dried lime powder
- 1 teaspoon coriander
- 2 teaspoons cumin
- ½ teaspoon cinnamon
- 1 teaspoon salt
- 1 teaspoon pepper
- 1 to 2 tablespoons olive oil
- Quick yogurt sauce (see recipe)

Direction

- Heat broiler. Peel and devein shrimp.
- Combine lime powder, coriander, cumin, cinnamon, salt and pepper in a small bowl and mix well. Add enough olive oil to form a paste about the texture of wet sand.
- Rub shrimp all over with spice paste, then place on broiler pan and broil about 4 inches from heat for 2 minutes. Turn (tongs are best for this) and continue to broil until just cooked through, about 2 minutes more. Serve with quick yogurt sauce.

47. Broiled Steak With Pineapple And Onion Salsa

Serving: 4 servings | Prep: | Cook: |Ready in: 30mins

Ingredients

- 1 pineapple, peeled, cored and cut into thick rings (canned rings are O.K.; drain excess syrup)
- 1 large onion, cut into thick slices
- 3 tablespoons olive oil
- 1 tablespoon minced fresh chile, like jalapeno or Thai, or to taste, or dried red chile flakes or cayenne to taste
- 2 tablespoons chopped basil or mint leaves
- 2 tablespoons lime juice
- Salt and freshly ground black pepper
- 2 12- to 16-ounce sirloin strip or ribeye steaks, preferably at room temperature

Direction

- Start broiler; set rack about 4 inches from heat source. Brush pineapple and onion slices with olive oil and put on a baking sheet. Broil, turning once or twice, until soft and slightly charred, about 8 minutes total. Remove slices as they finish cooking and chop into bite-size chunks, saving as much juice as possible. When finished, set a cast-iron pan under broiler and let sit for about 10 minutes.
- In a bowl, combine pineapple and onions with chile, basil and lime juice. Sprinkle with salt and pepper and stir to combine. Let sit for about 5 minutes, then taste and add more chile, lime or salt to taste.
- Season steaks with salt and pepper. When pan is very hot, carefully remove from oven and add steaks; return to oven immediately. Broil steaks 6 to 10 minutes for rare to medium rare. (Timing will depend on thickness of meat and broiler heat; check by feel or by making a small slit in one steak and peeking in.) Serve steaks hot, with salsa.

Nutrition Information

- 731: calories;
- 36 grams: carbohydrates;
- 24 grams: sugars;
- 50 grams: fat;
- 19 grams: saturated fat;
- 26 grams: monounsaturated fat;
- 1129 milligrams: sodium;
- 2 grams: trans fat;
- 3 grams: polyunsaturated fat;
- 5 grams: dietary fiber;
- 39 grams: protein;

48. Broiled Tomatoes

Serving: 6 servings | Prep: | Cook: |Ready in: 15mins

Ingredients

- 6 medium red ripe tomatoes
- 24 slivers garlic
- Salt to taste if desired
- Freshly ground pepper to taste
- 3 tablespoons olive oil
- 4 tablespoons grated Parmesan cheese
- 4 tablespoons chopped fresh basil

Direction

- Preheat the broiler to high, 500 degrees.
- Cut the tomatoes in half and arrange, cut side up, in a baking dish. Insert 2 garlic slivers in each half.
- Sprinkle with salt, pepper and olive oil. Sprinkle with the cheese.
- Place under the broiler for about 5 minutes until bubbling and the garlic tips start to brown. Remove garlic, sprinkle with basil and serve.

Nutrition Information

- 126: calories;
- 9 grams: fat;
- 7 grams: carbohydrates;
- 338 milligrams: sodium;
- 5 grams: protein;
- 3 grams: sugars;
- 6 grams: monounsaturated fat;
- 1 gram: polyunsaturated fat;
- 2 grams: dietary fiber;

49. Broiled Tuna Couscous Salad

Serving: 4 servings | Prep: | Cook: | Ready in: 25mins

Ingredients

- The tuna:
- 1 1 1/4-pound skinless and boneless tuna steak, about 1 inch thick
- Salt and freshly ground pepper to taste
- 1 tablespoon olive oil
- 2 sprigs fresh thyme, or 1 teaspoon dried
- The couscous:
- 1 tablespoon olive oil
- 4 tablespoons finely chopped onion
- 1 teaspoon finely chopped garlic
- 1 teaspoon ground cumin
- 1 cup water
- Salt and freshly ground pepper to taste
- 1 cup couscous
- The salad dressing:
- 4 tablespoons red-wine vinegar
- 6 tablespoons olive oil
- 2 tablespoons light soy sauce
- ½ teaspoon finely chopped jalapeno pepper, or to taste
- ¼ teaspoon Tabasco sauce
- 1 cup finely diced celery
- 1 ½ cups diced, peeled and seeded tomatoes
- 2 teaspoons finely minced chopped garlic
- ½ cup coarsely chopped fresh basil, coriander, chervil or parsley
- 2 tablespoons fresh lemon juice
- 2 teaspoons grated orange rind
- Salt and freshly ground pepper to taste

Direction

- Preheat broiler to high, or preheat outdoor grill.
- To prepare tuna, put it on a plate and sprinkle both sides with salt and pepper and brush with a mixture of the oil and thyme. Cover closely with plastic wrap and let stand until ready to broil or grill.
- If broiling, arrange steak on a rack and place under broiler, about 6 inches from heat source. Broil 4 minutes with door partly open. Turn steak and continue broiling, leaving door open, about 4 minutes more.
- If grilling, put steak on hot grill and cover. Cook 4 minutes. Turn fish, cover grill and cook about 4 minutes more. Remove fish; let cool.
- To prepare couscous, heat oil in a small saucepan. Add onion, garlic and cumin and cook, stirring, until vegetables are wilted. Add water, salt and pepper. Bring to a boil and add

couscous, stirring. Cover closely. Remove from heat and let stand 5 minutes. Put in a bowl to cool.
- Meanwhile, combine all ingredients for salad dressing in a large bowl. Blend well with a wire whisk. Check for seasoning.
- Cut tuna into bite-size pieces and add to the couscous in the bowl. Pour dressing over all and toss well. Serve immediately.

50. Broiled Veal Chops With Anchovy Butter

Serving: 4 servings | Prep: | Cook: | Ready in: 25mins

Ingredients

- 3 tablespoons olive oil
- 4 loin veal chops, about 3/4 pound each
- ¼ teaspoon ground cumin
- 2 tablespoons coarsely chopped rosemary leaves
- 2 tablespoons finely chopped shallots
- Salt to taste if desired
- Freshly ground pepper to taste
- 1 tablespoon finely chopped anchovies or anchovy paste
- 4 tablespoons butter, preferably at room temperature
- 2 tablespoons chopped fresh coriander

Direction

- Preheat a charcoal or gas grill or preheat broiler to high.
- Spoon oil into a flat dish and add chops in one layer, turning to coat on all sides. Sprinkle with cumin, rosemary, shallots, salt and pepper. Set aside.
- Meanwhile, combine chopped anchovies or anchovy paste, butter, salt, pepper and coriander in a bowl. Blend thoroughly.
- When ready to cook chops, scrape marinade with herbs from sides of each chop, returning the marinade with herbs to the dish. Put marinade in a warm place. If using a grill, cook the chops about 10 minutes, turning them often.
- If using a broiler, arrange chops on a rack and place about 2 inches from the source of heat. Leave broiler door partly open and cook chops about 5 minutes. Turn them and continue broiling 2 minutes longer.
- Return chops to the marinade in the dish and brush to coat both sides. Spoon anchovy butter over chops and serve.

Nutrition Information

- 564: calories;
- 42 grams: fat;
- 17 grams: saturated fat;
- 0 grams: sugars;
- 18 grams: monounsaturated fat;
- 3 grams: polyunsaturated fat;
- 2 grams: carbohydrates;
- 43 grams: protein;
- 1 gram: dietary fiber;
- 875 milligrams: sodium;

51. Bruschetta Dinner Salad

Serving: 2 servings | Prep: | Cook: | Ready in: 20mins

Ingredients

- 4 large slices of dense, crusty Italian bread
- 2 tablespoons olive oil
- 1 clove garlic
- 1 ½ tablespoons balsamic vinegar
- 1 teaspoon Dijon mustard
- 1 large bunch arugula
- 2 pounds assorted ripe tomatoes

Direction

- Turn on broiler, if using.
- Brush olive oil lightly over one side of each bread slice, using no more than 1 tablespoon

all together. Cut garlic clove and rub oiled side of bread with the cut side of garlic.
- Prepare stove-top grill, if using. Grill or broil bread on prepared side until it browns.
- Whisk the remaining oil with the vinegar and mustard.
- Trim, wash and dry the arugula, and set aside.
- Wash, trim and thickly slice the tomatoes, leaving any cherry or tiny pear-shaped tomatoes whole.
- Arrange arugula on two plates. Cut toasted bread in half and place the side brushed with oil up. Arrange bread on top of arugula. Arrange tomato slices on the bread, and scatter the remaining tomatoes on the arugula. Sprinkle the dressing over the tomatoes. Then, turn over the tomatoes that are on top of the bread so that the dressing seeps into the bread.

Nutrition Information

- 413: calories;
- 18 grams: fat;
- 0 grams: trans fat;
- 11 grams: monounsaturated fat;
- 55 grams: carbohydrates;
- 9 grams: dietary fiber;
- 3 grams: polyunsaturated fat;
- 17 grams: sugars;
- 13 grams: protein;
- 460 milligrams: sodium;

52. Brussels Sprouts And Potato Gratin With Taleggio

Serving: Four servings | Prep: | Cook: | Ready in: 1hours

Ingredients

- 3 cups brussels sprouts, trimmed
- 3 medium baking potatoes, peeled and cut into 1/8-inch thick slices
- 1 ½ teaspoons salt
- Freshly ground pepper to taste
- ½ cup chicken broth, homemade or low-sodium canned
- ¼ cup heavy cream
- ⅓ cup grated taleggio

Direction

- Preheat the oven to 350 degrees. Bring a large pot of water to a boil. Add the brussels sprouts and blanch for 8 minutes. Drain well and cut sprouts in half.
- Place half of the potatoes in an 8-inch round gratin pan, in slightly overlapping layers. Season with some of the salt and pepper. Spread half of the brussels sprouts over the potatoes and season with salt and pepper. Repeat the layers, seasoning each one. Pour the chicken broth over the top and drizzle on the cream. Cover with aluminum foil. Bake until the potatoes are tender, about 45 minutes.
- Preheat the broiler. Sprinkle the top of the gratin with the cheese. Place under the broiler until the cheese is melted and beginning to brown. Divide among 4 plates and serve immediately.

Nutrition Information

- 280: calories;
- 11 grams: protein;
- 7 grams: saturated fat;
- 3 grams: sugars;
- 1 gram: polyunsaturated fat;
- 37 grams: carbohydrates;
- 5 grams: dietary fiber;
- 679 milligrams: sodium;

53. Buffalo Chicken Dip

Serving: 6 to 8 servings | Prep: | Cook: | Ready in: 20mins

Ingredients

- 1 tablespoon unsalted butter
- 2 cups shredded, cooked chicken
- ½ cup Buffalo-style hot sauce
- ½ teaspoon fresh lemon juice
- ¼ cup sour cream
- 4 ounces cream cheese, cut into pieces and softened
- ½ cup freshly shredded white Cheddar cheese
- ¼ cup crumbled blue cheese
- 1 ½ teaspoons finely chopped chives, or to taste
- Celery sticks, carrot sticks, bread, potato chips, and-or tortilla chips, for serving

Direction

- Heat the oven to 375 degrees. In an 8-inch cast-iron or ovenproof skillet, melt the butter over medium-high heat. Add the chicken and hot sauce and simmer until the sauce has thickened and reduced by half, 2 to 3 minutes.
- Turn off the heat, then stir in the lemon juice, sour cream and cream cheese until combined. Sprinkle the Cheddar cheese over the top.
- Bake until bubbling around the edges and the cheese has melted, about 10 minutes. If you'd like the top to get browned, run it under the broiler for a minute or two.
- Immediately garnish with blue cheese and chives. Serve with chips, bread or vegetables for dipping.

Nutrition Information

- 179: calories;
- 0 grams: dietary fiber;
- 4 grams: monounsaturated fat;
- 1 gram: sugars;
- 12 grams: protein;
- 548 milligrams: sodium;
- 14 grams: fat;
- 7 grams: saturated fat;

54. Burnt Passion Fruit Curd

Serving: 4 servings | Prep: | Cook: |Ready in: 2hours30mins

Ingredients

- 4 eggs
- 2 egg yolks
- 1 cup fresh passion-fruit juice (from about 6 large ripe fruits, pulp removed, puréed in a blender for 1 minute and sieved; see note)
- 2 tablespoons fresh lime juice
- ¼ cup heavy cream
- 1 cup sugar
- Pinch of salt
- ½ cup unsalted butter, at room temperature, cut into 1-tablespoon pieces
- ¼ cup superfine sugar

Direction

- Combine all the ingredients except the butter and superfine sugar in a metal nonreactive bowl and beat together until the 1 cup of sugar is completely dissolved. Prepare an ice bath in a bowl slightly bigger than the bowl used to beat the ingredients. Put the bowl with the egg mixture over simmering water and cook, beating constantly, for 10 minutes, or until the curd thickens, being careful not to let the egg mixture curdle. Beat in the butter. Transfer the bowl to the ice bath and beat the curd until it is cold, about 5 minutes.
- Spoon the curd into four cold, shallow gratin dishes. Cover and refrigerate for at least 2 hours.
- When ready to serve, heat the broiler to maximum heat. Spread 1 1/816 inch of superfine sugar evenly over the surface of each dish. Place under broiler close to flame until the sugar caramelizes. (You can also use a mini-blowtorch.) Serve immediately.

Nutrition Information

- 617: calories;

- 0 grams: dietary fiber;
- 71 grams: sugars;
- 150 milligrams: sodium;
- 35 grams: fat;
- 1 gram: trans fat;
- 10 grams: monounsaturated fat;
- 73 grams: carbohydrates;
- 20 grams: saturated fat;
- 2 grams: polyunsaturated fat;
- 7 grams: protein;

55. California Sandwiches

Serving: 6 servings | Prep: | Cook: | Ready in: 20mins

Ingredients

- 1 tablespoon extra-virgin olive oil
- 1 teaspoon soy sauce
- Juice of 1 lime
- 1 pound skinless and boneless chicken breasts
- 1 ripe Haas avocado
- 2 teaspoons chili powder
- ¾ cup plain nonfat yogurt
- 1 cup radish sprouts
- ¼ cup grated carrot
- 12 slices multigrain bread

Direction

- Preheat a grill or broiler. Mix the olive oil with the soy sauce and one tablespoon of the lime juice. Brush this mixture on the chicken and grill or broil the chicken until it is lightly browned and cooked through. Set aside.
- Halve the avocado, remove the pit and peel off the skin. Cut the avocado into slices and gently toss them with the remaining lime juice and the chili powder.
- Mix the yogurt with the sprouts and the grated carrot. Spoon this mixture on the slices of bread. Top six of the slices of bread with the avocado slices. Slice the chicken one-half inch thick against the grain and arrange the slices of chicken on the avocado. Cover with the remaining slices of bread, yogurt-side down. Cut the sandwiches in half and serve.

Nutrition Information

- 386: calories;
- 27 grams: protein;
- 17 grams: fat;
- 4 grams: polyunsaturated fat;
- 0 grams: trans fat;
- 33 grams: carbohydrates;
- 7 grams: sugars;
- 8 grams: monounsaturated fat;
- 376 milligrams: sodium;

56. Canard Grille (Broiled Duck)

Serving: 4 servings | Prep: | Cook: | Ready in: 1hours

Ingredients

- 1 duck, 4 to 6 pounds, with giblets
- 1 bay leaf
- Salt and freshly ground pepper to taste
- 2 tablespoons olive oil
- 1 clove garlic, peeled and split

Direction

- Cut the duck or have it cut as follows: Cut off the thighs with legs attached. Cut off the wing tips and reserve, along with the carcass, for soup. Cut off the second wing joint. Cut off the two breast portions (with the main wing bones attached) from the carcass. Trim around the breast and thigh portions to cut away all peripheral skin, that is to say the outer edges.
- Put the breasts, thighs, second wing joints, neck, liver and gizzard in a large bowl.
- Chop the bay leaf as finely as possible on a flat surface. Put the chopped bay leaf in a small mixing bowl and add salt and pepper to taste and the oil. Mix well. Rub the duck pieces with the mixture and let stand until ready to cook.

- When ready to cook, arrange the breast, thigh and leg and wing portions skin side up in one layer in a flat baking dish. Add the neck, liver and gizzard so that they, too, will be exposed to the broiler heat.
- If the broiler and oven have separate temperature controls, preheat broiler to high and oven to 425 degrees. If they have the same temperature control, preheat broiler to high.
- Place duck under the broiler about three or four inches from the source of heat. Broil about five minutes until skin is golden brown. Turn the pieces.
- Broil duck on second side about five minutes or until golden brown.
- If the broiler and oven have the same temperature controls, turn the oven heat to 425 degrees. Let the duck bake in the oven 10 minutes.
- Turn the pieces skin side up and continue baking 10 minutes. Rub the outside of the duck skin with the garlic and then put the garlic in the baking dish. Continue baking five or 10 minutes and serve.

57. Cannelloni With Bitter Greens And Artichoke Saute

Serving: Six first-course servings | Prep: | Cook: | Ready in: 2hours15mins

Ingredients

- The pasta:
- 2 ¼ cups all-purpose flour
- 1 teaspoon kosher salt
- 3 eggs
- 3 tablespoons olive oil
- The filling and saute:
- 1 ¼ pounds spinach, stemmed
- ¾ pound mesclun
- ¼ pound arugula, stemmed
- 5 tablespoons olive oil
- 1 clove garlic, peeled
- 2 egg yolks
- ⅛ teaspoon ground nutmeg
- 2 teaspoons kosher salt
- Freshly ground pepper to taste
- 1 cup freshly grated Parmesan cheese
- 1 cup chicken broth, homemade or low-sodium canned
- 12 fresh baby artichokes

Direction

- To make the pasta, place the flour, salt, eggs and olive oil in a food processor and process until well combined. Turn the mixture out on a work surface and press the dough together. Knead until smooth. Wrap in a barely damp towel and let stand for 1 hour.
- Meanwhile, to make the filling, toss together the spinach, mesclun and arugula. Heat 1 tablespoon of olive oil in a large skillet. Add 2/3 of the greens to the skillet and set the rest aside. With the garlic clove pierced on the tines of a fork, stir the greens until wilted and tender, about 5 minutes. When cool enough to handle, press the excess moisture from the greens. Place in a food processor with the egg yolks, nutmeg, 1 teaspoon of salt, pepper, 2 tablespoons of olive oil and 1/2 cup of Parmesan. Process until smooth. Scrape into a bowl and refrigerate until ready to use.
- Divide the pasta dough in half. Roll out as thin as possible, making a rectangle slightly larger than 12 inches by 15 inches. Trim to 12 inches by 15 inches and then cut into 3-inch-by-4-inch rectangles. Repeat with the remaining dough. Let the pasta dry slightly while bringing a large pot of water to a boil. Have a bowl of ice water nearby and 2 dry towels, laid flat. Drop 6 pieces of pasta in the boiling water, wait 10 seconds, lift them out with tongs and place in the ice water. Lay the pieces flat on the towels to drain. Repeat with the remaining pasta.
- Preheat the oven to 350 degrees. Oil a medium-size shallow baking dish. Place 2 tablespoons of the filling in a line across the short side of 1 of the pasta rectangles. Roll the pasta around the filling to form a tube. Repeat

until all of the filling is used. (You may have some pasta left over.) Place the cannelloni in the dish and pour the chicken broth over them. Set aside.
- Stem the artichokes and pull off the tough outer leaves. Cut them in quarters. Bake the pasta for 10 minutes. Meanwhile, heat 2 tablespoons of olive oil in a large skillet over medium heat. Add the artichokes and saute, stirring, for 5 minutes. Add the remaining greens and saute until artichokes are tender, about 5 minutes longer. Season with 1 teaspoon of salt and pepper to taste and keep warm.
- Sprinkle the remaining cheese over the pasta and place under the broiler until lightly browned, about 3 minutes. Divide the artichoke mixture among 6 plates, top with 3 cannelloni and serve immediately.

Nutrition Information

- 645: calories;
- 0 grams: trans fat;
- 3 grams: polyunsaturated fat;
- 77 grams: carbohydrates;
- 21 grams: dietary fiber;
- 5 grams: sugars;
- 1447 milligrams: sodium;
- 7 grams: saturated fat;
- 28 grams: fat;
- 16 grams: monounsaturated fat;
- 30 grams: protein;

58. Caribbean Jerked Pork Tenderloins

Serving: Four servings | Prep: | Cook: | Ready in: 35mins

Ingredients

- 3 tablespoons allspice berries
- 1 teaspoon ground cinnamon
- ½ teaspoon ground nutmeg
- 4 teaspoons ground coriander
- 6 scallions, finely chopped
- 3 cloves garlic, peeled and chopped
- 1 Scotch bonnet chili, with seeds
- 2 tablespoons dark rum
- 6 tablespoons water
- 1 ½ teaspoons salt
- Freshly ground pepper to taste
- 2 pork tenderloins

Direction

- Grind the allspice berries in a spice grinder and transfer to a blender. Add the cinnamon, nutmeg, coriander, scallions, garlic, chili, rum, water, salt and pepper and blend until a smooth paste forms, scraping down the sides of the jar as needed. Place the pork tenderloins in a shallow baking dish. Wearing rubber gloves, rub the paste all over the pork. Refrigerate several hours or overnight.
- Preheat broiler. Place the pork 4 inches under the broiler and broil, turning once, until pork is only slightly pink in the center, about 12 to 15 minutes. Let stand for 5 minutes. Cut into 1/4-inch-thick slices and serve.

Nutrition Information

- 353: calories;
- 3 grams: dietary fiber;
- 4 grams: monounsaturated fat;
- 2 grams: polyunsaturated fat;
- 1 gram: sugars;
- 10 grams: fat;
- 0 grams: trans fat;
- 8 grams: carbohydrates;
- 53 grams: protein;
- 735 milligrams: sodium;

59. Caribbean Sweet Potato Soup With Gingered Shrimp

Serving: Six servings | Prep: | Cook: |Ready in: 1hours35mins

Ingredients

- The soup:
- 6 small sweet potatoes (about 3 1/2 pounds), peeled and cut into 1-inch-thick pieces
- 2 ¼ cups unsweetened coconut milk
- 6 cups chicken broth, homemade or low-sodium canned
- 1 teaspoon kosher salt, plus more to taste
- 1 ½ tablespoons fresh lime juice
- The condiments:
- 3 tablespoons minced fresh ginger
- 3 tablespoons fresh lemon juice
- 2 tablespoons canola oil
- ¼ teaspoon kosher salt
- 1 ½ pounds large shrimp, shelled and deveined
- 4 large bananas, peeled and cut across into 1/2-inch-thick slices
- 1 cup unsweetened coconut flakes, lightly toasted
- 1 cup sliced almonds, toasted
- ½ cup coarsely chopped cilantro
- Tabasco sauce

Direction

- To make the soup, combine the sweet potatoes, 1 cup of coconut milk and the chicken broth in a large saucepan. Bring to a boil, lower heat and simmer until the potatoes are soft, about 15 minutes. Place in a food processor and puree until smooth. Mix in the remaining coconut milk and the salt. Reheat before serving, and stir in the lime juice and additional salt, if needed.
- To make the condiments, combine the ginger, lemon juice, oil and salt in a shallow dish. Add the shrimp and toss to coat. Refrigerate for 1 hour. Preheat the broiler. Remove the shrimp from the marinade and broil until cooked through, about 5 minutes. Set aside. Place the bananas on a greased baking sheet and broil until nicely browned, about 3 minutes. Place the shrimp, bananas, coconut, almonds and cilantro in separate bowls.
- Ladle the soup into 6 bowls. Serve, passing the condiments, including Tabasco, separately.

Nutrition Information

- 807: calories;
- 11 grams: monounsaturated fat;
- 32 grams: protein;
- 1500 milligrams: sodium;
- 44 grams: fat;
- 4 grams: polyunsaturated fat;
- 79 grams: carbohydrates;
- 12 grams: dietary fiber;
- 25 grams: sugars;
- 26 grams: saturated fat;
- 0 grams: trans fat;

60. Carrot And Leek Frittata With Tarragon

Serving: Six servings | Prep: | Cook: |Ready in: 50mins

Ingredients

- 2 tablespoons extra virgin olive oil
- 1 ½ cups finely sliced or diced carrot
- 1 ½ cups finely sliced leeks
- Salt
- freshly ground pepper to taste
- 2 garlic cloves, minced
- 8 eggs
- 2 tablespoons milk
- ¼ cup finely chopped tarragon

Direction

- Heat 1 tablespoon of the oil over medium heat in a 10-inch heavy nonstick skillet. Add the carrots and leeks. Cook, stirring often, until

tender, five to eight minutes. Stir in the garlic, season to taste with salt and pepper. Cook, stirring, for 30 seconds to one minute, and remove from the heat.
- Beat the eggs and milk together in a large bowl. Stir in salt to taste (about 1/2 teaspoon), pepper, the cooked carrots and leeks, and the tarragon.
- Clean and dry the pan, and return to the burner, set on medium-high. Heat the remaining tablespoon of olive oil in the skillet. Drop a bit of egg into the pan, and if it sizzles and cooks at once, the pan is ready. Pour in the egg mixture. Tilt the pan to distribute the eggs and filling evenly over the surface. Shake the pan gently, tilting it slightly with one hand while lifting up the edges of the frittata with a spatula in your other hand, to let the eggs run underneath during the first few minutes of cooking.
- Turn the heat to low, cover and cook 10 minutes, shaking the pan gently every once in a while. From time to time, remove the lid, tilt the pan and loosen the bottom of the frittata with a wooden spatula so that it doesn't burn. The bottom should turn a golden color. The eggs should be just about set; cook a few minutes longer if they're not.
- Meanwhile, heat the broiler. Uncover the pan and place under the broiler, not too close to the heat, for one to three minutes, watching very carefully to make sure the top doesn't burn (at most, it should brown very slightly and puff under the broiler). Remove from the heat, shake the pan to make sure the frittata isn't sticking, and allow it to cool for at least five minutes and for as long as 15 minutes. Loosen the edges with a wooden or plastic spatula. Carefully slide from the pan onto a large round platter. Cut into wedges or into smaller bite-size diamonds. Serve hot, warm, at room temperature or cold.

Nutrition Information

- 158: calories;
- 285 milligrams: sodium;
- 3 grams: sugars;
- 2 grams: polyunsaturated fat;
- 1 gram: dietary fiber;
- 10 grams: fat;
- 0 grams: trans fat;
- 5 grams: monounsaturated fat;
- 8 grams: protein;

61. Celery Root Au Gratin

Serving: 4 servings | Prep: | Cook: |Ready in: 30mins

Ingredients

- 1 large celery root, about 2 pounds
- 2 potatoes, about 1 pound
- Salt to taste, if desired
- Freshly ground pepper to taste
- ¼ teaspoon freshly grated nutmeg
- 2 tablespoons butter
- ⅓ cup heavy cream
- ¼ cup freshly grated Parmesan cheese

Direction

- Peel celery root and cut into 1-inch cubes. There should be 6 to 7 cups.
- Peel potatoes and cut into 1-inch cubes. Combine potatoes and celery-root pieces in a saucepan. Add water to cover and salt to taste. Bring to a boil and cook about 15 minutes or until vegetable pieces are tender.
- Meanwhile, preheat broiler to high.
- Drain vegetables and pour them into the bowl of a food processor. Blend thoroughly and add salt, pepper, nutmeg, butter and cream. Blend well.
- Spoon and scrape mixture into a small baking dish and smooth over the top. Sprinkle evenly with Parmesan cheese.
- Place dish under broiler about 6 inches from heat. Broil about 5 minutes or until cheese is nicely browned and glazed.

Nutrition Information

- 298: calories;
- 873 milligrams: sodium;
- 10 grams: saturated fat;
- 0 grams: trans fat;
- 34 grams: carbohydrates;
- 6 grams: dietary fiber;
- 8 grams: protein;
- 16 grams: fat;
- 4 grams: sugars;
- 1 gram: polyunsaturated fat;

62. Charred Asparagus With Green Garlic Chimichurri

Serving: 4 servings | Prep: | Cook: | Ready in: 30mins

Ingredients

- 3 tablespoons finely chopped green garlic
- ½ cup finely chopped parsley
- 2 teaspoons finely chopped fresh oregano or 1 teaspoon dried oregano
- ½ cup extra-virgin olive oil, plus more for drizzling
- Salt and pepper
- 1 pound pencil-thin asparagus, tough ends snapped off
- 1 tablespoon red wine vinegar
- 4 ounces crumbled feta
- Handful of olives
- Crushed red pepper, to taste

Direction

- Heat a cast-iron pan or broiler, or prepare a charcoal grill. Make the chimichurri sauce: In a small bowl, stir together chopped green garlic, parsley, oregano, olive oil and 1/4 cup water. Season to taste with salt and pepper.
- Spread asparagus on a baking sheet, drizzle very lightly with oil and sprinkle with salt.
- Transfer asparagus to hot cast-iron pan or to a grill grate that is placed very close to live coals; alternatively if broiling, place pan as close to broiler element as possible. Let asparagus cook for 4 to 5 minutes, until nicely charred, with a few burnt and blistered spots. Asparagus cooked this way tastes best if slightly undercooked and still bright green.
- Put cooked asparagus on a platter. Stir vinegar into chimichurri and spoon sauce generously over spears. Top with crumbled feta and olives, then sprinkle with crushed red pepper and serve.

Nutrition Information

- 358: calories;
- 34 grams: fat;
- 8 grams: saturated fat;
- 21 grams: monounsaturated fat;
- 3 grams: sugars;
- 9 grams: carbohydrates;
- 7 grams: protein;
- 446 milligrams: sodium;

63. Charred Lamb And Eggplant With Date Yogurt Chutney

Serving: 4 servings | Prep: | Cook: | Ready in: 1hours

Ingredients

- ¾ cup plain yogurt
- 1 teaspoon grated lemon zest
- 2 ½ teaspoons lemon juice
- 2 fat garlic cloves, finely chopped
- 8 tablespoons extra virgin olive oil, more for drizzling
- 1 pound boneless leg of lamb, cut into 1-inch chunks
- 1 ¾ teaspoons kosher salt
- 1 ¼ teaspoons black pepper
- 1 pound eggplant, cut into 3/4-inch cubes
- 4 dates, pitted and finely chopped
- ¼ cup chopped cilantro
- 3 tablespoons sliced almonds

- Chopped fresh mint, for garnish

Direction

- In a medium bowl, whisk together the yogurt, lemon zest, lemon juice and garlic. Whisk in 5 tablespoons of the oil.
- Season the meat with 1 teaspoon salt and 1 teaspoon pepper and transfer to a large, nonreactive bowl. Pour half the yogurt mixture over the meat and toss well. Cover tightly with plastic wrap and refrigerate at least 3 hours or overnight.
- Heat the oven to 425 degrees. Toss the eggplant with the remaining 3 tablespoons oil, 3/4 teaspoon salt and 1/4 teaspoon pepper. Spread on a baking sheet and roast, tossing occasionally, until eggplant is golden brown and tender, 20 to 30 minutes. Scrape into a bowl. Whisk the dates and cilantro into the remaining yogurt mixture and toss with the warm eggplant.
- Adjust the oven to broil, with a rack 2 inches from the heat. Remove meat from marinade, wiping off any excess, and transfer to a large baking sheet. Drizzle lamb with a little oil. Broil until golden and cooked to desired doneness, about 4 minutes for medium rare. Let the meat rest for 5 minutes.
- In a small skillet over medium-high heat, toast almonds, tossing occasionally, until golden brown, about 3 minutes.
- Divide meat among serving plates and spoon eggplant next to the meat. Garnish with almonds and mint.

Nutrition Information

- 395: calories;
- 22 grams: sugars;
- 25 grams: protein;
- 718 milligrams: sodium;
- 21 grams: fat;
- 0 grams: trans fat;
- 2 grams: polyunsaturated fat;
- 8 grams: saturated fat;
- 9 grams: monounsaturated fat;
- 29 grams: carbohydrates;
- 6 grams: dietary fiber;

64. Cheddar Cheese Crostini

Serving: 24 crostini | Prep: | Cook: | Ready in: 30mins

Ingredients

- 1 baguette cut into 1/2-inch diagonal slices (or 8 slices country-style bread cut into 3-by-3-inch slices 1/2-inch thick)
- Dijon mustard
- ¼ pound good-quality cheddar cheese
- Cayenne pepper

Direction

- Preheat oven to 400 degrees. Bake the slices of bread until lightly browned (about 10 minutes). The slices may be toasted under a broiler or over a grill instead.
- Preheat broiler. Spread the slices with mustard, topped with slices of cheddar cheese and sprinkle with cayenne. Brown under the broiler and arrange on a serving platter.

65. Cheese Croutons

Serving: Eighteen cheese croutons | Prep: | Cook: | Ready in: 15mins

Ingredients

- 1 baguette
- 3 tablespoons olive oil
- ½ cup finely grated Gruyere or asiago cheese

Direction

- Preheat the broiler.
- Cut the bread on the bias into 18 slices one-quarter inch thick. Arrange the slices flat on a

baking sheet and place them under the broiler about four inches from the source of heat. Broil for 30 seconds, or until golden brown.
- Turn the slices over and brush with the olive oil. Sprinkle the center of each slice with the grated cheese. Return the slices to the broiler, and broil until they are golden brown and the cheese is melted.

Nutrition Information

- 78: calories;
- 2 grams: monounsaturated fat;
- 9 grams: carbohydrates;
- 144 milligrams: sodium;
- 3 grams: protein;
- 1 gram: sugars;
- 0 grams: dietary fiber;

66. Cherry Bread Pudding

Serving: Four servings | Prep: | Cook: | Ready in: 1hours15mins

Ingredients

- 1 ½ pounds fresh cherries, washed, stemmed and pitted
- ⅓ cup sugar
- ⅔ cup water
- 2 tablespoons fresh lemon juice, plus more to taste
- 8 2/3-inch slices stale coarse country-style bread, crust removed
- 2 tablespoons unsalted butter, melted
- Confectioners' sugar

Direction

- Place the cherries in a nonreactive saucepan and sprinkle with the sugar. Let stand for 30 minutes, stirring often. Stir in the water, place over medium-high heat and bring to a boil. Reduce heat and simmer gently for 10 to 15 minutes. Remove from heat and let cool.
- Stir in lemon juice. Refrigerate until cold.
- Preheat broiler. Lightly butter a 9-inch nonreactive skillet, preferably one that would be attractive to serve from. Brush 1 side of each bread slice with butter and place, buttered side up, in the skillet, slightly overlapping, in 1 layer. Set under broiler to lightly toast the bread. Cool completely.
- Strain the cherries, reserving the juice. Ladle the cherry juice over the bread and make sure that all of the bread is completely saturated with juice. Scatter the cherries over the top. Place the skillet over medium heat and bring the juices to a boil. Cover with foil and cook for 5 minutes. Remove from heat and let the pudding cool to room temperature in the pan. Sprinkle the top with confectioners' sugar and serve.

Nutrition Information

- 255: calories;
- 4 grams: dietary fiber;
- 0 grams: polyunsaturated fat;
- 2 grams: monounsaturated fat;
- 51 grams: carbohydrates;
- 3 grams: protein;
- 6 grams: fat;
- 42 grams: sugars;
- 39 milligrams: sodium;

67. Chick Pea And Pesto Canapes

Serving: 24 - 30 canapes | Prep: | Cook: | Ready in: 25mins

Ingredients

- 24 to 30 thin slices French baguette bread
- 1 cup cooked, drained chick peas (fresh or canned)
- 3 tablespoons lemon juice
- 3 tablespoons prepared pesto
- Salt and freshly ground black pepper

- 2 egg whites
- 3 tablespoons freshly grated Parmesan cheese

Direction

- Preheat broiler. Lightly toast the baguette rounds and arrange them on a foil-lined baking sheet.
- Puree the chick peas in a food processor along with the lemon juice and the pesto. Season to taste with salt and pepper. Transfer to a bowl.
- Beat the egg whites with a pinch of salt until they hold firm peaks but are still creamy. Stir one-fourth of the egg whites into the chick pea mixture, then fold in the rest.
- Spoon some of this mixture onto each of the toasted bread rounds and sprinkle each with a little of the cheese. Place under the broiler and broil until lightly browned.
- Transfer to a serving platter and serve.

Nutrition Information

- 31: calories;
- 1 gram: sugars;
- 0 grams: dietary fiber;
- 4 grams: carbohydrates;
- 2 grams: protein;
- 72 milligrams: sodium;

68. Chicken Paved With Tomatoes

Serving: 4 to 6 servings | Prep: | Cook: | Ready in: 30mins

Ingredients

- 6 skinless and boneless chicken breasts (about 2 1/2 pounds)
- 3 tablespoons extra-virgin olive oil
- 3 tablespoons finely chopped imported black olives or olive paste
- 3 medium-ripe tomatoes, sliced thin
- Freshly ground black pepper
- 1 tablespoon finely minced fresh basil

Direction

- Preheat a grill or broiler. Brush the chicken breasts with one-and-a-half tablespoons of the oil. Grill or broil the chicken until it is lightly browned on both sides and just cook through, six to eight minutes on each side.
- Spread the olives or olive paste on the top of each chicken breast and cover with overlapping slices of tomato. Brush with remaining olive oil and season with pepper.
- If you used a grill, move the hot coals to one side and place a sheet of heavy-duty foil on the grill rack not directly over the coals. Place the chicken breasts on the foil, tomato side up, and cover the grill for five minutes, just long enough to allow the tomatoes to warm. If you used a broiler, turn it off and return the chicken breasts to the broiler for about five minutes.
- Sprinkle the chicken with basil and serve.

Nutrition Information

- 332: calories;
- 21 grams: fat;
- 0 grams: trans fat;
- 11 grams: monounsaturated fat;
- 2 grams: carbohydrates;
- 1 gram: sugars;
- 128 milligrams: sodium;
- 5 grams: saturated fat;
- 4 grams: polyunsaturated fat;
- 32 grams: protein;

69. Chicken Roulades With Shrimp

Serving: Eight servings | Prep: | Cook: | Ready in: 45mins

Ingredients

- The roulades:

- 4 to 6 skinless, boneless chicken or capon breast halves, about 1 1/4 pounds
- 7 large shrimp, about 1 1/2 pounds
- 25 fresh coriander leaves
- Salt to taste, if desired
- 4 thin slices lean salt pork, about 2 ounces
- 32 thin, julienne strips carrot, each about 2 inches long
- 32 thin, julienne strips hot green pepper
- 32 thin, julienne strips scallions or green onions
- Oil for brushing the roulades
- The sauce:
- ½ teaspoon coriander seeds
- ½ teaspoon caraway seeds
- 2 teaspoons finely minced garlic
- 1 tablespoon corn, peanut or vegetable oil
- ½ cup finely sliced shallots
- ¼ cup light soy sauce
- ½ cup rich chicken broth
- ½ teaspoon dark brown sugar

Direction

- There are several ways that these roulades may be cooked. They may be broiled, charcoal-grilled or cooked in a skillet with a little oil. Preheat a broiler or charcoal grill or have a skillet ready.
- Place the breast halves on a flat surface and cut off enough of the end pieces to make five ounces. Put the end pieces into the container of a food processor or electric blender and add the shrimp, coriander leaves and salt. Blend until it has the consistency of hamburger meat.
- Meanwhile, put the salt pork slices in a small skillet and cook, turning the pieces often, until they are well browned and slightly crisp. Remove the slices from the skillet, and when they are cool enough to handle, cut them lengthwise into 32 thin, julienne strips.
- Put the chicken breast halves on a flat surface and cut them on the diagonal into approximately 16 thin slices. Pound each slice until it is quite thin and almost transparent. Spoon an equal amount of the ground shrimp-and-chicken mixture into the center of each slice. Smear this filling evenly over each piece. Stack two pieces each of the salt pork, carrot, green pepper and green onion over the center of the filling. Roll each slice over neatly and tightly, like small sausages, to enclose the filling.
- Arrange four of the filled chicken pieces close together and run two skewers parallel and crosswise through the centers to hold the groupings of four together. Brush each grouping on all sides with a little oil.
- To prepare the sauce, grind together the coriander seeds, caraway seeds and garlic, preferably in a mortar and pestle or in a small spice mill or grinder.
- Heat one tablespoon of oil in a small skillet and add the sliced shallots. Cook briefly, stirring, and add the ground spice mixture. Add the soy sauce, chicken broth and brown sugar and bring to the boil. Let simmer about five minutes.
- Meanwhile, cook the skewered chicken roulades as desired - under the broiler, on a grill or in a skillet. Cook about four or five minutes or less on one side. Turn the roulades and cook about four or five minutes on the second side. Spoon the sauce over the roulades and serve.

70. Chicken Skewers With Peanut Sauce

Serving: 4 servings | Prep: | Cook: | Ready in: 30mins

Ingredients

- ½ cup natural peanut butter, preferably chunky
- 1 tablespoon curry paste or curry powder, or to taste
- ½ teaspoon salt
- ¾ cup fresh or canned coconut milk, approximately
- 1 tablespoon nam pla or soy sauce

- 1 tablespoon lime juice
- 1 ½ to 2 pounds boneless chicken thighs, cut into large chunks
- Chopped fresh cilantro leaves for garnish
- Lime wedges

Direction

- Start charcoal or gas grill or heat broiler; fire should be moderately hot, and rack should be at least 4 inches from heat. If using wood skewers, soak them in water.
- Put peanut butter in a small saucepan over medium heat; add curry paste or powder, salt and enough coconut milk to achieve a creamy but quite thick consistency. Cook over low heat, whisking, until smooth; do not boil. Cool a bit, then stir in nam pla and lime juice.
- Marinate chicken in this mixture for 5 minutes to an hour. Skewer chicken chunks, then grill or broil slowly, until nicely browned and cooked through, 10 minutes or longer. Serve hot, garnished with cilantro and accompanied by lime.

Nutrition Information

- 723: calories;
- 10 grams: carbohydrates;
- 2 grams: dietary fiber;
- 4 grams: sugars;
- 23 grams: monounsaturated fat;
- 11 grams: polyunsaturated fat;
- 41 grams: protein;
- 669 milligrams: sodium;
- 59 grams: fat;
- 20 grams: saturated fat;
- 0 grams: trans fat;

71. Chicken Teriyaki

Serving: 8 servings | Prep: | Cook: | Ready in: 30mins

Ingredients

- 1 cup soy sauce
- 1 cup granulated sugar
- 1 ½ teaspoons brown sugar
- 6 cloves garlic, crushed in a press
- 2 tablespoons grated fresh ginger
- ¼ teaspoon freshly ground black pepper
- 1 3-inch cinnamon stick
- 1 tablespoon pineapple juice
- 8 skinless, boneless chicken thighs
- 2 tablespoons cornstarch

Direction

- In a small saucepan, combine all ingredients except cornstarch and chicken. Bring to boil over high heat. Reduce heat to low and stir until sugar is dissolved, about 3 minutes. Remove from heat and let cool. Discard cinnamon stick and mix in 1/2 cup water.
- Place chicken in a heavy-duty sealable plastic bag. Add soy sauce mixture, seal bag, and turn to coat chicken. Refrigerate for at least an hour, ideally overnight.
- Remove chicken and set aside. Pour mixture into a small saucepan. Bring to a boil over high heat, then reduce heat to low. Mix cornstarch with 2 tablespoons water and add to pan. Stir until mixture begins to thicken, and gradually stir in enough water (about 1/2 cup) until sauce is the consistency of heavy cream. Remove from heat and set aside.
- Preheat a broiler or grill. Lightly brush chicken pieces on all sides with sauce, and broil or grill about 3 minutes per side. While chicken is cooking, place sauce over high heat and bring to a boil, then reduce heat to a bare simmer, adding water a bit at a time to keep mixture at a pourable consistency. To serve, slice chicken into strips, arrange on plates, and drizzle with sauce.

Nutrition Information

- 459: calories;
- 7 grams: saturated fat;
- 10 grams: monounsaturated fat;
- 1873 milligrams: sodium;

- 27 grams: protein;
- 25 grams: fat;
- 0 grams: trans fat;
- 5 grams: polyunsaturated fat;
- 31 grams: carbohydrates;
- 1 gram: dietary fiber;
- 26 grams: sugars;

72. Chicken Wings Stuffed With Chevre

Serving: 12 servings | Prep: | Cook: | Ready in: P1DT20mins

Ingredients

- 6 ounces goat cheese, softened
- 2 scallions, finely chopped
- 24 chicken wings
- 3 large cloves garlic, minced
- 2 tablespoons fresh rosemary, minced
- 2 tablespoons kosher salt
- ½ teaspoon freshly ground black pepper
- ½ cup olive oil

Direction

- Stir together the cheese and scallions. Separate the wings at the joint and save the tips for another purpose, like making soup. Loosen the skin over the tops, making a pocket between the skin and the meat. Fill each pocket with about 1 tablespoon of the cheese mixture. Do not overfill.
- Combine the garlic, rosemary, salt, pepper and oil in a large bowl. Add the wings and coat well. Refrigerate for several hours, or up to one day.
- Preheat the broiler. Broil the wings until the skin is browned and the chicken is cooked through, about 8 minutes.

Nutrition Information

- 216: calories;
- 0 grams: sugars;
- 2 grams: polyunsaturated fat;
- 19 grams: fat;
- 5 grams: saturated fat;
- 10 grams: monounsaturated fat;
- 1 gram: carbohydrates;
- 12 grams: protein;
- 180 milligrams: sodium;

73. Chicken Wing Salad With Toasted Garlic Vinaigrette

Serving: 4 servings | Prep: | Cook: | Ready in: 45mins

Ingredients

- ½ cup extra virgin olive oil
- 10 cloves garlic, peeled
- ½ teaspoon cayenne, or to taste
- Salt
- 16 chicken wings
- ¼ cup sherry vinegar or other good vinegar, or to taste
- 6 cups romaine lettuce, washed, dried and torn
- Freshly ground black pepper

Direction

- Prepare a grill or preheat a broiler; the fire should be moderately hot and the rack 4 to 6 inches from the heat source. Put olive oil in a narrow saucepan and add garlic. Turn heat to medium-low and when garlic begins to sizzle, swirl pan occasionally so the garlic rolls about in the oil. When garlic is lightly browned and tender (a thin-bladed knife will penetrate easily), turn off heat.
- Combine 2 tablespoons garlic oil with cayenne and a big pinch salt; toss wings in the mixture. Grill or broil, turning occasionally (do not scorch), until wings are crisp and cooked through, about 20 minutes.

- Meanwhile, once oil has cooled, put it in a blender with the garlic, a pinch salt and vinegar. Blend until smooth; if too thick, add a little more oil, some hot water or, if it is not bright enough for your taste, more vinegar. Toss with greens and black pepper. Serve salad and chicken wings together.

Nutrition Information

- 458: calories;
- 0 grams: trans fat;
- 26 grams: monounsaturated fat;
- 2 grams: dietary fiber;
- 1 gram: sugars;
- 19 grams: protein;
- 513 milligrams: sodium;
- 40 grams: fat;
- 8 grams: saturated fat;
- 6 grams: polyunsaturated fat;
- 5 grams: carbohydrates;

74. Chimichurri Hanger Steak

Serving: 4 servings | Prep: | Cook: | Ready in: 45mins

Ingredients

- For the chimichurri hanger steak
- 1 cup packed flat-leaf parsley
- ½ jalapeño, seeded
- 1 garlic clove
- 2 tablespoons minced mint leaves
- 6 tablespoons extra virgin olive oil
- 1 tablespoon red wine vinegar
- ¼ teaspoon crushed red chili flakes
- Salt
- pepper, to taste
- Cayenne, to taste
- 3 tablespoons panko
- 1 hanger steak, about 2 pounds

Direction

- Mince parsley, jalapeño and garlic and mix in a bowl with mint, oil and vinegar. Season with chili flakes, salt, pepper and cayenne until it has a kick. Reserve 3 tablespoons and add panko to rest.
- Butterfly steak with a sharp knife, slicing it not quite all the way through, so it opens it like a book. Lightly pound any thicker areas to make meat more uniform. Spread chimichurri-panko mix on one side of cut surfaces, fold other side over and fasten the edge with metal or wooden skewers. Coat outside of steak with reserved chimichurri. Chill 3 hours.
- Light grill or broiler and, while it heats, allow steak to come to room temperature. Grill or broil steak to medium rare, about 6 to 8 minutes per side depending on heat. Let rest 10 minutes, remove skewers and cut in thick slices.

Nutrition Information

- 638: calories;
- 49 grams: fat;
- 14 grams: saturated fat;
- 28 grams: monounsaturated fat;
- 639 milligrams: sodium;
- 2 grams: trans fat;
- 4 grams: carbohydrates;
- 1 gram: dietary fiber;
- 0 grams: sugars;
- 46 grams: protein;

75. Chinese Glazed Chicken

Serving: 2 servings | Prep: | Cook: | Ready in: 15mins

Ingredients

- 12 ounces skinless, boneless chicken breasts
- 4 tablespoons finely chopped onion
- 1 tablespoon coarsely grated ginger
- 1 tablespoon reduced- or low-sodium soy sauce

- 2 tablespoons dry sherry
- 1 ½ tablespoons honey
- 1 teaspoon minced garlic in oil
- 2 tablespoons chopped cilantro leaves (optional)

Direction

- Turn broiler on and cover broiler pan with aluminum foil.
- Wash and dry chicken. Cut each breast into quarters. Put chicken in the broiler pan.
- Combine onion, ginger, soy sauce, sherry, honey and garlic in oil. Spoon some over chicken and put under broiler 2 or 3 inches from source of heat. Broil until chicken begins to brown, about 7 minutes. Turn and spoon remaining glaze over chicken and continue broiling until chicken is done, 10 to 12 minutes total.
- Chop cilantro. Serve chicken with its pan juices, sprinkling cilantro over the top.

Nutrition Information

- 379: calories;
- 14 grams: sugars;
- 366 milligrams: sodium;
- 16 grams: fat;
- 5 grams: saturated fat;
- 0 grams: trans fat;
- 7 grams: monounsaturated fat;
- 18 grams: carbohydrates;
- 1 gram: dietary fiber;
- 3 grams: polyunsaturated fat;
- 37 grams: protein;

76. Chipotle Chicken Sausage

Serving: About 1 pound of sausages | Prep: | Cook: | Ready in: 5mins

Ingredients

- 1 pound ground dark-meat chicken
- 3 tablespoons finely chopped scallion
- 1 tablespoon finely chopped chipotle chilies in adobo
- 1 ½ teaspoons kosher salt
- 1 teaspoon dried oregano
- 1 teaspoon ground cumin
- Olive oil for cooking

Direction

- In a large bowl, combine all ingredients and mix well. Form sausage mixture into desired shape: cylinders or patties. Chill for up to 5 days, freeze for up to 3 months, or use immediately.
- Brush sausages with oil and grill or broil them until browned and cooked through. Or fry them in a little oil until well browned all over.

Nutrition Information

- 176: calories;
- 6 grams: monounsaturated fat;
- 1 gram: carbohydrates;
- 14 grams: protein;
- 192 milligrams: sodium;
- 13 grams: fat;
- 3 grams: polyunsaturated fat;
- 0 grams: sugars;

77. Clam Frittata

Serving: 3 to 4 servings as a lunch course with a simple green salad | Prep: | Cook: | Ready in: 15mins

Ingredients

- 6 very large fresh eggs, beaten until smooth
- 1 small tomato, peeled and squeezed to remove seeds and excess juice, and chopped
- 1 cup shredded Parma prosciutto ham (about 3 ounces)

- ½ cup freshly grated Parmigiano-Reggiano cheese
- ½ cup half-and-half or cream
- 2 tablespoons extra-virgin olive oil
- 1 tablespoon fresh thyme leaves (no stems)
- 1 tablespoon minced fresh garlic
- 1 tablespoon unsalted butter, softened
- Freshly ground pepper
- A few drops hot sauce
- 1 ½ cups shucked cherrystone or chowder clams, chopped medium fine
- ½ cup loosely packed shredded basil leaves

Direction

- Place the top oven rack about 8 inches from the flame. Preheat the broiler. Tightly wrap the handle of a 9-inch nonstick skillet with a double thickness of heavy-duty aluminum foil.
- Beat the eggs until smooth. Add the tomato, ham, cheese and half-and-half and stir to mix well.
- Heat the oil in the prepared skillet over medium heat and add thyme and garlic. Stir until the oil is aromatic, about 2 minutes. Slowly pour in the egg mixture while stirring slowly. Stir in the butter, pepper and hot sauce. When curds begin to form, reduce the heat to medium-low and stir in the clams and basil. Cook until the egg mixture thickens, adjusting the heat if necessary so the bottom does not scorch. (Or place the skillet over a pot of simmering water and cook eggs as in a double boiler or bain marie.)
- When the eggs have mostly set and only a thin, uncooked layer remains on top, place the skillet under the broiler, stirring once after 2 minutes, until the top is lightly browned, about 5 minutes. Serve while warm.

Nutrition Information

- 414: calories;
- 0 grams: trans fat;
- 11 grams: monounsaturated fat;
- 3 grams: polyunsaturated fat;
- 8 grams: carbohydrates;
- 1 gram: dietary fiber;
- 2 grams: sugars;
- 27 grams: fat;
- 34 grams: protein;
- 1401 milligrams: sodium;
- 10 grams: saturated fat;

78. Cleopatra's Caesar Salad

Serving: 4 main-dish salads | Prep: | Cook: | Ready in: 20mins

Ingredients

- Olive-oil-flavored nonstick spray
- 3 to 4 slices sourdough bread, cut 1/2 inch thick
- 3 or 4 large cloves garlic
- 8 tablespoons finely grated Parmigiano Reggiano
- 1 cup low-fat buttermilk
- 1 teaspoon Dijon mustard
- 2 teaspoons lemon juice
- 6 drops Worcestershire sauce
- 2 flat anchovy fillets, drained, dried and minced
- 2 teaspoons minced parsley
- Few shakes salt
- Freshly ground black pepper
- 20 cups romaine lettuce torn into bite-size pieces (2 or 3 heads)

Direction

- Turn the oven to 450 degrees.
- Spray the bread on both sides with nonstick spray; then rub with the cut side of several garlic cloves, reserving 1 clove for the dressing. Toast the bread for about 10 minutes, on the bottom shelf of the oven, until brown, turning once.
- Spoon the grated cheese into a small bowl. Stir in the buttermilk, and blend well.
- Mince 1 clove of garlic, and add to the mixture with mustard, lemon juice, Worcestershire,

anchovies, parsley, salt and pepper, whisk to blend.
- For each salad, mix together 1/4 of the croutons with 5 cups of romaine and 1/4 of the salad dressing, and toss.

Nutrition Information

- 577: calories;
- 2 grams: polyunsaturated fat;
- 12 grams: sugars;
- 29 grams: protein;
- 1347 milligrams: sodium;
- 7 grams: monounsaturated fat;
- 18 grams: fat;
- 0 grams: trans fat;
- 77 grams: carbohydrates;
- 8 grams: dietary fiber;

79. Colombian Corn And Cheese Arepas

Serving: 11 large arepas | Prep: | Cook: | Ready in: 1hours

Ingredients

- 3 cups (about 1 pound) precooked white corn flour, like harina P.A.N.
- 2 tablespoons sugar
- 5 tablespoons unsalted butter, melted
- 1 ½ pounds soft fresh cheese like queso blanco or queso fresco (or mozzarella) coarsely grated (about 4 cups, well packed)
- 8 ounces aged cow's-milk cheese, preferably Mexican cotija (or Manchego or Parmesan), coarsely grated (about 2 cups)
- 1 ½ teaspoons salt

Direction

- Combine the flour and sugar in a large bowl. Gradually add 3 cups warm water, mixing with your fingers, then work in 4 tablespoons of the butter. Knead to a soft dough.
- One cup at a time, knead in the cheese. Add 1 to 2 tablespoons more water if the mixture seems dry. Taste the dough (some cheeses are very salty), then knead in salt to taste, 1/2 teaspoon at a time. Continue kneading until the dough feels soft and smooth, with no lumps. Set aside to rest for at least 15 minutes, covered with a damp cloth.
- Heat the broiler or a grill over high heat. Divide dough into 11 portions, roughly 5 ounces or 1/2 cup each. Roll into balls between your palms and set aside on a tray covered with a damp kitchen towel. Flatten each ball into a thick circle, 3 1/2 inches in diameter, flat on both sides. Return to tray and keep covered.
- Line broiler or grill rack with aluminum foil and brush foil lightly with remaining 1 tablespoon butter. Arrange arepas on foil and cook about 4 inches from the heat source, turning once, until both sides are golden brown and speckled — about 10 minutes per side. Serve immediately, for breakfast (like corn muffins) or as an accompaniment to soups or stews (like corn bread).

Nutrition Information

- 472: calories;
- 7 grams: monounsaturated fat;
- 2 grams: polyunsaturated fat;
- 3 grams: sugars;
- 16 grams: saturated fat;
- 1 gram: trans fat;
- 36 grams: carbohydrates;
- 20 grams: protein;
- 727 milligrams: sodium;
- 28 grams: fat;

80. Composed Salad With Green Olive And Garlic Vinaigrette

Serving: Four servings | Prep: | Cook: |Ready in: 1hours

Ingredients

- The salad:
- 4 artichokes
- 1 lemon, halved
- 4 medium zucchini, cut into 1/4-inch rounds
- 16 cups stemmed chicory
- ½ teaspoon olive oil
- 4 red bell peppers, roasted, peeled, seeded and cut into 1/4 inch strips
- 12 1/4-inch slices baguette, toasted
- The vinaigrette:
- ½ cup pitted and chopped green olives
- 4 cloves garlic, peeled and minced
- 2 tablespoons plus 2 teaspoons fresh lemon juice
- 2 tablespoons plus 2 teaspoons olive oil
- Salt and freshly ground pepper to taste

Direction

- To make the salad, cut the stems off the artichokes so they will stand straight. Remove the tough outer leaves and cut 1 1/2 inches off the top of each artichoke. Rub all surfaces with the lemon halves. Bring a large pot of water to the boil. Place the artichokes in a steamer basket and steam until the bottoms are tender when pierced with a knife, about 30 minutes. Set the artichokes aside and reserve 1/2 cup of the steaming liquid. When the artichokes are cool enough to handle, scoop out the choke.
- Preheat broiler. Place the zucchini slices on a baking sheet and broil just until the tops are browned, about 1 minute. Set aside. Wash but do not dry the chicory. Heat the olive oil in a large skillet over medium-high heat. Add the chicory, toss for a few seconds, cover with a lid and immediately remove from the heat. Let stand for 5 minutes.
- Meanwhile, to make the vinaigrette, whisk together the olives, garlic, lemon juice and olive oil in a small bowl. Whisk in the reserved artichoke steaming liquid. Season with salt and pepper. Divide the chicory among 4 large plates, mounding it in the center of each. Arrange the artichokes, zucchini and red peppers around the chicory. Spoon the vinaigrette over all, place 3 toast slices on each plate and serve immediately.

Nutrition Information

- 245: calories;
- 12 grams: sugars;
- 8 grams: protein;
- 0 grams: trans fat;
- 13 grams: dietary fiber;
- 2 grams: polyunsaturated fat;
- 9 grams: monounsaturated fat;
- 29 grams: carbohydrates;
- 1232 milligrams: sodium;

81. Cool Ziti With Eggplant And Tomatoes

Serving: 4 to 6 servings | Prep: | Cook: |Ready in: 45mins

Ingredients

- 2 pounds ripe tomatoes, cut in wedges
- Olive oil
- Salt and pepper
- 2 or 3 garlic cloves, minced
- ½ teaspoon peperoncino (hot red pepper flakes)
- 2 teaspoons capers, rinsed and roughly chopped
- 2 medium eggplants, about 1 pound
- 12 ounces ziti or other short pasta
- ¼ pound ricotta salata or mild feta, at room temperature
- 1 small bunch basil, for garnish

Direction

- Heat broiler. Put tomato wedges in a shallow baking dish in one layer. Drizzle with 3 tablespoons olive oil and season generously with salt and pepper. Broil tomatoes about 2 inches from heat until softened and lightly charred, 10 to 15 minutes. Set aside until cool, and then add garlic, peperoncino and capers. Stir gently to distribute.
- Slice eggplant into long strips about 1/4-inch thick. Paint both sides of eggplant strips with olive oil and season with salt and pepper. Cook eggplant strips on a stovetop grill, in a cast-iron pan or over hot coals, about two minutes per side. Cut into 1-inch pieces. Set aside.
- Boil the pasta in abundantly salted water until al dente, then drain and rinse briefly. Blot dry and put in a wide serving bowl. Add tomato mixture and eggplant. Toss gently to distribute. Taste for salt and hot pepper and adjust.
- Crumble cheese over top. Drizzle with a little more oil and garnish with torn basil leaves.

Nutrition Information

- 344: calories;
- 9 grams: fat;
- 4 grams: monounsaturated fat;
- 6 grams: dietary fiber;
- 720 milligrams: sodium;
- 1 gram: polyunsaturated fat;
- 54 grams: carbohydrates;
- 8 grams: sugars;
- 12 grams: protein;

82. Coquilles St. Jacques Portugaise (Scallops With Peppers And Capers)

Serving: 4 servings | Prep: | Cook: | Ready in: 15mins

Ingredients

- 2 pounds (2 pints) bay scallops
- Salt to taste if desired
- Freshly ground pepper to taste
- 2 tablespoons olive oil
- 4 tablespoons butter
- ¾ cup finely chopped sweet green pepper
- ½ teaspoon finely minced garlic
- ¼ cup drained capers
- ½ cup fine fresh bread crumbs
- ¼ cup dry white wine
- ¾ cup finely chopped sweet red pepper

Direction

- Preheat the broiler to high.
- Sprinkle the scallops with salt and pepper.
- Heat the oil in a large, heavy skillet and add the scallops. Cook over very high heat, stirring, about 2 minutes. Transfer the scallops to a baking dish that will hold the scallops compactly in one layer. Set aside briefly.
- To the skillet add two tablespoons of the butter. When it is melted and hot, add the chopped red and green peppers and the garlic. Cook, stirring, until wilted, about 1 minute.
- Add the capers. Stir. Add the bread crumbs and wine. Heat thoroughly. Spoon the mixture over the scallops.
- Dot the top with the remaining two tablespoons butter and place under the broiler. Let cook about 4 minutes.

Nutrition Information

- 402: calories;
- 2 grams: dietary fiber;
- 21 grams: carbohydrates;
- 3 grams: sugars;
- 1159 milligrams: sodium;
- 20 grams: fat;
- 9 grams: saturated fat;
- 0 grams: trans fat;
- 8 grams: monounsaturated fat;
- 30 grams: protein;

83. Corn Con Cotija (Courtesy Of Martine Garcia)

Serving: 6 servings | Prep: | Cook: | Ready in: 30mins

Ingredients

- 6 ears of fresh, ripe sweet corn (corn should be eaten on the day it is picked)
- 1 cup Mexican sour cream or more to taste
- 4 ounces cotija grated on the fine side of a 4-sided grater (about 1 1/2 cups) or more to taste

Direction

- The corn may be boiled, in which case remove the husks, place corn in a pot of rapidly boiling water and remove to a warm platter after 5 minutes. Then cover with a towel. Or it may be roasted, in which case remove the outer husk, brush the ears with cooking oil and place them beneath a preheated broiler and broil 3 inches from the heat source, turning from time to time, until the kernels begin to brown, about 15 minutes in all.
- When corn is cool enough to be handled, spread it with sour cream, then roll in grated cotija.

Nutrition Information

- 433: calories;
- 18 grams: saturated fat;
- 0 grams: trans fat;
- 9 grams: monounsaturated fat;
- 1069 milligrams: sodium;
- 31 grams: fat;
- 7 grams: sugars;
- 19 grams: protein;
- 2 grams: dietary fiber;
- 23 grams: carbohydrates;

84. Corn And Green Bean Salad With Tomatillo Dressing

Serving: Serves six generously | Prep: | Cook: | Ready in: 20mins

Ingredients

- For the dressing
- ¼ pound fresh tomatillos, husked
- 1 small serrano or 1/2 jalapeño chili
- 1 tablespoon fresh lime juice
- 10 cilantro sprigs
- 1 tablespoon chopped onion, soaked in cold water for five minutes, drained and rinsed
- 1 garlic clove, peeled
- 3 tablespoons extra virgin olive oil
- Salt to taste
- For the salad
- Kernels from 2 ears corn
- ¾ pound green beans, trimmed and cut in 2-inch lengths about 3 cups
- 1 large or 2 medium tomatoes, cut in 1/4-inch dice
- 4 radishes, cut in half lengthwise then sliced thin in half-moons
- 2 tablespoons minced chives
- Lettuce leaves for the platter or bowl
- ¼ cup crumbled queso fresco (1 ounce)

Direction

- Preheat the broiler. Cover a baking sheet with foil and place the tomatillos on top, stem side down. Place under the broiler at the highest rack setting and broil two to five minutes, until charred on one side. Turn over and broil on the other side for two to five minutes, until charred on the other side. Remove from the heat and transfer to a blender, tipping in any juice that may have accumulated on the baking sheet. Add the chili, lime juice, cilantro sprigs, onion, garlic and olive oil to the blender and blend until smooth. Taste and adjust salt, and set aside.
- Steam the corn kernels (or steam the entire ear, then cut the kernels off) and beans above one

inch of boiling water for five minutes, until tender. Remove from the heat, refresh with cold water and drain on paper towels. Place in a bowl and toss with the tomato, radishes, chives and the dressing. Line a platter or wide bowl with the lettuce leaves, top with the salad, sprinkle on the crumbled cheese and serve.

Nutrition Information

- 106: calories;
- 8 grams: fat;
- 2 grams: saturated fat;
- 7 grams: carbohydrates;
- 298 milligrams: sodium;
- 0 grams: trans fat;
- 5 grams: monounsaturated fat;
- 1 gram: polyunsaturated fat;
- 3 grams: protein;
- 4 grams: sugars;

85. Corn Seafood Stew With Avocado And Chiles

Serving: 4 to 6 servings | Prep: | Cook: | Ready in: 1hours

Ingredients

- 4 medium tomatillos, husked
- 2 medium poblano chiles
- 1 large jalapeño
- 5 large ears corn, shucked
- ½ tablespoon grapeseed or olive oil
- 4 garlic cloves, sliced
- 2 small shallots (or 1 large), halved lengthwise and sliced
- 2 packed cups cilantro leaves and stems, plus more leaves for garnish
- ½ cup packed parsley leaves and stems
- Fine sea salt, as needed
- 2 cups vegetable, chicken or seafood stock, preferably homemade
- ¾ pound squid, tentacles separated, bodies cut into 1-inch rings
- ¾ pound shelled shrimp, cut into 1-inch pieces
- ½ pound firm white fish fillets, cut into 1-inch pieces
- 2 limes, cut into wedges
- Diced avocado, for garnish
- Sliced radishes, for garnish
- Shredded green cabbage, for garnish
- Tostadas, for garnish (optional)

Direction

- Heat a grill or broiler. If grilling, grill tomatillos, poblanos and jalapeño until well charred all over, 3 to 7 minutes per side. If broiling, spread them out on a large rimmed baking sheet. Broil until charred all over, 3 to 7 minutes per side. Transfer vegetables to a large bowl, cover with a plate or foil, and let cool.
- Grill or broil corn until golden brown in spots, 3 to 4 minutes per side. Let cool, then use your heaviest knife to slice two of the cobs crosswise into 2-inch rounds. Cut kernels off remaining 3 ears and reserve.
- In a medium skillet over high heat, add oil. When hot but not smoking, add garlic and shallots and cook, sautéing, until well browned, 2 to 3 minutes. Transfer to a blender.
- Bring a kettle of water to a boil. Place cilantro and parsley in a colander in the sink. Pour boiling water over herbs to wilt them, then immediately run cold water over them to cool them down. Press hard on herbs and squeeze to remove excess water. Transfer herbs to blender with shallots.
- When chiles are cool enough to handle, remove skins, seeds and stems, and discard. Add peeled chiles and tomatillos to blender along with a large pinch of salt. Purée the mixture, adding a tablespoon or 2 of water if needed to make everything move, until it is thick but pourable. Taste and add more salt, if needed. It should be well seasoned.
- In a pot or large skillet, bring the stock to a simmer. Add fish and seafood and cook until

it's just cooked through, 1 to 3 minutes. Stir 1 cup of chile purée into the seafood mixture and season aggressively with freshly squeezed lime juice from some of the wedges, and salt to taste. Taste and add more chile purée if you like. Stir in corn kernels.
- To serve, spoon stew into bowls and top with rounds of corn on the cob, more lime wedges, avocado, radishes, cabbage and cilantro leaves, with tostadas on the side if you like.

Nutrition Information

- 298: calories;
- 30 grams: protein;
- 2 grams: polyunsaturated fat;
- 37 grams: carbohydrates;
- 6 grams: dietary fiber;
- 895 milligrams: sodium;
- 5 grams: fat;
- 1 gram: saturated fat;
- 0 grams: trans fat;
- 11 grams: sugars;

86. Country Omelet

Serving: 6 servings | Prep: | Cook: |Ready in: 20mins

Ingredients

- 3 tablespoons canola oil
- 1 tablespoon unsalted butter
- 2 onions (about 3/4 pound), peeled and sliced
- 1 ¼ pounds potatoes, peeled and sliced thin
- 1 large tomato (about 12 ounces), sliced thin
- 8 large eggs
- ½ cup coarsely chopped chives
- ¾ teaspoon salt
- ½ teaspoon freshly ground pepper

Direction

- Heat the oil and butter in a nonstick skillet until hot but not smoking. Add the onions and potatoes and cook, covered, for about 10 minutes, stirring the mixture every 3 to 4 minutes. Arrange the tomato slices so they cover most of the surface of the potato-and-onion mixture, cover, and cook for 1 minute.
- Meanwhile, break the eggs into a bowl, add the chives, salt and pepper, and mix together with a fork. Add the egg mixture to the skillet and stir gently with the tines of the fork for about 1 minute to allow the eggs to flow between the potatoes. Then place the skillet under a hot broiler, 3 or 4 inches from the heat, and cook for about 3 minutes, until eggs are set.
- Invert onto a platter, cut into wedges and serve.

Nutrition Information

- 278: calories;
- 0 grams: trans fat;
- 3 grams: polyunsaturated fat;
- 5 grams: sugars;
- 396 milligrams: sodium;
- 4 grams: dietary fiber;
- 24 grams: carbohydrates;
- 11 grams: protein;
- 16 grams: fat;
- 7 grams: monounsaturated fat;

87. Crab Meat Au Gratin

Serving: 4 servings | Prep: | Cook: |Ready in: 25mins

Ingredients

- 3 tablespoons unsalted butter
- 2 tablespoons all-purpose flour
- 1 ½ cups milk
- 1 pinch cayenne pepper
- ⅛ teaspoon freshly grated nutmeg
- Salt and freshly ground white pepper to taste
- ¾ cup heavy cream
- ¼ cup dry sherry

- 1 egg yolk
- 4 tablespoons finely chopped shallots
- 1 pound fresh lump crab meat, shell and cartilage removed, if any
- 4 tablespoons freshly grated Gruyere or Parmesan cheese

Direction

- Preheat the broiler to high.
- Melt two tablespoons of the butter in a saucepan over medium heat. Add the flour and blend well. Do not brown. Add the milk and cook, stirring with a whisk, until blended and smooth. Season with cayenne pepper, nutmeg, salt and pepper.
- Add the cream, bring to a boil and simmer briefly about 3 to 4 minutes. Stir in half of the sherry, beat in the egg yolk well and remove from heat.
- Melt the remaining tablespoon of butter in a nonstick skillet over medium-high heat. Add the shallots and cook them briefly until wilted. Add the crab meat and cook briefly, stirring gently. Sprinkle with the remaining sherry.
- Spoon the crab meat into a baking dish and smooth over with a spatula. Cover with the hot sauce and spoon it over with a rubber spatula. Sprinkle with the cheese.
- Place the dish under the broiler until golden brown and bubbling hot.

Nutrition Information

- 479: calories;
- 895 milligrams: sodium;
- 34 grams: fat;
- 20 grams: saturated fat;
- 9 grams: monounsaturated fat;
- 12 grams: carbohydrates;
- 30 grams: protein;
- 0 grams: dietary fiber;
- 2 grams: polyunsaturated fat;
- 7 grams: sugars;

88. Crab And Spinach Mornay

Serving: 4 servings | Prep: | Cook: | Ready in: 45mins

Ingredients

- 1 pound crab meat, preferably lump
- 1-1/4 pounds fresh spinach
- 4 tablespoons butter
- 3 tablespoons flour
- Salt to taste if desired
- Freshly ground pepper to taste
- ⅛ teaspoon cayenne pepper
- 1-3/4 cups milk
- ⅓ cup heavy cream
- ⅛ teaspoon freshly grated nutmeg
- 2 tablespoons finely diced cheese, preferably Gruyere or Swiss
- 2 tablespoons finely chopped shallots
- 2 tablespoons freshly grated Parmesan cheese

Direction

- Preheat oven to 350 degrees.
- Pick over crab meat carefully to remove and discard pieces of shell or cartilage. Do not break up the pieces of crab; leave them as whole as possible. Set aside.
- Pick over spinach to remove tough stems or blemished leaves. Rinse well and drain. Set aside.
- Heat 3 tablespoons butter in a saucepan and add flour, stirring rapidly with a whisk. Add salt, pepper and cayenne. When blended, stir in milk, cream and nutmeg. Let simmer, stirring often from the bottom, about 10 minutes. Add cheese and stir until melted.
- Put spinach in a deep skillet or casserole without water. Cook, stirring often, until the leaves wilt. Drain. Press or squeeze to extract as much liquid as possible from the leaves. Chop spinach until it is medium fine.
- Heat remaining tablespoon of butter in a skillet and add 1 tablespoon shallots. Cook briefly, stirring, and add spinach. Add salt and pepper. Spoon mixture into a baking dish (an

oval dish measuring 14 by 8 by 2 inches is ideal).
- Spoon crab into a smaller ovenproof dish and sprinkle with remaining tablespoon of chopped shallots. Place in oven and bake 5 minutes. Scatter crab meat over spinach and smooth it to make an even layer. Spoon cheese sauce over all and smooth it over. Sprinkle Parmesan cheese evenly on top.
- Place dish in oven and bake 10 minutes. Heat broiler. Let broil, leaving the door partly ajar, about 2 minutes or until nicely glazed on top. Serve.

Nutrition Information

- 446: calories;
- 7 grams: sugars;
- 34 grams: protein;
- 4 grams: dietary fiber;
- 981 milligrams: sodium;
- 28 grams: fat;
- 17 grams: carbohydrates;
- 0 grams: trans fat;
- 2 grams: polyunsaturated fat;

89. Creamy Gruyere Potatoes

Serving: Four servings | Prep: | Cook: | Ready in: 1hours

Ingredients

- 4 medium baking potatoes, peeled and cut across into 1/8-inch slices
- 1 ½ teaspoons kosher salt
- Freshly ground pepper to taste
- 1 tablespoon unsalted butter, cut into small pieces
- 1 ½ cups half-and-half
- 1 cup grated Gruyere cheese

Direction

- Preheat the oven to 350 degrees. Arrange half of the potato slices in slightly overlapping layers in a deep-dish pie plate or small shallow casserole dish. Sprinkle with 3/4 teaspoon of the salt and pepper to taste. Dot with half of the butter pieces.
- Repeat the layers. Pour the half-and-half over the potatoes. Bake until the potatoes are tender, about 45 minutes.
- Remove the dish from the oven and preheat the broiler. Sprinkle the cheese over the potatoes and broil until melted and lightly browned. Divide among 4 plates and serve.

Nutrition Information

- 451: calories;
- 17 grams: protein;
- 24 grams: fat;
- 7 grams: monounsaturated fat;
- 0 grams: trans fat;
- 1 gram: polyunsaturated fat;
- 43 grams: carbohydrates;
- 3 grams: dietary fiber;
- 5 grams: sugars;
- 794 milligrams: sodium;
- 15 grams: saturated fat;

90. Creamy Mussel Stew With Peas, Fennel And Lemon

Serving: 2 servings | Prep: | Cook: | Ready in: 40mins

Ingredients

- 1 large fennel bulb
- 2 tablespoons extra virgin olive oil, more for brushing
- 1 large leek, white part only, cleaned and finely chopped
- 4 garlic cloves, smashed and peeled
- Pinch red pepper flakes
- ¾ cup dry white wine
- 3 tablespoons Pernod

- 2 pounds fresh mussels, rinsed
- ⅔ cup chicken or vegetable stock
- ½ pound fresh English peas, shelled 1/2 cup
- 2 tablespoons crème fraîche
- ¼ teaspoon finely grated lemon zest
- Fine sea salt
- 2 slices country-style bread, 1/2-inch-thick

Direction

- Chop and reserve 1/4 cup fennel fronds. Peel and discard the outer layers from the bulb, then finely chop the bulb and coarsely chop the stems.
- Heat the oil in a large pot over medium-high heat. Add the chopped fennel bulb, leek and garlic cloves. Cook until the fennel and leek are golden, 5 to 7 minutes. Add the pepper flakes and cook 30 seconds. Stir in the fennel stems, wine and Pernod. Cook, stirring to scrape up any browned bits from the bottom of the pan, 2 minutes.
- Add the mussels to the pot. Cover tightly and cook until most of the mussels have opened, 5 to 7 minutes (discard any remaining closed mussels). Transfer to a large bowl and cover loosely with foil.
- Heat the broiler. Strain the liquid in the pot through a fine sieve into a small saucepan, pressing down on the solids with a spoon. Add the stock and bring to a simmer over medium heat. Stir in the peas and cook until just tender, 2 to 3 minutes. Whisk in the crème fraîche, lemon zest, salt and chopped fennel fronds. Cover to keep warm.
- Drizzle the bread with oil and place it under the broiler until just golden, about 1 minute. Place a slice of bread into each of two bowls. Mound the mussels on top of the bread, then ladle the broth over everything.

91. Croque Monsieur With Gruyere Cheese

Serving: Eight servings | Prep: | Cook: | Ready in: 15mins

Ingredients

- 2 ounces butter
- 16 slices sandwich bread
- About 2 1/2 tablespoons Dijon mustard, or to taste
- 8 slices lean ham
- 8 slices Gruyere cheese
- 2 ounces finely grated Gruyere

Direction

- Preheat the broiler.
- Butter 8 slices of the bread and arrange them on a baking sheet, buttered side down. Smear the top side with Dijon to taste and top with the ham, the sliced cheese and the remaining bread. Butter the top of each sandwich.
- Place under the broiler, about 2 to 3 inches from the flame. Broil for about 3 minutes or until top slice is golden brown. Turn the sandwiches over and broil for an additional 1 to 2 minutes. Sprinkle each with the grated Gruyere and broil for 1 minute or until the cheese is melted.

Nutrition Information

- 399: calories;
- 12 grams: saturated fat;
- 7 grams: monounsaturated fat;
- 2 grams: polyunsaturated fat;
- 30 grams: carbohydrates;
- 22 grams: protein;
- 0 grams: trans fat;
- 3 grams: dietary fiber;
- 4 grams: sugars;
- 918 milligrams: sodium;

92. Crostini With Porcini Butter And Summer Truffles

Serving: 48 crostini | Prep: | Cook: | Ready in: 15mins

Ingredients

- 8 ounces high quality lightly salted or unsalted butter at room temperature
- Salt
- 4 tablespoons porcini powder
- ½ cup canned summer truffle peelings
- 2 French baguettes
- 4 tablespoons minced parsley for garnish, optional
- Black pepper

Direction

- Preheat the broiler. Grind dried porcini in a spice grinder, producing about 1/2 cup of powder. The excess will keep for about a year in a jar. Or buy porcini powder online or at some food shops.
- In small bowl, combine the butter and 4 tablespoons of porcini powder. Add salt to taste.
- Slice the baguettes into very thin slices. Place on a sheet pan and toast until golden brown on both sides.
- Spread about 1 teaspoon of porcini butter on the baguette slices. Add a good pinch of truffles, and sprinkle with minced parsley if you like and a few grinds of pepper.
- Spread about 1 teaspoon of butter on the baguette slices. Add a good pinch of truffles, and sprinkle with minced parsley and a few grinds of pepper if you like.

Nutrition Information

- 69: calories;
- 1 gram: protein;
- 7 grams: carbohydrates;
- 76 milligrams: sodium;
- 4 grams: fat;
- 2 grams: saturated fat;
- 0 grams: dietary fiber;

93. Croutons With Parmesan

Serving: 16 to 24 croutons | Prep: | Cook: | Ready in: 15mins

Ingredients

- 1 loaf of French bread like a baguette
- 1 large garlic clove peeled and left whole
- 2 tablespoons olive oil
- 4 tablespoons grated Parmesan cheese

Direction

- Preheat oven broiler.
- Rub the bread's crust all over with the garlic clove.
- Slice the bread on the bias 1/4 inch thick. Arrange the slices in a baking dish, brush with the oil and sprinkle with Parmesan cheese.
- Place under the broiler until golden brown on one side. Turn and brown lightly on the reverse side.

Nutrition Information

- 214: calories;
- 8 grams: fat;
- 2 grams: sugars;
- 0 grams: trans fat;
- 4 grams: monounsaturated fat;
- 9 grams: protein;
- 1 gram: dietary fiber;
- 27 grams: carbohydrates;
- 431 milligrams: sodium;

94. Crusty Broiled Cod With Littlenecks And Chouriço

Serving: 4 servings | Prep: | Cook: | Ready in: 40mins

Ingredients

- ½ cup panko, lightly toasted
- ¼ cup chopped parsley
- 3 tablespoons minced garlic
- 1 tablespoon lemon zest
- ¼ cup extra-virgin olive oil, divided
- 4 5-ounce pieces cod fillet, about 1 to 1 1/2 inches thick
- 1 lemon, quartered
- 2 tablespoons medium or hot smoked paprika
- Salt
- Cracked black pepper
- ½ pound chouriço, diced medium
- 12 littleneck clams, well washed
- ½ cup dry white wine

Direction

- Heat broiler (to high if you have the option).
- Combine panko, parsley, garlic, lemon zest and 2 tablespoons of olive oil in a small bowl, mix well and set aside.
- Rub cod and lemon quarters all over with remaining oil, sprinkle with paprika, salt and pepper, then place in 9-by-12-inch shallow baking dish or disposable foil pan. Arrange chouriço and clams around cod and pour in wine. Place under broiler on top rack (about 3 to 4 inches from flame) and broil, turning dish back to front after about 5 minutes, until fish is almost opaque and littlenecks are open, 10 to 12 minutes.
- Sprinkle panko mixture over the cod and return to broiler until crumbs are crispy golden brown, another 2 to 3 minutes.
- Split cod, clams, chouriço, and lemon among 4 shallow bowls, pour pan juices around and serve.

Nutrition Information

- 350: calories;
- 16 grams: fat;
- 2 grams: dietary fiber;
- 0 grams: trans fat;
- 34 grams: protein;
- 616 milligrams: sodium;
- 10 grams: monounsaturated fat;
- 14 grams: carbohydrates;
- 1 gram: sugars;

95. Cumin Chicken With Black Bean Sauce

Serving: 2 servings | Prep: | Cook: | Ready in: 30mins

Ingredients

- 8 ounces boneless, skinless chicken breasts
- 1 teaspoon ground cumin
- ½ teaspoon ground coriander
- 1 15-ounce can no-salt-added black beans
- 1 large clove garlic
- ½ to 1 Serrano chili
- 2 tomatillos, to yield 3 tablespoons chopped
- Few sprigs cilantro, to yield 2 tablespoons chopped
- 1 small onion, to yield 1 tablespoon chopped
- 1 small green pepper, to yield 4 teaspoons chopped
- 2 teaspoons lime juice
- ⅛ teaspoon salt
- Freshly ground black pepper to taste

Direction

- Preheat broiler, if using. Wash and dry the chicken, and rub the breasts on both sides with cumin and coriander.
- Rinse and drain the beans.
- Turn on the food processor, and put garlic through feed tube. Wash, trim and seed the chili, add as much as you like to the food processor and process until finely chopped. Chop the tomatillos. Wash and chop the cilantro. Chop the onion and the green pepper.
- To the garlic and chili in the food processor add the beans, tomatillos, cilantro, onion, green pepper, lime juice, salt and pepper, and process until mixture is pureed.

- Prepare stove-top grill, if using. Broil or grill chicken, browning on both sides and cooking until chicken is no longer pink, about 10 minutes.
- Heat the bean puree in a pot slowly until warm.
- Place the bean puree in the middle of each of two dinner plates. Place the chicken on top, and top with mango salsa.

Nutrition Information

- 376: calories;
- 45 grams: carbohydrates;
- 17 grams: dietary fiber;
- 40 grams: protein;
- 496 milligrams: sodium;
- 4 grams: sugars;
- 1 gram: polyunsaturated fat;
- 0 grams: trans fat;

96. Cumin Lamb Meatballs With Tahini Yogurt Dipping Sauce

Serving: 2 to 4 servings | Prep: | Cook: | Ready in: 20mins

Ingredients

- 3 garlic cloves, minced
- 1 ¼ teaspoons coarse kosher salt, plus a pinch
- 1 pound ground lamb
- 2 teaspoons cumin seeds
- ½ teaspoon hot sauce, more for serving
- Black pepper, to taste
- ½ teaspoon chile powder
- 1 scallion, minced
- 2 tablespoons finely chopped parsley
- Olive oil, for greasing pan
- ¼ cup plain yogurt
- ¼ cup tahini
- Fresh lemon juice, to taste

Direction

- Heat broiler with an oven rack placed 3 inches below heat source.
- Using a mortar and pestle or the flat side of a knife, make a paste with garlic and a pinch of salt. Put half the garlic paste in a large bowl and add lamb, 1 teaspoon of the salt, cumin, hot sauce, pepper, chile powder, scallion and 1 tablespoon parsley. Mix to combine.
- Shape lamb mixture into 1 1/2-inch meatballs and place on an oiled rimmed baking sheet. Make sure meatballs are spaced at least 1 inch apart. Transfer baking sheet to oven and broil meatballs for 8 to 10 minutes, or until browned on top and slightly pink on the inside.
- Meanwhile, combine yogurt, tahini, remaining garlic paste,1/4 teaspoon salt and the lemon juice to taste.
- Transfer cooked meatballs to a serving platter or individual plates and serve with tahini sauce and extra hot sauce, if you like. Garnish with the remaining parsley.

Nutrition Information

- 448: calories;
- 38 grams: fat;
- 16 grams: monounsaturated fat;
- 2 grams: dietary fiber;
- 22 grams: protein;
- 13 grams: saturated fat;
- 6 grams: carbohydrates;
- 1 gram: sugars;
- 363 milligrams: sodium;

97. Curried Grilled Jumbo Shrimp

Serving: Four servings | Prep: | Cook: | Ready in: 2hours30mins

Ingredients

- 1 ½ pounds jumbo shrimp
- 4 cloves garlic
- 2 small red chilies, chopped

- 2 teaspoons sugar
- ¾ teaspoon salt
- ½ cup finely chopped coriander leaves
- 1 teaspoon curry paste or powder
- 1 tablespoon vegetable oil
- 4 cups cooked white rice, warm

Direction

- Use scissors to cut down the back of the shrimp, through the shell, to remove the vein. Gently loosen the shell around the shrimp, but keep it in place. Set aside. In a mortar, pound the garlic and chilies to a coarse paste (or use a mini food processor or chop to a paste with a knife). Add the sugar and salt and pound or chop to a finer paste. Stir in the coriander, curry and oil.
- Gently pull open the shell of each shrimp and, dividing the coriander paste evenly, push some of it down the back of the shrimp where the vein was and under the shell a bit. Close up the shell around the shrimp. Marinate at room temperature at least 2 hours or, covered, in the refrigerator up to 4 hours.
- Preheat a grill or broiler. Grill or broil the shrimp until the shells are charred on one side and the shrimp is cooked halfway through, about 3 minutes. Turn and cook on the other side for 1 to 3 minutes. Serve immediately with the rice.

Nutrition Information

- 415: calories;
- 28 grams: protein;
- 972 milligrams: sodium;
- 6 grams: fat;
- 1 gram: dietary fiber;
- 0 grams: trans fat;
- 3 grams: sugars;
- 60 grams: carbohydrates;

98. Curried Beef Skewers

Serving: Ten servings | Prep: | Cook: | Ready in: 25mins

Ingredients

- ¼ cup curry powder
- ½ cup peanut oil
- 2 pounds beef filet, cut into 1-inch cubes
- Kosher salt to taste

Direction

- Place the curry powder in a small heavy skillet over very low heat. Stir constantly until toasted and fragrant, being careful not to burn it, about 10 minutes. Place in a large bowl and let cool. Stir in the oil. Add the beef and toss to coat well. Refrigerate overnight.
- Bring the beef to room temperature. Preheat a grill or broiler. Thread the beef onto 6-inch skewers, using 3 cubes for each. Grill or broil until medium rare, about 1 minute per side. Sprinkle with salt, place on a platter and serve.

Nutrition Information

- 327: calories;
- 18 grams: protein;
- 242 milligrams: sodium;
- 27 grams: fat;
- 8 grams: saturated fat;
- 12 grams: monounsaturated fat;
- 4 grams: polyunsaturated fat;
- 1 gram: dietary fiber;
- 0 grams: sugars;

99. Curry Spiced Lamb Burgers

Serving: 4 burgers | Prep: | Cook: | Ready in: 20mins

Ingredients

- 1 ½ pounds boneless lamb shoulder, cut into chunks

- 1 medium (or 1/2 large) onion, peeled and cut into chunks
- 1 fresh chili, preferably jalapeño, seeded and minced
- 1 teaspoon ground coriander
- 1 teaspoon ground cumin
- ½ teaspoon turmeric
- Salt
- freshly ground black pepper to taste
- Diced mango to garnish (optional)
- green and red pepper to garnish (optional)
- red onion to garnish (optional)
- scallion to garnish (optional)
- shredded carrot to garnish (optional)
- shredded lettuce, to garnish (optional)

Direction

- If grilling or broiling, heat should be medium-high and rack about 4 inches from fire. Put lamb and onion into a food processor (in batches if your machine is small) and pulse until coarsely ground. Put in a bowl with chili, coriander, cumin and turmeric, and sprinkle with salt and pepper. Mix, handling the meat as little as possible, until combined. Taste and adjust seasonings. Handling meat as lightly as possible to avoid compressing it, shape it into 4 or more burgers.
- To broil or grill, cook about 3 minutes on each side for rare and another minute per side for each increasing stage of doneness. For stovetop, heat a large skillet over medium heat for 2 or 3 minutes, then add patties; cook, undisturbed, for about 2 minutes, then rotate them so they brown evenly. Turn once and cook for a total of about 6 minutes for rare.
- Garnish with diced mango, green and red pepper, red onion and scallion, and with shredded carrot and lettuce.

Nutrition Information

- 469: calories;
- 29 grams: protein;
- 481 milligrams: sodium;
- 16 grams: saturated fat;
- 3 grams: polyunsaturated fat;
- 4 grams: carbohydrates;
- 1 gram: sugars;
- 37 grams: fat;
- 0 grams: trans fat;
- 15 grams: monounsaturated fat;

100. Cyrus's Express Bread And Butter Pudding

Serving: 8 servings | Prep: | Cook: | Ready in: 1hours15mins

Ingredients

- 11 slices white bread
- 1 cup melted butter
- ¾ cup diced mixed fruit
- 1 ½ tablespoons whole charoli nuts or finely chopped pistachios
- 15 almonds, skins on, very finely chopped
- 2 12-ounce cans evaporated milk
- 1 14-ounce can sweetened condensed milk
- 6 large eggs
- 7 tablespoons sugar
- 1 teaspoon cardamom powder
- ¾ teaspoon grated nutmeg
- 1 teaspoon rose water
- 1 teaspoon vanilla extract

Direction

- Preheat oven to 375 degrees. Generously brush each slice of bread on both sides with butter. Cut each slice into two triangles. Brush a 13-by-9-inch baking dish with butter and lay the bread in, overlapping the slices. Sprinkle with fruit, working a little between slices, and sprinkle with nuts.
- Combine milks and whisk in the eggs until very smooth. Whisk in sugar, cardamom, nutmeg, rose water and vanilla. Pour over the bread, up to 1/2 inch from the rim.
- Place the dish in a bain-marie and pour in 1/3-inch of boiling water. Bake for 1 hour (add

more water if necessary) or until a knife inserted comes out clean. If the pudding is not golden and crisp on top, place under the broiler to brown. Serve warm or cold.

Nutrition Information

- 712: calories;
- 69 grams: carbohydrates;
- 49 grams: sugars;
- 41 grams: fat;
- 12 grams: monounsaturated fat;
- 3 grams: polyunsaturated fat;
- 2 grams: dietary fiber;
- 20 grams: protein;
- 413 milligrams: sodium;
- 23 grams: saturated fat;
- 1 gram: trans fat;

101. Deviled Chicken Thighs

Serving: 4 servings | Prep: | Cook: | Ready in: 20mins

Ingredients

- 8 chicken thighs, or a mixture of thighs and drumsticks
- Salt and freshly ground black pepper
- ⅓ cup Dijon mustard
- ⅓ cup minced shallots, onion or scallion
- ¼ teaspoon ground cayenne pepper or Tabasco sauce, or to taste
- Minced parsley for garnish, optional

Direction

- Heat the broiler to its maximum, and set the rack about 4 inches from the heat. Season the chicken with salt and pepper on both sides, and place it in a pan, skin side up. Broil, watching carefully, until the skin is golden brown, about 5 minutes.
- Meanwhile, combine the mustard, shallots and cayenne. (If you have a small food processor, you can chop the shallots by throwing them in with the mustard and pulsing the machine on and off a few times.)
- When the chicken has browned, remove it from oven, and turn it. Spread just a teaspoon or so of the mustard mixture on the underside of the chicken, and broil about 5 minutes. Turn the chicken, and spread the remaining mixture on the upper, or skin side. Broil until mustard begins to brown.
- At this point, the chicken may be done. (There will be only the barest trace of pink near the bone; an instant-read thermometer inserted into the meat will read 160 degrees.) If it is not done, turn off the broiler and leave the chicken in the oven 5 more minutes or so. Garnish and serve.

Nutrition Information

- 683: calories;
- 11 grams: polyunsaturated fat;
- 5 grams: carbohydrates;
- 775 milligrams: sodium;
- 14 grams: saturated fat;
- 0 grams: trans fat;
- 21 grams: monounsaturated fat;
- 1 gram: sugars;
- 50 grams: protein;
- 2 grams: dietary fiber;

102. Easy Party Paella

Serving: 20 to 24 servings | Prep: | Cook: | Ready in: 2hours30mins

Ingredients

- 5 pounds chicken wings (30 to 40 wings)
- 8 tablespoons olive oil
- Juice of 2 lemons
- 1 teaspoon ground cumin
- Salt and freshly ground black pepper
- 40 mussels, scrubbed and debearded

- 1 cup dry white wine
- 3 pounds chorizo sausage
- 2 large onions, chopped
- 2 large sweet red peppers, cored, seeded and chopped
- 1 large green pepper, cored, seeded and chopped
- 6 cloves garlic, minced
- 2 teaspoons oregano
- 5 cups long grain rice
- 1 28-ounce can whole plum tomatoes
- 6 cups well-flavored chicken stock
- ½ teaspoon powdered saffron
- 3 pounds cooked shelled shrimp
- ½ cup drained capers
- 3 tablespoons minced fresh parsley
- Lemon wedges for garnish

Direction

- Disjoint the chicken wings, discarding the wing tips or reserving them for making stock. Place the remaining wing pieces in a large bowl. Mix three tablespoons of the olive oil with the lemon juice and cumin. Season this mixture to taste with salt and pepper. Pour over the chicken wings, cover and allow to marinate one to four hours.
- Up to two hours before serving time, steam the mussels. Bring the wine to a simmer in a large pot, add the mussels, cover tightly and cook over medium heat until they open, about 10 minutes. Leave the mussels in the covered pan until shortly before serving time.
- Saute the chorizos over medium heat in a six-quart casserole until they are cooked through, 15 to 20 minutes. Remove them from the casserole, draining them well, and set them aside on a plate covered with a paper towel. Leave the fat in the casserole. Add the remaining olive oil to the casserole.
- Add the onions and peppers to the casserole and cook over low heat, stirring, until the vegetables are soft but not brown. Stir in the garlic, cook briefly, then add the oregano. Stir in the rice and cook for several minutes, stirring, until the rice is well coated with the other ingredients. Remove the casserole from the heat.
- Drain the canned tomatoes, pricking them to drain the liquid inside. Reserve all the tomato liquid and chop the tomatoes fine. Stir the chopped tomatoes in with the rice.
- Measure the reserved tomato liquid. You should have about a cup and a half. Add a little water if necessary to make this amount. Place the tomato liquid in a saucepan along with the chicken stock and bring to a simmer. Stir in the saffron, remove from the heat and allow to steep for 10 minutes. Meanwhile, slice the cooled chorizo into rounds a half-inch thick.
- Place the casserole over medium-low heat and bring to a simmer. Stir in the pieces of chorizo, then stir in the tomato and chicken stock seasoned with the saffron. Bring to a simmer and add salt and pepper, if necessary. Cover and cook over low heat until all of the liquid is absorbed and the rice is done, which should take about 20 minutes. Set aside, covered for at least 20 minutes.
- While the rice is cooking, remove the shrimps from the refrigerator so they can come to room temperature.
- Preheat a broiler. Place the marinated chicken wings on a broiling pan and broil until they are browned and cooked through, about 25 minutes. Turn them once during the cooking. Transfer them to a large platter or bowl, cover with foil and set aside.
- To serve, spoon the rice gently into one or more large mixing bowls to fluff it. Do not fill the bowls more than half full or you will have rice all over the floor. Taste the rice for seasoning and add more salt and pepper, if necessary, so that the seasoning will need no further adjusting.
- Gently fold the capers, parsley, shrimp and chicken wings in with the rice.
- Warm a large serving platter or shallow bowl. Even a big paella pan can be used as a serving dish. Transfer some or all of the paella to the platter or bowl. If there is not enough room for all the paella on one platter, you can use two

platters or keep some of the paella reserved in the kitchen for refilling the platter.
- Briefly reheat the mussels in their broth, then arrange them, in their shells, around the edge of the platter, alternating them with the lemon wedges. Place the platter on the buffet table along with serving spoons. After all the guests have served themselves, rearrange the paella on the platter, refilling the platter, if necessary, or transferring the remaining paella to a smaller platter so it continues to look attractive.

Nutrition Information

- 752: calories;
- 21 grams: monounsaturated fat;
- 45 grams: carbohydrates;
- 2 grams: dietary fiber;
- 46 grams: protein;
- 1419 milligrams: sodium;
- 41 grams: fat;
- 13 grams: saturated fat;
- 6 grams: polyunsaturated fat;
- 4 grams: sugars;
- 0 grams: trans fat;

103. Eggplant Parmagiano

Serving: 4 to 6 servings | Prep: | Cook: | Ready in: 1hours

Ingredients

- 2 medium eggplants, about 1 1/2 pounds
- Salt
- Olive oil
- 2 cloves garlic, finely minced
- 1 ½ cups drained canned plum tomatoes, crushed
- Freshly ground black pepper
- 1 cup freshly grated parmagiano-reggiano cheese

Direction

- Remove the leaves from the eggplants and cut the eggplants lengthwise into slices one-half-inch thick. Sprinkle liberally with salt, place in a collander and allow to drain for about 30 minutes.
- While the eggplant is draining, heat two tablespoons of olive oil in a heavy saucepan, add the garlic and saute lightly for a few seconds. Add the tomatoes and cook over medium heat for 15 minutes. Season the sauce to taste with salt and pepper.
- Rinse and dry the eggplants. Arrange them in a single layer on one or two oiled baking sheets, brush with olive oil and broil in a hot broiler until the slices are lightly browned. Alternatively you can pan grill the slices in a hot nonstick skillet.
- Preheat oven to 375 degrees.
- Brush an oblong baking dish about 9 by 12 inches with a tablespoon or two of the sauce. Spread about half the grilled eggplant slices, slightly overlapping, in the baking dish. Season with salt and pepper to taste. Spread half the sauce over the eggplant and top with half the cheese. Repeat the layers. Drizzle a little olive oil over the top.
- Bake about 20 minutes.

Nutrition Information

- 129: calories;
- 9 grams: fat;
- 3 grams: dietary fiber;
- 8 grams: carbohydrates;
- 4 grams: sugars;
- 0 grams: trans fat;
- 1 gram: polyunsaturated fat;
- 6 grams: protein;
- 403 milligrams: sodium;

104. Eggplant And Beef Creole

Serving: 2 servings | Prep: | Cook: |Ready in: 30mins

Ingredients

- 1 pound eggplant
- Nonstick cooking spray
- 12 ounces whole onion or 11 ounces chopped, ready-cut onion (2 1/4 to 2 1/2 cups)
- 1 teaspoon olive oil
- 2 large cloves garlic
- 8 ounces extra-lean ground beef
- 8 ounces whole yellow or red bell pepper or 7 ounces chopped, ready-cut pepper (1 1/2 cups)
- 3 cups canned plum tomatoes, drained
- ¼ cup dry red wine
- 2 sprigs fresh oregano to yield 1 tablespoon chopped
- ⅛ teaspoon hot red pepper flakes or more to taste
- ⅛ teaspoon salt
- Freshly ground black pepper to taste

Direction

- Turn on the broiler and cover broiler rack with aluminum foil. Wash and trim eggplant, but do not peel. Slice off both ends. Cut remaining eggplant into 1/4-inch thick slices and spray lightly with pan spray. Arrange in pan, and broil 2 to 3 inches from heat source, about 5 to 7 minutes.
- Chop whole onion. Heat nonstick pan large enough to hold all the ingredients until it is very hot. Spray pan and add 1 teaspoon oil; reduce heat to medium high and saute onions until they begin to soften and turn golden.
- Mince and add garlic. After 30 seconds, push the onions and garlic to one side. Add ground beef, breaking it into small pieces. Stir and brown.
- Turn eggplant, spray with pan spray and continue broiling to brown on second side.
- Wash, dry, trim, seed and chop pepper. When beef is brown, stir in the peppers and the onion mixture.
- Drain the tomatoes, and squeeze them in hands to crush. Add to pan along with the wine.
- Remove the eggplant.
- Wash and dry the oregano and chop; stir in with the hot pepper flakes.
- Cut up the eggplant and stir into the pan, seasoning with salt and pepper.

Nutrition Information

- 507: calories;
- 19 grams: fat;
- 4 grams: polyunsaturated fat;
- 0 grams: trans fat;
- 53 grams: carbohydrates;
- 26 grams: sugars;
- 257 milligrams: sodium;
- 10 grams: monounsaturated fat;
- 16 grams: dietary fiber;
- 32 grams: protein;

105. Eggplant And Feta With Fusilli

Serving: 2 servings | Prep: | Cook: |Ready in: 45mins

Ingredients

- Nonstick pan spray
- 1 ½ pounds eggplant
- 8 ounces whole onion or 7 ounces chopped, cut onion (1 1/2 cups)
- 2 teaspoons olive oil
- 2 large cloves garlic
- 2 medium-large ripe tomatoes
- 1 tablespoon tomato paste
- 2 tablespoons balsamic vinegar
- 1 or 2 sprigs oregano to yield 2 teaspoons chopped

- Fresh thyme sprigs, enough to yield 1 teaspoon thyme leaves
- 8 oil-cured olives like Moroccan or Italian
- 8 ounces short pasta like fusilli or penne (fresh, if possible)
- ⅛ teaspoon salt
- Freshly ground black pepper to taste
- 1 or 2 sprigs parsley to yield 2 tablespoons chopped
- 3 tablespoons feta cheese
- 2 slices crusty country bread

Direction

- Turn on broiler. Bring water to boil for pasta in covered pot.
- Wash and trim the eggplant (do not peel) and cut into 1/4-inch-thick slices. Cover broiler pan with aluminum foil and arrange slices on pan. Spray tops of eggplant with pan spray, and broil 2 or 3 inches from source of heat until tops are brown.
- Chop all the onion. Heat a nonstick pan large enough to hold all the sauce ingredients until it is very hot. Reduce heat to medium high, and add oil. Saute the onion until it begins to soften and brown.
- Meanwhile, mince the garlic; chop the tomatoes. Check the eggplant: if it is browned, turn, spray with nonstick spray and continue to broil. It takes about 10 minutes broiling time to cook the eggplant.
- Add the garlic to the onions when they have softened, and saute for 30 seconds. Stir in tomatoes, tomato paste and vinegar; reduce heat to low and continue cooking.
- Chop the oregano and thyme, and add to the sauce as it cooks.
- Cook the pasta.
- When the eggplant is ready, cut it into small chunks (about 1 inch) and stir into the sauce.
- Pit the olives, and chop and add to the sauce. Season with salt and pepper.
- Wash and chop the parsley.
- When the pasta is cooked, drain and stir in the sauce. Stir in the cheese and parsley, and serve with the bread.

Nutrition Information

- 890: calories;
- 29 grams: sugars;
- 23 grams: fat;
- 0 grams: trans fat;
- 5 grams: polyunsaturated fat;
- 147 grams: carbohydrates;
- 21 grams: dietary fiber;
- 28 grams: protein;
- 698 milligrams: sodium;
- 6 grams: saturated fat;
- 11 grams: monounsaturated fat;

106. Eggplant And Tomatoes Au Gratin

Serving: 4 servings | Prep: | Cook: | Ready in: 40mins

Ingredients

- 1 slender eggplant about 3 inches in diameter, about 1 pound
- 4 plum tomatoes, about 1/2 pound, cored
- Salt to taste if desired
- Freshly ground pepper to taste
- 3 tablespoons olive oil
- 2 tablespoons finely chopped parsley
- 2 teaspoons minced garlic
- ¼ cup finely chopped onion
- ¼ cup freshly grated Parmesan cheese

Direction

- Preheat broiler to high.
- Trim off and discard ends of eggplant. Cut eggplant into 16 slices of equal thickness. Set aside.
- Cut each tomato lengthwise into 1/4-inch slices. There should be 16 slices. Sprinkle with salt and pepper.

- Arrange eggplant slices in one layer on a baking sheet. Brush top of each slice with 1 tablespoon of oil.
- Sprinkle with salt and pepper.
- Place eggplant slices under broiler about 4 inches from source of heat. Let broil about 3 minutes and turn slices. Broil about 3 minutes more. Take care that eggplant does not burn.
- Arrange eggplant and tomato slices in baking dish, slightly overlapping.
- Blend parsley, garlic and onion and sprinkle mixture over eggplant and tomatoes.
- Dribble remaining 2 tablespoons oil over top and sprinkle evenly with cheese.
- Place dish under broiler about 6 to 7 inches from source of heat and broil about 3 minutes.
- Adjust oven temperature to 450 degrees. Put vegetables in oven and bake 3 minutes. Serve.

Nutrition Information

- 169: calories;
- 1 gram: polyunsaturated fat;
- 5 grams: protein;
- 7 grams: sugars;
- 523 milligrams: sodium;
- 12 grams: carbohydrates;
- 3 grams: saturated fat;
- 8 grams: monounsaturated fat;

107. Eggplant, Tomato And Onion Pasta

Serving: 3 servings | Prep: | Cook: | Ready in: 25mins

Ingredients

- 2 quarts water
- 1 ½ pounds eggplant, baby or white Oriental or regular
- 4 teaspoons olive oil
- 1 pound onions, diced
- 8 or 9 ounces fresh shell pasta, multicolored assortment, if possible
- 1 pound ripe field tomatoes, diced
- 1 tablespoon coarsely grated ginger
- 1 teaspoon sugar
- 1 tablespoon reduced-sodium soy sauce
- Freshly ground black pepper to taste

Direction

- Turn on broiler and cover pan with double thickness of aluminum foil.
- Bring water to boil in covered pot for pasta. regular size into 1/2-inch thick slices. Place on broiler pan and brush cut sides sparingly with touch of oil, using about 1 teaspoon. Broil about two inches from source of heat, about 7 to 10 minutes until tops are brown and flesh is soft.
- Heat remaining 3 teaspoons of oil in non-stick skillet and saute onions until soft and golden.
- Cook pasta, according to package directions.
- Add tomatoes and ginger to onions and cook a few minutes while removing the flesh from the eggplant by cutting it from the skin. Cut coarsely and add the flesh to tomato mixture with sugar, soy sauce and pepper. Cook a few minutes to meld flavors and heat through.
- Drain pasta and mix with tomato mixture.

108. Eggs Florentine

Serving: 4 servings | Prep: | Cook: | Ready in: 30mins

Ingredients

- 4 large eggs
- 2 pounds fresh spinach or 1 1/2 packages frozen chopped spinach, defrosted
- ½ teaspoon unsalted butter
- For the sauce:
- 2 ½ tablespoons unsalted butter
- ⅓ cup flour
- 2 cups milk, skim milk or half-and-half
- ½ teaspoon salt
- Few grindings of black pepper
- Pinch of nutmeg

- ¾ cup grated Gruyere cheese

Direction

- Bring 2 inches of water to a boil in a 9-inch saucepan. Break each egg into a demitasse cup with a rounded bottom. Smoothly pour eggs into water, and poach 2 to 3 minutes, until as firm as desired. Remove with a slotted spoon to a bowl of warm water.
- If using fresh spinach, stem, wash well and cook in a heavy pan until limp. Drain thoroughly in a sieve, pressing to remove as much water as possible. Pulse in a food processor until coarsely chopped, and strain again. If using frozen spinach, defrost in a sieve under hot running water. Press with the back of a spoon to remove as much water as possible.
- Butter inside of 9-inch pie plate or quiche dish with 1/2 teaspoon butter.
- To make the sauce, melt butter over low heat. Remove from heat, and stir in flour. Whisk thoroughly. Whisk in milk or half-and-half. Stir into the corners to incorporate any bits of flour and butter, and whisk again. Place over low heat, and whisk and stir constantly for 8 minutes. Put in food processor, and process until completely smooth. Combine half the sauce with spinach, 1/2 teaspoon salt, pepper and pinch of nutmeg.
- Preheat broiler, placing rack at highest level. Stir 1/2 cup cheese into remaining sauce.
- Make a smooth layer of the spinach in the buttered pan. With the back of a kitchen spoon make 4 depressions that do not touch and that are about 1 inch from the edge of the pan.
- Drain eggs. Place one in each depression. Divide sauce to cover eggs. Do not let sauce touch sides of pan. Sprinkle remaining cheese all over the top. Place pan on a cookie sheet, and broil 4 minutes.

Nutrition Information

- 406: calories;
- 25 grams: protein;
- 14 grams: saturated fat;
- 2 grams: polyunsaturated fat;
- 23 grams: carbohydrates;
- 0 grams: trans fat;
- 7 grams: sugars;
- 5 grams: dietary fiber;
- 771 milligrams: sodium;

109. Eggs Kejriwal

Serving: 2 servings | Prep: | Cook: | Ready in: 10mins

Ingredients

- 1 tablespoon softened butter
- 2 thick slices Pullman bread
- 2 teaspoons mustard
- 4 ounces Cheddar cheese, grated
- 1 serrano chile, finely sliced
- 2 tablespoons cilantro leaves, washed and chopped
- 1 tablespoon minced red onion
- 2 eggs
- Salt and pepper, to taste
- Ketchup (optional)

Direction

- Butter the bread on both sides, and lightly brown in a frying pan (use the pan you like most for frying eggs). Smear one side of the toasts with mustard, and transfer to a sheet pan, mustard-side up. Turn on the broiler.
- Mix together the cheese, chile, cilantro and onion, then split the mixture evenly between the toasts. Place under the broiler just until the cheese is melted.
- While the cheese is melting, fry the eggs in the same pan you used to make the toast, until the white edges are crisp, but the yolks are still soft. Gently loosen the eggs from the pan, and slide one on top of each toast. Season with salt and pepper, and serve with ketchup on the side, if you like.

Nutrition Information

- 428: calories;
- 30 grams: fat;
- 1 gram: trans fat;
- 17 grams: carbohydrates;
- 23 grams: protein;
- 16 grams: saturated fat;
- 8 grams: monounsaturated fat;
- 2 grams: sugars;
- 631 milligrams: sodium;

110. Endives Au Gratin

Serving: 6 servings | Prep: | Cook: | Ready in: 1hours

Ingredients

- 8 large endives
- 1 tablespoon butter
- 1 tablespoon lemon juice
- 1 teaspoon sugar
- ⅓ cup water
- Salt and freshly ground pepper to taste
- Butter for greasing the dish
- ⅓ cup grated Gruyere cheese
- 2 tablespoons melted butter

Direction

- Trim off the bottom of each endive. Place the endives in a heavy saucepan and add the butter, lemon juice, sugar, water, salt and pepper. Cover tightly, bring to a boil and simmer 30 minutes or until the endives are tender.
- Preheat the broiler.
- Drain the endives and press gently to remove any excess moisture.
- Arrange the endives in a buttered baking dish large enough to hold them in one layer. Sprinkle the cheese evenly over them and add the melted butter. Place under the broiler until the cheese is golden brown.

Nutrition Information

- 112: calories;
- 5 grams: carbohydrates;
- 1 gram: sugars;
- 281 milligrams: sodium;
- 10 grams: fat;
- 6 grams: saturated fat;
- 0 grams: polyunsaturated fat;
- 3 grams: protein;

111. Fig Brochettes With Tapioca Cream

Serving: 12 servings | Prep: | Cook: | Ready in: 1hours

Ingredients

- 8 cups milk
- 5 cinnamon sticks, broken into pieces
- 13 large egg yolks
- 6 tablespoons lightly packed light brown sugar, plus more for dusting the figs
- ¼ cup quick-cooking tapioca
- 24 black mission figs, halved
- 24 whole cinnamon sticks

Direction

- In a large saucepan, combine 4 cups of the milk and the cinnamon-stick pieces. Over medium-high heat, bring the milk just to a boil, remove from the heat, cover and allow to infuse for 10 minutes. Strain the mixture through a fine sieve, discard the cinnamon and return the milk to the pan.
- In a large bowl, whisk together the yolks and the sugar until thick and light-colored. Gradually whisk the hot milk into the yolk mixture. Return to the pan and cook over medium heat, stirring constantly with a wooden spoon until the mixture is slightly thickened and just coats the back of the spoon, about 15 to 20 minutes. (Do not allow it to boil.) Immediately remove from the heat and

strain into a large, clean bowl. Cover with plastic wrap and refrigerate.
- In a large saucepan over medium-high heat, bring the remaining 4 cups of milk just to a boil. (If a skin forms on the milk, remove it with a spoon.) Sprinkle the tapioca over the milk and cook, stirring, until the mixture is thick and the tapioca pearls are translucent, about 15 to 20 minutes. Remove from the heat, cover and refrigerate. When chilled, combine with the custard.
- Preheat the broiler. Skewer 2 fig halves on each cinnamon stick and place on a baking sheet. Sprinkle them with brown sugar and broil until the sugar is caramelized. Spoon the tapioca cream into serving dishes and top each with two warm brochettes.

Nutrition Information

- 288: calories;
- 82 milligrams: sodium;
- 11 grams: fat;
- 5 grams: saturated fat;
- 43 grams: carbohydrates;
- 6 grams: dietary fiber;
- 9 grams: protein;
- 4 grams: monounsaturated fat;
- 1 gram: polyunsaturated fat;
- 32 grams: sugars;

112. Fillets Of Scrod

Serving: 6 servings | Prep: | Cook: | Ready in: 20mins

Ingredients

- ½ cup extra virgin olive oil
- 6 cloves garlic
- ½ cup fresh basil
- ½ cup fresh parsley
- Juice of 2 limes (1/2 cup)
- Salt and pepper to taste
- 6 scrod fillets
- 1 cup cherry tomatoes

Direction

- Preheat the broiler. Place an oven rack six inches below the heat. Line a baking sheet with aluminum foil. Combine the oil, garlic, basil, parsley, lime juice, salt and pepper in a food processor and purée.
- Rinse fish; pat dry. Pour mixture on both sides of fish. Place on baking sheet and broil for 5 minutes. Place tomatoes around fish and broil for 5 to 8 more minutes. Remove and serve.

Nutrition Information

- 368: calories;
- 20 grams: fat;
- 3 grams: saturated fat;
- 5 grams: carbohydrates;
- 42 grams: protein;
- 716 milligrams: sodium;
- 13 grams: monounsaturated fat;
- 2 grams: polyunsaturated fat;
- 1 gram: sugars;

113. Fillets Of Shad Stuffed With Swiss Chard

Serving: 2 servings | Prep: | Cook: | Ready in: 30mins

Ingredients

- 2 shad fillets with skin on
- Juice of 1 lemon
- 1 pound of Swiss chard
- 1 tablespoon unsalted butter
- 1 tablespoon olive oil
- 2 shallots, minced
- Coarse salt and freshly ground pepper to taste
- 1 tablespoon peanut or vegetable oil
- Lemon quarters for garnish

Direction

- Put the fillets of shad on a plate and squeeze the lemon juice over the flesh. Remove the stems from the Swiss chard and carefully wash the leaves in several changes of water. Drain and chop.
- Melt the butter in a frying pan with the olive oil and soften the shallots. Add the chard and cook it until it is wilted. Season with salt and pepper and set aside.
- Preheat broiler. Take a piece of foil twice the width of the shad fillet and put the shad skin down on one side of the foil so later you can turn the fillet over onto the other side of the foil. Place the Swiss chard in the middle of the fillet and close the overhanging flaps of flesh over it. Flip the fish over on the foil so it is now skin side up. Sprinkle with the peanut oil.
- Broil the shad until the skin is crisp (about five minutes). Using the foil as a lever, turn the fish over. Broil until done, about three to four minutes and serve with the lemon wedges.

Nutrition Information

- 633: calories;
- 22 grams: carbohydrates;
- 37 grams: protein;
- 1212 milligrams: sodium;
- 7 grams: dietary fiber;
- 45 grams: fat;
- 11 grams: saturated fat;
- 0 grams: trans fat;
- 8 grams: sugars;

114. Fish With Cilantro And Garlic

Serving: 2 servings | Prep: | Cook: | Ready in: 20mins

Ingredients

- Fresh cilantro to yield 1/4 cup coarsely chopped
- Fresh parsley to yield 1/4 cup coarsely chopped
- 2 large cloves garlic
- ¼ teaspoon ground cumin
- ⅛ to ¼ teaspoon hot pepper flakes
- 2 tablespoons lemon juice
- 2 teaspoons olive oil
- 10 ounces red snapper or grouper

Direction

- Turn on the broiler, and cover broiler pan with aluminum foil.
- Wash, dry and coarsely chop cilantro and parsley. Mince cilantro, parsley and garlic in food processor.
- Add the cumin, hot pepper flakes, lemon juice and olive oil, and process until well blended.
- Wash fish, and cut in half. Place in a single layer on foil, and spread cilantro mixture evenly over fish.
- Broil fish four inches from heat, according to the Canadian rule: measure fish at the thickest part, and cook 8 to 10 minutes to the inch.

Nutrition Information

- 196: calories;
- 0 grams: dietary fiber;
- 30 grams: protein;
- 97 milligrams: sodium;
- 7 grams: fat;
- 1 gram: sugars;
- 4 grams: monounsaturated fat;
- 3 grams: carbohydrates;

115. Flounder In Orange Sauce With Pine Nuts

Serving: 2 servings | Prep: | Cook: | Ready in: 10mins

Ingredients

- ¾ pound flounder or sole fillet

- 1 tablespoon olive oil plus a few drops
- 2 tablespoons raisins
- 2 tablespoons pine nuts
- 2 tablespoons orange juice concentrate
- 1 teaspoon lemon juice
- 1 teaspoon water
- 1 tablespoon chopped parsley

Direction

- Heat broiler. Arrange fish on broiler pan and rub them with a few drops of oil. Broil about 2 inches from source of heat, 4 to 5 minutes, depending on thickness of fillets. Do not turn them.
- Heat 1 tablespoon of oil in small skillet. Saute raisins and pine nuts over medium heat 2 to 3 minutes, until nuts begin to color. Stir in orange juice concentrate, lemon juice and water and simmer to heat.
- When fish is cooked, arrange on serving plates and spoon sauce over. Sprinkle with parsley.

Nutrition Information

- 271: calories;
- 7 grams: sugars;
- 4 grams: polyunsaturated fat;
- 10 grams: carbohydrates;
- 506 milligrams: sodium;
- 16 grams: fat;
- 1 gram: dietary fiber;
- 23 grams: protein;
- 2 grams: saturated fat;
- 0 grams: trans fat;

116. Four Seasons Oysters In Champagne Veloute

Serving: 6 servings | Prep: | Cook: | Ready in: 45mins

Ingredients

- 24 oysters on the half shell
- 3 tablespoons lightly salted butter
- 3 tablespoons all-purpose flour
- ⅓ to ½ cup fish stock
- Juice from 24 oysters
- ½ cup brut Champagne
- ¼ cup heavy cream
- ¼ cup chopped mixed fresh herbs
- Freshly ground black pepper, to taste
- Rock salt (optional)

Direction

- Remove the oysters from the shells and refrigerate. Reserve the oyster liquid and the shells.
- Melt butter in a 2 1/2-quart saucepan and stir in the flour. Cook for 2 minutes without letting the mixture brown. Add enough fish stock to the oyster juice to make 1 cup. Gradually beat this into the flour mixture and when thickened and smooth, let the sauce simmer gently for about 20 minutes, whisking often to prevent the sauce from sticking to the pan.
- Stir in 1/4 cup of the Champagne and the cream. Simmer until the mixture is reduced to 1 cup, whisking often.
- In a separate pan, heat the remaining 1/4 cup Champagne with the herbs and cook until the liquid is almost evaporated. Add the mixture to the sauce and season with pepper.
- Preheat broiler. Line a baking pan large enough to hold the shells in a single layer with rock salt or crumpled foil to hold them steady. Rinse and dry the shells and place in the pan.
- Put an oyster on each shell and spoon about 1 heaping teaspoon of sauce over each. Glaze briefly under the broiler, transfer to individual plates and serve at once.

Nutrition Information

- 446: calories;
- 25 grams: carbohydrates;
- 1 gram: sugars;
- 39 grams: protein;
- 501 milligrams: sodium;

- 4 grams: polyunsaturated fat;
- 0 grams: trans fat;
- 19 grams: fat;
- 8 grams: saturated fat;

117. Fragrant Citrus Couscous With Pork

Serving: 3 servings | Prep: | Cook: | Ready in: 35mins

Ingredients

- 1 pound mushrooms
- 4 ounces whole onion or 3 ounces ready-cut onion (1 cup)
- 1 teaspoon olive oil
- 6 ounces pork tenderloin
- 1 tablespoon cumin
- Cayenne pepper to taste
- 1 tablespoon lemon rind
- 1 tablespoon orange rind
- ⅓ cup dried apricots
- 1 cup whole-wheat couscous
- ½ cup chopped parsley
- ½ cup chopped mint
- 1 large tomato
- ¼ teaspoon salt

Direction

- Preheat broiler, or prepare top-of-the-stove grill.
- Wash, dry, trim and slice the mushrooms; chop the whole onion.
- Heat oil in large nonstick pot, and saute mushrooms and onions in hot oil to soften.
- Cut tenderloin into 1/4-inch-thick pieces, and rub each side with 2 teaspoons of the cumin and a sprinkling of the cayenne. Broil or grill until brown on both sides, about 5 minutes.
- Meanwhile, grate lemon and orange rind; chop apricots.
- Follow package directions for making couscous. Add water to onions and mushrooms; bring to boil. Stir in couscous, lemon and orange rind, apricots, remaining cumin and cayenne; cover, and turn off heat.
- Cut cooked pork into bite-size pieces, and stir into couscous.
- Wash, dry and chop parsley and mint; wash, trim and chop tomato. When cosucous is done, add parsley, mint and tomato. Season with salt and serve.

Nutrition Information

- 411: calories;
- 5 grams: fat;
- 1 gram: polyunsaturated fat;
- 0 grams: trans fat;
- 2 grams: monounsaturated fat;
- 256 milligrams: sodium;
- 68 grams: carbohydrates;
- 9 grams: dietary fiber;
- 14 grams: sugars;
- 26 grams: protein;

118. French Crepes

Serving: About 12 six-inch crepes | Prep: | Cook: | Ready in: 2hours25mins

Ingredients

- ¾ cup sifted flour
- Pinch of salt
- 2 eggs
- 1 cup milk
- 2 tablespoons clarified butter
- 1 cup fruit perserves
- Confectioners' sugar (optional)

Direction

- Mix the flour and salt. Beat eggs and milk just until well blended. Stir into flour mixture until smooth. Stir in butter. Set aside for at least one-half hour and up to two hours. (Batter

may also be kept overnight but may have to be thinned with a little milk before using. It should be just a little thicker than heavy cream.)
- Heat a six- to seven-inch crepe pan. (See note.)
- Spoon a small amount of batter into the pan, tipping the pan so the batter just coats the entire bottom.
- Cook about two minutes, until the underside is golden, flip over and cook the second side about 30 seconds, until lightly browned. Stack finished crepes on a plate and repeat with remaining batter.
- Spread a spoonful of preserves on each crepe, roll the crepes or fold them in quarters and warm in the oven before serving. Tops of filled crepes may be dusted with confectioners' sugar and if the crepes are placed under the broiler very briefly the sugar will caramelize.

Nutrition Information

- 76: calories;
- 9 grams: carbohydrates;
- 44 milligrams: sodium;
- 4 grams: fat;
- 2 grams: protein;
- 0 grams: dietary fiber;
- 1 gram: sugars;

119. Frisee Salad With Fish And Chips (Salmon And Seaweed)

Serving: 6 to 8 servings | Prep: | Cook: | Ready in: 40mins

Ingredients

- For the salmon:
- ⅓ cup olive oil flavored with herbes de Provence, or best-quality extra-virgin olive oil
- 1 salmon fillet, preferably from a wild fish, weighing at least 1 pound
- 1 ounce of dulse (see note)
- 3 tablespoons grape seed oil or other oil that tolerates high temperatures
- 12 basil leaves preserved in oil (optional)
- 2 tablespoons sage vinegar or flavorful wine vinegar
- For the chive salad cream:
- 3 tablespoons basil vinegar or flavorful wine vinegar
- 8 tablespoons basil oil or best-quality extra-virgin olive oil
- Pinch of salt
- Freshly ground black pepper to taste
- 2 tablespoons creme fraiche (see note)
- ⅓ cup finely slivered fresh chives
- 2 bunches curly endive or chicory frisee, rinsed and dried

Direction

- Rub the 1/3 cup of olive oil into the salmon and set aside to marinate at least 1 hour. Preheat grill or broiler to high heat and grill salmon 3 minutes to a side, until it is thoroughly seared on the outside but barely warm in the center. Remove from heat and set aside.
- To prepare the dulse, first peel and stretch the pieces to separate them. Heat the grape seed oil in a skillet over high heat until oil is smoking. Add the pieces of seaweed a few at a time to the smoking oil. They will curl flat and brown almost immediately. Remove from heat, drain on paper towels and set aside. Saute basil leaves; drain and set aside. Sprinkle the sage vinegar over the seaweed and basil.
- To prepare the salad cream, first whisk together the vinegar and oil. Add salt and pepper. Beat in creme fraiche until mixture is thoroughly homogeneous and creamy. Add chives just before serving. Pour over the endive and toss to mix and coat the leaves completely.
- To serve, put a mound of greens on each plate. Cut the salmon in very thin slices and distribute on top of each salad mound.

Sprinkle the salmon slices with seaweed "chips" and serve immediately.

Nutrition Information

- 272: calories;
- 55 milligrams: sodium;
- 29 grams: fat;
- 4 grams: protein;
- 17 grams: monounsaturated fat;
- 6 grams: polyunsaturated fat;
- 1 gram: dietary fiber;
- 0 grams: sugars;

120. Frittata With Sorrel, Potatoes And Prosciutto

Serving: 2 to 3 servings | Prep: | Cook: | Ready in: 40mins

Ingredients

- 2 medium potatoes, peeled and diced
- 1 small onion, chopped
- 3 tablespoons olive oil
- 5 eggs
- Coarse salt and freshly ground pepper to taste
- 1 cup sorrel leaves, washed and cut into julienne
- 1 teaspoon fresh thyme leaves
- 2 ounces prosciutto, cut into julienne
- 1 tablespoon fresh basil or tarragon leaves

Direction

- Saute the potatoes and the onion in two tablespoons olive oil until the onions are soft and the potatoes lightly browned and cooked through.
- Beat the eggs together in a bowl and season with salt and pepper. Add the sorrel, thyme and prosciutto and mix together.
- Preheat broiler. Heat the remaining oil in a skillet or a large omelet pan. Add the potato-onion mixture to the eggs and mix thoroughly.
- Cook the omelet over moderate heat until the bottom is set. Finish cooking under a hot broiler until the top is puffed but the omelet is still slightly liquid underneath. Sprinkle with basil or tarragon and serve.

Nutrition Information

- 388: calories;
- 13 grams: monounsaturated fat;
- 30 grams: carbohydrates;
- 4 grams: dietary fiber;
- 18 grams: protein;
- 674 milligrams: sodium;
- 5 grams: saturated fat;
- 0 grams: trans fat;
- 3 grams: sugars;
- 22 grams: fat;

121. Frittata With Turnips And Olives

Serving: 6 servings. | Prep: | Cook: | Ready in: 1hours15mins

Ingredients

- 1 pound firm medium-size or small turnips
- Salt
- 2 tablespoons extra virgin olive oil
- 2 teaspoons fresh thyme leaves, chopped
- 6 eggs
- 1 tablespoon milk
- Freshly ground pepper
- ½ cup chopped flat-leaf parsley
- 1 ounce imported black olives, pitted and chopped, about 1/3 cup (optional)
- 1 or 2 garlic cloves, minced or puréed (optional)

Direction

- Peel the turnips and grate on the large holes of a box grater or with a food processor. Salt generously and leave to drain in a colander for 30 minutes. Take up handfuls and squeeze tightly to rid the turnips of excess water.
- Heat 1 tablespoon of the olive oil over medium-low heat in a wide saucepan or skillet and add the turnips and the thyme. When the turnips are sizzling, cover and cook gently, stirring often, for about 15 minutes, until they are tender. If they begin to stick to the pan or brown, add a tablespoon of water. Season to taste with salt and pepper. Remove from the heat and allow to cool slightly.
- Beat the eggs and milk in a bowl and season to taste with salt and pepper. Stir in the parsley, chopped olives and garlic. Add the turnips and mix together.
- Heat the remaining olive oil over medium-high heat in a heavy 10-inch skillet, preferably nonstick. Hold your hand above it; it should feel hot. Drop a bit of egg into the pan, and if it sizzles and cooks at once, the pan is ready. Pour in the egg mixture. Swirl the pan to distribute the eggs and filling evenly over the surface. Shake the pan gently, tilting it slightly with one hand while lifting up the edges of the frittata with a spatula in your other hand, to let the eggs run underneath during the first few minutes of cooking. Once a few layers of egg have cooked during the first couple of minutes of cooking, turn the heat down to very low, cover (use a pizza pan if you don't have a lid that will fit your skillet) and cook 10 minutes, shaking the pan gently every once in a while. From time to time, remove the lid and loosen the bottom of the frittata with a spatula, tilting the pan, so that the bottom doesn't burn.
- Meanwhile, heat the broiler. Uncover the pan and place under the broiler, not too close to the heat, for 1 to 3 minutes, watching very carefully to make sure the top doesn't burn (at most, it should brown very slightly and puff under the broiler). Remove from the heat, shake the pan to make sure the frittata isn't sticking and allow it to cool for at least 5 minutes (the frittata is traditionally eaten warm or at room temperature). Loosen the edges with a spatula. Carefully slide from the pan onto a large round platter. Cut into wedges or into smaller bite-size diamonds. Serve warm, at room temperature or cold.

Nutrition Information

- 127: calories;
- 1 gram: polyunsaturated fat;
- 9 grams: fat;
- 2 grams: dietary fiber;
- 3 grams: sugars;
- 305 milligrams: sodium;
- 0 grams: trans fat;
- 5 grams: monounsaturated fat;
- 6 grams: protein;

122. Frittata With Zucchini, Goat Cheese And Dill

Serving: 6 servings | Prep: | Cook: | Ready in: 40mins

Ingredients

- 2 tablespoons extra virgin olive oil
- 1 pound zucchini, grated (about 4 cups)
- 2 garlic cloves, minced
- Salt
- freshly ground pepper to taste
- 8 eggs
- 2 ounces goat cheese, crumbled (about 1/2 cup)
- ¼ cup chopped fresh dill

Direction

- Heat 1 tablespoon of the oil over medium heat in a 10-inch heavy nonstick skillet. Add the zucchini. Cook, stirring, until the zucchini begins to wilt, about two minutes. Stir in the garlic. Cook for another minute or until the zucchini has just wilted — it should still be

bright green. Season to taste with salt and pepper, and remove from the heat.
- Beat the eggs in a large bowl with the goat cheese. Add salt and pepper, and stir in the zucchini and the dill.
- Clean and dry the pan, and return to the burner, set on medium-high. Heat the remaining tablespoon of olive oil in the skillet. Drop a bit of egg into the pan; if it sizzles and cooks at once, the pan is ready. Pour in the egg mixture. Tilt the pan to distribute the eggs and filling evenly over the surface. Shake the pan gently, tilting it slightly with one hand while lifting up the edges of the frittata with the spatula in your other hand, to let the eggs run underneath during the first few minutes of cooking.
- Turn the heat to low, cover and cook 10 minutes, shaking the pan gently every once in a while. From time to time, remove the lid, tilt the pan and loosen the bottom of the frittata with a wooden spatula so that it doesn't burn. The bottom should have a golden color. The eggs should be just about set; cook a few minutes longer if they're not.
- Meanwhile, heat the broiler. Uncover the pan and place under the broiler, not too close to the heat, for one to three minutes, watching very carefully to make sure the top doesn't burn (at most, it should brown very slightly and puff under the broiler). Remove from the heat, and shake the pan to make sure the frittata isn't sticking. Allow it to cool for at least five minutes and for as long as 15 minutes. Loosen the edges with a wooden or plastic spatula. Carefully slide from the pan onto a large round platter. Cut into wedges or into smaller bite-size diamonds. Serve hot, warm, at room temperature or cold.

Nutrition Information

- 178: calories;
- 4 grams: carbohydrates;
- 5 grams: saturated fat;
- 0 grams: trans fat;
- 2 grams: sugars;
- 1 gram: dietary fiber;
- 11 grams: protein;
- 375 milligrams: sodium;
- 13 grams: fat;
- 6 grams: monounsaturated fat;

123. Gabriella Marriotti's Egg And Eggplant Appetizer

Serving: Eight or more appetizer servings | Prep: | Cook: | Ready in: P1DT30mins

Ingredients

- 1 eggplant, about 1 pound
- 3 hard-cooked eggs
- Salt to taste, if desired
- Freshly ground pepper to taste
- ½ cup drained small capers
- 2 tablespoons finely minced garlic
- 1 2-ounce can anchovies, drained and finely chopped
- 1 cup finely chopped parsley
- 1 cup olive oil, approximately
- 2 tablespoons red-wine vinegar, approximately

Direction

- Preheat a charcoal grill or a kitchen broiler.
- Cut off the ends of the eggplant. Cut the eggplant into slices about one-quarter-inch thick. There should be about 18 slices.
- Remove the yolks from the eggs and put them through a fine sieve. Finely chop the whites. Combine the two. Put in a mixing bowl.
- Place the eggplant slices, a few at a time, over the charcoal or under the broiler and cook, turning once, about 45 seconds on each side. The partly cooked slices will be slightly limp.
- Remove the slices and sprinkle with salt and pepper.
- Add the capers, garlic, anchovies and parsley to the eggs and toss to blend well.

- Line a six-cup loaf pan lengthwise with one layer of eggplant slices. Sprinkle with one tablespoon oil and one-half teaspoon vinegar. Cover with one-quarter cup of the egg mixture. Add another layer of eggplant slices and sprinkle as before with the same amount of oil and vinegar. Add another layer of the egg mixture and cover with a layer of eggplant slices. Sprinkle with the same amount of oil and vinegar.
- Continue making layers until all the eggplant slices and the egg mixture are used, ending with the egg mixture. Sprinkle that final layer with one tablespoon of vinegar and 10 tablespoons of olive oil. Press down with the fingers. Cover closely with clear plastic wrap and let stand 24 hours in the refrigerator.
- When ready, the dish may be cut into crosswise slices, but ideally the eggplant slices should be rolled individually, with the egg filling in the center. Serve one or two rolled slices as an appetizer.

Nutrition Information

- 297: calories;
- 21 grams: monounsaturated fat;
- 3 grams: polyunsaturated fat;
- 5 grams: protein;
- 2 grams: sugars;
- 410 milligrams: sodium;
- 29 grams: fat;
- 4 grams: saturated fat;

124. Garlic Croutons

Serving: 4 to 6 servings | Prep: | Cook: | Ready in: 15mins

Ingredients

- 1 loaf of French bread
- 2 garlic cloves, peeled
- 2 tablespoons olive oil
- Freshly ground pepper to taste

Direction

- Preheat broiler.
- Rub the bread's crust all over with the garlic cloves. Cut the bread into 1/2-inch thick slices and sprinkle one side with the olive oil and pepper.
- Place the bread slices on a baking sheet under the broiler until they are golden. Turn and broil on the other side until brown.

Nutrition Information

- 178: calories;
- 3 grams: monounsaturated fat;
- 26 grams: carbohydrates;
- 5 grams: protein;
- 301 milligrams: sodium;
- 6 grams: fat;
- 1 gram: dietary fiber;
- 0 grams: trans fat;
- 2 grams: sugars;

125. Garlicky Steak With Carrot, Walnut And Dill Salad

Serving: 4 servings | Prep: | Cook: | Ready in: 20mins

Ingredients

- 1 lemon
- 1 ½ teaspoons kosher salt
- ½ teaspoon black pepper
- 4 garlic cloves, pressed or minced
- 1 teaspoon ground coriander
- ½ cup full-fat plain Greek yogurt
- ⅓ cup olive oil
- 1 ¼ pounds flank steak
- 4 large carrots
- ⅓ cup walnuts, toasted
- ¼ cup roughly chopped dill

Direction

- Zest the lemon and combine zest in a bowl with 1 teaspoon salt, the pepper, garlic and coriander, and rub with your fingers to make an even paste. Stir 1 teaspoon mixture into yogurt, and set aside. Pour 3 tablespoons olive oil over the remaining mixture. Rub on both sides of the steak; place the steak in a bowl or a large resealable bag and set aside for 30 minutes, or refrigerate up to overnight.
- Meanwhile, make the salad: Juice the lemon into a large bowl, and whisk together with the remaining 2 tablespoons olive oil and 1/2 teaspoon salt. Shave the carrots into the bowl with a vegetable peeler or a mandoline, making long, thin shavings (like ribbons). Toss together with the dressing and walnuts and set aside while you grill the steak.
- Light the grill or heat the broiler. Remove the steak from the marinade and brush off any excess. (A dry steak yields a better, crisper sear.) Grill the meat over direct heat until char lines appear and meat is done to taste, 5 minutes per side for medium-rare, or broil until charred, 3 to 5 minutes per side.
- Let the meat rest for 5 minutes before slicing against the grain. Toss the dill with the carrot salad. Spread a thin layer or a dollop of lemon-garlic yogurt on each plate, and top with the steak and salad.

Nutrition Information

- 480: calories;
- 34 grams: protein;
- 9 grams: saturated fat;
- 11 grams: carbohydrates;
- 3 grams: dietary fiber;
- 5 grams: sugars;
- 18 grams: monounsaturated fat;
- 4 grams: polyunsaturated fat;
- 672 milligrams: sodium;

126. Ginger Glazed Loin Lamb Chops

Serving: 2 servings | Prep: | Cook: | Ready in: 20mins

Ingredients

- 4 loin lamb chops, about 3/4 pound total
- 4 tablespoons ginger marmalade, jalapeno jelly or other hot-sweet preserve

Direction

- Turn on broiler, if using. Line pan with aluminum foil.
- Wash and dry chops; trim all excess fat.
- Prepare stove-top grill, if using.
- If grilling, cook chops on one side until brown. Turn over, and spread some of preserves on browned top. Continue cooking to brown chop on second side, about 7 minutes for medium rare. Turn chops once more, spread with remaining preserves and serve. If broiling, brown chops on each side, and spread each side with preserves when finished cooking.

Nutrition Information

- 959: calories;
- 35 grams: saturated fat;
- 6 grams: polyunsaturated fat;
- 19 grams: sugars;
- 78 grams: fat;
- 0 grams: dietary fiber;
- 33 grams: protein;
- 140 milligrams: sodium;
- 32 grams: monounsaturated fat;
- 28 grams: carbohydrates;

127. Glazed Pork

Serving: 8 to 10 servings | Prep: | Cook: | Ready in: 30mins

Ingredients

- ½ cup dry white wine
- 2 tablespoons soy sauce
- 1 tablespoon Chinese oyster sauce
- 1 teaspoon sweet paprika
- ½ teaspoon cinnamon
- 5 tablespoons honey
- 1 ½ tablespoons cornstarch
- 1 pound pork shoulder, about 6 inches long

Direction

- Combine wine, soy sauce, oyster sauce, paprika, cinnamon and honey in a saucepan. Add 2 tablespoons water. Bring to a simmer. Mix cornstarch with 2 tablespoons cold water and whisk into sauce. Cook until thickened. Remove from heat and let cool.
- Place pork in a heavy resealable plastic bag. Add half the sauce and mix well with pork. Seal bag and refrigerate overnight. Refrigerate remaining sauce.
- Bring pork to room temperature and heat a grill or broiler. Sear pork, turning once or twice, until glazed, browned and cooked through, 6 to 10 minutes, depending on the heat of the grill. A thermometer should read 145 degrees.
- Just before serving, slice pork 1/2 inch thick. Baste with reserved sauce. Serve immediately if desired.

Nutrition Information

- 156: calories;
- 9 grams: sugars;
- 256 milligrams: sodium;
- 8 grams: protein;
- 3 grams: saturated fat;
- 4 grams: monounsaturated fat;
- 1 gram: polyunsaturated fat;
- 11 grams: carbohydrates;
- 0 grams: dietary fiber;

---

128. Gordon Hamersley's Boned Stuffed Leg Of Lamb

Serving: Eight servings | Prep: | Cook: | Ready in: 1hours

Ingredients

- 1 8-pound (approximately) leg of lamb (weighed with the bone), boned and butterflied
- Bones from the lamb
- ½ large onion, unpeeled
- 2 carrots, scrubbed but unpeeled
- 2 stalks of celery, with leaves
- 1 ½ tablespoons tomato paste
- 1 ½ cups dry red wine
- Approximately 3 cups water or chicken stock
- 4 cloves garlic
- 1 bay leaf
- 6 whole peppercorns
- 1 bunch green kale
- 3 tablespoons, plus 1/4-cup, olive oil
- 3 sweet red peppers
- 3 ounces jumbo Kalamata olives, pitted (about 18 olives)
- 1 shallot
- 1 teaspoon dried thyme
- 1 teaspoon dried oregano
- Kosher salt
- Cracked black pepper

Direction

- Preheat the oven to 375 degrees. Place the lamb bones in a roasting pan and roast for about 45 minutes. Roughly chop the unpeeled onion, the carrots and the celery and add to the roasting pan with the tomato paste. Mix to distribute the vegetables and coat them with tomato paste and fat from the lamb. Return to the oven and roast an additional 15 minutes.
- Remove bones and vegetables from the pan and place them in a stock pot that is just large enough to hold them comfortably. Deglaze the roasting pan with the red wine over high heat and add to the stock pot. Then add enough chicken stock or water to just cover the bones

in the pan. Bring to a boil, skim any scum that rises and add a pinch of salt, two cloves of garlic, the bay leaf and peppercorns. Lower the heat to simmering, partially cover the stock pot and simmer for at least two hours. At the end of this time, the stock should have a destinctive lamb flavor.
- Remove stock from the heat and strain through a coarse sieve. Return strained stock to the pan and cook briskly to reduce and thicken the stock. You should have about four cups of sauce when it is reduced.
- While the sauce is cooking, clean and rinse the kale, stripping the leaves from the ribs. Discard the ribs. In a saute pan over medium high heat saute the kale in three tablespoons of olive oil until it is softened but still a little crisp to the bite. (You may need to add a bit of water to keep the kale from burning.) Remove from the heat and set aside.
- Roast the red peppers over a gas flame, an electric grill or in a preheated broiler, turning until the outsides are blackened. Place in a paper bag for about 15 minutes to soften the skins. Then peel the peppers, discard the seeds and inner membranes and cut in thick slices.
- Roughly chop the olives together with the peeled shallot and remaining garlic cloves. Mix in dried herbs.
- Spread the butterflied lamb out on a countertop, skin side down. If the butcher has left the nugget of fat on the inside of the leg, remove and discard it. Layer the kale over the lamb, then layer the strips of red pepper over that. Sprinkle the olives, garlic and shallot pieces over the pepper strips, then sprinkle salt and cracked black pepper and about half the one-quarter cup of olive oil over the vegetables.
- Roll the lamb leg, securing the stuffing, and tie it in several places with butcher's twine, tucking in the loose flaps at both ends. The result will be a long cylinder.
- Preheat the oven to 400 degrees. Place the lamb roll on a rack in a roasting pan and roast for exactly one hour. Remove from the oven and set aside to rest for 15 minutes. Carve in thick (one-half to three-quarter-inch) slices and serve on heated plates with a little of the hot sauce. Pass the rest of the sauce in a sauce boat.

Nutrition Information

- 916: calories;
- 26 grams: monounsaturated fat;
- 16 grams: carbohydrates;
- 4 grams: dietary fiber;
- 58 grams: fat;
- 23 grams: saturated fat;
- 5 grams: polyunsaturated fat;
- 6 grams: sugars;
- 70 grams: protein;
- 1668 milligrams: sodium;

129. Gratin Of Brussels Sprouts With Parmesan

Serving: Four servings | Prep: | Cook: | Ready in: 1hours

Ingredients

- 4 cups brussels sprouts, trimmed
- 1 ½ teaspoons melted unsalted butter
- 1 ½ teaspoons salt
- Freshly ground pepper to taste
- 1 cup chicken broth, homemade or low-sodium canned
- ¾ cup bread crumbs
- 3 tablespoons freshly grated Parmesan cheese

Direction

- Preheat the oven to 350 degrees. Bring a large pot of water to a boil. Add the brussels sprouts and blanch for 2 minutes. Drain. Place in a 9-inch round gratin dish or pie plate and toss with the butter, 1 teaspoon of the salt and pepper. Pour the chicken broth over the brussels sprouts. Cover with aluminum foil

and bake until tender, about 45 minutes. Drain and return the sprouts to the pan.
- Preheat the broiler. Combine the bread crumbs, Parmesan, remaining salt and pepper to taste and sprinkle the mixture over the brussels sprouts. Place under the broiler until lightly browned. Divide among 4 plates and serve.

Nutrition Information

- 195: calories;
- 25 grams: carbohydrates;
- 11 grams: protein;
- 6 grams: fat;
- 3 grams: saturated fat;
- 2 grams: monounsaturated fat;
- 1 gram: polyunsaturated fat;
- 0 grams: trans fat;
- 4 grams: sugars;
- 421 milligrams: sodium;

130. Gratin Of Zucchini And Yellow Squash

Serving: 4 servings | Prep: | Cook: | Ready in: 15mins

Ingredients

- 2 small zucchini, about 3/4 pound
- 2 small yellow squash, about 3/4 pound
- 2 tablespoons olive oil
- ½ cup finely chopped onion
- 2 teaspoons finely chopped garlic
- 2 sprigs fresh thyme, chopped, or 1/2 teaspoon dried
- Salt and freshly ground pepper to taste
- 3 medium-size ripe tomatoes, cored and cut into thin slices
- 2 tablespoons basil leaves cut into small strips
- 2 tablespoons freshly grated Parmesan cheese

Direction

- Preheat the broiler.
- Rinse the zucchini and squash and pat them dry. Trim off the ends but do not peel them. Slice them in thin slices crosswise.
- Heat 1 tablespoon olive oil in a nonstick skillet and when hot add the zucchini, squash, onion, garlic and thyme. Saute over high heat, shaking the pan and tossing the vegetables gently. Add salt and pepper and cook for a total of 5 minutes.
- Spoon the mixture into a casserole or baking dish. Smooth the top and arrange the sliced tomatoes in a circular pattern to cover the top. Add salt and pepper and sprinkle with the strips of basil leaves and the cheese. Drizzle the remaining oil over all.
- Place under the broiler for 3 to 4 minutes or until light brown.

Nutrition Information

- 158: calories;
- 9 grams: fat;
- 16 grams: carbohydrates;
- 4 grams: dietary fiber;
- 5 grams: protein;
- 701 milligrams: sodium;
- 2 grams: saturated fat;
- 6 grams: monounsaturated fat;
- 1 gram: polyunsaturated fat;

131. Green Garlic Toast

Serving: 8 servings | Prep: | Cook: | Ready in: 15mins

Ingredients

- Slices of crusty bread
- ½ cup unsalted butter (1 stick), softened
- ½ cup grated Parmesan
- 2 ½ tablespoons chopped young green garlic stalks, white and green parts
- 1 tablespoon minced chives
- ¼ teaspoon black pepper

- ¼ teaspoon fine sea salt, more to taste
- Large pinch red chile flakes
- 1 regular (not green) garlic clove, halved

Direction

- Heat the broiler. Place the bread slices on a baking sheet and broil them, flipping them halfway through cooking time, until golden on both sides. Keep warm.
- In a bowl, stir together the butter, cheese, green garlic, chives, pepper, salt and chile.
- Rub the toast with the cut side of the regular garlic clove, then spread with the green garlic butter. Broil toast again for 30 seconds to 2 minutes, until the tops lightly brown and the butter melts. Serve hot or warm.

Nutrition Information

- 144: calories;
- 4 grams: monounsaturated fat;
- 1 gram: polyunsaturated fat;
- 3 grams: protein;
- 118 milligrams: sodium;
- 13 grams: fat;
- 8 grams: saturated fat;
- 0 grams: sugars;

132. Green Papaya Salad With Shrimp

Serving: 4 servings | Prep: | Cook: | Ready in: 30mins

Ingredients

- Salt and pepper
- 12 large shrimp, peeled
- 4 cups peeled, shredded, seeded green papaya or Granny Smith apple or jicama or a combination
- 2 cups mung bean sprouts
- 1 cup roughly chopped cilantro leaves
- ½ cup roughly chopped mint leaves
- ½ cup trimmed and chopped scallions
- 1 teaspoon Vietnamese chili-garlic paste, or to taste
- 2 limes, juiced
- ¼ cup Thai fish sauce (nam pla)
- 1 tablespoon brown or palm sugar
- ½ cup chopped dry-roasted peanuts

Direction

- Salt the shrimp, then grill or broil them, or put them in a saucepan with salted water to cover. Bring water almost to a boil, then turn off heat. Let shrimp sit in water until cool. When cool, slice in half lengthwise.
- In a large bowl, toss together papaya, sprouts, herbs and scallions. Whisk together chili-garlic paste, lime juice, fish sauce and sugar, along with a little salt and a lot of pepper. Taste and adjust seasoning. Toss dressing with papaya-herb mixture, then top with shrimp and peanuts. Toss again at table, and serve.

Nutrition Information

- 234: calories;
- 31 grams: carbohydrates;
- 7 grams: dietary fiber;
- 12 grams: protein;
- 3 grams: polyunsaturated fat;
- 10 grams: fat;
- 1 gram: saturated fat;
- 0 grams: trans fat;
- 5 grams: monounsaturated fat;
- 18 grams: sugars;
- 1559 milligrams: sodium;

133. Green Pea Guacamole

Serving: 6 to 8 servings | Prep: | Cook: | Ready in: 45mins

Ingredients

- ½ pound fresh sweet peas, shucked (about 1/2 to 2/3 cup peas)
- 2 small jalapeños
- 2 tablespoons packed cilantro leaves, chopped, more for garnish
- ¾ teaspoon salt, more as needed
- 3 small ripe avocados, mashed
- 2 scallions, whites only, sliced as thin as possible (about 1/4 cup)
- Zest of 1 lime
- Juice of 1 lime, more as needed
- 1 tablespoon toasted sunflower seeds
- Flaky sea salt, for serving
- Tortilla chips, for serving
- Lime wedges, for serving

Direction

- Bring a medium pot of salted water to a boil and prepare a bowl with water and ice. Plunge peas into the boiling water and cook until al dente, about 1 minute. Drain peas and immediately transfer to the ice bath. Drain.
- Heat broiler to high and broil one of the jalapeños on a heatproof pan. Cook, turning occasionally, until jalapeño is completely charred. Transfer to a small bowl, cover tightly in plastic wrap and let sit for 15 minutes. When cool enough to handle, use a towel to wipe off the charred skin. Halve, seed and devein the roasted jalapeño. Then halve, seed, and mince the remaining raw jalapeño.
- In a blender or the bowl of a food processor, purée peas (reserving 2 tablespoons for garnish) with roasted jalapeño, minced raw jalapeño, cilantro and 1/4 teaspoon salt. Process until almost smooth but still a little chunky.
- In a medium bowl, combine mashed avocado, scallions, lime zest, lime juice, remaining 1/2 teaspoon salt and the pea purée. Adjust salt and lime juice as needed and garnish with fresh peas, sunflower seeds and flaky sea salt. Serve with tortilla chips and lime wedges.

Nutrition Information

- 112: calories;
- 9 grams: carbohydrates;
- 1 gram: sugars;
- 6 grams: monounsaturated fat;
- 5 grams: dietary fiber;
- 2 grams: protein;
- 211 milligrams: sodium;

134. Grilled Bread Salad

Serving: 4 to 6 servings | Prep: | Cook: | Ready in: 45mins

Ingredients

- 1 small baguette (about 8 ounces) or other crusty bread
- ¼ cup extra virgin olive oil
- ¼ cup fresh lemon juice
- 2 tablespoons diced shallot, scallion or red onion
- ¼ teaspoon minced garlic (optional)
- 1 ½ pounds tomatoes, chopped
- Salt and freshly ground black pepper to taste
- ¼ cup or more roughly chopped basil or parsley

Direction

- Start gas or charcoal grill, or preheat broiler; rack should be 4 to 6 inches from heat source. Cut bread lengthwise into quarters. Grill or broil the bread, watching carefully and turning as each side browns and chars slightly; total time will be less than 10 minutes. Remove, and set aside.
- While bread cools, mix together next five ingredients in a large bowl. Mash tomatoes with back of a fork to release all of their juices. Season to taste with salt and pepper. Cut bread into 1/2- to 1-inch cubes (no larger), and toss them with the dressing.
- Let bread sit for 20 to 30 minutes, tossing occasionally and tasting a piece every now and then. The salad is at its peak when the bread is

fairly soft but some edges remain crisp, but you can serve it before or after it reaches that state. When it's ready, stir in basil or parsley, and serve.

Nutrition Information

- 206: calories;
- 2 grams: polyunsaturated fat;
- 24 grams: carbohydrates;
- 3 grams: dietary fiber;
- 6 grams: sugars;
- 5 grams: protein;
- 11 grams: fat;
- 0 grams: trans fat;
- 7 grams: monounsaturated fat;
- 407 milligrams: sodium;

135. Grilled California Goat Cheese On Toast

Serving: 4 to 8 servings | Prep: | Cook: | Ready in: 30mins

Ingredients

- ½ pound round or rounds of goat cheese
- Freshly ground pepper to taste
- 2 teaspoons coarsely chopped fresh thyme, or 1/2 teaspoon dried
- 2 tablespoons extra-virgin olive oil
- 8 bread rounds cut to the diameter of the cheese rounds, each about half an inch thick

Direction

- Preheat the broiler to high.
- Slice the rounds crosswise into eight pieces of more or less equal thickness.
- Arrange the slices of cheese in one layer in a shallow dish or plate. Sprinkle with equal amounts of pepper, thyme and oil. Let marinate for at least 15 minutes.

- Toast the bread on both sides and arrange the rounds on a baking sheet. Arrange one slice of cheese on each bread round. Pour any remaining oil over the cheese.
- Place under the broiler about one or two minutes or just until piping hot. Serve on hot plates.

Nutrition Information

- 252: calories;
- 0 grams: sugars;
- 194 milligrams: sodium;
- 21 grams: fat;
- 7 grams: monounsaturated fat;
- 2 grams: carbohydrates;
- 11 grams: saturated fat;
- 1 gram: polyunsaturated fat;
- 15 grams: protein;

136. Grilled Chicken And Pineapple Salad

Serving: 2 servings | Prep: | Cook: | Ready in: 35mins

Ingredients

- 1 small fennel bulb (3/4 cup)
- 1 large pineapple (1 1/2 cups)
- 8 ounces skinless, boneless chicken
- 8 ounces fresh corkscrew pasta
- 8 large black Italian, Greek or French olives
- 1 tablespoon grated onion
- 1 teaspoon anchovy paste
- 1 teaspoon dry mustard
- 1 teaspoon Dijon mustard
- 4 teaspoons Worcestershire sauce
- ½ cup plain nonfat yogurt
- 1 teaspoon raspberry or balsamic vinegar
- 1 bunch arugula
- Freshly ground black pepper

Direction

- If using a broiler, turn it on.
- For the pasta, bring water to boil in a covered pot.
- Wash, trim and chop fennel finely and place in large serving bowl.
- Cut pineapple into small pieces. You will need about 3/4 of the pineapple to make 1 1/2 cups. Add to fennel.
- If using a stove-top grill, prepare. Grill or broil chicken until it is brown on both sides, about 10 minutes, depending on thickness of pieces.
- Cook pasta according to package directions.
- Cut up olives and grate onion; add to bowl along with anchovy paste, mustards, Worcestershire sauce, yogurt and vinegar.
- Wash, trim and dry arugula.
- When chicken is cooked, remove and cut into julienne strips; add to bowl.
- Drain pasta and add to bowl. Season with pepper.
- Arrange arugula on two serving plates and top with chicken salad. Add two slices of crusty French or Italian bread.

Nutrition Information

- 818: calories;
- 9 grams: monounsaturated fat;
- 111 grams: carbohydrates;
- 44 grams: protein;
- 8 grams: dietary fiber;
- 21 grams: sugars;
- 486 milligrams: sodium;
- 22 grams: fat;
- 6 grams: saturated fat;
- 0 grams: trans fat;
- 5 grams: polyunsaturated fat;

137. Grilled Chicken Breasts With Turmeric And Lime

Serving: 4 to 6 servings | Prep: | Cook: | Ready in: 15mins

Ingredients

- 4 to 6 skinless, boneless chicken breasts, about 1 1/2 pounds
- 2 tablespoons olive oil
- 3 tablespoons freshly squeezed lime juice
- ½ teaspoon chile powder
- ½ teaspoon ground turmeric
- 2 teaspoons chopped fresh or crushed dried rosemary leaves
- 1 teaspoon finely minced garlic
- Salt to taste if desired
- Freshly ground pepper to taste
- 2 tablespoons melted butter

Direction

- Heat a grill or the broiler.
- Put the oil in a mixing bowl; and lime juice, chile powder, turmeric, rosemary, garlic, salt and pepper. Stir to blend well and add the chicken pieces. Turn them in the marinade to coat well. Cover and set aside until ready to cook. If they are to be marinated for a long period, refrigerate them.
- Place chicken pieces on the grill or on the rack under the broiler. Cover the grill or close the door to the broiler. Cook about 2 to 3 minutes and turn the pieces. Continue cooking until done, about 2 to 3 minutes on the grill, possibly a little longer under the broiler.
- Remove the pieces and brush the tops with the melted butter.

Nutrition Information

- 236: calories;
- 17 grams: fat;
- 6 grams: saturated fat;
- 0 grams: sugars;
- 8 grams: monounsaturated fat;
- 2 grams: carbohydrates;
- 19 grams: protein;
- 307 milligrams: sodium;

138. Grilled Chicken Thighs With Sauce Au Chien

Serving: 4 servings | Prep: | Cook: | Ready in: 30mins

Ingredients

- 1 tablespoon peeled and slivered or minced garlic
- 6 scallions, trimmed and minced
- 1 Scotch bonnet or jalapeno pepper, stemmed, seeded and minced, or chili paste or crushed red pepper flakes to taste (start with 1/2 teaspoon)
- Salt and fresh black pepper
- ½ teaspoon ground allspice, or to taste
- 1 tablespoon peanut or canola oil
- 8 chicken thighs, about 2 pounds
- Juice of 1 lime

Direction

- Prepare a charcoal or gas grill, or preheat the broiler. While it is heating, prepare the sauce: in a small bowl, combine the garlic, scallions, chili, salt, allspice and oil. Add 1/2 cup boiling water; stir and set aside.
- Sprinkle the chicken with salt and pepper, and grill or broil, turning 2 or 3 times, until it is cooked through, about 15 minutes. Taste the sauce, and add more chili, salt, pepper or allspice if needed. Stir in the lime juice. Serve the chicken hot or at room temperature, passing the sauce at the table.

Nutrition Information

- 409: calories;
- 30 grams: fat;
- 7 grams: carbohydrates;
- 0 grams: trans fat;
- 13 grams: monounsaturated fat;
- 2 grams: sugars;
- 27 grams: protein;
- 704 milligrams: sodium;

139. Grilled Chicken Topped With Mixed Melon Salsa

Serving: Four servings | Prep: | Cook: | Ready in: 25mins

Ingredients

- 1 cup ripe honeydew melon, cut into 1/4-inch dice
- 1 cup ripe cantaloupe, cut into 1/4-inch dice
- 1 teaspoon grated fresh ginger
- 3 tablespoons minced scallion
- 1 teaspoon seeded and minced jalapeno
- 1 tablespoon fresh lime juice
- ¾ teaspoon salt
- 2 chicken breasts, boned, skinned and split
- Freshly ground pepper to taste

Direction

- In a medium bowl, toss together the melons, ginger, scallion and jalapeno. Mix in the lime juice and 1/4 teaspoon of salt. Refrigerate until cold.
- Heat a grill or broiler. Season the chicken breasts with the remaining salt and pepper to taste. Grill or broil until cooked through, about 4 minutes per side. Divide among 4 plates and top with the salsa. Serve immediately.

Nutrition Information

- 185: calories;
- 8 grams: fat;
- 0 grams: trans fat;
- 3 grams: monounsaturated fat;
- 7 grams: sugars;
- 431 milligrams: sodium;
- 2 grams: polyunsaturated fat;
- 9 grams: carbohydrates;
- 1 gram: dietary fiber;
- 19 grams: protein;

140. Grilled Cornish Hens With Pecan Crust

Serving: 4 servings | Prep: | Cook: |Ready in: 45mins

Ingredients

- 4 Cornish hens, about 1 pound each, split in half for broiling
- Salt and freshly ground pepper to taste
- 4 tablespoons Dijon mustard
- 2 tablespoons white vinegar
- 2 tablespoons Worcestershire sauce
- 3 tablespoons olive oil
- ⅓ cup finely chopped toasted pecans
- 2 tablespoons finely chopped scallions
- 1 tablespoon chopped fresh sage or 2 teaspoons dried
- 2 tablespoons melted butter
- 2 tablespoons finely chopped parsley

Direction

- Preheat the oven to broil.
- With a mallet or meat pounder, flatten the hens. Sprinkle them with salt and pepper. Arrange the halves in one layer in a baking dish.
- Place the mustard, vinegar and Worcestershire sauce in a small mixing bowl, and blend well with a wire whisk. Brush both sides of the hens with the mixture.
- Brush the hens with oil, and place skin side down in a baking dish. Place under the broiler about 4 inches from the heat source, and cook for about 10 minutes, basting occasionally. Turn, and continue cooking for about 10 minutes or until lightly browned. Baste often.
- Blend the pecans, scallions and sage. Sprinkle the hens with the mixture and the melted butter.
- Reduce heat to 400 degrees and continue cooking for about 10 minutes, basting occasionally, until the hens are nicely browned. Sprinkle with parsley.

Nutrition Information

- 780: calories;
- 0 grams: trans fat;
- 11 grams: polyunsaturated fat;
- 3 grams: dietary fiber;
- 1 gram: sugars;
- 49 grams: protein;
- 61 grams: fat;
- 17 grams: saturated fat;
- 30 grams: monounsaturated fat;
- 6 grams: carbohydrates;
- 1206 milligrams: sodium;

141. Grilled Duck Legs With Frisee Salad

Serving: 2 servings | Prep: | Cook: |Ready in: 35mins

Ingredients

- 2 duck legs
- 1 duck liver
- Coarse salt and freshly ground pepper to taste
- 1 tablespoon butter
- 1 tablespoon Madeira or dry sherry
- 8 slices French bread for croutons
- 1 tablespoon chopped parsley
- 1 small head frisee (also called curly endive)
- For the dressing:
- 1 to 2 tablespoons fresh lemon juice (or to taste)
- ¼ cup hazelnut oil
- ¼ cup toasted hazelnuts
- 2 tablespoons duck cracklings (optional)

Direction

- Turn the legs skin side down. Cut along each thigh bone and remove it. Preheat oven to 325 degrees.
- Remove the sinews from the duck liver. Season and saute in butter over high heat for three minutes. Pour in the Madeira or sherry

- and cook another minute. Mash the livers until smooth and set aside.
- Bake the bread in the oven for 10 minutes and allow to cool.
- Meanwhile, heat grill or broiler. Season the duck legs and broil for five minutes on the flesh side and eight minutes on the skin side.
- Spread the liver mixture on the croutons and sprinkle with chopped parsley. Wash and dry the frisee and place it in a salad bowl.
- Combine the lemon juice and hazelnut oil and season to taste with salt and pepper. Garnish with hazelnuts and toss the salad in the dressing. Divide the salad between two warm plates, place a duck leg on each one and sprinkle with liver croutons around the side. Sprinkle with duck cracklings if you like.

142. Grilled Fish Setubal Style

Serving: 4 servings | Prep: | Cook: | Ready in: 35mins

Ingredients

- large garlic clove, peeled, crushed and chopped
- ⅓ cup olive oil
- 4 pieces of firm-textured, white-meat fish (see note)
- ¼ pound (1 stick) unsalted butter
- 6 tablespoons dry white wine
- Juice of 2 medium-size oranges
- Juice of 1 medium-size lemon
- ¼ teaspoon salt
- ¼ teaspoon freshly ground black pepper
- 2 small oranges, thinly sliced (see note)
- ¼ cup minced Italian parsley

Direction

- Steep garlic in olive oil at room temperature for several hours. Brush fish well on both sides with oil, cover and refrigerate until shortly before ready to cook. Reserve remaining oil and let stand at room temperature.
- Make the sauce: In a small heavy saucepan set over low heat, let butter melt and turn to a rich topaz brown. Watch carefully so that butter does not burn. Add wine, orange and lemon juices, salt and pepper, and boil, uncovered and stirring occasionally, for 15 to 20 minutes, until sauce is reduced to a syrup. Set off heat until shortly before serving.
- When ready to grill fish, preheat broiler and set broiler rack about 6 inches below heat. Oil broiler pan, then brush fish generously on both sides with remaining oil. Lay fish on broiler rack over pan and grill, about 5 minutes to a side, just until fish flakes. (Boned fish fillets will cook more quickly than small whole fish.)
- While fish broil, pour sauce into a medium-size skillet and set over lowest heat. Lay orange slices in the sauce, covering skillet bottom. When fish are done, remove from heat and place on a large heated platter. Using a spatula, carefully lift orange slices from sauce and set aside. Add chopped parsley to sauce and stir to mix well. Drizzle orange-parsley sauce over fish in platter, then arrange orange slices, slightly overlapping, over the fish. Serve immediately.

Nutrition Information

- 595: calories;
- 18 grams: saturated fat;
- 1 gram: trans fat;
- 3 grams: dietary fiber;
- 11 grams: sugars;
- 34 grams: protein;
- 236 milligrams: sodium;
- 44 grams: fat;
- 20 grams: monounsaturated fat;
- 16 grams: carbohydrates;

143. Grilled Flank Steak With Worcestershire Butter

Serving: 6 servings | Prep: | Cook: | Ready in: 45mins

Ingredients

- For the steak:
- 1 ½ pounds flank steak
- Fine sea salt and freshly ground black pepper
- 6 thyme sprigs
- 3 garlic cloves, finely grated or mashed to a paste
- 1 jalapeño, minced
- 2 tablespoons minced chives, plus more for serving
- 2 tablespoons Worcestershire sauce
- 1 tablespoon coconut palm sugar or dark brown sugar
- 1 tablespoon fresh lemon juice, plus more as needed
- 3 ripe plum tomatoes
- Extra-virgin olive oil
- 3 scallions, white and green parts, thinly sliced
- Handful of torn fresh basil, plus more for serving
- For the Worcestershire butter:
- ½ cup unsalted butter (1 stick), softened
- 1 tablespoon chopped fresh thyme
- 1 tablespoon minced chives
- 2 teaspoons Worcestershire sauce
- 1 garlic clove, grated or mashed to a paste
- Finely grated zest of 1 lemon
- ¼ teaspoon fine sea salt, plus more to taste
- ½ teaspoon freshly ground black pepper

Direction

- Season steak all over with 1 teaspoon salt and 1/2 teaspoon pepper. In a bowl or resealable bag, combine thyme, garlic, jalapeño, chives, Worcestershire sauce, sugar and lemon juice. Add meat and let marinate in the refrigerator for at least 2 hours and up to overnight.
- Prepare the Worcestershire butter: In a bowl, mash together the butter, thyme, chives, Worcestershire sauce, garlic, lemon zest, salt and pepper.
- Spoon the butter onto a piece of parchment paper or plastic wrap, form into a log and wrap well. Chill for at least 2 hours before using.
- Light the grill or heat the broiler, arranging the rack about 4 inches from the heat source. Grill tomatoes, or broil them on a rimmed baking pan, turning them, until charred on all sides, about 2 to 4 minutes per side. Transfer to a cutting board to cool.
- Brush off any pieces of marinade clinging to the steak, pat steak dry and coat it lightly with oil. Grill or broil steak until it reaches desired doneness, 3 to 5 minutes per side for medium-rare (125 degrees).
- Transfer steak to a cutting board. Slice butter into coins and place them on the steak to melt slightly. Let steak rest for 5 minutes while you prepare the tomatoes.
- Roughly chop tomatoes and place in a bowl with scallions, basil, a pinch of salt and pepper, a drizzle of olive oil and a squeeze of lemon juice. Toss well, adding more salt or lemon juice, or both, to taste.
- Slice the steak thinly, across the grain, and serve with the charred tomato mixture spooned on top. Garnish with more chives and torn basil, if you like.

144. Grilled Goat's Cheese And Eggplant, From Chris Cox

Serving: 8 servings | Prep: | Cook: | Ready in: 30mins

Ingredients

- 2 medium eggplants (about 2 1/2 pounds)
- Coarse salt
- 3 to 4 tablespoons extra-virgin olive oil
- 2 to 3 ripe round tomatoes
- ½ pound soft white goat's cheese
- For the sauce:

- 1 ½ pounds ripe Italian plum tomatoes
- Coarse salt and freshly ground pepper to taste
- Fresh basil leaves to garnish

Direction

- Slice the eggplant thin and sprinkle with salt. Allow to drain in a colander for an hour.
- Preheat broiler.
- Pat the eggplant dry with paper towels and brush the slices on both sides with the olive oil. Place them on a broiling pan lined with aluminum foil and broil them lightly, turning once, until the slices are golden but not overbrowned. Cool.
- Meanwhile, make the tomato sauce, or puree. Boil the tomatoes in their skins for 10 minutes. Drain and, when cool enough to handle, peel the skins. Squeeze out the juice and seeds and discard. Place the pulp in a food processor. Process until smooth and pour into a noncorrosive saucepan. The puree should be quite thick. Season with salt and pepper and set aside.
- Slice the round tomatoes thin. Place two slices eggplant per person, overlapping them slightly, on a broiling pan lined with foil. (You should have eight portions.) Top each portion with a slice or two of tomato and a generous tablespoon of goat's cheese. Set aside.
- Preheat broiler. Broil the eggplant until the cheese is browned and bubbling. While it is cooking, warm the tomato sauce.
- Place the eggplant portions on individual plates, with a pool of sauce on the side. Garnish with basil and serve.

Nutrition Information

- 180: calories;
- 5 grams: dietary fiber;
- 6 grams: monounsaturated fat;
- 1 gram: polyunsaturated fat;
- 7 grams: sugars;
- 8 grams: protein;
- 699 milligrams: sodium;
- 12 grams: carbohydrates;

145. Grilled Lamb

Serving: 2 servings | Prep: | Cook: | Ready in: 20mins

Ingredients

- 8 ounces boneless leg of lamb
- 1 tablespoon fresh or frozen ginger
- 1 clove garlic
- 1 teaspoon brown sugar
- 1 tablespoon reduced-sodium soy sauce
- 1 teaspoon ground coriander

Direction

- If using a broiler, turn it on.
- Wash and trim lamb.
- Grate the ginger and mince the garlic. Mix with sugar, soy sauce and coriander in a bowl large enough to hold the lamb. Add the lamb and set aside.
- If using a top-of-the-stove grill, prepare it. Grill or broil lamb about 10 minutes, basting with marinade occasionally. Slice thinly and serve.

Nutrition Information

- 254: calories;
- 22 grams: protein;
- 321 milligrams: sodium;
- 17 grams: fat;
- 7 grams: monounsaturated fat;
- 1 gram: dietary fiber;
- 3 grams: carbohydrates;
- 2 grams: sugars;

146. Grilled Lamb Fillet

Serving: Two servings | Prep: | Cook: | Ready in: 15mins

Ingredients

- 1 rack of lamb, about 2 pounds, boned and in a solid piece
- ½ tablespoon extra-virgin olive oil
- Pinch kosher salt
- ½ teaspoon coarsely ground black pepper
- Tomato onion chutney (see recipe)

Direction

- Preheat the broiler or barbecue grill.
- Rub both sides of the meat with the olive oil. Sprinkle with salt and pepper.
- Broil or grill the lamb to the desired degree of doneness. About five minutes on each side should be medium-rare.
- Set the lamb aside to cool to room temperature before slicing. Cut the meat into slices no more than one-half-inch thick. When ready to serve, arrange the slices in a fanlike pattern on individual plates and serve with the the chutney.

147. Grilled Leeks With Romesco Sauce

Serving: 6 servings | Prep: | Cook: | Ready in: 2hours

Ingredients

- For the romesco sauce
- 1 medium red pepper, roasted, peeled, seeds and membranes removed
- 6 ounces tomatoes (1 large or 2 roma)
- 1 thick slice (about 1 ounce) baguette or country-style bread, lightly toasted
- 1 large garlic clove, peeled
- ¼ cup toasted almonds, or a combination of almonds and skinned roasted hazelnuts
- ½ to 1 teaspoon pure ground chili powder or red pepper flakes, to taste pepper flakes are hotter
- 2 teaspoons chopped fresh Italian parsley
- ½ teaspoon sweet paprika or Spanish smoked paprika (pimentón)
- Salt
- freshly ground pepper to taste
- 1 tablespoon sherry vinegar
- ¼ cup extra virgin olive oil, as needed
- For the leeks
- 6 fat leeks, or 12 baby leeks
- 2 tablespoons extra virgin olive oil
- Salt
- freshly ground pepper

Direction

- Make the romesco sauce. Preheat the broiler, and cover a baking sheet with foil. Place the tomatoes on the baking sheet, and place under the broiler at the highest setting. Broil for two to four minutes until charred on one side. Turn over, and broil on the other side for two to four minutes until charred. Remove from the heat, transfer to a bowl and allow to cool. Peel and core.
- Turn on a food processor fitted with the steel blade, and drop in the garlic cloves. When the garlic is chopped and adheres to the sides of the bowl, stop the machine and scrape down the sides. Add the toasted almonds (or almonds and hazelnuts), bread and chili powder or flakes to the bowl. Process into a paste. Scrape down the sides of the bowl, and add the pepper, tomatoes, parsley, paprika, salt and pepper. Process until smooth. With the machine running, add the vinegar and olive oil in a slow stream. Process until well mixed, then scrape into a bowl. Taste and adjust seasoning, adding salt as desired. If possible, allow the sauce to stand for an hour at room temperature before using.
- Cut away the dark green ends of the leeks. Trim the root end. Cut fat leeks lengthwise into quarters, and rinse thoroughly under cold water to wash away any sand. If your leeks are 1/2 inch in diameter they needn't be cut; if they are between 1/2 inch and an inch, you can just cut them in half.

- Bring an inch of water to a boil in the bottom of a steamer. Place the leeks in the steamer, and steam 10 minutes. Transfer to a bowl, and toss with the olive oil and salt and pepper to taste.
- Prepare a medium-hot grill. Grill the steamed leeks for five minutes, turning often, just until grill marks appear. Remove from the heat, and serve with romesco sauce.

Nutrition Information

- 219: calories;
- 10 grams: carbohydrates;
- 3 grams: protein;
- 250 milligrams: sodium;
- 20 grams: fat;
- 2 grams: polyunsaturated fat;
- 0 grams: trans fat;
- 14 grams: monounsaturated fat;

148. Grilled Leg Of Lamb With Mustard Seeds

Serving: 6 to 8 servings | Prep: | Cook: | Ready in: 3hours

Ingredients

- 1 8-pound leg of lamb, boned, butterflied and trimmed of fat, inside and out (ask butcher)
- Salt and freshly ground pepper to taste
- ¼ cup olive oil
- 5 tablespoons mustard seeds
- 1 teaspoon ground cumin
- 1 tablespoon finely chopped garlic
- 4 sprigs fresh thyme or 1 teaspoon dried
- 1 teaspoon fennel seeds
- 2 tablespoons chopped fresh rosemary or 1 tablespoon dried
- 2 bay leaves, crumbled
- 4 tablespoons fresh lemon juice
- 2 cups red wine
- 2 tablespoons butter, melted
- 4 tablespoons finely chopped parsley

Direction

- Lay lamb out flat, and sprinkle with salt and pepper on all sides.
- Put oil in baking dish large enough to hold lamb. Add lamb, and sprinkle on both sides with mustard seeds, cumin, garlic, thyme, fennel seeds, rosemary, bay leaves, lemon juice and red wine. Turn and rub lamb so it is evenly coated with the ingredients. Marinate in a cool place for 1 or 2 hours, or in a refrigerator up to 6 hours. If lamb is refrigerated, let it return to room temperature before cooking.
- Preheat a charcoal grill or oven broiler.
- Remove lamb from marinade and reserve marinade. If a grill is used, put lamb flat on grill. If broiler is used, place lamb under broiler 4 to 5 inches from heat. Cook lamb uncovered on grill or under broiler about 15 minutes. Turn and cook 10 to 15 minutes on second side. For medium or well-done meat, cook longer.
- Meanwhile, in a baking pan large enough to hold lamb, bring reserved marinade to a boil, stirring until the liquid is reduced by half. Remove from heat, and swirl in butter and parsley. Transfer lamb to marinade pan, cover loosely with foil and keep warm. Let meat rest 10 to 15 minutes before serving. Slice thinly and serve with pan gravy.

Nutrition Information

- 905: calories;
- 25 grams: saturated fat;
- 0 grams: trans fat;
- 28 grams: monounsaturated fat;
- 1252 milligrams: sodium;
- 62 grams: fat;
- 5 grams: carbohydrates;
- 1 gram: sugars;
- 67 grams: protein;

149. Grilled Maple Chicken With Corn Relish

Serving: 2 servings | Prep: | Cook: | Ready in: 20mins

Ingredients

- 8 ounces skinless, boneless chicken breast
- 2 tablespoons orange juice
- 1 tablespoon maple syrup
- 1 or 2 sprigs fresh tarragon to yield 2 teaspoons tarragon leaves
- 2 cups frozen corn kernels
- 1 teaspoon water
- ½ teaspoon cumin
- ½ jalapeno pepper
- 1 small red onion to yield 1/4 cup chopped
- 8 ounces whole red bell pepper or 7 ounces chopped ready-cut red bell pepper
- 10 sprigs cilantro to yield 2 tablespoons chopped
- 2 tablespoons defrosted orange juice concentrate
- ¼ teaspoon salt
- Freshly ground black pepper to taste

Direction

- Turn on broiler, if using, and cover broiler pan with aluminum foil.
- Wash and dry chicken, and cut into 1/2-inch-wide strips. Combine orange juice and maple syrup, add tarragon and marinate chicken in mixture while preparing the rest of the meal.
- Over low heat, cook corn in water with cumin for just a few minutes, until corn is tender.
- Trim, seed and mince jalapeno. Finely chop onion. Wash, trim, seed and chop red pepper. Wash and chop cilantro.
- Prepare stove-top grill, if using. Grill or broil chicken strips for a couple of minutes. Baste with marinade, and then turn and grill a minute or two longer, until done.
- To make relish, combine corn with jalapeno, onion, red pepper, cilantro, orange juice concentrate, salt and pepper. Serve the chicken strips with the corn relish and the banana curry. (See recipe below.)

Nutrition Information

- 482: calories;
- 31 grams: protein;
- 20 grams: sugars;
- 13 grams: fat;
- 3 grams: polyunsaturated fat;
- 0 grams: trans fat;
- 5 grams: monounsaturated fat;
- 59 grams: carbohydrates;
- 8 grams: dietary fiber;
- 383 milligrams: sodium;

150. Grilled Marinated Lamb Brochettes

Serving: 4 servings | Prep: | Cook: | Ready in: 1hours

Ingredients

- 1 ½ pounds boneless lean loin or leg of lamb
- 16 pearl white onions
- 3 tablespoons red wine vinegar
- ½ cup dry white wine
- 2 garlic cloves, crushed
- 2 teaspoons grated lemon rind
- 2 teaspoons ground cumin
- 1 tablespoon chopped fresh rosemary or 1 tablespoon dried
- 2 teaspoons chopped fresh thyme leaves or 1 teaspoon dried
- 2 teaspoons honey
- Salt and freshly ground pepper to taste
- 2 tablespoons olive oil
- 1 bunch watercress for garnishing

Direction

- Cut the lamb into 16 1 1/2-inch cubes.

- Peel the onions, then steam or parboil them until nearly cooked but firm. Drain.
- Combine onions, vinegar, white wine, garlic, grated lemon, cumin, rosemary, thyme, honey, salt and pepper to taste. Blend well, then add the lamb and marinate for 30 minutes or longer.
- Meanwhile, preheat oven broiler or grill to high.
- Drain the meat, reserving the marinade. Thread onto 4 skewers, alternating between the lamb cubes and onions on each skewer.
- Brush the skewers with the oil and the reserved marinade.
- Broil under high heat 3 minutes on each side for rare, brushing often with the marinade. Cook longer if desired.
- Serve immediately. Garnish with the watercress.

Nutrition Information

- 664: calories;
- 15 grams: monounsaturated fat;
- 9 grams: dietary fiber;
- 24 grams: sugars;
- 32 grams: fat;
- 12 grams: saturated fat;
- 3 grams: polyunsaturated fat;
- 53 grams: carbohydrates;
- 38 grams: protein;
- 1689 milligrams: sodium;

151. Grilled Marinated Quail

Serving: 12 servings | Prep: | Cook: | Ready in: 20mins

Ingredients

- 24 semiboneless quail
- 12 tablespoons fresh thyme leaves
- 6 tablespoons olive oil
- 6 garlic cloves, peeled and quartered
- Freshly ground black pepper, to taste
- 1 ½ cups dry red wine

Direction

- Wash and dry quail.
- Combine remaining ingredients and place in noncorrosive container large enough to hold quail. Place quail in marinade, turning to coat both sides. Cover. Refrigerate for at least 2 hours, or overnight, turning occasionally.
- To cook, heat broiler(s). Cover broiler pan with 2 layers of aluminum foil and arrange quail on foil. If you have only one broiler, you will have to cook the quail in 2 batches. Broil 2 inches from source of heat for 5 minutes on each side. Remove metal frame holding quail open and serve with polenta (see recipe).

Nutrition Information

- 514: calories;
- 33 grams: fat;
- 8 grams: saturated fat;
- 0 grams: sugars;
- 43 grams: protein;
- 118 milligrams: sodium;
- 14 grams: monounsaturated fat;
- 7 grams: polyunsaturated fat;
- 4 grams: carbohydrates;
- 1 gram: dietary fiber;

152. Grilled Moroccan Lamb Sausage

Serving: 4 servings | Prep: | Cook: | Ready in: 23mins

Ingredients

- 1 ⅓ pounds lean lamb, ground with 2/3 pound lamb, pork or beef fat
- 2 tablespoons water
- 1 ½ tablespoons minced garlic
- 2 tablespoons chopped fresh cilantro
- 2 tablespoons chopped fresh parsley

- 2 tablespoons paprika
- 1 ½ teaspoons ground cumin
- 1 ½ teaspoons ground coriander
- 1 ¼ teaspoons cinnamon
- ¾ teaspoon cayenne pepper or to taste
- 1 ¼ teaspoons salt
- ½ teaspoon freshly ground pepper
- 2 tablespoons olive oil
- 2 feet hog casing (optional)
- 1 large green pepper, cored and cut into 8 pieces (optional)
- 2 medium-size onions, peeled and quartered (optional)

Direction

- Combine all ingredients except the olive oil and the three optional items in a large bowl and mix well. If making sausages, use the sausage attachment on a heavy-duty mixer, stuff the casing with the mixture and twist and tie to make eight 4-inch links. Or shape into eight 3-inch-long lozenges, slightly fatter in the middle, formed around metal skewers or into 8 patties.
- Preheat grill or broiler.
- If the sausages are in casings, prick with a fork 2 to 3 times and brush with oil. Grill or broil 3 to 4 minutes on each side until cooked through. For lozenges, brush with oil and cook 3 to 4 minutes on each side. For patties, brush with oil and grill 4 to 5 minutes on each side or saute over high heat.
- If desired, sausages may be threaded on four skewers alternately with green pepper pieces and onion quarters before grilling.

153. Grilled Polenta With Chanterelles

Serving: 6 servings | Prep: | Cook: | Ready in: 30mins

Ingredients

- 1 13-ounce package instant polenta
- 2 tablespoons olive oil plus additional oil for brushing the polenta
- 1 pound chanterelles
- 1 clove garlic, minced (green part removed)
- 2 shallots, minced
- ¼ pound white mushrooms, sliced
- Coarse salt and freshly ground pepper to taste
- ½ cup dry white wine or vermouth
- 1 teaspoon fresh thyme leaves
- 1 to 2 tablespoons chopped Italian parsley
- Grated Parmesan cheese

Direction

- Make the polenta according to the directions on the package. When it is cooked pour it into a pan about eight inches square and cool.
- When the polenta has cooled, cut it into eight slices about two inches wide and four inches long. Brush the polenta on both sides with one tablespoon olive oil and place the slices on an oiled broiling rack. Set aside.
- Cut the base off the stems of the chanterelles. If the mushrooms are very gritty, rinse them quickly under cold running water and pat them dry. Otherwise, clean them with a soft paint or pastry brush. Cut the large mushrooms into bite-size pieces; leave the smaller ones whole.
- Preheat broiler. In a skillet, soften the garlic with the shallots in the remaining olive oil. Add the mushrooms, season to taste with salt and pepper and cook over moderate heat for 10 to 15 minutes. Add the wine and cook until it has evaporated. Stir in the thyme and parsley and keep warm.
- Grill the polenta for three to four minutes on each side, until golden.
- Arrange the polenta pieces on four serving plates and top them with the mushroom mixture. Sprinkle with Parmesan cheese and serve.

Nutrition Information

- 305: calories;
- 2 grams: fat;

- 0 grams: monounsaturated fat;
- 6 grams: dietary fiber;
- 4 grams: sugars;
- 465 milligrams: sodium;
- 1 gram: polyunsaturated fat;
- 62 grams: carbohydrates;
- 7 grams: protein;

154. Grilled Pork Satay

Serving: 6 servings | Prep: | Cook: | Ready in: 45mins

Ingredients

- For the meat:
- 1 pound boneless pork loin
- 2 tablespoons coriander seeds or 2 tablespoons ground coriander
- 2 teaspoons ground cumin
- For the marinade:
- 10 shallots, peeled and trimmed
- 2 cloves garlic
- 1 small knob fresh ginger
- ¼ thumb-sized piece turmeric or 1/2 teaspoon turmeric powder
- 4 stalks lemon grass, sliced fine
- 2 tablespoons soy sauce
- 2 tablespoons light brown sugar
- For the peanut sauce:
- 10 shallots, peeled and trimmed
- 8 cloves garlic, peeled
- 2 stalks lemon grass, trimmed
- ½ cup crunchy peanut butter
- 1 cup coconut milk (or canned, unsweetened milk)
- 2 tablespoons tamarind juice or pineapple juice
- 2 teaspoons hot chili paste
- 2 tablespoons light brown sugar
- 1 tablespoon soy sauce
- 30 to 35 bamboo skewers, covered with cold water and soaked for 20 minutes

Direction

- Trim meat, and cut into thin, angled slices about 3 inches long and 1 inch wide. Place in a bowl. In an ungreased saute pan, heat the coriander seeds and cumin for several minutes over medium heat to bring out flavor. Add to the bowl.
- Prepare the marinade. In a food processor fitted with a steel blade or in a blender with the motor running, add the shallots, garlic, ginger, turmeric, lemon grass, soy sauce and brown sugar. Blend to a fine paste, and add to the meat. Toss lightly to coat. Cover with plastic wrap, and let marinate for 30 minutes.
- Prepare the peanut sauce. In a food processor fitted with a steel blade or in a blender with the machine running, puree the shallots, garlic, lemon grass, peanut butter, coconut milk, tamarind juice, chili paste, brown sugar and soy sauce.
- Thread the meat slices through the bamboo skewers, and prepare a fire for grilling or the broiler. Place on a baking sheet about 3 inches from the source of heat. Grill 6 to 7 minutes, turning once, until the pork is cooked. Remove and serve the sauce for dipping.

Nutrition Information

- 538: calories;
- 8 grams: dietary fiber;
- 3 grams: polyunsaturated fat;
- 54 grams: carbohydrates;
- 24 grams: sugars;
- 26 grams: fat;
- 11 grams: saturated fat;
- 0 grams: trans fat;
- 28 grams: protein;
- 514 milligrams: sodium;

155. Grilled Quail

Serving: 4 servings | Prep: | Cook: | Ready in: 20mins

Ingredients

- 8 partly boned quail
- ¼ cup balsamic vinegar
- 1 cup extra virgin olive oil
- 2 tablespoons honey
- ½ cup loosely packed thyme sprigs
- 1 tablespoon freshly ground black pepper

Direction

- Check quail for any stray bone fragments or feathers. If there are V-shaped grilling pins protruding (these shape the partly boned birds), leave them in place. Rinse, and pat dry with paper towels.
- In large mixing bowl, combine vinegar, olive oil, honey, thyme and black pepper. Add quail, and toss gently to coat. Cover, and set aside in a cool place for 2 hours, or refrigerate overnight.
- Preheat grill or broiler. Remove quail from marinade, and place near hottest part of grill or broiler. Cook until exteriors are browned and meat is just pink when sliced at the leg bones, about 3 to 5 minutes a side. Remove grilling pins, and serve immediately.

Nutrition Information

- 961: calories;
- 81 grams: fat;
- 49 grams: monounsaturated fat;
- 12 grams: polyunsaturated fat;
- 11 grams: sugars;
- 44 grams: protein;
- 16 grams: carbohydrates;
- 3 grams: dietary fiber;
- 122 milligrams: sodium;
- 15 grams: saturated fat;

156. Grilled Quail With Oyster Sauce

Serving: 6 servings | Prep: | Cook: | Ready in: 50mins

Ingredients

- The quail:
- 12 quail, main body bones and wings removed but with leg and thigh bones intact, about 3 pounds ready-to-cook weight
- Salt to taste if desired
- Freshly ground pepper to taste
- 6 slices regular bacon, each slice cut in half crosswise
- ¼ cup olive oil
- 1 tablespoon balsamic vinegar
- 1 tablesoon finely minced fresh thyme
- The oyster sauce:
- 1 tablespoon butter
- ¼ cup country ham or prosciutto, finely chopped
- ¼ cup leeks, both white and green parts, finely minced
- 2 cups heavy cream
- 2 tablespoons finely chopped pimento
- 1 cup (1/2 pint) small oysters, drained

Direction

- Preheat the oven to 475 degrees.
- Sprinkle the quail inside and out with salt and pepper, and arrange them in a baking dish. Wrap the breast of each quail with half a slice of bacon, folding it under and neatly overlapping the ends. The quail should be placed, breast-side-up, in the baking dish.
- Blend the oil, vinegar and thyme, and spoon an equal amount of the sauce over each quail. Place in the oven, and bake 13 to 15 minutes. Put under the broiler briefly to crisp the bacon.
- To prepare the oyster sauce, heat the butter in a heavy skillet or casserole, and add the prosciutto and leeks. Cook about 1 minute, stirring, and add the cream and pimento. Cook over relatively high heat about 10 minutes or until reduced to about 1 cup.
- Put the oysters in a small skillet, and cook over moderately high heat, shaking the skillet briefly until the oysters just start to bubble. Take care not to overcook the oysters, or they will toughen. Drain the oysters, and add them

to the sauce. Spoon the sauce over the quail and serve immediately.

Nutrition Information

- 1199: calories;
- 103 grams: fat;
- 39 grams: saturated fat;
- 59 grams: protein;
- 1110 milligrams: sodium;
- 0 grams: trans fat;
- 42 grams: monounsaturated fat;
- 15 grams: polyunsaturated fat;
- 7 grams: carbohydrates;
- 1 gram: dietary fiber;
- 3 grams: sugars;

157. Grilled Quail Wrapped In Grape Leaves On White Bean Salad

Serving: Two servings | Prep: | Cook: |Ready in: 45mins

Ingredients

- The quail:
- 1 cup vegetable oil
- 1 large white onion, thinly sliced
- 1 teaspoon soy sauce
- 6 bay leaves
- 10 whole black peppercorns
- 4 boneless quails, split in half lengthwise
- 8 large untorn grape leaves, blotted dry
- 1 large red bell pepper, cut into 1-inch squares
- The salad:
- 4 ounces Great Northern beans, soaked overnight
- 1 red onion, thinly sliced
- 1 medium-sized tomato, coarsely chopped
- 2 tablespoons olive oil
- 1 tablespoon fresh lemon juice
- ½ teaspoon sumac, optional (see note)
- Salt to taste
- 2 tablespoons torn mint leaves

Direction

- Combine the oil, onion, soy sauce, bay leaves and peppercorns together in a nonreactive dish just large enough to hold the quails in one layer. Add the quails, turning to coat them with the marinade. Cover and refrigerate them for eight hours, or overnight. Baste once during this time.
- Bring a large pot of water to a boil. Add the beans, cook them until just tender, about 35 to 45 minutes, then drain. While the beans are still warm, add the red onion, tomato, olive oil, lemon juice, sumac if used, salt and mint leaves.
- While the beans are cooking, eat a charcoal grill or a broiler. Remove the quails from the marinade. Spread the grape leaves out flat. Place a half quail on the lower edge of each leaf. Roll up the bird in the leaf, turning in the sides as you roll. Run a skewer through the roll crosswise and add a piece of red pepper. Repeat with three more rolls and pieces of pepper per skewer.
- Once the salad has been made and the charcoal is hot, place the skewers on the grill and cook the quails for five minutes, then turn them over and cook the second side for five minutes more. Serve the quail rolls on top of the bean salad.

158. Grilled Salmon With Sage

Serving: 4 servings | Prep: | Cook: |Ready in: 1hours

Ingredients

- 1 salmon fillet, about 1 1/2 to 2 pounds
- 2 lemons
- 2 tablespoons Dijon mustard
- ½ cup olive oil
- Freshly ground pepper to taste
- About 24 sage leaves

- Coarse sea salt to taste

Direction

- Wipe the salmon fillet dry with paper towels. Combine the juice of one lemon, mustard, two tablespoons olive oil and pepper in a small bowl. Chop six sage leaves and add them. Mix thoroughly and spread the mixture on both sides of the salmon. Allow to marinate about 30 minutes.
- Meanwhile, preheat grill or broiler. Heat the remaining olive oil in a small frying pan and saute the sage leaves until they are crisp. Drain them on paper towels.
- Season the salmon with salt and grill or broil the fillet about six minutes on each side or until it reaches the desired degree of doneness. Sprinkle with sauteed sage leaves, garnish with remaining lemon cut into quarters and serve.

Nutrition Information

- 685: calories;
- 7 grams: carbohydrates;
- 1 gram: sugars;
- 10 grams: saturated fat;
- 0 grams: trans fat;
- 27 grams: monounsaturated fat;
- 4 grams: dietary fiber;
- 42 grams: protein;
- 625 milligrams: sodium;
- 55 grams: fat;
- 11 grams: polyunsaturated fat;

159. Grilled Salmon With Shrimp

Serving: 4 servings | Prep: | Cook: |Ready in: 50mins

Ingredients

- 1 ½ pounds boneless fillet of salmon with skin left on
- 8 large shrimp, about 1/2 pound
- ¼ cup olive oil
- Salt to taste if desired
- Freshly ground pepper to taste
- 1 tablespoon chopped fresh thyme
- ¼ teaspoon dried hot red pepper flakes
- 1 tablespoon fresh lemon juice
- 3 tablespoons melted butter
- 2 tablespoons finely chopped parsley

Direction

- Preheat charcoal or gas grill, or broiler, to high.
- Cut salmon into 4 pieces of equal size and set aside.
- Place each shrimp on a flat surface and cut through back of shell, leaving shell and underside feelers intact. Open each shrimp butterfly fashion and devein.
- Pour oil into a flat dish and add shrimp and salmon. Turn pieces to coat on all sides. Sprinkle all over with salt, pepper, thyme, pepper flakes and lemon juice. Cover with plastic wrap and let stand at room temperature about 10 to 15 minutes.
- When ready to cook, remove seafood from marinade. Pour marinade into small saucepan. If using a broiler, arrange salmon skin side up on a baking sheet. Place under broiler about 4 inches from source of heat. Leave broiler door partly open. Broil 1 1/2 minutes on one side and turn. Arrange shrimp shell side down around salmon and place under broiler. Cook 2 minutes and turn shrimp. Leave broiler door totally open. Continue cooking salmon and shrimp 1 minute.
- If using a charcoal or gas grill, place salmon pieces skin side down on grill and cook about 1 1/2 minutes. Turn salmon and place shrimp shell side down. Continue cooking 2 minutes, turning shrimp occasionally.
- Transfer pieces to a heated platter. Add melted butter to reserved marinade and bring to a

boil. Pour butter mixture over seafood. Sprinkle with chopped parsley and serve.

Nutrition Information

- 595: calories;
- 46 grams: fat;
- 13 grams: saturated fat;
- 19 grams: monounsaturated fat;
- 1 gram: dietary fiber;
- 43 grams: protein;
- 0 grams: sugars;
- 9 grams: polyunsaturated fat;
- 2 grams: carbohydrates;
- 602 milligrams: sodium;

160. Grilled Sea Scallops (Sign Of The Dove)

Serving: 4 appetizer servings | Prep: | Cook: | Ready in: 18mins

Ingredients

- 2 cups fish stock
- 2 ounces unsalted butter at room temperature
- 3 ounces assorted sliced mushrooms, wild or cultivated
- ½ teaspoon fresh thyme leaves
- 8 ounces mixed greens like Swiss chard, turnip greens, baby kale or spinach, in small pieces
- 12 ounces sea scallops
- Salt and white pepper to taste
- Olive oil for grilling

Direction

- Preheat grill or broiler.
- Bring stock to boil in a saucepan; whisk in butter bit by bit.
- Add mushrooms and thyme and reduce stock by half.
- Add greens and simmer until greens are wilted.
- Season scallops with salt and pepper and brush with oil. Grill or broil just until done, 2 to 4 minutes, depending on size of scallops.
- Remove greens and mushrooms from stock and arrange on four salad-size plates and keep warm. Consistency of stock will depend on how much water the greens gave off. For a lightly thickened stock, you may need to reduce the mixture more.
- Arrange scallops on greens, slicing large scallops, and finish with thickened stock.

Nutrition Information

- 230: calories;
- 17 grams: fat;
- 8 grams: saturated fat;
- 0 grams: trans fat;
- 6 grams: carbohydrates;
- 1 gram: sugars;
- 15 grams: protein;
- 692 milligrams: sodium;

161. Grilled Seasoned Lamb With Greek Potato Salad

Serving: 2 servings | Prep: | Cook: | Ready in: 45mins

Ingredients

- 1 pound tiny new potatoes
- 1 large clove garlic
- 1 small clove garlic
- ¼ teaspoon hot-pepper flakes
- Few shakes of cinnamon
- 8 ounces butterflied leg of lamb
- 1 bunch arugula
- 2 cups nonfat plain yogurt
- 2 tablespoons white-wine vinegar
- 8 ounces Kirby cucumbers
- 6 cherry tomatoes
- 5 Greek Kalamata olives, or Italian or French black olives

- Freshly ground black pepper to taste

Direction

- Turn on broiler if using.
- Scrub potatoes, and cook in water to cover in covered pot until they are tender, 10 to 20 minutes, depending on size.
- Put large clove of garlic through press, then mix in a small bowl with hot-pepper flakes and cinnamon. Using your fingers, rub mixture into both sides of the lamb. Prepare stove top grill, if using. Broil or grill lamb for 2 to 5 minutes, until it is browned but still pink inside.
- Trim the tough stems from the arugula, wash thoroughly and dry.
- Mix the yogurt and vinegar in a small bowl. Wash, trim and cut the cucumbers into half-inch pieces or smaller, and add to the bowl; mince the remaining clove of garlic, and add.
- Cut the cooked lamb into julienne strips, and set aside.
- Wash and halve the tomatoes, and add to the yogurt. Pit and chop the olives, and add; season with pepper.
- Cut cooked potatoes into halves or quarters, depending on size, and add to yogurt mixture.
- Arrange the arugula on two plates. Place sliced lamb to one side, potato salad on the other.

Nutrition Information

- 626: calories;
- 19 grams: fat;
- 9 grams: dietary fiber;
- 26 grams: sugars;
- 362 milligrams: sodium;
- 8 grams: monounsaturated fat;
- 2 grams: polyunsaturated fat;
- 72 grams: carbohydrates;
- 44 grams: protein;

162. Grilled Shrimp With Coriander Salsa

Serving: 4 servings | Prep: | Cook: | Ready in: 20mins

Ingredients

- 1 pound large or medium shrimp, unpeeled
- Coarse salt
- ½ to ¾ cup olive oil
- 2 green chilies, minced (less if very hot)
- 1 small clove garlic, minced
- ½ small red onion, minced
- ½ cup coriander leaves, chopped
- Juice 1 to 2 limes

Direction

- Preheat broiler. Soak the shrimp in heavily salted iced water for 10 minutes. Drain, rinse and pat dry. Sprinkle lightly with olive oil.
- Combine the remaining ingredients in a small bowl to make a sauce. Correct seasoning and set aside.
- Broil the shrimp (be careful not to overcook them). Serve immediately, passing the sauce separately.

Nutrition Information

- 400: calories;
- 646 milligrams: sodium;
- 5 grams: saturated fat;
- 0 grams: trans fat;
- 7 grams: carbohydrates;
- 1 gram: dietary fiber;
- 2 grams: sugars;
- 35 grams: fat;
- 25 grams: monounsaturated fat;
- 4 grams: polyunsaturated fat;
- 16 grams: protein;

163. Grilled Shrimp With Oil And Basil Sauce

Serving: 4 servings | Prep: | Cook: | Ready in: 25mins

Ingredients

- 1 ½ teaspoons finely minced garlic
- 1 ½ teaspoons finely chopped shallots
- 1 ½ teaspoons Dijon-style mustard
- ⅓ cup dry white wine
- ⅓ cup freshly squeezed lemon juice
- ¾ cup olive oil
- ⅓ cup finely chopped fresh basil
- 24 jumbo shrimp, about 1 1/4 pounds, shelled and deveined

Direction

- Combine garlic, shallots, mustard, wine, lemon juice, olive oil and basil in a bowl. Stir to blend. Add shrimp and stir to coat. Let stand until ready to cook.
- When ready to cook, preheat an outdoor or indoor grill to high, or preheat a broiler to high.
- Remove shrimp from marinade and pour marinade into a small saucepan. Arrange shrimp 6 to a skewer, pushing the skewer through the tail section, then the head section, so shrimp will lie flat on grill or under broiler (see note). Arrange them barely touching and without crowding.
- Place skewers on grill or on rack under broiler, about 6 inches from source of heat, and cook about 3 minutes or until shrimp can be lifted from grill or rack without sticking. Turn skewers and cook about 2 minutes longer.
- Meanwhile, bring marinade to a boil and simmer about 2 minutes.
- Remove shrimp from skewers and arrange them symmetrically on 4 plates. Spoon the sauce over the shrimp and serve.

Nutrition Information

- 416: calories;
- 6 grams: saturated fat;
- 0 grams: dietary fiber;
- 7 grams: protein;
- 41 grams: fat;
- 30 grams: monounsaturated fat;
- 4 grams: polyunsaturated fat;
- 3 grams: carbohydrates;
- 1 gram: sugars;
- 295 milligrams: sodium;

164. Grilled Skewered Sausages

Serving: 4 servings | Prep: | Cook: | Ready in: 27mins

Ingredients

- 4 fresh sweet Italian, pork or turkey sausages
- 24 1-inch cubes country bread
- 2 to 3 tablespoons extra-virgin olive oil

Direction

- Prick the sausages in several places. Place in water to cover and simmer about 10 minutes. Drain and cut each into 5 pieces.
- Preheat the grill or broiler.
- Thread four skewers, starting with a bread cube, putting 6 pieces of bread and 5 pieces of sausage on each skewer. Brush very lightly with olive oil.
- Place the skewers on a very hot grill or four inches from the source of heat in the broiler, turning until the bread and the sausage are golden and crusty on all sides.

Nutrition Information

- 390: calories;
- 0 grams: trans fat;
- 42 grams: carbohydrates;
- 5 grams: sugars;
- 20 grams: protein;
- 771 milligrams: sodium;

- 16 grams: fat;
- 3 grams: dietary fiber;
- 8 grams: monounsaturated fat;
- 4 grams: polyunsaturated fat;

165. Grilled Striped Bass With Mango Salsa

Serving: 4 servings | Prep: | Cook: | Ready in: 30mins

Ingredients

- 2 not-overly-ripe mangoes, or 3 peaches, skin removed and cut into 1/2-inch dice
- Salt and pepper
- Dried red chili flakes or cayenne
- 2 limes, juiced
- 1 tablespoon olive or peanut oil, plus more as needed
- 2 pounds striped bass, red snapper, sea bass or grouper, in one or two fillets, preferably with skin
- ½ cup (about) chopped cilantro leaves

Direction

- Start a grill or preheat a broiler. Combine fruit with a sprinkle of salt, chili flakes or cayenne, lime juice and a tablespoon of olive oil. Rub both sides of fish lightly with oil and sprinkle with salt and pepper.
- Grill or broil fish, skin side down. If grill has a cover, use it, and grill 8 to 12 minutes, or until fish is done. Remove carefully with a large spatula.
- If grill does not have a cover, brush top of fish with oil after 4 or 5 minutes and turn it carefully with a large spatula. Continue to cook, skin side up, until fish is done; remove carefully.
- To broil, put fish in a nonstick broiling pan and adjust the oven rack so top of fillet is no more than 4 inches from the heat source. Broil without turning, until top is nicely browned and fish is done. If fish appears to be browning too quickly, move the rack a couple of inches farther from the heat.
- Brush fish once more with oil; garnish salsa with cilantro, then serve fish and salsa together.

166. Grilled Swordfish With Tomatillo Sauce

Serving: 4 servings | Prep: | Cook: | Ready in: 35mins

Ingredients

- 2 swordfish steaks about 1-inch thick (about 1 1/2 to 2 pounds)
- 2 tablespoons olive oil
- For the sauce:
- 3 cloves garlic, unpeeled
- 1 pound tomatillos
- 2 jalapeno chilies, seeded and sliced
- 1 to 2 teaspoons sugar (or to taste)
- ⅓ cup dry white wine
- 1 tablespoon white-wine vinegar
- 2 tablespoons unsalted butter
- Coarse salt and freshly ground pepper to taste
- ⅓ cup fresh coriander leaves
- Coriander sprigs to garnish

Direction

- Cut the swordfish steaks in half. Wipe them dry with paper towels and coat them on both sides with the olive oil. Set aside.
- Make the sauce. Boil the garlic for 10 minutes. Peel the cloves, mash them and set aside. Chop the tomatillos coarsely and put them in a saucepan with the chilies, sugar, wine and vinegar. Cook until soft, stirring frequently. Add the garlic. Taste to see if more sugar or vinegar is needed and season with salt and pepper. Add the butter to thicken the sauce.
- Pour the sauce into a food processor with the garlic cloves and add the coriander leaves. Puree, taste and correct seasoning. Set aside.

- Preheat broiler or coals. Broil the fish steaks six inches from the heat for about five minutes on each side or until cooked. Meanwhile, reheat the sauce.
- To serve, pour some sauce on each of four individual plates. Put the steaks on top and sprinkle with coriander leaves.

Nutrition Information

- 463: calories;
- 0 grams: trans fat;
- 4 grams: polyunsaturated fat;
- 7 grams: sugars;
- 41 grams: protein;
- 841 milligrams: sodium;
- 27 grams: fat;
- 8 grams: saturated fat;
- 11 grams: carbohydrates;
- 3 grams: dietary fiber;
- 13 grams: monounsaturated fat;

167. Grilled Tuna With Herbs

Serving: 4 servings | Prep: | Cook: | Ready in: 15mins

Ingredients

- 1 slab of tuna, preferably from the belly portion, about 1 3/4 pounds
- Salt to taste if desired
- Freshly ground pepper to taste
- ¼ cup olive oil
- 6 sprigs fresh thyme
- 2 cloves garlic, peeled and cut into very thin slices
- 2 tablespoons freshly squeezed lemon juice
- 4 strips lemon rind
- ⅛ teaspoon dried hot red pepper flakes
- 1 tablespoon melted butter

Direction

- Preheat charcoal or gas grill or broiler to high.
- Sprinkle tuna with salt and pepper on both sides. Place oil in a flat dish and add thyme, garlic, lemon juice, lemon rind and hot red pepper flakes. Add tuna and coat on both sides.
- Remove tuna from the marinade.
- Add butter to marinade, and place the dish in a warm place.
- If tuna is to be cooked on a charcoal or gas grill, place it directly on the grill, fatty side down, and cook, turning often, 5 to 6 minutes. If it is to be cooked under a broiler, arrange tuna on a rack, fatty side up. Broil about 2 inches from heat, leaving broiler door partly open. Cook 3 minutes and turn; continue cooking 2 minutes. Transfer tuna to marinade. Turn tuna to coat on both sides. Cut into thin slices and serve.

Nutrition Information

- 203: calories;
- 183 milligrams: sodium;
- 4 grams: saturated fat;
- 2 grams: polyunsaturated fat;
- 3 grams: carbohydrates;
- 11 grams: protein;
- 1 gram: dietary fiber;
- 17 grams: fat;
- 0 grams: sugars;

168. Grilled Tuna With Red Peppers

Serving: Four servings | Prep: | Cook: | Ready in: 1hours15mins

Ingredients

- 6 tablespoons fresh lemon juice
- 4 tablespoons, plus 1 teaspoon, olive oil
- 1 teaspoon chopped rosemary
- 2 cloves garlic, peeled and minced
- Freshly ground pepper to taste

- 4 6-ounce tuna steaks
- 4 red bell peppers, cored, halved, seeded and deribbed
- Salt to taste

Direction

- Combine the lemon juice, 4 tablespoons olive oil, rosemary, garlic and ground pepper in a shallow dish. Add the tuna and turn to coat well on all sides. Let marinate for 1 hour, turning tuna from time to time.
- Preheat a grill or broiler. Brush the remaining teaspoon of olive oil over both sides of the pepper halves. Grill or broil the tuna and peppers until the tuna is charred on the outside but still pink in the center, about 4 minutes per side, and until the peppers are crisp-tender, about 3 minutes per side. Divide among 4 plates, season the tuna with salt and pepper to taste and serve immediately.

Nutrition Information

- 351: calories;
- 2 grams: polyunsaturated fat;
- 0 grams: trans fat;
- 3 grams: dietary fiber;
- 43 grams: protein;
- 15 grams: fat;
- 10 grams: carbohydrates;
- 6 grams: sugars;
- 759 milligrams: sodium;

169. Grilled Tuna With Salad

Serving: 4 servings | Prep: | Cook: | Ready in: 25mins

Ingredients

- 1 bonito or tuna fillet with skin left on, about 1 pound
- 2 tablespoons olive oil, plus oil for greasing the grill
- Salt to taste if desired
- Freshly ground pepper to taste
- 4 sprigs fresh thyme
- ¼ teaspoon dried hot red pepper flakes
- lettuce salad with tomato dressing

Direction

- Preheat an outdoor grill or the oven broiler.
- Put the tuna on a flat surface and cut away and discard the dark center streak or bones. Spoon the olive oil over the fish and sprinkle with salt, ground pepper, thyme and pepper flakes.
- If an outdoor grill is used, rub the rack lightly with olive oil. Place the fish, skin side up, on the grill. If the broiler is used, place the fish on a rack, skin side up, about 4 inches from the heat. Cook 3 minutes and turn; cook for another 3 minutes. If you wish the fish to be well done, cook 5 minutes on each side.
- Remove the fish and cut it into thin diagonal slices.
- Arrange one-quarter of the salad greens on each of four large plates. Arrange an equal number of fish slices on each plate, placing them in the center of the greens.
- Spoon equal amounts of the salad dressing over the salad greens and around the fish. Serve any remaining salad dressing on the side. Serve while the fish is still warm.

170. Grilled Veal Chop Sicilian Style

Serving: 2 servings | Prep: | Cook: | Ready in: 30mins

Ingredients

- 1 medium-size tomato, seeded and diced
- ½ tablespoon diced red onion
- 7 black olives, pitted and sliced into quarters
- 1 tablespoon capers
- 1 tablespoon chopped fresh basil
- Pinch dried hot red chili peppers

- 2 tablespoons extra-virgin olive oil
- 2 tablespoons red-wine vinegar
- Salt and freshly ground pepper to taste
- 2 large veal loin chops, 1/2 to 3/4 inch thick
- ½ bunch arugula, washed and stems removed

Direction

- Mix the tomato, onion, olives, capers, basil, chili peppers, 1 tablespoon of the olive oil and the vinegar together in a bowl. Add salt and pepper.
- Preheat a grill or broiler. Brush the veal chops with the remaining olive oil. Place them on a hot grill or under the broiler, and cook, turning them once. For medium rare to medium, cooking time is 10 to 15 minutes.
- To serve, line individual plates with a bed of arugula. Remove the chops from the grill or broiler and place on the arugula and top each with the tomato mixture. Grind black pepper over the top.

Nutrition Information

- 442: calories;
- 31 grams: fat;
- 8 grams: saturated fat;
- 1 gram: trans fat;
- 18 grams: monounsaturated fat;
- 6 grams: carbohydrates;
- 3 grams: sugars;
- 2 grams: dietary fiber;
- 34 grams: protein;
- 751 milligrams: sodium;

171. Grilled Veal Chops With Morels

Serving: 4 servings | Prep: | Cook: | Ready in: 30mins

Ingredients

- 4 veal loin or rib chops, one inch thick
- 1 tablespoon olive oil
- 1 tablespoon fresh thyme leaves
- Coarse salt and freshly ground pepper to taste
- 1 ounce dried morels, soaked in warm water for 30 minutes
- ½ pound fresh morels
- 1 tablespoon lemon juice
- ½ cup chicken stock
- 2 shallots, minced
- 4 tablespoons unsalted butter
- ¼ cup dry vermouth
- ½ cup creme fraiche
- 1 tablespoon parsley, minced

Direction

- Preheat broiler or grill.
- Coat the veal chops on both sides with the olive oil, thyme, salt and pepper and set aside.
- Scoop the dried morels up from their soaking liquid and squeeze them, letting them drain back into the bowl. Strain the soaking liquid through several layers of cheesecloth. Rinse the morels under running water and slice them.
- Prepare the fresh morels. Rinse them quickly under running water and dry them with paper towels. Slice the tops and stems. Place them in a saucepan with the dried morels, the morel soaking liquid, the lemon juice and chicken stock and cook over low heat for 15 minutes.
- Meanwhile, grill the chops to desired doneness. They are medium when the flesh is pale pink (when you cut near the bone). While the chops are cooking, soften the shallots in the butter in the skillet. Add the morels with their cooking liquid, the vermouth and the creme fraiche, and cook them over high heat until the mixture has formed a thick sauce. Correct seasoning and keep warm.
- Place the veal chops on four heated plates. Pour the sauce next to the chops, dividing it evenly among the four plates and garnish the chops with parsley.

Nutrition Information

- 884: calories;
- 74 grams: fat;
- 12 grams: carbohydrates;
- 4 grams: sugars;
- 40 grams: protein;
- 972 milligrams: sodium;
- 28 grams: saturated fat;
- 1 gram: trans fat;
- 26 grams: monounsaturated fat;
- 10 grams: polyunsaturated fat;
- 3 grams: dietary fiber;

172. Halibut Steaks With Pesto Sauce

Serving: 4 servings | Prep: | Cook: | Ready in: 1hours20mins

Ingredients

- 2 halibut steaks, cut in half
- 4 tablespoons pesto sauce (see above)
- Coarse salt and freshly ground pepper to taste
- 2 limes or lemons

Direction

- Wipe the steaks dry with paper towels. Spread the pesto on both sides of the steaks and allow them to sit for an hour at room temperature.
- Heat coals or broiler and grill the steaks on both sides until cooked. Remove from heat, season with salt and pepper and serve, garnished with lemon or lime, cut in half.

Nutrition Information

- 252: calories;
- 8 grams: fat;
- 1 gram: sugars;
- 5 grams: carbohydrates;
- 39 grams: protein;
- 583 milligrams: sodium;

173. Halloumi Tzaganaki

Serving: Serves 4 to 6 as meze | Prep: | Cook: | Ready in: 25mins

Ingredients

- 1 large (8-ounce) Vidalia onion
- 2 tablespoons, plus 2 teaspoons, extra-virgin olive oil, or as needed
- 12 anchovy fillets in oil, drained
- ½ cup finely julienned roasted red peppers
- ½ cup pitted Kalamata olives
- 16 capers
- ¼ cup loosely packed parsley leaves
- ¼ cup loosely packed young dill fronds (if older and coarse, roughly chop)
- ¼ cup loosely packed mint leaves
- 1 ½ teaspoons freshly squeezed lemon juice, or as needed
- Kosher salt and freshly ground black pepper
- 8 ounces halloumi cheese, cut crosswise into 1/4-inch-thick slices
- Rustic bread, for serving

Direction

- Preheat a grill or broiler to high. Cut the onion crosswise into 1/2-inch slices, keeping the rings intact. Lay the slices in one layer on a baking sheet and drizzle with 1 tablespoon of the olive oil. Grill or broil, flipping once, until browned and crispy on the edges, about 5 minutes per side. Cool to room temperature.
- In a medium mixing bowl, combine the onions, anchovies, red peppers, olives, capers, parsley, dill and mint. Dress with the lemon juice, 2 teaspoons olive oil, 1/2 teaspoon salt and 1/4 teaspoon pepper, adjusting the amounts as needed to taste.
- Place a 10-inch skillet over medium-high heat. Add 1 tablespoon olive oil. When hot, sear the halloumi until browned on both sides. Transfer to a platter and top with salad and serve with bread.

Nutrition Information

- 247: calories;
- 0 grams: trans fat;
- 1 gram: dietary fiber;
- 7 grams: carbohydrates;
- 3 grams: sugars;
- 637 milligrams: sodium;
- 19 grams: fat;
- 8 grams: monounsaturated fat;
- 12 grams: protein;

174. Hamburgers (With Goat Cheese)

Serving: 4 servings | Prep: | Cook: | Ready in: 30mins

Ingredients

- 2 pounds very lean ground beef, preferably top round
- Salt to taste if desired
- Freshly ground pepper to taste
- ¼ pound goat cheese
- 2 tablespoons chopped fresh tarragon or half the amount dried, optional

Direction

- Preheat broiler to high.
- Divide beef into 4 portions. Shape each into hamburger-shaped rounds, each about an inch thick. Sprinkle with salt and pepper. Place wire rack on baking dish and arrange patties over it. Put meat under broiler, inch or two from source of heat, and leave broiler door slightly ajar. Cook about 3 minutes on one side if you wish meat rare. If you prefer it more well done cook up to 6 minutes on one side, then turn and continue cooking 2 to 4 minutes.
- Meanwhile, crumble cheese and top each portion of meat with equal portions of cheese, pressing to keep mounds of cheese intact. Return cheese-topped patties to broiler and let broil about 2 minutes until the cheese is browned on top and partly melted.
- Sprinkle top of each patty with chopped tarragon.

Nutrition Information

- 458: calories;
- 0 grams: sugars;
- 55 grams: protein;
- 595 milligrams: sodium;
- 25 grams: fat;
- 11 grams: saturated fat;
- 9 grams: monounsaturated fat;
- 1 gram: polyunsaturated fat;

175. Hamburgers With Garlic And Shallot Butter

Serving: 4 servings | Prep: | Cook: | Ready in: 20mins

Ingredients

- 1 ½ pounds ground beef, preferably sirloin
- Salt to taste, if desired
- ½ teaspoon freshly ground pepper
- 2 tablespoons Dijon-style mustard
- 3 tablespoons finely chopped shallots
- ¼ cup dry white wine
- 1 tablespoon finely minced garlic
- 4 tablespoons butter at room temperature
- 2 tablespoons finely chopped parsley

Direction

- Put meat into a mixing bowl and add salt, pepper and mustard. Blend well, using your fingers. Divide mixture into four portions and shape each into a patty.
- Combine shallots and wine in a small saucepan. Cook over moderately high heat about 3 minutes or until the wine is almost evaporated. Remove from heat and let cool

briefly. Add garlic, butter and parsley and blend well.
- Burgers may be broiled or cooked in a hot skillet. If they are to be broiled, preheat the broiler to high. Place burgers on a rack and place them under broiler about two or three inches from the source of heat. Cook about 5 minutes, turning burgers occasionally. If burgers are to be cooked in a skillet, heat the skillet, preferably a cast-iron one, until very hot. Brush it lightly with oil. Add burgers and cook about 2 minutes on one side. Turn and cook about 3 minutes longer, turning them occasionally.
- Smear top of each burger immediately with herb butter and serve.

Nutrition Information

- 492: calories;
- 36 grams: fat;
- 0 grams: trans fat;
- 14 grams: monounsaturated fat;
- 17 grams: saturated fat;
- 1 gram: sugars;
- 3 grams: carbohydrates;
- 35 grams: protein;
- 507 milligrams: sodium;

176. Hard Shell Clams With Parsley Pesto

Serving: 4 or more servings | Prep: | Cook: | Ready in: 20mins

Ingredients

- 2 cups parsley leaves (thin stems are O.K.), washed
- Salt
- ½ clove garlic, more to taste
- ½ cup extra virgin olive oil, or more
- 1 tablespoon sherry vinegar or lemon juice
- 2 dozen hardshell clams (littlenecks or cherrystones), washed and scrubbed

Direction

- Turn on broiler and put a large cast-iron skillet under it while you make parsley pesto. Combine parsley with a pinch of salt, garlic and about half the oil in a food processor or blender. Process, stopping to scrape down sides of container if necessary, and adding rest of oil gradually. Add vinegar or lemon juice, then a little water to thin mixture slightly. Taste and adjust seasoning.
- Carefully remove skillet from broiler, add clams to it and return to broiler. They should all open more or less at once, within 10 minutes; remove them as soon as they do to preserve their juices, and put on a plate. Dab each with parsley sauce and serve hot. (Any clams that do not open are safe to eat; open them with a dull knife, or continue to broil a few minutes longer.)

Nutrition Information

- 326: calories;
- 1 gram: dietary fiber;
- 540 milligrams: sodium;
- 28 grams: fat;
- 4 grams: saturated fat;
- 20 grams: monounsaturated fat;
- 0 grams: sugars;
- 3 grams: polyunsaturated fat;
- 5 grams: carbohydrates;
- 14 grams: protein;

177. Harissa

Serving: | Prep: | Cook: | Ready in: 1hours10mins

Ingredients

- 2 ounces dried red chili, such as Nora or Ancho, stemmed and seeded

- 1 fleshy red bell or pimento pepper
- 1 teaspoon tomato paste
- 1 teaspoon red-wine vinegar
- Salt to taste
- 1 cup extra-virgin olive oil
- 2 teaspoons coriander seeds, toasted
- 2 teaspoons cumin seeds, toasted
- ½ teaspoon caraway seeds, toasted
- 3 garlic cloves, peeled
- Cayenne pepper to taste

Direction

- On a sheet tray, toast the dried chili peppers in a 350-degree oven until they start to smell good. Be careful not to burn them, as they go from nicely toasted to burned in a matter of seconds. Place in a bowl and cover with hot water, leaving them to rehydrate for about 20 minutes.
- Grill or broil the bell or pimento pepper until well charred and blistered. Seal in a paper bag for 20 minutes to steam. Scrape the charred skin off the pepper and remove, discarding the seeds and stem. Avoid the temptation to rinse the pepper while cleaning it, as its delicious oils would be lost.
- Drain the chilies and place in a blender jar with the roasted pepper, tomato paste, vinegar, a good pinch of salt and about a quarter of the olive oil. Blend to a thick, fairly smooth paste, adding more oil as needed to facilitate blending. Transfer to a medium bowl.
- Coarsely grind the toasted spices in a mortar and add to the pepper mixture. Pound the garlic cloves to a paste with a pinch of salt in the mortar and add to the mixture. Slowly mix in the rest of the oil with a spoon, not being overly concerned with creating an even consistency. Taste and adjust with salt and cayenne. The oil will rise and stay somewhat separate from the chili solids, allowing the harissa to be preserved in the fridge for months. Just stir together before using it. The oil itself is a delicious flavoring agent.

Nutrition Information

- 268: calories;
- 20 grams: monounsaturated fat;
- 5 grams: carbohydrates;
- 2 grams: dietary fiber;
- 0 grams: sugars;
- 1 gram: protein;
- 4 grams: saturated fat;
- 28 grams: fat;
- 3 grams: polyunsaturated fat;
- 121 milligrams: sodium;

178. Herb Polenta With Red Bell Pepper Sauce

Serving: 6 servings | Prep: | Cook: | Ready in: 2hours45mins

Ingredients

- For the herb polenta:
- 4 tablespoons extra virgin olive oil
- 1 cup milk
- 1 clove garlic, finely chopped
- ½ cup regular (10 minute) Cream of Wheat
- 2 large eggs
- ¼ cup plus 2 tablespoons finely grated Parmigiano-Reggiano
- 1 well-packed cup thinly shredded spinach leaves
- 12 large basil leaves, thinly shredded
- 2 tablespoons finely chopped parsley or chervil
- Salt and freshly ground black pepper
- Sprigs of fresh oregano, for garnish
- For the red bell pepper sauce:
- 1 large red bell pepper
- ½ anchovy, chopped, or 1/2 teaspoon anchovy paste, optional
- 2 cloves garlic, chopped
- 2 tablespoons extra virgin olive oil
- ¼ cup chicken stock or broth, or as needed
- ½ teaspoon sugar

- Salt and freshly ground black pepper
- Vegetable oil for baking sheet

Direction

-
-

Nutrition Information

- 295: calories;
- 0 grams: trans fat;
- 1 gram: dietary fiber;
- 9 grams: protein;
- 328 milligrams: sodium;
- 21 grams: fat;
- 5 grams: saturated fat;
- 13 grams: monounsaturated fat;
- 2 grams: polyunsaturated fat;
- 17 grams: carbohydrates;
- 4 grams: sugars;

179. Herb Crumbed Broiled Tomatoes

Serving: Four servings | Prep: | Cook: | Ready in: 15mins

Ingredients

- 1 ½ teaspoons olive oil
- 2 large cloves garlic, peeled and minced
- ½ cup bread crumbs
- 2 tablespoons chopped Italian parsley
- 2 teaspoons chopped fresh thyme
- ½ teaspoon kosher salt
- Freshly ground pepper to taste
- 4 medium tomatoes, ripe but firm, cut in half crosswise, seeds scooped out

Direction

- Preheat the broiler. Heat the olive oil in a medium-size nonstick skillet. Add the garlic and cook, stirring constantly, for 30 seconds. Stir in the bread crumbs and remove from heat. Stir in the parsley, thyme, salt and pepper. Place the tomatoes on a baking sheet and sprinkle heavily with the crumbs. Broil just until the crumbs are lightly browned. Serve immediately.

Nutrition Information

- 96: calories;
- 2 grams: dietary fiber;
- 4 grams: sugars;
- 334 milligrams: sodium;
- 3 grams: protein;
- 0 grams: saturated fat;
- 1 gram: polyunsaturated fat;
- 16 grams: carbohydrates;

180. Herb Marinated Chicken Wings Stuffed With Scallion Goat Cheese

Serving: Twelve servings | Prep: | Cook: | Ready in: 25mins

Ingredients

- 6 ounces goat cheese, softened
- 2 scallions, finely chopped
- 24 chicken wings
- 3 large cloves garlic, peeled and finely chopped
- 2 tablespoons chopped fresh rosemary
- 1 teaspoon kosher salt
- ½ teaspoon freshly ground pepper
- ½ cup olive oil

Direction

- Stir together the goat cheese and scallions. Separate the chicken wings at the small joint and save the wing tips for another purpose, like stock. Loosen the skin over the top of the remaining portions, making a pocket between the skin and meat. Fill each pocket with about

- 1 teaspoon of the goat cheese mixture; do not overfill.
- Combine the garlic, rosemary, salt, pepper and oil in a large bowl. Add the chicken wings and turn to coat well. Refrigerate for several hours.
- Preheat the broiler. Place the chicken wings on a broiler pan with a drip tray and broil until the skin is browned and chicken is cooked through, about 8 minutes.

Nutrition Information

- 216: calories;
- 19 grams: fat;
- 5 grams: saturated fat;
- 10 grams: monounsaturated fat;
- 0 grams: sugars;
- 2 grams: polyunsaturated fat;
- 1 gram: carbohydrates;
- 12 grams: protein;
- 180 milligrams: sodium;

181. Homemade Merguez

Serving: About 1 pound of sausages | Prep: | Cook: | Ready in: 15mins

Ingredients

- ½ teaspoon cumin seeds
- ½ teaspoon coriander seeds
- ½ teaspoon fennel seeds
- 1 pound ground lamb
- 2 tablespoons fresh cilantro, finely chopped; more for serving
- 2 garlic cloves, minced
- 1 ½ teaspoons kosher salt
- 1 teaspoon paprika
- ½ teaspoon cayenne pepper, or to taste
- Olive oil, for cooking
- Harissa, for serving (optional)

Direction

- In a small skillet over medium-low heat, toast cumin, coriander and fennel seeds until fragrant, 1 to 2 minutes. Transfer warm spices to a spice grinder and grind well, or use a mortar and pestle and pound seeds.
- In a large bowl, combine all ingredients and mix well. Form lamb mixture into desired shape (1-inch-thick by 5-inch-long cigars make nice merguez, but fatter cylinders or patties will also work). Chill for up to 5 days, freeze for up to 3 months, or use immediately.
- Brush sausages with oil and grill or broil them until browned and cooked through. Or fry them in a little oil until well browned all over. Serve with more cilantro and harissa on the side, if desired.

Nutrition Information

- 228: calories;
- 8 grams: monounsaturated fat;
- 2 grams: polyunsaturated fat;
- 1 gram: carbohydrates;
- 0 grams: sugars;
- 13 grams: protein;
- 185 milligrams: sodium;
- 19 grams: fat;

182. Huevos Rancheros

Serving: Four servings | Prep: | Cook: | Ready in: 45mins

Ingredients

- 1 ½ cups dried black beans
- 3 large cloves garlic
- 1 dried chipotle chili
- Sea salt, to taste
- 5 tablespoons lard, goose or duck fat, or corn oil
- 6 large, ripe tomatoes (about 2 1/2 pounds)
- 2 serrano chilis
- 2 poblano chilis
- 1 large white onion

- 1 bunch cilantro, plus a bit for garnish
- Butter, for frying
- 8 large eggs
- Sour cream, for garnish

Direction

- Place the beans, two of the garlic cloves and the chipotle chili in a saucepan, cover with water in a saucepan and simmer until the beans are very soft. Drain, season with salt to taste, and discard the chili. (The beans may be prepared in advance and refrigerated, but should be allowed to return to room temperature prior to frying.)
- Melt three tablespoons of the lard over medium heat in a heavy bottomed frying pan. Mash the cooked beans with a potato masher or large spoon, to prevent spattering, and add to the pan. Fry until the beans have a firm but fairly smooth consistency; set aside and keep warm.
- Place the tomatoes in a heavy pan or on a griddle, either under the broiler or on top of the stove, and roast until the skin blisters and blackens. Do not peel.
- Over an open flame or under the broiler, roast the poblano and serrano chilis until their skin blisters and starts to blacken. Peel the poblanos and slice them into long, thin strips. (The smaller serranos need not be peeled.)
- Finely chop the onion and the remaining garlic, melt the remaining lard in a heavy-bottomed frying pan, and add the onions and garlic to it. Cook over medium to low heat until cooked through but not browned. Core the roasted tomatoes. In a food processor or mill, make a rough puree of the tomatoes, with their skins, and the roasted serrano chilis. Add the puree to the cooked onion and garlic. Firmly tie the bunch of fresh cilantro and add it. Cook for 15 minutes over medium heat, or until the sauce thickens a little. Season to taste with salt. Remove and discard the cilantro.
- Fry the eggs sunnyside up in a little butter. Spoon generous quantities of salsa ranchero onto plates and place two fried eggs on top of each serving. Criss-cross strips of roasted poblano chili on top of the eggs. Serve the beans on the side and garnish with a spoonful of sour cream and a sprig of cilantro.

Nutrition Information

- 1202: calories;
- 28 grams: monounsaturated fat;
- 7 grams: polyunsaturated fat;
- 52 grams: saturated fat;
- 3 grams: trans fat;
- 64 grams: carbohydrates;
- 16 grams: dietary fiber;
- 12 grams: sugars;
- 33 grams: protein;
- 1486 milligrams: sodium;
- 93 grams: fat;

183. Indoor S'mores

Serving: 6 to 9 servings | Prep: | Cook: |Ready in: 10mins

Ingredients

- Oil for baking sheet
- 36 graham crackers (to make your own, see recipe here)
- 4 ounces semisweet chocolate, melted
- 18 large marshmallows

Direction

- Preheat broiler. Cover small baking sheet with foil, and lightly oil the foil.
- Put graham crackers top side down on a cutting board or another baking sheet. Slather each graham cracker with chocolate.
- Put marshmallows on the foil-covered baking sheet, and broil a few seconds, until tops are browned. Turn over to brown the other side.
- Put a toasted marshmallow on half of the chocolate-coated graham crackers. Top each

with another graham, chocolate side down, and serve.

Nutrition Information

- 415: calories;
- 4 grams: polyunsaturated fat;
- 74 grams: carbohydrates;
- 3 grams: dietary fiber;
- 5 grams: protein;
- 0 grams: trans fat;
- 35 grams: sugars;
- 307 milligrams: sodium;
- 12 grams: fat;

184. Iranian Herb And Walnut Frittata

Serving: Serves 6 | Prep: | Cook: | Ready in: 1hours10mins

Ingredients

- 8 eggs
- ½ cup plain yogurt (may use low-fat but not nonfat)
- ½ teaspoon rose water
- ½ teaspoon salt, or to taste
- Freshly ground pepper
- 4 cups, loosely packed, parsley leaves and cilantro (may use other herbs like mint, tarragon, dill or basil if you can't tolerate cilantro), finely chopped
- ⅓ cup finely chopped walnuts
- 2 tablespoons extra virgin olive oil
- 1 bunch scallions, white and green parts, finely chopped
- 2 garlic cloves or 1 bulb spring garlic, minced

Direction

- Beat the eggs in a large bowl. Add the yogurt, rose water, and salt and pepper and beat well. Add the herbs and walnuts, stir together and let sit for 30 minutes, stirring every so often.
- Heat one tablespoon of the oil in a 10-inch nonstick skillet over medium heat and add the scallions. Cook, stirring, until tender, about 3 minutes. Add the garlic and cook, stirring, until fragrant, 30 seconds to a minute. Remove from the heat and add to the eggs. Stir together.
- Add the remaining tablespoon of oil to the pan and swirl to coat evenly. Heat over medium-high heat until a drop of egg sizzles and sets within seconds of adding it to the pan. Stir the frittata mixture and add it to the pan, scraping in every last bit with a rubber spatula. Shake the pan gently, tilting it slightly with one hand while lifting up the edges of the frittata with the spatula in your other hand, to let the eggs run underneath during the first few minutes of cooking. Once a few layers of egg have cooked during the first couple of minutes of cooking, turn the heat down to low, cover the pan and cook over low heat for 10 minutes, shaking the pan gently every once in a while. From time to time remove the lid and loosen the bottom of the omelet with a wooden spatula, tilting the pan, so that the bottom doesn't burn. It will however turn golden. The eggs should be just about set; cook a few minutes longer if they're not.
- Meanwhile, heat the broiler. Uncover the pan and place under the broiler, not too close to the heat, for 1 to 3 minutes, watching very carefully to make sure the top doesn't burn (at most, it should brown very slightly and puff under the broiler). Remove from the heat, shake the pan to make sure the frittata isn't sticking and allow it to cool for at least 5 minutes and for up to 15. Loosen the edges with a wooden or plastic spatula. Carefully slide from the pan onto a large round platter. Cut into wedges and serve hot, warm, at room temperature

Nutrition Information

- 168: calories;
- 311 milligrams: sodium;
- 12 grams: fat;
- 3 grams: saturated fat;
- 0 grams: trans fat;
- 6 grams: carbohydrates;
- 2 grams: sugars;
- 10 grams: protein;

185. Italian Wedding Soup With Turkey Meatballs

Serving: 4 servings | Prep: | Cook: | Ready in: 30mins

Ingredients

- 12 cups chicken broth
- 2 tablespoons olive oil, plus additional for greasing and serving
- 1 pound lean ground turkey
- ½ cup panko bread crumbs
- ⅓ packed cup fresh parsley leaves, finely chopped
- 1 egg, lightly beaten
- 3 to 4 garlic cloves, minced
- 1 teaspoon kosher salt
- ½ teaspoon black pepper
- ½ cup freshly grated Parmesan cheese, plus more for serving
- ¾ cup orzo, ditalini, acini di pepe or another small soup pasta
- 3 packed cups baby spinach or kale, thinly sliced
- 1 lemon, zested and halved
- ¼ cup fresh dill, oregano or basil, roughly chopped (optional)

Direction

- Combine the chicken broth and 2 tablespoons oil in a large pot and bring to a boil.
- Meanwhile, add the turkey, panko, parsley, egg, garlic, salt, pepper and 1/2 cup Parmesan to a large bowl. Mix with a fork or clean hands until combined. Gently roll the mixture into 12 medium (2-inch) or 20 small (1 1/2-inch) meatballs and transfer to a baking sheet lined with lightly oiled aluminum foil or a silicone baking mat.
- Heat the broiler to high and set an oven rack 6 to 8 inches from the heat. Broil the meatballs until brown on two sides, turning halfway through, about 3 to 4 minutes per side.
- Add the pasta to the boiling broth and cook over medium until al dente, then lower the heat to a low simmer.
- Add the meatballs to the broth and simmer on low until completely warmed through, 3 to 5 minutes, stirring occasionally. Remove from the heat, and add the spinach and lemon zest, stirring well, to wilt. Season with salt and pepper to taste.
- Divide the soup among four bowls. Drizzle each with olive oil, sprinkle with more Parmesan and squeeze a bit of lemon over the top. Scatter the dill over the top, or stir in.

Nutrition Information

- 669: calories;
- 49 grams: carbohydrates;
- 2 grams: dietary fiber;
- 13 grams: sugars;
- 0 grams: trans fat;
- 29 grams: fat;
- 8 grams: saturated fat;
- 14 grams: monounsaturated fat;
- 5 grams: polyunsaturated fat;
- 51 grams: protein;
- 1797 milligrams: sodium;

186. Jeremiah Tower's Duck With Endive Salad

Serving: 4 servings | Prep: | Cook: | Ready in: 40mins

Ingredients

- 4 duck legs
- 2 duck livers
- Coarse salt and freshly ground pepper
- 2 tablespoons butter
- 2 tablespoons Madeira or dry sherry
- 16 small slices bread for croutons
- 3 tablespoons chopped tomatoes
- 1 tablespoon chopped fresh parsley
- 2 tablespoons fresh lemon juice
- ¼ cup hazelnut or walnut oil
- 1 large head curly endive, washed and spin-dried
- ½ cup hazelnuts, toasted and skinned

Direction

- Turn the legs skin side down. Cut along each thigh bone and remove them.
- Heat the oven to 325 degrees.
- Remove the sinews from the duck livers. Season and then saute over high heat in the butter for three minutes. Pour in the Madeira or sherry and cook for another minute. Puree the liver and juices in a food processor or through a food mill until smooth; then set aside.
- Bake the bread for 10 minutes and then let cool.
- Heat grill or broiler. Season the duck legs and grill or broil for five minutes on the flesh side and eight minutes on the skin side. Spread the liver puree on the croutons and put half a teaspoon of the chopped tomatoe on each crouton and sprinkle with chopped parsley.
- Dissolve salt and pepper in the lemon juice and whisk in the oil. Toss the endive and hazelnuts in the dressing. Put the salad on warm plates, a duck leg on top of each salad, the liver croutons around the salads.

Nutrition Information

- 1258: calories;
- 36 grams: saturated fat;
- 0 grams: trans fat;
- 55 grams: monounsaturated fat;
- 10 grams: carbohydrates;
- 2 grams: sugars;
- 771 milligrams: sodium;
- 120 grams: fat;
- 22 grams: polyunsaturated fat;
- 3 grams: dietary fiber;
- 34 grams: protein;

187. Jerusalem Artichokes Or Sun Chokes Au Gratin (Topinambours Au Gratin)

Serving: 6 servings | Prep: | Cook: | Ready in: 45mins

Ingredients

- 1 pound Jerusalem artichokes, 8 to 10
- Salt to taste, if desired
- 4 tablespoons butter
- 4 tablespoons flour
- 1 ½ cups milk
- Freshly ground pepper to taste
- ⅛ teaspoon freshly grated nutmeg
- 2 tablespoons finely chopped onion
- ¼ cup heavy cream
- Pinch of cayenne pepper
- 1 cup grated Swiss or Gruyere cheese
- 1 egg yolk

Direction

- Preheat the broiler.
- Using a small regular or swivel-bladed paring knife, peel the artichokes. If the artichokes are very large, cut them in half. Ideally, the artichokes or pieces of artichoke should be of uniform size or the size of the smallest whole artichoke.
- Put the artichokes in a saucepan. Add cold water to cover and salt to taste. Bring to the boil. Let simmer about 10 to 15 minutes or until tender but still a little crisp. Drain well.
- Meanwhile, melt three tablespoons of the butter in a saucepan and add the flour, stirring

with a wire whisk. Add the milk, stirring rapidly with the whisk. Add salt, pepper and nutmeg.
- Cut the hot artichokes into not-too-small bite-size cubes or wedges. There should be about two cups.
- Heat one tablespoon of butter in a saucepan and add the onion. Cook until wilted. Add the artichoke pieces, cream and cayenne. Bring to a boil and add the white sauce. Blend well. Bring to a simmer. Add three-quarters cup of the grated cheese and stir until melted. Add the egg yolk and let simmer about 15 seconds.
- Pour and scrape the mixture into a baking dish. Sprinkle with the remaining cheese.
- Place under the broiler and let stand until bubbling and nicely glazed on top.

Nutrition Information

- 315: calories;
- 21 grams: carbohydrates;
- 6 grams: monounsaturated fat;
- 1 gram: polyunsaturated fat;
- 2 grams: dietary fiber;
- 13 grams: saturated fat;
- 0 grams: trans fat;
- 11 grams: protein;
- 441 milligrams: sodium;

188. Kasu Cod

Serving: Four servings | Prep: | Cook: | Ready in: 20mins

Ingredients

- 4 black cod (sablefish) steaks or other cod as available
- ½ teaspoon kosher salt
- 1 cup sake kasu (see notes)
- 2 ¼ tablespoons dark brown sugar
- ½ to ¾ cup water
- The garnish:
- 1 cup ocean salad or 4 nori leaves, toasted (see notes)

Direction

- Rinse the steaks and pat them dry. Salt on both sides.
- Using a fork or a food processor, mash the sake lees with sugar and water to make a thick paste. Place a third of the paste in the bottom of a plastic bag, put two of the steaks on top of the paste and cover them with another third of the paste. Repeat with the remaining two steaks, covering them with remaining paste. Seal the bag and refrigerate for 24 hours.
- When ready to broil or grill the steaks, scrape off the paste (which can be reused if refrigerated) and broil the fish close to the heat for four minutes on one side, three minutes on the other.
- Garnish the steaks with pickled seaweed or toasted nori leaves, cut into julienne strips.

189. Kosher Pot Roast (Brisket)

Serving: 12 - 15 servings | Prep: | Cook: | Ready in: 4hours

Ingredients

- 1 whole brisket, 6 to 7 pounds
- 2 tablespoons beef fat rendered from the brisket, or vegetable oil
- 2 large onions, sliced very thin
- 1 cup well-seasoned beef stock
- Salt and freshly ground black pepper to taste

Direction

- Preheat broiler.
- Place the brisket on a rack in a broiling pan and broil until the outside is browned on both sides.
- Preheat oven to 350 degrees.

- Heat the beef fat in a large roasting pan or a 7- to 8-quart heat-proof casserole and saute the onions. When the onions are brown, stir in the stock. Place the meat in the pan or casserole, cutting it in half if necessary. Cover the pan and place in the oven.
- Bake the brisket for three to four hours, or until very tender. Allow to cool, then refrigerate overnight.
- Remove congealed fat from the sauce and reheat the meat in the sauce. Season the sauce with salt and pepper. Slice and serve the meat in the sauce or with sauce on the side.

Nutrition Information

- 612: calories;
- 586 milligrams: sodium;
- 0 grams: trans fat;
- 21 grams: monounsaturated fat;
- 2 grams: polyunsaturated fat;
- 3 grams: carbohydrates;
- 1 gram: sugars;
- 38 grams: protein;
- 49 grams: fat;
- 19 grams: saturated fat;

190. Lamb Chops

Serving: 4 servings | Prep: | Cook: | Ready in: 30mins

Ingredients

- 12 rib or loin lamb chops (about 2 1/2 pounds total); have the butcher "French" the rib chops (trim and scrape the top portions of the bones clean)
- ¼ cup coarsely chopped rosemary
- 4 cloves garlic, peeled and crushed with the side of a knife
- Extra-virgin olive oil, for sprinkling
- Coarse sea salt or kosher salt
- Freshly ground black pepper

Direction

- In the morning, get out a large bowl or dish. In it, combine the lamb chops with the rosemary and garlic. Sprinkle enough olive oil over the chops to coat them lightly. Toss to coat, then cover with plastic wrap and refrigerate until an hour before dinner, giving them a stir every few hours.
- An hour before serving, set out the chops to bring them to room temperature. Preheat a grill to medium high or a broiler. Season the chops with salt and pepper. Grill for 2 to 3 minutes on each side, turning them just once, so that they are nicely browned on the edges but still quite pink inside. Pile onto a warm serving platter and set on the table.

Nutrition Information

- 907: calories;
- 76 grams: fat;
- 13 grams: polyunsaturated fat;
- 767 milligrams: sodium;
- 2 grams: carbohydrates;
- 0 grams: sugars;
- 50 grams: protein;
- 24 grams: saturated fat;
- 1 gram: dietary fiber;
- 28 grams: monounsaturated fat;

191. Lamb Chops With Red Leicester Potato Cake

Serving: 4 servings | Prep: | Cook: | Ready in: 40mins

Ingredients

- 3 large potatoes, peeled
- 2 large onions
- 2 tablespoons olive oil
- Salt and freshly ground black pepper to taste
- Finely chopped fresh thyme leaves
- 6 ounces red Leicester cheese, thinly sliced

- 12 rib lamb chops

Direction

- Coarsely grate the potatoes and onions and place them in a large bowl. Heat the oil in a large, heavy-bottomed frying pan set over medium heat. Spread half the potatoes and onions across the bottom and season with salt, pepper and thyme. Layer the cheese evenly over the top. Add the rest of the potatoes and onions and press down to form a cake.
- Cook slowly on one side until golden and crisp, 10 to 12 minutes. (Lower the heat if it begins to brown too quickly.) Turn and cook on the other side.
- Meanwhile, preheat the broiler or prepare a charcoal grill. Season the lamb chops with salt and pepper and grill or broil to desired doneness, 10 to 15 minutes.
- Cut the potato cake into four wedges and place them on dinner plates. Lay three chops over each and serve.

192. Lamb Chops, Yellow Pepper Tarragon Sauce

Serving: 2 servings | Prep: | Cook: | Ready in: 40mins

Ingredients

- 4 spring loin lamb chops
- 3 tablespoons olive oil
- 3 yellow peppers
- 1 tablespoon tarragon vinegar
- 1 medium onion, coarsely chopped
- 1 clove garlic, crushed
- Coarse salt and freshly ground white pepper to taste
- 2 tablespoons fresh tarragon leaves

Direction

- Wipe the lamb chops dry with paper towels. Sprinkle with one-and-a-half tablespoons olive oil and set aside.
- Seed the peppers and cut into quarters. Cut the quarters in half.
- Place the peppers in a small heavy saucepan with the remaining olive oil, vinegar, onion and garlic. Season with salt and pepper. Cover and cook over low heat for about 20 minutes, or until the onions and peppers are soft.
- Puree the pepper mixture in a food processor and pass the mixture through a strainer. Keep warm. Meanwhile, preheat broiler.
- Broil the lamb chops until browned on the outside and pink in the middle. Place two chops on two heated plates and pour small pool of yellow pepper sauce next to them. Sprinkle the sauce with tarragon leaves and serve.

Nutrition Information

- 1133: calories;
- 8 grams: polyunsaturated fat;
- 37 grams: protein;
- 99 grams: fat;
- 24 grams: carbohydrates;
- 4 grams: dietary fiber;
- 2 grams: sugars;
- 1379 milligrams: sodium;
- 38 grams: saturated fat;
- 47 grams: monounsaturated fat;

193. Lamb Medallions With Curry Sauce

Serving: 4 servings | Prep: | Cook: | Ready in: 40mins

Ingredients

- 2 boneless, skinless racks of lamb, each about 1 1/4 pounds, plus the bones, leaving them in slabs
- Salt to taste if desired

- Freshly ground pepper to taste
- 4 teaspoons plus 1 tablespoon curry powder
- 2 tablespoons butter
- ¼ cup finely chopped onion
- ½ cup fresh or canned chicken broth
- ½ cup heavy cream

Direction

- Preheat the broiler to high.
- Cut each rack crosswise into eight flat medallions, each about half an inch thick. Sprinkle with salt and pepper. Set aside.
- Rub the slabs of lamb bones with curry powder, using about 2 teaspoons on each slab. Arrange the slabs on a flat baking dish.
- Heat the butter in a heavy skillet large enough to hold the pieces of meat in one layer. Add the medallions and cook without crowding until nicely browned on one side, about 45 seconds to one minute. Turn and cook on the second side about the same length of time. Transfer the pieces of meat to a warm serving dish.
- Place the slabs of bones under the broiler and let brown as you continue making the sauce. Broil about 2 1/2 minutes on each side.
- Add the onion and remaining tablespoon of curry powder to the butter remaining in the skillet in which the medallions cooked. Cook, stirring, until onion is wilted. Add the broth and any juices that have accumulated around the pieces of meat. Cook about 2 minutes or until the sauce has thickened slightly. Add the cream and cook briefly, about one minute.
- Line a saucepan with a sieve, preferably of the sort known in French kitchens as a chinois. Pour in the sauce. Press, using a plastic or rubber spatula, to extract most of the juices from the solids. There should be about two-thirds of a cup of sauce.
- Pour the sauce into the center of a hot serving dish and surround the sauce with the medallions of meat.
- Remove the slabs of bones and cut between each bone. Arrange the bones over the sauce. Serve with rice.

Nutrition Information

- 944: calories;
- 42 grams: saturated fat;
- 34 grams: monounsaturated fat;
- 5 grams: carbohydrates;
- 32 grams: protein;
- 851 milligrams: sodium;
- 89 grams: fat;
- 0 grams: trans fat;
- 6 grams: polyunsaturated fat;
- 2 grams: dietary fiber;
- 1 gram: sugars;

194. Lamb With Red Wine And Dried Cherries

Serving: 2 servings | Prep: | Cook: | Ready in: 40mins

Ingredients

- 8 ounces boneless leg of lamb
- 1 large clove garlic
- ½ cup dry red wine
- 3 tablespoons dried cherries
- Salt and freshly ground black pepper to taste

Direction

- If using a broiler, turn it on.
- Wash, dry and remove excess fat from the lamb. Cut into 1/4-inch thick slices.
- Mash the garlic and combine with the wine in a bowl large enough to hold the lamb. Add the lamb, and turn it to coat it with wine. Allow the lamb to marinate until time to cook, or at least 10 minutes.
- If using a stove-top grill, prepare it. Remove the lamb from the marinade and broil or grill until it is brown on both sides and pink inside, 7 to 10 minutes total.
- Add the cherries to the wine marinade, and boil until it is reduced by half. When the lamb

is cooked, stir it into wine mixture. Season with salt and pepper, and serve.

Nutrition Information

- 340: calories;
- 16 grams: fat;
- 7 grams: monounsaturated fat;
- 1 gram: dietary fiber;
- 15 grams: carbohydrates;
- 10 grams: sugars;
- 21 grams: protein;
- 437 milligrams: sodium;

195. Lamb And Red Pepper Fajitas

Serving: 2 servings | Prep: | Cook: | Ready in: 35mins

Ingredients

- ½ pound boneless leg of lamb
- 2 teaspoons reduced-sodium soy sauce
- 1 tablespoon dry sherry
- 4 teaspoons red wine vinegar
- 1 teaspoon Dijon mustard
- 1 teaspoon honey
- 2 teaspoons grated fresh or frozen ginger
- 14 ounces julienned red bell pepper
- 1 tablespoon olive oil
- 1 bunch arugula
- 5 scallions
- 4 8-inch flour tortillas
- 4 tablespoons plain nonfat yogurt

Direction

- If using broiler, cover broiler rack with foil and preheat.
- Cut lamb in strips 1/4-inch thick, removing excess fat.
- Combine soy sauce, sherry, vinegar, mustard, honey and ginger.
- Stir lamb pieces into marinade to coat lamb well.
- Heat oil in a nonstick skillet until hot, and saute pepper until soft.
- Wash, dry and trim stems from arugula, and set aside.
- If using a stovetop grill, broil or grill lamb until medium rare, about 10 minutes.
- Wash, dry, trim and slice scallions and stir into cooked red peppers. Stir cooked lamb into red peppers.
- Heat two tortillas in a toaster oven for about 1 minute.
- Spoon 1 tablespoon of yogurt over each tortilla, top with a quarter of the arugula and a quarter of the lamb mixture. Roll up and serve.
- Repeat with remaining tortillas.

Nutrition Information

- 736: calories;
- 15 grams: monounsaturated fat;
- 5 grams: polyunsaturated fat;
- 74 grams: carbohydrates;
- 32 grams: fat;
- 9 grams: dietary fiber;
- 0 grams: trans fat;
- 20 grams: sugars;
- 37 grams: protein;
- 1051 milligrams: sodium;

196. Loin Of Pork With Peaches And Apricots

Serving: 12 to 14 servings | Prep: | Cook: | Ready in: 2hours30mins

Ingredients

- ¾ pound dried peaches and apricots, soaked overnight in water to cover
- 1 4-pound boneless loin of pork, rolled and tied
- Coarse salt and freshly ground pepper to taste

- 3 cloves garlic, minced
- 1 cup sage leaves
- ½ cup white-wine vinegar
- 1 cup dry white wine

Direction

- Simmer the dried fruits in their soaking liquid until they are tender (about 15 minutes) and allow them to cool. If the butcher has already tied the pork loin, untie it. Season the meat with salt and pepper, sprinkle with garlic and half the sage leaves and stuff it with peaches and apricots. Bind the meat again to form a roll.
- Preheat the oven to 350 degrees. Using a heavy Dutch oven or enameled casserole just large enough for the pork, brown the meat under a broiler on all sides or on top of the stove. Remove it from the casserole and add the vinegar and the wine, scraping up the cooking juices over medium heat.
- Return the pork to the casserole and cover. Cook, basting from time to time, for about two hours, or until the temperature on a meat thermometer registers 155 degrees, which is high enough to kill any trichinosis bacteria. For the last 30 minutes, uncover the pork so that it browns. Do not overcook the pork or it will be dry and tough.
- Remove the pork from the cooking juices and put it on a platter. Keep it warm on the back of the stove. Bring the juices to a boil and skim off excess fat. Add any excess fruit to the sauce and heat through. To serve the pork, slice it thin and arrange it on a serving platter. Spoon on the sauce and decorate with chopped sage leaves.

Nutrition Information

- 297: calories;
- 1 gram: polyunsaturated fat;
- 24 grams: carbohydrates;
- 496 milligrams: sodium;
- 26 grams: protein;
- 11 grams: fat;

- 2 grams: monounsaturated fat;
- 0 grams: trans fat;
- 6 grams: dietary fiber;
- 13 grams: sugars;

197. Macaroni With Cheese

Serving: 4 servings | Prep: | Cook: | Ready in: 25mins

Ingredients

- 1 ½ cups uncooked elbow macaroni
- Salt to taste if desired
- 1 cup milk
- ½ cup heavy cream
- ⅛ teaspoon freshly grated nutmeg
- ¼ cup freshly grated Parmesan cheese

Direction

- Measure out the macaroni and set aside.
- Bring 3 quarts of water to a boil and add salt and macaroni. Stir frequently and cook until tender, about 12 minutes. Drain thoroughly.
- Return the macaroni to the kettle and add the milk, cream and nutmeg. Bring to a boil and cook about 4 minutes or until the liquid is absorbed. Pour the macaroni into a flat baking dish.
- Meanwhile, preheat the broiler to high.
- Sprinkle the top of the macaroni evenly with cheese. Place the dish under the broiler and broil until the top is lightly browned.

Nutrition Information

- 314: calories;
- 1 gram: dietary fiber;
- 33 grams: carbohydrates;
- 4 grams: monounsaturated fat;
- 5 grams: sugars;
- 10 grams: protein;
- 319 milligrams: sodium;
- 15 grams: fat;

- 9 grams: saturated fat;

198. Macaroni And Beef Casserole

Serving: 4 servings | Prep: | Cook: | Ready in: 30mins

Ingredients

- 2 quarts water
- Salt to taste
- 1 ½ cups elbow macaroni
- 1 tablespoon olive oil
- 1 cup chopped onions
- ¼ cup chopped celery
- ¼ cup chopped green pepper
- 2 teaspoons finely chopped garlic
- 1 pound lean ground beef chuck or round steak
- Freshly ground pepper to taste
- 1 tablespoon chopped fresh oregano (or 1 teaspoon dried)
- 2 tablespoons chopped fresh basil or Italian parsley
- ½ cup canned crushed tomatoes
- 2 tablespoons butter
- 2 tablespoons flour
- 2 cups milk
- 2 cups cubed or shredded Cheddar cheese
- Cayenne pepper to taste
- ¼ teaspoon freshly grated nutmeg
- 2 tablespoons grated Parmesan cheese

Direction

- Bring the water with salt to a boil. Add the macaroni; stir and simmer until tender, about 5 minutes. Do not overcook. Drain and rinse under cold water.
- In a skillet, heat the oil and add the onions, celery, green pepper and garlic. Cook, stirring, until wilted. Add the meat, salt and pepper. Cook, stirring, until the meat loses its red color. Add the oregano, basil and tomatoes. Cook, stirring, for 5 minutes. Add the cooked macaroni. Blend well and set aside. Keep warm.
- Meanwhile, melt the butter in a saucepan, and stir in the flour with a wire whisk until well-blended. Add the milk, stirring rapidly, and bring to a simmer. Cook, stirring, for about 5 minutes.
- Remove the sauce from the heat, and stir in the Cheddar cheese, cayenne, nutmeg, and more salt and pepper to taste. Stir until the cheese melts.
- Preheat broiler.
- Spoon the macaroni mixture into a baking dish measuring 7 by 10 by 2 1/2 inches. Pour the cheese sauce evenly over the macaroni mixture. Sprinkle with Parmesan cheese, and place under the broiler (about 4 to 5 inches from the heat source) until it is hot, bubbling and lightly browned.

Nutrition Information

- 763: calories;
- 41 grams: fat;
- 1 gram: trans fat;
- 13 grams: monounsaturated fat;
- 2 grams: polyunsaturated fat;
- 11 grams: sugars;
- 21 grams: saturated fat;
- 49 grams: carbohydrates;
- 4 grams: dietary fiber;
- 52 grams: protein;
- 2138 milligrams: sodium;

199. Maine Coast Lobster Rolls

Serving: 6 servings | Prep: | Cook: | Ready in: 20mins

Ingredients

- 1 pound cooked lobster meat
- 4 stalks crisp, cold celery
- 1 to 1 ¼ cups Hellmann's mayonnaise

- 6 hot dog rolls, top-sliced (not side-sliced)
- Paprika (optional)
- Capers (optional)
- 4 tablespoons butter, melted (optional)

Direction

- Cut the lobster into 1/2-inch pieces and place in a bowl. Chop the celery into medium-fine pieces and stir into lobster. Stir in just enough mayonnaise to coat the lobster mixture.
- As is traditional in Maine lobster shacks, fry the rolls in a skillet or on a griddle in butter. Otherwise, toast them on both sides under a broiler. Add the lobster salad and sprinkle with paprika and a few capers.

Nutrition Information

- 479: calories;
- 1 gram: dietary fiber;
- 0 grams: trans fat;
- 21 grams: polyunsaturated fat;
- 22 grams: carbohydrates;
- 3 grams: sugars;
- 17 grams: protein;
- 801 milligrams: sodium;
- 36 grams: fat;
- 6 grams: saturated fat;
- 9 grams: monounsaturated fat;

200. Maple Mustard Salmon With Mango

Serving: 2 servings | Prep: | Cook: | Ready in: 20mins

Ingredients

- 2 tablespoons apple cider vinegar
- 1 teaspoon Dijon mustard
- 2 tablespoons maple syrup
- Freshly ground black pepper to taste
- 10 ounces skinless salmon fillet
- 1 large firm mango

Direction

- Turn on broiler, if using, and cover broiler pan with aluminum foil.
- Mix the vinegar, mustard, maple syrup and pepper to taste in a large bowl.
- Wash and dry the salmon, and place in the marinade, turning to coat.
- Prepare stove-top grill, if using. Grill salmon on both sides, following the Canadian rule: measure salmon at thickest part and cook 8 to 10 minutes to the inch.
- Peel and cube mango; heat the remaining marinade until it boils.
- When salmon is cooked, top with heated marinade and mango and serve.

Nutrition Information

- 455: calories;
- 31 grams: protein;
- 116 milligrams: sodium;
- 20 grams: fat;
- 0 grams: trans fat;
- 6 grams: polyunsaturated fat;
- 3 grams: dietary fiber;
- 35 grams: sugars;
- 4 grams: saturated fat;
- 40 grams: carbohydrates;

201. Marinated Broiled Tuna Steaks With Sauce Nicoise

Serving: 4 servings | Prep: | Cook: | Ready in: 1hours

Ingredients

- 4 center-cut tuna steaks about an inch thick and 6 ounces each
- Salt and freshly ground pepper to taste
- 6 tablespoons olive oil
- 4 sprigs fresh thyme or 2 teaspoons dried
- 2 crumbled bay leaves

- 4 small sprigs fresh rosemary or 2 teaspoons dried
- ⅛ teaspoon red pepper flakes
- 4 ripe plum tomatoes
- ½ cup sliced fennel
- ½ cup sliced red onions
- 2 teaspoons coarsely chopped garlic
- 4 pitted black olives
- 2 teaspoons grated lemon rind
- 2 tablespoons red wine vinegar
- 4 tablespoons coarsely chopped fresh basil or parsley

Direction

- Preheat broiler to high or turn on charcoal outdoor grill.
- Place the tuna in a dish and sprinkle both sides with salt and pepper. Brush both sides with 2 tablespoons olive oil. Add the thyme, bay leaves, rosemary and pepper flakes. Cover with plastic wrap and let it stand for 20 minutes.
- Place the tomatoes in boiling water for about 9 seconds. Drain and pull away the skin. Cut and discard the core and chop the tomatoes coarsely.
- Place the remaining olive oil in a small saucepan over medium-high heat. When it's hot, add the fennel, onions and garlic. Cook briefly until wilted. Add the tomatoes, olives, lemon rind, vinegar, salt and pepper to taste. Cover and simmer for 5 minutes.
- Transfer the mixture into a blender or food processor. Add 3 tablespoons of the basil, then blend for 5 to 7 seconds, taking care that it remain coarse. Transfer the sauce to a saucepan, check for seasoning, reheat briefly. Keep warm.
- If broiling, arrange the tuna steaks on a rack and place under the broiler about 5 inches from the heat source. Broil 4 minutes with the door partly open. Turn the steaks, and, leaving the door open, continue broiling about 3 minutes longer. The steaks should not be overcooked.
- If grilling, place the steaks on a hot grill and cover. Cook for 4 minutes. Turn the fish, cover the grill and continue cooking for about 3 minutes. Serve with the prepared sauce around the fish and sprinkle with the remaining basil.

Nutrition Information

- 249: calories;
- 3 grams: sugars;
- 0 grams: trans fat;
- 15 grams: monounsaturated fat;
- 2 grams: polyunsaturated fat;
- 8 grams: protein;
- 370 milligrams: sodium;
- 21 grams: fat;

202. Marinated Hamburgers

Serving: 6 hamburgers | Prep: | Cook: |Ready in: 4hours

Ingredients

- 2 pounds ground beef round
- 6 fresh bay leaves, crumpled
- 8 cloves garlic, minced
- 2 ½ cups dry white wine
- ½ cup lemon juice
- 2 tablespoons red wine vinegar
- 1 tablespoon extra virgin olive oil
- Salt and freshly ground black pepper to taste

Direction

- Put 6 patties on a flat, nonreactive baking dish. Place a bay leaf under each burger and sprinkle the garlic over them.
- Stir the wine, lemon juice, vinegar and oil together and pour over the patties. Sprinkle with salt and pepper to taste. Cover and refrigerate, turning the burgers several times, for at least 3 hours. Half an hour before cooking, remove the bay leaves and drain the

patties on paper. Grill, broil or fry in a hot cast-iron skillet, 3 to 6 minutes per side. Serve on warmed rolls.

Nutrition Information

- 366: calories;
- 647 milligrams: sodium;
- 15 grams: fat;
- 5 grams: saturated fat;
- 7 grams: monounsaturated fat;
- 1 gram: sugars;
- 6 grams: carbohydrates;
- 34 grams: protein;

203. Marinated Pork

Serving: 2 servings | Prep: | Cook: | Ready in: 20mins

Ingredients

- 8 ounces pork tenderloin
- Fresh or frozen ginger to yield 1 tablespoon coarsely grated
- 1 teaspoon toasted sesame oil
- 2 tablespoons dry red or white wine
- 1 tablespoon hoisin sauce

Direction

- Turn on broiler, and cover pan with aluminum foil.
- Wash, dry and trim fat from tenderloin. Cut in half crosswise.
- Grate ginger, and combine with sesame oil, wine and hoisin sauce. Marinate pork in the mixture until it is time to broil.
- Broil pork two or three inches from source of heat 10 to 15 minutes, until meat is slightly pink inside, turning once. Slice and serve.

Nutrition Information

- 188: calories;

- 0 grams: dietary fiber;
- 3 grams: monounsaturated fat;
- 4 grams: carbohydrates;
- 24 grams: protein;
- 189 milligrams: sodium;
- 7 grams: fat;
- 2 grams: sugars;

204. Marinated Pork Tenderloin

Serving: 2 servings | Prep: | Cook: | Ready in: 25mins

Ingredients

- 2 tablespoons hoisin sauce
- ½ teaspoon five-spice powder
- ½ teaspoon minced garlic
- 1 tablespoon coarsely shredded ginger
- 2 tablespoons white wine
- 12 ounces pork tenderloin

Direction

- Mix the hoisin, five-spice powder, garlic, ginger and wine in bowl large enough to hold pork.
- Wash and dry the tenderloin and marinate in the hoisin mixture while you prepare the rest of the meal, or for up to a full day.
- Remove pork from marinade, reserving marinade, and cut off thinner part of tenderloin. Heat broiler or stove-top grill, and cook all the tenderloin, allowing 10 to 12 minutes for the thicker part, and less than 10 minutes for the thinner.
- Heat marinade. Slice tenderloin and spoon sauce over it.

Nutrition Information

- 256: calories;
- 7 grams: fat;
- 2 grams: monounsaturated fat;

- 0 grams: trans fat;
- 9 grams: carbohydrates;
- 1 gram: dietary fiber;
- 5 grams: sugars;
- 36 grams: protein;
- 348 milligrams: sodium;

205. Maureen Abood's Eggplant With Lamb, Tomato And Pine Nuts

Serving: 8 servings | Prep: | Cook: | Ready in: 2hours

Ingredients

- 2 large firm eggplants, cut into 1/2-inch slices
- 4 tablespoons extra-virgin olive oil
- 2 teaspoons kosher salt, more as needed
- 1 medium yellow onion, finely diced
- 2 garlic cloves, minced
- 1 pound ground lamb or beef (80 percent lean)
- ½ teaspoon ground cinnamon
- Black pepper
- ½ tablespoon unsalted butter
- ½ cup pine nuts
- 1 (28-ounce) can tomato sauce, or 3 1/2 cups homemade sauce (see recipe)
- 12 ounces fresh mozzarella, sliced

Direction

- Heat broiler and line a baking sheet with foil or parchment.
- Brush both sides of eggplant slices with 2 tablespoons olive oil and sprinkle with 1 teaspoon salt. Arrange slices on prepared baking sheet and broil in batches until they are deep mahogany brown, turning once halfway through, 5 to 7 minutes per side.
- Adjust the oven to 375 degrees with rack positioned in the center.
- In a large skillet, heat 1 tablespoon of the remaining olive oil over medium heat. Add onion and sauté until translucent, but not browned, stirring occasionally, about 5 minutes. Add garlic and cook until fragrant, about 1 minute. Add ground lamb or beef, stirring frequently and breaking up meat into very small pieces with the side of a metal spoon. Season with remaining teaspoon salt, cinnamon and pepper. Sauté until meat is just cooked through. Taste and add more salt or pepper, or both, as needed.
- In a medium skillet, melt butter over medium heat. Add pine nuts and reduce heat to medium-low. Stir nuts to coat them with butter and continue stirring constantly until nuts are golden brown, 2 to 4 minutes. Keep a close watch over the nuts; they can burn quickly once they begin to brown. Transfer nuts to a bowl while still warm and salt them lightly.
- Coat a 13-by-9-by-2-inch baking dish with remaining 1 tablespoon of olive oil. Spread 1/2 cup of tomato sauce in the bottom of the dish. Lay 1/3 of the eggplant slices in a single layer over the sauce, covering as much surface area of the bottom of the dish as possible. Spoon half the meat evenly over eggplant. Pour 1/3 of the remaining tomato sauce evenly over meat. Sprinkle with 1/3 of the pine nuts. Layer again with eggplant, meat, tomato sauce and pine nuts. Finish with a layer of eggplant and cover with more tomato sauce, sprinkling top with pine nuts.
- Pour 1 cup warm water around the perimeter of the baking dish. (Sauce will thicken as it bakes.) Cover pan with foil and bake for 90 minutes. Remove foil and top eggplant evenly with mozzarella. Bake for 15 minutes longer, uncovered, or until the cheese is bubbling and golden. Serve eggplant warm, over rice.

Nutrition Information

- 478: calories;
- 18 grams: carbohydrates;
- 7 grams: dietary fiber;
- 23 grams: protein;
- 854 milligrams: sodium;

- 5 grams: polyunsaturated fat;
- 0 grams: trans fat;
- 15 grams: monounsaturated fat;
- 10 grams: sugars;
- 37 grams: fat;
- 13 grams: saturated fat;

- 2 grams: sugars;
- 5 grams: carbohydrates;
- 4 grams: protein;
- 115 milligrams: sodium;
- 16 grams: fat;
- 3 grams: saturated fat;

206. Mesclun Salad With Roasted Peppers

Serving: 4 servings | Prep: | Cook: | Ready in: 25mins

Ingredients

- 1 large sweet red pepper
- 4 tablespoons extra-virgin olive oil
- 2 tablespoons white wine vinegar
- 2 tablespoons freshly grated Parmesan cheese
- Freshly ground black pepper to taste
- 6 cups mesclun
- 1 tablespoon finely minced chives

Direction

- Using a long fork, hold the pepper over an open flame and turn it slowly to char the skin all over. This can also be done under a broiler or on a grill. Put the charred pepper in a pastic or paper bag and seal the bag for five minutes. Remove the pepper from the bag and scrape off all the charred skin. Remove the core, seeds and ribs from the inside of the pepper and cut the pepper in strips. Toss in a dish with two tablespoons of the oil.
- Beat the remaining oil with the vinegar and cheese. Season with pepper.
- Put the mesclun in a salad bowl and toss with the peppers and the cheese dressing. Sprinkle with chives and serve.

Nutrition Information

- 170: calories;
- 10 grams: monounsaturated fat;

207. Mexican White Shrimp In Champagne Sauce

Serving: 4 servings | Prep: | Cook: | Ready in: 30mins

Ingredients

- 1 tablespoon unsalted butter
- ¼ cup peeled and finely minced shallots
- 1 clove garlic, peeled and finely minced
- 1 cup Champagne
- 1 sprig tarragon, plus additional chopped for garnish
- ½ cup cream
- Kosher salt and freshly ground white pepper to taste
- 1 ½ pounds medium shrimp, preferably Mexican white, shelled and deveined

Direction

- In a medium saucepan, melt the butter over medium heat and add the shallots and garlic. Saute, stirring, until the shallots are slightly softened, about 2 to 3 minutes. Add the Champagne and tarragon sprig and simmer gently until reduced by half, about 15 minutes. Remove the tarragon sprig and add the cream. Simmer for another 5 minutes. Season to taste with salt and white pepper. Set aside.
- Preheat the broiler and lay the shrimp in a roasting pan large enough to hold them in one layer. Sprinkle them with salt and brush 1/4 cup of the Champagne sauce over them with a pastry brush. Broil, turning once, until the shrimp are just cooked through, about 5 minutes.

- Gently reheat the remaining sauce over low heat. Divide the shrimp among 4 plates and spoon the sauce over them. Garnish with chopped tarragon and serve immediately.

Nutrition Information

- 304: calories;
- 0 grams: dietary fiber;
- 4 grams: monounsaturated fat;
- 1 gram: polyunsaturated fat;
- 6 grams: carbohydrates;
- 16 grams: fat;
- 9 grams: saturated fat;
- 2 grams: sugars;
- 24 grams: protein;
- 979 milligrams: sodium;

208. Middle Eastern Inspired Herb And Garlic Chicken

Serving: 4 to 6 servings | Prep: | Cook: |Ready in: 40mins

Ingredients

- 6 boneless skinless chicken thighs (about 1 3/4 pounds)
- 6 garlic cloves, grated on a Microplane or minced
- Juice and zest of 2 lemons
- 3 tablespoons extra-virgin olive oil, more for serving
- 2 tablespoons minced fresh parsley, more for serving
- 2 tablespoons minced fresh mint
- 1 tablespoon minced fresh thyme
- 1 tablespoon minced fresh oregano or marjoram
- 1 ½ teaspoons kosher salt, more as needed
- 1 tablespoon sesame seeds, more for garnish (optional)
- ¾ teaspoon sumac, more for garnish (optional)
- ⅔ cup plain Greek yogurt, preferably whole milk yogurt
- ¼ teaspoon ground black pepper

Direction

- Combine chicken with all but 1 teaspoon of the grated garlic (save that teaspoon for the yogurt sauce), the zest and juice of 1 lemon, oil, parsley, mint, thyme, oregano, 1 1/2 teaspoons salt, and the sesame seeds and sumac, if using. Cover and marinate for 15 to 30 minutes at room temperature; you can refrigerate it for up to 24 hours.
- Heat grill or broiler. If grilling, cook chicken over high heat until charred in spots, 4 to 7 minutes. Flip pieces and continue grilling until just cooked through, another 4 to 7 minutes. If broiling, arrange a rack 3 to 4 inches from flame. Line a rimmed baking sheet with foil and spread chicken out in a single layer. Broil chicken, turning halfway through cooking, until well colored and charred in spots, 4 to 7 minutes per side. Be careful that it doesn't burn.
- While chicken cooks, place yogurt in a small bowl. Stir in the reserved grated garlic and lemon zest and season to taste with salt. Serve the chicken drizzled with olive oil, remaining lemon juice to taste, black pepper, parsley and sesame seeds and sumac, if using, with the yogurt alongside for dipping.

Nutrition Information

- 187: calories;
- 11 grams: fat;
- 6 grams: monounsaturated fat;
- 17 grams: protein;
- 2 grams: sugars;
- 0 grams: trans fat;
- 5 grams: carbohydrates;
- 1 gram: dietary fiber;
- 447 milligrams: sodium;

209. Miso Broiled Scallops

Serving: 4 servings | Prep: | Cook: | Ready in: 20mins

Ingredients

- ½ cup white miso
- 2 tablespoons mirin, fruity white wine or dry white wine
- ½ cup minced onion
- Salt and cayenne pepper
- 1 ½ pounds scallops
- Juice of one lime

Direction

- Put miso in a bowl. Add mirin or wine. Whisk until smooth, adding more mirin if needed. Stir in onion, a pinch of salt and of cayenne. Combine scallops, let sit 10 minutes. Cook right away, or cover and refrigerate for up to a day. When ready to cook, heat a broiler (or grill), setting the rack as close as possible to the heat source.
- Broil until lightly browned, without turning, 3 to 5 minutes, or grill, turning once after 2 to 3 minutes. Sprinkle with lime juice, and serve.

Nutrition Information

- 205: calories;
- 3 grams: sugars;
- 1 gram: polyunsaturated fat;
- 0 grams: trans fat;
- 18 grams: carbohydrates;
- 25 grams: protein;
- 1950 milligrams: sodium;

210. Miso Glazed Eggplant

Serving: Serves 4 as an appetizer or side dish | Prep: | Cook: | Ready in: 45mins

Ingredients

- 2 long Japanese eggplants or 4 small Italian eggplants (about 3/4 pound)
- Salt to taste
- 1 teaspoon sesame oil, plus additional for the baking sheet
- 1 tablespoon mirin
- 1 tablespoon sake
- 2 tablespoons white or yellow miso
- 1 tablespoon sugar

Direction

- Cut the eggplants in half lengthwise and cut off the stem and calyx. Using the tip of a paring knife, cut an incision down the middle of each half, making sure not to cut through the skin, but cutting down to it. Salt the eggplant lightly and let sit for 10 minutes. Meanwhile preheat the oven to 425 degrees. Line a baking sheet with foil or parchment and brush with sesame oil.
- Blot the eggplants with paper towels and place, cut side down, on the baking sheets. Roast for 15 to 20 minutes, until the skin is beginning to shrivel and the flesh is soft. Remove from the oven, carefully turn the eggplants over, and preheat the broiler.
- To make the glaze, combine the mirin and sake in the smallest saucepan you have and bring to a boil over high heat. Boil 20 seconds, taking care not to boil off much of the liquid, then turn the heat to low and stir in the miso and the sugar. Whisk over medium-low heat without letting the mixture boil, until the sugar has dissolved. Remove from the heat and whisk in the sesame oil.
- Brush the eggplants with the miso glaze, using up all of the glaze. Place under the broiler, about 2 inches from the heat, and broil for about 1 minute, until the glaze begins to bubble and looks shiny. Remove from the heat. Allow to cool if desired or serve hot. To serve, cut the eggplant halves on the diagonal into 1- to 1-1/2-inch slices.

Nutrition Information

- 117: calories;
- 2 grams: fat;
- 0 grams: saturated fat;
- 1 gram: polyunsaturated fat;
- 9 grams: dietary fiber;
- 13 grams: sugars;
- 684 milligrams: sodium;
- 22 grams: carbohydrates;
- 4 grams: protein;

211. Miso Glazed Fish

Serving: 4 servings | Prep: | Cook: | Ready in: 3hours30mins

Ingredients

- ¼ cup mirin
- ¼ cup sake
- 3 tablespoons white or yellow miso paste
- 1 tablespoon sugar
- 2 teaspoons dark sesame oil
- 4 salmon, trout, Arctic char, mahi mahi or black cod fillets, about 6 ounces each

Direction

- Combine the mirin and sake in the smallest saucepan you have and bring to a boil over high heat. Boil 20 seconds, taking care not to boil off much of the liquid, then turn the heat to low and stir in the miso and the sugar. Whisk over medium heat without letting the mixture boil until the sugar has dissolved. Remove from the heat and whisk in the sesame oil. Allow to cool. Transfer to a wide glass or stainless steel bowl or baking dish.
- Pat the fish fillets dry and brush or rub on both sides with the marinade, then place them in the baking dish and turn them over a few times in the marinade remaining in the dish. Cover with plastic wrap and marinate for 2 to 3 hours, or for up to a day.
- Light the broiler or prepare a grill. Line a sheet pan with foil and oil the foil. Tap each fillet against the sides of the bowl or dish so excess marinade will slide off. Place skin side up on the baking sheet if broiling.
- Place the fish skin side down on the grill, or skin side up under the broiler, about 6 inches from the heat. Broil or grill for 2 to 3 minutes on each side, until the surface browns and blackens in spots. If necessary (this will depend on the thickness of the fillets) finish in a 400-degree oven, for about 5 minutes, until the fish is opaque and can be pulled apart easily with a fork.

Nutrition Information

- 450: calories;
- 36 grams: protein;
- 576 milligrams: sodium;
- 7 grams: monounsaturated fat;
- 4 grams: sugars;
- 1 gram: dietary fiber;
- 26 grams: fat;
- 6 grams: saturated fat;
- 8 grams: carbohydrates;

212. Mock Eggs Benedict

Serving: 4 servings | Prep: | Cook: | Ready in: 30mins

Ingredients

- 3 cups sauce Mornay (see recipe)
- 8 cups water
- ¼ cup white vinegar
- 4 tablespoons butter
- 8 thin slices cooked ham or prosciutto, about a quarter pound
- 8 eggs
- 4 English muffins, split in half
- ½ teaspoon paprika
- Parsley sprigs for garnish

Direction

- Prepare the sauce and set it aside.
- Preheat the broiler.
- Pour the water into a skillet (a heavy 10-inch stainless steel, aluminum or nonstick pan is suitable). Add the vinegar and bring to a simmer.
- Heat one tablespoon of the butter in a skillet (a 10- or 11 1/2-inch skillet is suitable). Add the ham slices and turn once. Let stand only enough to heat through, about one minute. Remove the skillet from the heat and let stand.
- Carefully break the eggs, one at a time, into the simmering water. Let simmer about three minutes. As gently as possible, using a heavy standard perforated kitchen spoon, turn the eggs in the water. Remove the skillet from the heat and let the eggs stand to the desired degree of doneness. Remember that the eggs will continue to cook even after the skillet is removed from the heat. The total cooking time, once the eggs are added to the water, is about five minutes. Time may vary, depending on the size of the eggs and their temperature.
- Line a dish with several layers of kitchen paper toweling. Using a perforated spoon, carefully remove the eggs onto the paper. Let drain briefly.
- Melt the remaining butter. Brush the muffin halves with melted butter and place cut side up under the broiler. Broil briefly until brown.
- Arrange two muffin halves browned side up on individual serving plates. Top each half with a slice of ham. Top each ham slice with a poached egg. Spoon an equal portion of sauce over each egg. Sprinkle with paprika. Garnish with parsley sprigs.

213. Monkfish Rolls

Serving: Serves 4 | Prep: | Cook: | Ready in: 20mins

Ingredients

- Salt
- 1 * pounds monkfish, cut into 3-inch pieces
- 1 ½ cups chopped celery
- 1 ½ tablespoons sliced scallions
- 1 ½ tablespoons sliced chives
- 1 teaspoon chopped tarragon
- ⅓ cup mayonnaise
- 1 tablespoon lemon juice
- Zest of one lemon
- Freshly ground black pepper
- 2 tablespoons butter, softened
- 4 hot-dog rolls

Direction

- Bring a large saucepan of salted water to a boil. Lower the heat to a simmer, add the monkfish and poach for 8 to 10 minutes, or until fully cooked. Drain, then remove the dark veins and membrane and discard. Pull the monkfish into bite-size pieces and place them in a large bowl.
- Add the celery, scallions, chives, tarragon, mayonnaise, lemon juice and zest. Season with salt and pepper. Blend until the fish is evenly coated with the dressing.
- Butter the cut sides of the hot-dog buns and toast either under a broiler or in a nonstick pan over medium heat. Fill each roll with a helping of monkfish salad.

Nutrition Information

- 401: calories;
- 24 grams: fat;
- 7 grams: saturated fat;
- 0 grams: trans fat;
- 21 grams: protein;
- 562 milligrams: sodium;
- 6 grams: monounsaturated fat;
- 11 grams: polyunsaturated fat;
- 25 grams: carbohydrates;
- 2 grams: dietary fiber;
- 4 grams: sugars;

214. More Vegetable Than Egg Frittata

Serving: 2 or 4 servings | Prep: | Cook: | Ready in: 30mins

Ingredients

- 2 tablespoons olive oil
- ½ onion, sliced (optional)
- Salt and black pepper
- 4 to 6 cups of any chopped or sliced raw or barely cooked vegetables
- ¼ cup fresh basil or parsley leaves, or 1 teaspoon chopped fresh tarragon or mint leaves, or any other herb
- 2 or 3 eggs
- ½ cup freshly grated Parmesan

Direction

- Put olive oil in a skillet (preferably nonstick or well-seasoned cast iron) and turn heat to medium. When fat is hot, add onion, if using, and cook, sprinkling with salt and pepper, until it is soft, 3 to 5 minutes. Add vegetables, raise heat and cook, stirring occasionally, until they soften, from a couple of minutes for greens to 15 minutes for sliced potatoes. Adjust heat so vegetables brown a little without scorching. (With precooked vegetables, just add them to onions and stir before proceeding.)
- When vegetables are nearly done, turn heat to low and add herb. Cook, stirring occasionally, until vegetables are tender.
- Meanwhile, beat eggs with some salt and pepper, along with cheese if you are using it. Pour over vegetables, distributing them evenly. Cook, undisturbed, until eggs are barely set, 10 minutes or so; run pan under broiler for a minute or two if top does not set. Cut into wedges and serve hot, warm or at room temperature.

Nutrition Information

- 237: calories;
- 7 grams: monounsaturated fat;
- 16 grams: carbohydrates;
- 5 grams: dietary fiber;
- 12 grams: protein;
- 380 milligrams: sodium;
- 0 grams: sugars;
- 14 grams: fat;
- 4 grams: saturated fat;
- 2 grams: polyunsaturated fat;

215. Moroccan Lamb

Serving: Serves 8 | Prep: | Cook: | Ready in: 1hours30mins

Ingredients

- 4 tablespoons paprika
- 2 tablespoons ground cumin
- 2 tablespoons ground coriander
- 2 teaspoons salt
- 1 teaspoon ground black pepper
- ⅛ teaspoon ground cardamom
- 1 6- to 7-pound leg of lamb, butterflied by your butcher

Direction

- Mix together the paprika, cumin, coriander, salt, pepper and cardamom. Rub lamb all over with these spices (or 1/2 cup zaatar) and refrigerate for 1 hour.
- On a very hot grill or under the broiler, grill or broil lamb, turning once, until cooked to the desired doneness, 10 to 20 minutes for medium rare depending on thickness of the lamb. Let rest on a cutting board for 10 minutes before slicing and serving.

Nutrition Information

- 621: calories;
- 2 grams: dietary fiber;

- 17 grams: monounsaturated fat;
- 4 grams: polyunsaturated fat;
- 18 grams: saturated fat;
- 3 grams: carbohydrates;
- 0 grams: sugars;
- 54 grams: protein;
- 751 milligrams: sodium;
- 42 grams: fat;

216. Mousse De Poivrons Doux (Red Pepper Mousse)

Serving: Four to six servings | Prep: | Cook: | Ready in: 2hours45mins

Ingredients

- 3 to 4 large red bell peppers
- ½ teaspoon salt
- 1 cup heavy cream

Direction

- Preheat the broiler with the rack set to leave the peppers about two inches from the heat, then broil the whole peppers for approximately 10 minutes, turning them as their skins blister and turn black. Remove the peppers from the broiler and, when they are cool enough to handle, peel, seed and quarter them.
- Place the peppers and salt in a small saucepan, without water, and slowly bring to a simmer. Cover and cook gently, stirring occasionally, until the peppers are very thick and have given up most of their liquid, about an hour or an hour and a half, depending on the moisture content of of the peppers. Place the cooked peppers in a sieve to drain off any remaining liquid. Drain them for several hours or overnight.
- Puree the peppers in a food processor until smooth. There should be about a half a cup.
- Place a whisk, or the beaters for an electric mixer, and a bowl in the freezer for at least one hour.
- Take the cold whisk, or beaters, and bowl and whip the cream until very stiff. Carefully fold in the pepper puree to make a mousse. Using two spoons, form small oval shapes of the mousse. Place two to three ovals on each plate and serve.

Nutrition Information

- 167: calories;
- 4 grams: monounsaturated fat;
- 1 gram: polyunsaturated fat;
- 7 grams: carbohydrates;
- 2 grams: protein;
- 9 grams: saturated fat;
- 15 grams: fat;
- 5 grams: sugars;
- 213 milligrams: sodium;

217. Mrs. Sebastiani's Malfatti

Serving: Serves 12 | Prep: | Cook: | Ready in: 30mins

Ingredients

- 2 pounds fresh spinach (weighed after trimming) or 2 packages frozen
- 6 ounces crusty Italian bread (about half a loaf)
- Hot water
- 1 onion, finely chopped
- 1 clove garlic, finely chopped
- 2 tablespoons olive oil
- ½ to 1 cup dry, coarse bread crumbs
- 1 cup freshly grated Parmesan cheese, plus more for serving
- ½ cup chopped parsley
- 1 teaspoon salt
- ¼ teaspoon freshly ground black pepper
- 1 teaspoon dried basil
- 4 eggs, lightly beaten
- Flour

- 3 cups hot tomato sauce, preferably homemade

Direction

- Cook the fresh spinach in the water clinging to the leaves after washing, or cook the frozen according to package instructions. Drain over a bowl, squeezing out as much water as possible — do this in small handfuls so you can press out the most water — and chop. Reserve the water.
- Briefly soak the bread in the reserved spinach water plus enough hot water to cover and squeeze dry.
- Sauté the onion and garlic in the olive oil until tender, 3 to 5 minutes. Mix the spinach, bread, sautéed onion and garlic and put through the finest blade of a meat grinder or pulse in a food processor until chopped, then scrape into a mixing bowl.
- Add 1/2 cup of the dry bread crumbs, the cup of Parmesan, parsley, salt, pepper and basil. Stir in the eggs. With lightly floured hands, gently shape the mixture into sausagelike links, 1 inch round by 3 inches long. If they do not hold together, add more bread crumbs. Lay on a baking sheet.
- Bring a large pot of salted water to a boil. Drop the links, one at a time, into the boiling water. Reduce the heat to let the water barely simmer and cook until the malfatti float to the surface, 1 to 2 minutes. Remove with a slotted spoon, drain on paper towels and place in a greased baking dish, large enough to fit the malfatti in a single layer.
- Spoon the tomato sauce over the links, sprinkle with lots of cheese and broil to reheat.

Nutrition Information

- 184: calories;
- 7 grams: fat;
- 3 grams: monounsaturated fat;
- 21 grams: carbohydrates;
- 4 grams: sugars;
- 0 grams: trans fat;
- 1 gram: polyunsaturated fat;
- 11 grams: protein;
- 633 milligrams: sodium;

218. Mushroom Soup Gratinée

Serving: 6 servings | Prep: | Cook: | Ready in: 1hours

Ingredients

- 3 tablespoons extra-virgin olive oil
- 1 pound cremini mushrooms, very finely minced, as for duxelles
- 1 large red onion, sliced thin
- 4 cloves garlic, sliced
- 1 ½ pounds shiitake mushrooms, stems discarded, sliced thin
- Salt
- 5 cups mushroom or vegetable stock
- 1 cup dry red wine
- 2 tablespoons red miso
- Ground black pepper to taste
- ½ teaspoon ground cloves
- ½ teaspoon ground ginger
- 6 slices sourdough bread, about 3 inches in diameter
- 6 ounces Gruyère, shaved thin

Direction

- Heat oil in a large sauté pan. Add minced mushrooms and sauté on low until they glisten with moisture, about 5 minutes. Remove 1/3 cup and set aside. Add onion and garlic to pan and cook, stirring, until the onion wilts. Add shiitakes and a dusting of salt, increase heat to medium and sauté, stirring, until mushrooms have softened, 5 minutes or so. Stir in stock and wine, bring to a simmer and cook 15 minutes.
- Place miso in a dish and dissolve in a few tablespoons of the cooking liquid, then stir back into the pan. Add pepper to taste, cloves and ginger. Simmer, partly covered, about 30 minutes. Check consistency, adding a little

water if needed. Adjust salt and pepper. Soup can be finished and served at once, or set aside, then reheated and finished.
- To serve, heat broiler. Transfer soup to a 3-quart ovenproof dish or casserole. Toast bread. Spread reserved minced mushrooms on each slice and cover with cheese. Float slices on top of soup. Place dish under the broiler long enough to melt and lightly brown the cheese, then bring to the table and serve into bowls. Alternatively, the soup can be divided into individual oven-proof bowls, each topped with toast, mushrooms and cheese, and broiled.

Nutrition Information

- 669: calories;
- 12 grams: sugars;
- 29 grams: protein;
- 1424 milligrams: sodium;
- 7 grams: saturated fat;
- 0 grams: trans fat;
- 8 grams: dietary fiber;
- 3 grams: polyunsaturated fat;
- 89 grams: carbohydrates;
- 20 grams: fat;

219. Mussel And Spinach Gratin

Serving: Four ervings | Prep: | Cook: | Ready in: 40mins

Ingredients

- ½ cup dry white wine
- 2 pounds mussels, thoroughly scrubbed in several changes of water and bearded
- 2 pounds fresh spinach, picked over, washed, dried and stemmed
- Freshly grated nutmeg
- The hollandaise:
- 3 egg yolks
- 2 tablespoons mussel cooking liquid
- 8 tablespoons softened unsalted butter
- ¼ teaspoon salt
- 1 teaspoon lemon juice

Direction

- In a large, deep-sided saucepan combine the wine and mussels, and over high heat bring the mixture to a boil. Cover and cook just until the mussels open, about five minutes. Do not overcook. Remove from the heat. Remove the mussels with a strainer, then strain and reserve the mussel cooking liquid. Discard any mussels that do not open.
- Allow the mussels to cool slightly, and when they are not too hot to touch, remove them from their shells and set aside.
- Bring a large pot of salted water to a rolling boil. Add the spinach and cook just until soft, for one or two minutes. The spinach should remain a bright, vivid green. Immediately drain the spinach and rinse it thoroughly in cold water to set the color. Drain thoroughly, squeezing out any excess liquid. Season to taste with salt, freshly ground black pepper and freshly grated nutmeg and set aside.
- Preheat broiler.
- Prepare the hollandaise: In the top of a double boiler combine the egg yolks and mussel cooking liquid and beat with a whisk over hot but not boiling water until fluffy.
- Add a few spoonfuls of butter to the mixture and whisk continually until the butter has melted and the sauce begins to thicken. Be certain that the water in the bottom of the boiler remains hot but does not boil. Continue adding the butter, bit by bit, stirring constantly.
- Add the salt and lemon juice. Taste and adjust seasoning if necessary.
- Add several tablespoons of hollandaise to the spinach and toss. Divide the spinach among four six-inch round baking dishes and flatten it into a smooth bed. Sprinkle the mussels evenly over the spinach, then spoon hollandaise sauce over the mussels.

- Broil just until the top is crisp and brown. Serve immediately.

220. Mustard Marinated Breaded Chicken

Serving: Eight servings | Prep: | Cook: | Ready in: 1hours30mins

Ingredients

- The chicken:
- ½ cup plain nonfat yogurt
- 1 tablespoon Dijon mustard
- 1 ½ teaspoons sweet paprika
- ⅛ teaspoon cayenne
- 1 ½ teaspoons salt
- Freshly ground pepper to taste
- 1 pound boneless, skinless chicken breasts
- ¾ cup bread crumbs
- Olive oil spray
- The sauce:
- 6 tablespoons plain nonfat yogurt
- 6 tablespoons Dijon mustard
- ½ cup honey
- 1 tablespoon ground cumin

Direction

- To prepare the chicken, in a medium-size bowl combine the yogurt, mustard, paprika, cayenne, 1/2 teaspoon of salt and pepper to taste. Cut the chicken lengthwise into 1/4-inch-thick strips. Place the chicken in the bowl and toss to coat with the marinade. Cover and refrigerate for 1 hour.
- Meanwhile, to prepare the dipping sauce stir all of the ingredients together in a small bowl until well combined. Refrigerate if making ahead.
- Preheat the oven to 400 degrees. Place the bread crumbs in a shallow bowl and season with 1 teaspoon of the salt and pepper to taste. Roll the chicken strips in the bread crumbs to coat well. Thread each chicken strip onto 1 skewer.
- Spray a baking sheet lightly with the olive oil. Place the skewers on the pan and spray them lightly with the oil. Bake until the bread crumbs are browned and the chicken has cooked through, about 10 minutes per side. Set aside to cool. Refrigerate if making more than 1 hour ahead.
- Prepare a charcoal fire or preheat the broiler. Place the skewers on the grill or under the broiler until lightly charred and heated through, about 5 minutes per side. Serve hot with the dipping sauce.

Nutrition Information

- 205: calories;
- 20 grams: sugars;
- 16 grams: protein;
- 303 milligrams: sodium;
- 3 grams: fat;
- 1 gram: dietary fiber;
- 0 grams: trans fat;
- 28 grams: carbohydrates;

221. My Pain Catalan With Extra Tomatoes And Goat Cheese

Serving: 1 serving, or 2 servings as an appetizer | Prep: | Cook: | Ready in: 10mins

Ingredients

- 2 slices whole-wheat country bread
- 1 garlic clove, cut in half, or Dijon mustard to taste
- 1 large or 2 smaller ripe tomatoes in season
- Salt to taste
- ½ ounce goat cheese, crumbled or thinly sliced

Direction

- If desired, toast the bread. Rub with the cut side of the garlic clove or spread with mustard. Cut one of the tomatoes in half and rub the cut side against the bread until the bread is nicely saturated with the juice and pulp of the tomato. Slice the remaining tomato and layer over the bread. Season to taste with salt, crumble the goat cheese on top, add a few torn basil leaves if desired and enjoy.

Nutrition Information

- 218: calories;
- 461 milligrams: sodium;
- 5 grams: fat;
- 1 gram: polyunsaturated fat;
- 7 grams: sugars;
- 34 grams: carbohydrates;
- 4 grams: dietary fiber;
- 10 grams: protein;
- 3 grams: saturated fat;
- 0 grams: trans fat;

222. Naan (Indian Flatbread)

Serving: 8 pieces | Prep: | Cook: | Ready in: 1hours

Ingredients

- 1 envelope (2 1/2 teaspoons) dry yeast
- 2 tablespoons sugar
- 4 ½ to 5 cups all-purpose flour, more for dusting and rolling
- 2 teaspoons salt
- 1 teaspoon baking powder
- 3 tablespoons milk
- 2 tablespoons plain Greek yogurt
- 1 large egg, lightly beaten
- 2 tablespoons vegetable oil, more for the bowl
- 3 tablespoons ghee (Indian-style clarified butter) or melted unsalted butter

Direction

- In a small bowl, combine the yeast, sugar and 1/4 cup warm water (110 to 115 degrees). Let stand until foamy, 5 to 10 minutes.
- Place 4 1/2 cups flour, the salt and baking powder in the bowl of a food processor fitted with a dough blade or in mixer with a dough hook. Mix to blend. Add yeast mixture, milk, yogurt, egg, 2 tablespoons vegetable oil and 3/4 cup warm water. Knead dough until smooth and elastic, 2 to 3 minutes in a processor, 5 to 8 minutes in a mixer, 8 to 10 minutes by hand. Dough should be soft but not too sticky. Add flour as needed.
- Place dough in a large, lightly oiled bowl, turning to coat all sides. Cover bowl with plastic wrap, then a kitchen towel. Let the dough rise in a warm, draft-free spot until doubled, 1 to 1 1/2 hours.
- Punch down the dough and divide into 8 equal pieces. Roll them into balls, place them on a lightly floured baking sheet and cover with a slightly damp kitchen towel. Let rise until doubled in size, 40 to 60 minutes.
- If using a tandoor, heat it to about 450 degrees. If using the oven, place a pizza stone on the bottom rack and heat oven to 450 degrees. If using a barbecue grill, set it up for direct grilling and heat to medium-high.
- Roll out a dough ball on a lightly floured work surface into a disk about 6 inches in diameter. Roll and stretch one end to make a teardrop shape. Brush off any excess flour. Repeat with remaining dough.
- If using a tandoor, drape one piece of dough over the round cloth pillow called a gadhi. Press the bread onto the hot clay wall. Cook the naan until the top is puffed, blistered and browned, 1 to 2 minutes. Using a skewer, gently pry the bread off the tandoor wall, taking care not to scratch the clay. Brush the top of the bread with ghee or melted butter, then place in a cloth-lined basket for serving. Repeat with remaining dough.
- If using an oven, turn on the broiler. Lay 1 or 2 pieces of dough on the pizza stone. Cook until the bottoms are browned and the tops blister, puff and are lightly toasted, 2 to 4 minutes.

Remove from oven, brush tops with ghee or melted butter, and place in a cloth-lined basket for serving. Repeat with remaining dough.
- If using the grill, brush and oil the grate. Lightly brush top of dough with butter and place butter-side down on grate a few at a time (do not crowd the grate). Grill until the bottoms are browned and the tops start to puff and blister, 1 to 2 minutes. Lightly brush the tops with a little butter. Invert bread, and grill the other side until lightly browned, 1 to 2 minutes. Transfer to a cloth-lined basket, brushing tops of each with any remaining butter.

Nutrition Information

- 372: calories;
- 4 grams: sugars;
- 0 grams: trans fat;
- 1 gram: polyunsaturated fat;
- 61 grams: carbohydrates;
- 2 grams: dietary fiber;
- 243 milligrams: sodium;
- 10 grams: protein;

223. Napoleon Of Tuna With A Mosaic Salad

Serving: Four servings | Prep: | Cook: | Ready in: 30mins

Ingredients

- The salad:
- 1 ½ tablespoons lemon juice
- ¼ cup olive oil
- ½ teaspoon salt
- 1 teaspoon freshly ground pepper
- 2 artichoke hearts, cooked, cleaned and cut into 1/8-inch cubes
- 1 large, ripe tomato, peeled, seeded and cut into 1/8-inch cubes
- 4 large white mushrooms, cleaned, stemmed and cut into 1/8-inch cubes
- 1 small ripe avocado, peeled and cut into 1/8-inch cubes
- ¼ cup nicoise olives, pitted and coarsely chopped
- 2 ½ tablespoons chopped chives
- The napoleon of tuna:
- 1 10-ounce piece of fresh tuna, about 1 inch thick
- 1 tablespoon olive oil
- 6 slices good quality white sandwich bread, crusts removed, toasted and halved
- 1 clove garlic, peeled
- 4 tufts mache lettuce, rinsed and dried

Direction

- In a small bowl, whisk together the lemon juice, olive oil, salt and pepper. Put the artichoke hearts, tomato, mushrooms, avocado, olives and chives in a large glass or ceramic bowl, toss with half the dressing and set aside.
- Preheat the broiler. Brush the tuna with the olive oil. Place under the broiler, 4 inches from the heat and broil until rare at center, about 3 to 4 minutes per side. Brush both sides of the tuna steak with the remaining dressing. Refrigerate until cold.
- To assemble the napoleon, rub the toast with the garlic clove and discard the clove. With a sharp knife cut the tuna steak on an angle into 12 thin slices. Cover each piece of toast with one layer of sliced tuna; trim the edges. Stack three slices of toast to make each napoleon.
- Put each napoleon in the center of a serving plate. Spread a layer of the salad on top of each napoleon. Garnish with a tuft of mache.

Nutrition Information

- 439: calories;
- 0 grams: trans fat;
- 17 grams: monounsaturated fat;
- 31 grams: carbohydrates;
- 7 grams: dietary fiber;
- 5 grams: sugars;
- 25 grams: protein;

- 4 grams: saturated fat;
- 3 grams: polyunsaturated fat;
- 626 milligrams: sodium;

224. New Potato, Red Pepper And Chive Salad

Serving: 4 servings | Prep: | Cook: | Ready in: 25mins

Ingredients

- 2 pounds new potatoes
- 1 red pepper
- For the dressing:
- 1 tablespoon Dijon mustard
- 1 clove garlic
- 2 to 3 tablespoons Balsamic vinegar (or to taste)
- Coarse salt and freshly ground pepper to taste
- ¾ cup extra-virgin olive oil
- 1 bunch fresh chives, minced

Direction

- Steam the potatoes until tender (about 20 minutes).
- While the potatoes are cooking, cut the pepper into quarters, remove the stem and seeds and place the pepper face down on a broiling rack. Broil until skin is charred. Place in a paper bag a few minutes, then peel off the skin. Cut the pepper into dice.
- Make the dressing. Place the mustard in a bowl large enough to hold the potatoes. Peel the garlic and crush it into the mustard with a fork. Add the vinegar, salt and pepper. Gradually beat in the olive oil, creating an emulsion.
- When the potatoes are cooked, remove the garlic from the dressing. Add the potatoes and diced pepper and toss thoroughly. Add the chives and serve the salad at room temperature. Correct seasoning just before serving.

Nutrition Information

- 557: calories;
- 41 grams: fat;
- 0 grams: trans fat;
- 44 grams: carbohydrates;
- 5 grams: protein;
- 734 milligrams: sodium;
- 6 grams: dietary fiber;
- 30 grams: monounsaturated fat;
- 4 grams: polyunsaturated fat;

225. Nina Simonds's Broiled Halibut With Miso Glaze

Serving: 4 servings | Prep: | Cook: | Ready in: 15mins

Ingredients

- 1 teaspoon grated ginger
- 2 tablespoons mirin
- 3 tablespoons mellow white miso
- Vegetable oil for brushing pan
- 1 3/4-pound halibut fillet, cut into four pieces

Direction

- In small bowl, combine ginger, mirin and miso, and mix until smooth. Rub on flesh side of fish pieces. Marinate 30 minutes.
- Heat broiler. Brush broiling pan with oil. Lay fish in pan, skin side down, and broil for 7 to 9 minutes, until flesh flakes and glaze bubbles and browns. Serve with steamed sticky rice and sauteed greens.

Nutrition Information

- 243: calories;
- 6 grams: fat;
- 1 gram: sugars;
- 0 grams: trans fat;
- 3 grams: monounsaturated fat;
- 4 grams: carbohydrates;

- 38 grams: protein;
- 610 milligrams: sodium;

226. Ninh Hoah (Skewered Vietnamese Meatballs)

Serving: 6 first-course servings | Prep: | Cook: | Ready in: 20mins

Ingredients

- 1 pound ground pork
- ½ teaspoon freshly ground pepper
- 3 stalks lemongrass, tough outer leaves discarded and ends trimmed, minced
- 6 cloves garlic, minced
- 2 medium shallots, minced
- 1 tablespoon granulated sugar
- 2 ½ teaspoons cornstarch
- 1 tablespoon fish sauce
- 6 wooden or bamboo skewers, soaked in hot water for 10 minutes
- Lettuce leaves for garnish

Direction

- In a medium bowl, mix the pork, pepper, lemongrass, garlic, shallots, sugar, cornstarch and fish sauce. Cover and refrigerate for at least 4 hours and up to 12.
- Using your hands, divide the meat mixture into 18 equal portions and roll into individual balls. Gently push 3 meatballs onto each skewer.
- Preheat the broiler or a grill. Broil or grill the meatballs, turning once, until uniformly brown and crisp, about 4 to 5 minutes per side. Transfer to a serving platter lined with lettuce and serve with peanut sauce (see recipe) on the side.

227. Oatmeal Crème Brûlée With Almond And Orange

Serving: 6 servings | Prep: | Cook: | Ready in: 1hours30mins

Ingredients

- Butter for pans
- 1 cup cooked oatmeal
- 2 tablespoons light brown sugar
- 2 teaspoons freshly grated orange zest
- 2 cups heavy cream
- ½ cup granulated sugar, more for topping
- 1 cup blanched almonds, toasted and chopped
- 6 large egg yolks

Direction

- Preheat oven to 325 degrees. Lightly butter six small ramekins or brûlée dishes. Mix oatmeal, brown sugar and 1 teaspoon zest together. Divide among ramekins; smooth surface of mixture.
- In medium saucepan over medium heat, combine cream, granulated sugar, almonds and remaining orange zest. Heat, stirring frequently, about 4 minutes or until mixture is hot and sugar has dissolved (do not boil). Turn off heat and let infuse 10 minutes.
- In a medium bowl, whisk egg yolks. Strain cream mixture into egg yolks, whisking constantly; discard solids. Ladle cream and egg mixture into ramekins atop oatmeal. Transfer to a baking dish and pour in enough warm water to come halfway up sides of ramekins.
- Bake 40 to 50 minutes, until custards jiggle slightly when dish is moved and center is slightly runny; be careful not to overcook. Remove from water bath and cool. Refrigerate at least 2 hours or overnight.
- When ready to serve, evenly sprinkle each ramekin with about 1 tablespoon granulated sugar. Using a kitchen torch or under very hot broiler, carefully caramelize sugar until amber

brown. Serve immediately or chill again, uncovered, up to 4 hours.

Nutrition Information

- 527: calories;
- 5 grams: polyunsaturated fat;
- 15 grams: carbohydrates;
- 3 grams: dietary fiber;
- 6 grams: sugars;
- 0 grams: trans fat;
- 19 grams: monounsaturated fat;
- 22 grams: saturated fat;
- 11 grams: protein;
- 46 milligrams: sodium;
- 49 grams: fat;

228. Olivada

Serving: 6 servings | Prep: | Cook: | Ready in: 15mins

Ingredients

- 1 red pepper
- 1 cup Kalamata olives
- ½ red onion
- 1 clove garlic
- 1 rib celery
- 2 tablespoons balsamic vinegar
- 1 tablespoon oregano
- ½ cup extra-virgin olive oil

Direction

- Prepare the broiler. Char the red pepper, turning to cook on all sides. Let cool slightly, tear off blackened skin and remove seeds and veins.
- While pepper is roasting, pit the olives. Peel onion and garlic, trim celery and chop in large pieces.
- Combine all ingredients in food processor. Pulse until mixture is spreadable.
- Serve with bread or crackers.

Nutrition Information

- 202: calories;
- 20 grams: fat;
- 3 grams: saturated fat;
- 15 grams: monounsaturated fat;
- 2 grams: sugars;
- 5 grams: carbohydrates;
- 1 gram: protein;
- 155 milligrams: sodium;

229. One Pot French Onion Soup With Garlic Gruyère Croutons

Serving: 8 servings | Prep: | Cook: | Ready in: 5hours

Ingredients

- ¼ cup extra-virgin olive oil
- 4 pounds oxtail or beef shoulder, cut into 1- or 2-inch pieces
- Salt
- 8 medium onions
- 4 celery stalks, coarsely chopped
- 4 medium carrots, peeled and coarsely chopped
- 2 bay leaves
- 4 thyme sprigs
- 8 tablespoons (1 stick) unsalted butter
- Black pepper
- 1 cup port wine
- Lemon juice, to taste, optional
- 6 ounces baguette loaf, cut into 1/2-inch-thick slices
- 2 garlic cloves, halved
- 8 ounces Gruyère cheese

Direction

- Heat the oil in a 6-quart Dutch oven over high heat. Add the oxtail (or beef shoulder) in a single layer (work in batches, if necessary to

avoid crowding the pan), and sear until the undersides are brown (do not turn). Season generously with salt and transfer to a plate.
- Coarsely chop two of the onions; add to the pot, along with the celery, carrots, bay leaves and thyme. Lower heat to medium and cook, stirring occasionally, until vegetables are soft and beginning to caramelize, about 10 minutes. Return the beef to the pot. Pour in 8 cups water. Simmer mixture gently until the meat is very tender, 2 1/2 to 3 hours.
- Transfer beef to a bowl to cool for another use. Strain liquid into a bowl over a fine-mesh sieve; press gently on the solids with the back of a spatula to extract as much flavor as possible. Discard the solids; you should have about 10 cups broth (add water if necessary to equal 10 cups).
- Halve the remaining 6 onions through the root end, then peel and thinly slice them lengthwise. Melt the butter in the bottom of the Dutch oven over medium heat. Add the onions and cook, tossing occasionally, until deep golden-brown and caramelized, 45 minutes to 1 hour. Season with 1 teaspoon salt and black pepper. Pour in the port and cook, scraping up any browned bits from the bottom of the pan, for 3 minutes. Pour in the broth and simmer mixture over low heat for 30 minutes. Season with salt and lemon juice, if desired. (For a smaller group, you could refrigerate some of the soup and reheat it later.)
- While the broth simmers, heat the oven to 350 degrees. Arrange the bread slices on a baking sheet and toast until golden, about 12 minutes. Rub the garlic halves over the surface of the bread.
- Heat the broiler and arrange a rack 4 to 6 inches from the flame. Using a cheese slicer, thinly slice 3 ounces of Gruyère. Coarsely grate the remaining cheese. Float the broiled bread over the surface of the hot soup. Layer the cheese slices over the bread; scatter the grated cheese over it. Transfer the Dutch oven to the oven and broil until cheese is golden and bubbling, 3 to 5 minutes (watch to see that it does not burn).
- To serve, use kitchen shears or scissors to cut the bread and cheese into portions. Ladle soup, bread and cheese into individual bowls.

Nutrition Information

- 748: calories;
- 28 grams: carbohydrates;
- 4 grams: dietary fiber;
- 8 grams: sugars;
- 59 grams: protein;
- 1104 milligrams: sodium;
- 1 gram: trans fat;
- 3 grams: polyunsaturated fat;
- 42 grams: fat;
- 19 grams: monounsaturated fat;

230. Orange Glazed Pork

Serving: 2 servings | Prep: | Cook: |Ready in: 20mins

Ingredients

- 8 ounces pork tenderloin
- ½ teaspoon ground coriander
- 1 ½ teaspoons fresh rosemary or 1/2 teaspoon dried
- ½ teaspoon ground ginger
- ¼ cup orange juice concentrate
- Freshly ground black pepper to taste

Direction

- If using broiler, turn it on and cover broiler pan with aluminum foil.
- Wash and dry pork, and cut into four equal pieces.
- In a bowl just large enough to hold the pork, combine the coriander, rosemary, ginger and orange juice, and season with pepper. Add the pork, and turn to coat well on all sides.
- If using stove-top grill, prepare.

- Broil or grill pork until brown on all sides, basting with marinade, for 10 to 12 minutes, until just pink inside.

Nutrition Information

- 155: calories;
- 1 gram: polyunsaturated fat;
- 0 grams: dietary fiber;
- 2 grams: monounsaturated fat;
- 3 grams: sugars;
- 24 grams: protein;
- 60 milligrams: sodium;
- 4 grams: carbohydrates;

231. Oven Baked Tomatoes

Serving: 4 servings | Prep: | Cook: | Ready in: 15mins

Ingredients

- 4 red ripe, unblemished tomatoes, about 1 3/4 pounds
- Salt to taste if desired
- Freshly ground pepper to taste
- 2 tablespoons olive oil
- ¼ teaspoon fresh or dried chopped rosemary

Direction

- Preheat broiler to high.
- Cut away core of each tomato. Bring quantity of water to a boil. Add tomatoes and let stand about 30 seconds or slightly longer until skin can be pulled away easily.
- Cut each tomato lengthwise in half and set aside. Place each tomato, round side down, on clean cloth. Pull up edges of cloth to make bag to enclose each tomato half, one at a time, evenly. Squeeze bag gently to extract most of liquid and shape into balls.
- Arrange each tomato ball, round side up, in one layer in baking dish. Sprinkle with salt and pepper. Blend oil and rosemary and brush the tomatoes with mixture. Place under the broiler for 3 to 5 minutes.

Nutrition Information

- 83: calories;
- 7 grams: fat;
- 1 gram: protein;
- 5 grams: carbohydrates;
- 2 grams: dietary fiber;
- 3 grams: sugars;
- 303 milligrams: sodium;

232. Oven Dried Tomato And Zucchini Salad

Serving: Four servings | Prep: | Cook: | Ready in: 3hours30mins

Ingredients

- 5 teaspoons olive oil
- ½ teaspoon orange oil
- 16 plum tomatoes, cored and halved lengthwise
- 6 medium zucchini, trimmed, halved lengthwise and cut across into 1-inch pieces
- 4 teaspoons balsamic vinegar
- 2 teaspoons kosher salt
- Freshly ground pepper to taste
- 1 teaspoon chopped fresh thyme
- 4 teaspoons chopped fresh basil
- ½ cup crumbled goat cheese

Direction

- Preheat the oven to 275 degrees. Combine 2 teaspoons olive oil and the orange oil in a small bowl. Brush the tomatoes with the oil mixture lightly on all sides and place, cut side down on 2 baking sheets. Bake until reduced to one-third of their original size, about 3 hours; tomatoes should still be plump.

- Heat 1 teaspoon olive oil in a large, nonstick skillet over medium heat. Add the zucchini and saute until crisp-tender, about 5 minutes. Place in a large bowl and toss in the tomatoes. In another bowl, whisk together the vinegar, remaining olive oil, salt, pepper, thyme and basil. Add to the vegetables and toss.
- Preheat the broiler. Place the mixture in a shallow gratin dish or pie plate. Sprinkle with the goat cheese and broil until melted. Divide among 4 plates and serve.

Nutrition Information

- 218: calories;
- 4 grams: saturated fat;
- 0 grams: trans fat;
- 6 grams: dietary fiber;
- 21 grams: carbohydrates;
- 12 grams: fat;
- 1 gram: polyunsaturated fat;
- 15 grams: sugars;
- 10 grams: protein;
- 1082 milligrams: sodium;

233. Oysters With Bacon And Horseradish

Serving: 4 servings | Prep: | Cook: | Ready in: 30mins

Ingredients

- 4 ounces finely diced slab bacon
- 2 tablespoons minced onion
- 1 tablespoon flour
- ½ teaspoon dried thyme
- 1 cup dry white wine
- 1 ½ teaspoons bottled white horseradish
- Salt and freshly ground pepper to taste
- 12 oysters on the half shell
- 2 teaspoons dry breadcrumbs

Direction

- Put the bacon in a skillet and cook over medium heat until crisp and browned. Remove the bacon from the skillet, leaving the fat in the pan. Drain the bacon on paper towels and reserve.
- Add the onion to the skillet and saute in the bacon fat until tender and golden. Stir in the flour and thyme, then whisk in the wine. Cook, whisking constantly, until the mixture is smooth and thick. Stir in the horseradish and the bacon and season to taste with salt and pepper.
- Spread this mixture on top of each oyster. Sprinkle with breadcrumbs. The recipe can be prepared in advance up to this point and refrigerated until just before serving.
- Preheat a broiler. Arrange the oysters with their topping on a baking sheet. Put under the broiler and broil until lightly browned and bubbling, three to five minutes. Serve at once.

Nutrition Information

- 303: calories;
- 15 grams: fat;
- 5 grams: saturated fat;
- 6 grams: monounsaturated fat;
- 1 gram: sugars;
- 18 grams: protein;
- 0 grams: dietary fiber;
- 3 grams: polyunsaturated fat;
- 13 grams: carbohydrates;
- 571 milligrams: sodium;

234. Oysters With Miso Glaze

Serving: 4 to 6 servings | Prep: | Cook: | Ready in: 30mins

Ingredients

- 2 dozen oysters on the half shell, juices reserved
- Clam juice or fish stock, as needed

- 1 ½ tablespoons unsalted butter
- ½ cup minced shallots
- 4 teaspoons flour
- 1 tablespoon lemon juice
- 1 tablespoon red miso paste
- 1 cup heavy cream
- Salt and freshly ground white pepper
- ½ cup fine bread crumbs

Direction

- Arrange oysters on a baking sheet, using crumpled foil or rock salt to keep them steady. A large madeleine pan covered in foil is an excellent alternative. Measure the oyster juices and, if needed, add enough clam juice or fish stock to make 1/2 cup. Heat broiler.
- In a saucepan, melt butter over low heat. Add shallots and sauté until soft. Whisk in flour, cook briefly and add oyster juice and lemon juice, whisking until blended. Whisk in miso, then gradually whisk in cream. Cook 3 to 4 minutes. Season with salt and pepper. Mix in crumbs.
- Spoon mixture on oysters, covering them completely. Broil 5 minutes until glazed and bubbling. Serve.

Nutrition Information

- 382: calories;
- 23 grams: fat;
- 0 grams: trans fat;
- 22 grams: protein;
- 634 milligrams: sodium;
- 12 grams: saturated fat;
- 6 grams: monounsaturated fat;
- 3 grams: sugars;
- 1 gram: dietary fiber;

235. Paillard Of Portobello Mushroom Glazed With Balsamic Vinegar

Serving: 4 servings | Prep: | Cook: | Ready in: 1hours

Ingredients

- 2 tablespoons plus 2 teaspoons porcini-infused olive oil or extra-virgin olive oil
- 2 tablespoons balsamic vinegar
- 2 tablespoons minced shallot
- 2 cloves garlic, minced
- ¾ teaspoon minced rosemary
- ¾ teaspoon kosher salt
- 4 large (6-inch diameter) portobello mushrooms, stems removed
- 2 cups veal stock
- 1 tablespoon minced parsley

Direction

- In a very large bowl, whisk together 2 tablespoons of the oil, the vinegar, shallot, garlic, rosemary and salt. Thoroughly coat the mushrooms in the mixture and leave to marinate for 20 minutes.
- Preheat the broiler. Transfer mushrooms to a baking pan that has sides at least 3/4-inch high and is large enough to hold the mushrooms in a single layer. Broil the mushrooms, turning them once, until they are nicely browned and tender, about 15 to 20 minutes.
- Transfer the mushrooms to a platter and keep warm. Place the baking pan on top of the stove and add the stock and simmer over medium-high heat, stirring constantly, until the stock is thickened and reduced to about 1/3 cup.
- Remove from the heat, stir in the remaining 2 teaspoons of porcini oil and the parsley and pour the sauce over the mushrooms. Serve immediately.

Nutrition Information

- 127: calories;

- 1 gram: dietary fiber;
- 0 grams: trans fat;
- 7 grams: carbohydrates;
- 4 grams: protein;
- 532 milligrams: sodium;
- 9 grams: fat;

236. Pan Fried Pizza

Serving: At least 4 servings | Prep: | Cook: | Ready in: 2hours

Ingredients

- 2 cups all-purpose or bread flour, more as needed
- ¾ teaspoon instant yeast
- 1 teaspoon coarse salt
- 3 tablespoons extra virgin olive oil, more for cooking
- About 2 cups any light, fresh tomato sauce, warmed
- Sliced mozzarella to taste
- Salt and black pepper
- Prosciutto slices and basil leaves for topping (optional)

Direction

- Combine flour, yeast and salt in a food processor. Turn machine on and add 1/2 cup water and 2 tablespoons oil through feed tube. Process for about 30 seconds, adding more water, a tablespoon or so at a time, until mixture forms a ball and is slightly sticky to the touch. (If mixture becomes too sticky, add flour a tablespoon at a time.)
- Put one tablespoon olive oil in a bowl and turn dough ball in it. Cover bowl with plastic wrap and let rise until dough doubles in size, 1 to 2 hours. When dough is ready, re-form into a ball and divide it into 4 pieces; roll each piece into a ball. Place each piece on a lightly floured surface, sprinkle with a little flour, and cover with plastic wrap or a towel. Let rest until each puffs slightly, about 20 minutes.
- When ready to cook, press one ball into about a 10-inch round. Use a little flour, if needed, to prevent sticking and a rolling pin, if desired. Film a 10-inch skillet with olive oil and turn heat to medium. When oil shimmers, put dough in pan and adjust heat so it browns evenly without burning. (If dough puffs up unevenly in spots, push bubbles down.)
- Turn dough, then top browned side with tomato sauce, cheese, a bit of salt and pepper, and, if you like, prosciutto and/or basil leaves. If top is now heavily laden, cover pan and continue cooking, or run it under broiler, just until toppings become hot. With only a couple of toppings, just cook until bottom browns. Repeat with remaining dough; serve hot, warm or at room temperature.

237. Panqueque

Serving: Serves 6 to 12 | Prep: | Cook: | Ready in: 9hours20mins

Ingredients

- 1 cup flour
- 2 teaspoons sugar
- ½ teaspoon salt
- 4 large eggs
- 1 ¼ cups milk
- 1 tablespoon butter, more as needed
- 1 ¼ cups dulce de leche
- Sugar for sprinkling
- 1 pint vanilla ice cream

Direction

- In a medium bowl, sift together the flour, sugar and salt. In another bowl, beat together the eggs and milk. Stir in the flour mixture until smooth. Cover and let rest at room temperature for 30 to 60 minutes.

- Place a 7-inch crepe pan or nonstick skillet over medium heat. Melt 1 teaspoon butter to grease the pan; then ladle in 3 tablespoons batter, tilting the pan as you pour to coat the bottom. When it starts to brown, after about 30 seconds, flip and cook just until firm, 10 to 15 seconds. Use butter as necessary to keep the batter from sticking. Transfer to a plate to cool.
- Spread 1 tablespoons dulce de leche two-thirds of the way from the bottom to the top of each crepe. Fold the left and right sides over by 1 inches and then loosely roll up the crepe from bottom to top, finishing with the top flap of the crepe tucked under. The rolled crepes can be covered and refrigerated for up to 8 hours.
- To serve, preheat a broiler and arrange the panqueque on a broiling dish. Sprinkle with sugar and heat until caramelized. Place 1 or 2 crepes on each plate and top with vanilla ice cream.

Nutrition Information

- 280: calories;
- 0 grams: trans fat;
- 39 grams: carbohydrates;
- 8 grams: protein;
- 5 grams: saturated fat;
- 1 gram: dietary fiber;
- 27 grams: sugars;
- 228 milligrams: sodium;
- 10 grams: fat;
- 3 grams: monounsaturated fat;

238. Panzanella With Grilled Eggplant

Serving: 6 servings | Prep: | Cook: | Ready in: 40mins

Ingredients

- A 3/4-pound eggplant, sliced 1/2-inch thick
- A 6-inch piece French or Italian bread, crusts removed
- 2 large cloves garlic, split
- 1 ½ pounds ripe tomatoes, coarsely chopped
- ½ cup chopped sweet onion
- ¼ cup red wine vinegar
- 4 tablespoons extra-virgin olive oil
- 2 tablespoons slivered fresh basil leaves
- Salt and freshly ground black pepper

Direction

- Preheat grill or broiler. Grill or broil eggplant slices until nicely browned, turning once to brown both sides. Coarsely chop slices; set aside.
- Slice the bread one-half-inch thick and lightly toast the slices on the grill or under the broiler. Rub each slice with the cut side of the garlic. Dice the bread and mince the garlic.
- Combine tomatoes, onion and eggplant in bowl. Add minced garlic. Fold in vinegar and olive oil. Fold in bread, mixing well so it becomes moistened with vinegar, oil and juice of tomatoes. Fold in basil and season salad with salt and pepper. Set aside at least one-half-hour before serving.

Nutrition Information

- 131: calories;
- 486 milligrams: sodium;
- 9 grams: fat;
- 1 gram: polyunsaturated fat;
- 11 grams: carbohydrates;
- 5 grams: sugars;
- 2 grams: protein;
- 7 grams: monounsaturated fat;
- 3 grams: dietary fiber;

239. Parmesan Cheese Croutons

Serving: 4 servings | Prep: | Cook: | Ready in: 10mins

Ingredients

- 1 small loaf of french bread, like a baguette
- 1 large garlic clove, peeled
- 2 tablespoons olive oil
- 4 tablespoons Parmesan cheese or Romano

Direction

- Preheat broiler.
- Rub the outside of the bread with the garlic. Cut the bread into slices about 1/4-inch thick.
- Arrange the slices on a baking sheet and brush one side with oil.
- Place under the broiler until lightly browned on one side. Turn and repeat.
- Top each crouton with the Parmesan cheese. Place under the broiler until golden brown.

Nutrition Information

- 270: calories;
- 4 grams: saturated fat;
- 6 grams: monounsaturated fat;
- 1 gram: dietary fiber;
- 3 grams: sugars;
- 11 grams: protein;
- 12 grams: fat;
- 0 grams: trans fat;
- 30 grams: carbohydrates;
- 534 milligrams: sodium;

240. Parmesan Cheese Hard Rolls

Serving: 4 pieces | Prep: | Cook: | Ready in: 10mins

Ingredients

- 2 oval-shaped, crusty (kaiser) hard rolls
- 2 tablespoons melted butter
- 8 teaspoons freshly grated Parmesan cheese

Direction

- Preheat broiler to high.
- Split each roll in half sandwich-style. Brush with equal amounts of melted butter. Sprinkle each roll half with 2 teaspoons grated cheese.
- Arrange roll halves on a baking sheet, cut side up. Place under broiler several inches from the source of heat and broil until golden brown on top, 2 minutes or longer.

Nutrition Information

- 171: calories;
- 15 grams: carbohydrates;
- 0 grams: trans fat;
- 3 grams: monounsaturated fat;
- 6 grams: protein;
- 285 milligrams: sodium;
- 9 grams: fat;
- 5 grams: saturated fat;
- 1 gram: sugars;

241. Parsleyed Rack Of Lamb (Carre D'Agneau Persille)

Serving: 4 to 6 servings | Prep: | Cook: | Ready in: 30mins

Ingredients

- 2 racks of lamb, about 2 1/2 pounds combined weight
- Salt to taste if desired
- Freshly ground pepper to taste
- 4 tablespoons butter plus butter for greasing a baking dish
- ½ cup bread crumbs
- 3 tablespoons chopped parsley
- 1 clove garlic, finely minced
- 1 shallot, finely minced
- 1 teaspoon olive oil
- Sauce forestiere (see recipe)

Direction

- Have butcher saw off chine bone (flat, continuous bone at top of ribs), leaving meat exposed.
- Preheat broiler to high. If oven is heated separately, preheat it also to 500 degrees.
- Using fingers and sharp knife, pull and slice off top thick layer of fat from racks of lamb. When ready, loins and ribs should be almost clean of fat. Hack off ends of ribs, leaving about 1 1/2 inches of ribs intact and extending from meat.
- Rub with butter baking dish large enough to hold racks of lamb in layer and close together. Place racks, meat side down, in dish and dot ribs with 2 tablespoons of butter.
- Meanwhile, combine bread crumbs, parlsey, garlic, shallot and olive oil in bowl.
- Place racks under broiler and cook 2 or 3 minutes. Turn and cook 2 or 3 minutes.
- Sprinkle meaty side of ribs with bread-crumb mixture. Melt remaining 2 tablespoons of butter and pour over ribs. Place in oven and bake 8 to 10 minutes, depending on degree of doneness desired. Slice and serve with sauce forestiere.

Nutrition Information

- 267: calories;
- 23 grams: fat;
- 8 grams: monounsaturated fat;
- 9 grams: carbohydrates;
- 1 gram: sugars;
- 7 grams: protein;
- 11 grams: saturated fat;
- 0 grams: trans fat;
- 2 grams: polyunsaturated fat;
- 164 milligrams: sodium;

242. Pear Gratin With Mascarpone Custard

Serving: 6 servings | Prep: | Cook: | Ready in: 1hours15mins

Ingredients

- The custard:
- 1 cup milk
- 2 egg yolks
- 1 cup sugar
- ¼ cup flour
- 1 cup mascarpone
- 3 cups heavy cream
- 1 teaspoon pure vanilla extract
- The gratin:
- 6 tablespoons unsalted butter
- 1 cup sugar
- 6 pears, peeled, halved lengthwise, cores removed
- 2 pieces candied ginger, minced (optional)

Direction

- To make the custard, heat the milk in a heavy saucepan until it is almost boiling. In a separate bowl, beat egg yolks until they are light and pale-colored. Beat sugar into the yolks, tablespoon by tablespoon. Add flour and beat until smooth. Add heated milk to the yolk mixture in a slow stream, beating constantly. Beat until smooth. Return the mixture to the saucepan and cook, stirring constantly, until mixture comes to a boil. Boil for 2 minutes. Remove from heat and chill.
- When the mixture is thoroughly chilled, remove from refrigerator and whisk until smooth. Fold the mascarpone into the mixture. In a separate bowl, beat the cream until medium-stiff and fold into the custard mixture. Stir in vanilla and chill until ready to use.
- To make the gratin, preheat the oven to 450 degrees. Melt the butter in a large cast-iron skillet over medium heat. Add sugar and stir

constantly until a golden brown caramel develops. Remove from heat.
- Arrange the pear halves, cut side down, on top of the caramel and scatter minced ginger, if desired, over the pears. Cover the pears with foil and bake for 15 minutes or until tender when pierced with a skewer.
- Place two pear halves in each of six individual gratin dishes. Divide the caramel among the dishes. Pour about 1 cup of custard into each gratin dish, covering the pears. Place the gratin dishes on a baking sheet for easier handling and bake for 5 minutes. Remove from oven.
- Change the oven setting to broil. Place gratins on the upper rack of the oven and broil carefully until the custard bubbles and browns, about 1 1/2 minutes. Watch very carefully; do not burn.

Nutrition Information

- 1067: calories;
- 208 milligrams: sodium;
- 71 grams: fat;
- 43 grams: saturated fat;
- 0 grams: trans fat;
- 3 grams: polyunsaturated fat;
- 106 grams: carbohydrates;
- 8 grams: protein;
- 20 grams: monounsaturated fat;
- 6 grams: dietary fiber;
- 91 grams: sugars;

243. Pears With Raspberries And Meringue

Serving: 6 servings | Prep: | Cook: | Ready in: 1hours

Ingredients

- 3 pears, about 1 1/2 pounds
- 5 tablespoons lemon juice
- 3 cups water
- 1 ¾ cups sugar
- 1 vanilla bean or 1 teaspoon pure vanilla extract
- 3 cups whole red, ripe raspberries, or 3 cups strawberries cut in half
- 3 tablespoons orange juice
- 2 egg whites

Direction

- Peel the pears using a swivel-bladed paring knife. Cut away the stems.
- Combine enough water to cover the pears when added and 4 tablespoons lemon juice and add the pears as they are peeled.
- Cut the pears lengthwise in half. Scoop out the cores, and a little of the meat, of each half to form a nice-sized cavity.
- Combine the 3 cups water with 1 1/2 cups of the sugar and the vanilla bean or extract. Bring to the boil and add the pear halves and the remaining 1 tablespoon lemon juice. When the mixture returns to the boil reduce the heat and cook about 20 minutes or until pears are tender when pierced with a fork. Remove the pears and reserve 1 cup of the cooking liquid. Let the pears cool.
- Put half of the berries in the container of a food processor or electric blender and blend while gradually adding the reserved 1 cup of pear-cooking liquid and the orange juice. This mixture may be used as is, but it is best to put it through a fine sieve of the sort known in French kitchens as a chinois, pressing to extract as much liquid as possible. There should be about 1 1/3 cups.
- Fill the cavity of each pear with about 3 of the remaining berries. Quickly invert the pears on an ovenproof serving dish.
- Preheat the broiler.
- Beat the egg whites until stiff and gradually beat in the remaining 1/4 cup sugar. Continue beating until stiff. Spoon the resulting meringue into a pastry bag outfitted with a star-shaped tube (No. 3B). Squeeze out the meringue in star patterns over the pears. Pour the sauce around the pears. Place the dish

under the broiler about 4 inches from the source of heat. Broil briefly until the tips of the stars are browned. Garnish around the sauce with a circle of the remaining raspberries.

Nutrition Information

- 321: calories;
- 0 grams: polyunsaturated fat;
- 81 grams: carbohydrates;
- 5 grams: dietary fiber;
- 73 grams: sugars;
- 2 grams: protein;
- 22 milligrams: sodium;

244. Penne With Peppers And Cream

Serving: 4 servings | Prep: | Cook: | Ready in: 45mins

Ingredients

- 2 large sweet red peppers
- 1 large clove garlic, minced
- 2 oil-packed sun-dried tomatoes, well drained and minced
- Pinch hot red pepper flakes
- 2 tablespoons heavy cream
- salt
- ½ pound penne
- 2 tablespoons freshly grated Parmesan cheese

Direction

- Char peppers under a broiler or over an open flame. Place charred peppers in a plastic bag and keep it closed for a few minutes, then remove peppers and scrape off all the skin. Core, seed and chop peppers coarsely.
- Bring a large pot of water to a boil for the pasta.
- Heat a large nonstick skillet, add the peppers, garlic and sun-dried tomatoes and cook over medium heat until the peppers are tender, about five minutes.
- Stir in the pepper flakes and cream and cook a few minutes, until the cream has thickened slightly. Season to taste with salt and remove from the heat.
- When the water has boiled, add a generous pinch of salt and the penne. Cook the penne until it is al dente, about eight minutes. Drain it well and add it to the skillet.
- Return the skillet to the heat and cook, stirring for a minute or two, until the ingredients are well combined. Stir in the cheese and serve.

Nutrition Information

- 295: calories;
- 11 grams: protein;
- 1 gram: polyunsaturated fat;
- 2 grams: monounsaturated fat;
- 48 grams: carbohydrates;
- 4 grams: dietary fiber;
- 5 grams: sugars;
- 363 milligrams: sodium;
- 6 grams: fat;
- 3 grams: saturated fat;

245. Pepper Pasta With Crab (Fearrington House)

Serving: 4 servings | Prep: | Cook: | Ready in: 30mins

Ingredients

- 1 red ripe unblemished sweet red pepper
- ½ pound lump crab meat
- ½ cup raw or cooked ham, preferably country ham, cut into small cubes
- 1 ½ cups heavy cream
- 2 tablespoons jalapeno pepper sauce (see recipe), or use a bottled spicy Mexican table sauce
- ½ cup finely chopped scallions, green part and all

- ½ cup freshly shelled or frozen green peas
- 2 tablespoons freshly grated Parmesan cheese
- 1 tablespoon finely chopped fresh coriander
- Salt to taste, if desired
- Freshly ground pepper to taste
- 10 ounces fresh fettucine, or 3/4 pound dried

Direction

- Preheat the broiler to high. Place the pepper under the broiler flame, turning the pepper often so that the skin is blistered and charred all over. Remove the pepper and hold it under cold running water while peeling away the charred skin. Cut the pepper in half. Cut away and discard the seeds, veins and core. Pat the pepper dry. Cut the halves into very thin strips. There should be about one cup. Set aside.
- Pick over the crab meat to remove all trace of shell and cartilage. Set aside.
- If raw ham is used, put it into a 9- or 10-inch nonstick skillet. Cook, briefly, stirring, about 30 seconds. If cooked ham is used, put it in the skillet. Add all but half a cup of the crab meat, the cream, jalapeno pepper sauce and scallions. Bring to a boil and let cook over relatively high heat about two minutes.
- If fresh peas are used, add them to the sauce. If frozen peas are used, put them in a sieve, pour boiling water over them and set aside. Cook the sauce with the fresh peas about one minute.
- Add the pepper strips, grated cheese and the remaining half-cup of crab meat and frozen peas if used. Add salt to taste. Cook, stirring until the crab is heated through. Sprinkle the sauce with the chopped fresh coriander and a generous grinding of black pepper.
- Meanwhile, bring enough water to the boil to cook the pasta and add salt to taste. Add the pasta and cook until tender, about three minutes or to the desired degree of doneness.
- Drain the pasta and toss it in the sauce. Spoon equal portions into four hot plates.

Nutrition Information

- 1172: calories;
- 21 grams: monounsaturated fat;
- 5 grams: sugars;
- 8290 milligrams: sodium;
- 61 grams: fat;
- 30 grams: saturated fat;
- 0 grams: trans fat;
- 49 grams: carbohydrates;
- 2 grams: dietary fiber;
- 103 grams: protein;

246. Pepper Shrimp

Serving: Eight servings | Prep: | Cook: | Ready in: 35mins

Ingredients

- ½ cup fruity red wine, such as Beaujolais or red zinfandel
- 1 8-ounce can tomato sauce
- 1 teaspoon dried chervil
- 1 tablespoon lemon juice
- 1 teaspoon dry mustard
- 1 teaspoon dried oregano
- Salt to taste
- 2 teaspoons pepper
- ½ cup olive oil
- 2 cloves garlic, minced
- ½ cup loosely packed flat-leaved parsley, chopped
- 2 pounds medium shrimps, peeled and deveined

Direction

- In a bowl, whisk together the wine, tomato sauce, chervil, lemon juice, mustard, oregano, salt and pepper.
- Heat the oil in a skillet and cook the minced garlic over medium heat for 1 minute. Add the tomato-sauce mixture and bring to a boil, then

- lower the heat and simmer the mixture, stirring occasionally, for 10 minutes.
- Remove from heat and set aside to cool for 5 minutes. Stir in chopped parsley.
- Place the shrimp in a single layer in a nonmetal baking dish. Pour the sauce over the shrimp and marinate, covered, for 3 hours at room temperature, or overnight in the refrigerator.
- Preheat the broiler. Broil the shrimps about 6 inches from the heat for 10 minutes or until cooked through, turning once.

Nutrition Information

- 226: calories;
- 0 grams: trans fat;
- 10 grams: monounsaturated fat;
- 4 grams: carbohydrates;
- 16 grams: protein;
- 2 grams: polyunsaturated fat;
- 779 milligrams: sodium;
- 15 grams: fat;
- 1 gram: sugars;

247. Pepper And Snow Pea Salad

Serving: 4 servings | Prep: | Cook: | Ready in: 10mins

Ingredients

- 2 sweet red peppers, about 3/4 pound
- Salt to taste if desired
- ¾ pound snow peas
- 1 small red onion, peeled
- 1 tablespoon imported mustard
- 2 tablespoons red-wine vinegar
- Freshly ground pepper to taste
- ¼ cup olive oil
- ¼ cup finely chopped parsley

Direction

- Preheat broiler to high or heat charcoal grill. Place peppers under broiler or on grill and cook on all sides until skin is well charred. When cool enough to handle split in half, core and discard charred skin.
- Cut peppers lengthwise into thin strips. There should be about 1 cup. Put strips in salad bowl.
- Bring enough water to a boil to cover peas when added. Add salt to taste. Add peas and let boil 2 minutes. Drain in sieve. Run cold water briefly over peas and drain. Add to salad bowl.
- Cut onion in half, cut each half crosswise into thin slice and add to bowl.
- Put mustard and vinegar in separate bowl and add salt and pepper. Start beating vigorously with whisk while adding oil. Stir in parsley.
- Pour sauce over the vegetables and toss.

Nutrition Information

- 190: calories;
- 7 grams: sugars;
- 504 milligrams: sodium;
- 0 grams: trans fat;
- 10 grams: monounsaturated fat;
- 13 grams: carbohydrates;
- 4 grams: protein;
- 14 grams: fat;
- 2 grams: polyunsaturated fat;

248. Pickled Green Beans

Serving: 1 pint | Prep: | Cook: | Ready in:

Ingredients

- 6 to 7 ounces green beans
- 1 teaspoon coriander seeds
- 1 teaspoon mustard seeds
- ¼ teaspoon black peppercorns
- 3 sprigs fresh dill
- 1 bay leaf

- ½ cup white wine vinegar
- ½ cup sherry vinegar
- ½ cup water
- 1 tablespoon raw brown (turbinado) sugar
- 1 teaspoon fine sea salt
- 1 large garlic clove, quartered

Direction

- Rinse green beans and break off stem ends. Put them into a pint jar, standing them up and squeezing as many into the jar as you can. There should be 1/2 inch of head space in the jar, so you may have to trim down some of the beans. Once you've cut them down to fit, take them out of the jar and sterilize the jar in a boiling water bath for 5 to 10 minutes. Using a jar grip, carefully remove the jar from the water and tip out all water.
- Place coriander seeds, mustard seeds, peppercorns and bay leaf in jar and fill with beans, standing them up in the jar. Push dill sprigs down into the jar.
- In a small saucepan, combine the vinegars, water, sugar, salt and garlic and bring to a boil. Reduce heat slightly and simmer 2 minutes. Pour into jar with green beans. The beans should be covered but there should still be 1/4 to 1/2 inch head space. Push garlic down into the jar. Seal jar and allow to cool, then refrigerate for up to 2 months. For best results wait 2 days before eating.

Nutrition Information

- 88: calories;
- 0 grams: polyunsaturated fat;
- 15 grams: carbohydrates;
- 3 grams: dietary fiber;
- 9 grams: sugars;
- 2 grams: protein;
- 656 milligrams: sodium;
- 1 gram: fat;

249. Pineapple Avocado Salsa

Serving: 2 1/2 cups | Prep: | Cook: | Ready in: 15mins

Ingredients

- ¼ ripe pineapple, peeled, cored and finely chopped (about 1 1/2 cups)
- 2 tablespoons fresh lime juice
- 1 medium or 1/2 large avocado, cut in small dice (about 1/2 cup)
- ½ medium jicama, cut in small dice (about 1 cup)
- 1 to 2 jalapeño or serrano chiles, to taste (or more, to taste)
- Salt to taste
- ¼ cup chopped cilantro

Direction

- Combine all the ingredients in a bowl and gently toss together, taking care not to mash the avocado. Allow to sit for 15 to 30 minutes before serving, then toss again.

Nutrition Information

- 120: calories;
- 5 grams: monounsaturated fat;
- 14 grams: carbohydrates;
- 4 grams: sugars;
- 2 grams: protein;
- 406 milligrams: sodium;
- 7 grams: dietary fiber;
- 1 gram: polyunsaturated fat;

250. Pineapple Rhubarb Salsa And Shad

Serving: 4 servings | Prep: | Cook: | Ready in: 30mins

Ingredients

- 2 tablespoons cooking oil
- ½ cup finely diced onion

- 1 pound fresh rhubarb, finely diced
- ½ cup pineapple juice
- ½ cup sugar
- 1 cup finely chopped fresh pineapple
- 1 teaspoon finely minced, seeded fresh jalapeno pepper
- Salt and freshly ground black pepper to taste
- 1 large shad fillet, about 1 1/2 pounds

Direction

- Preheat a broiler.
- Heat a tablespoon of the oil in a skillet, add the onion and saute over medium heat until softened and golden brown. Stir in the rhubarb, pineapple juice and sugar and cook over medium-low heat, stirring often, until the rhubarb is tender, about 10 minutes. Remove from heat and fold in the fresh pineapple and jalapeno pepper. Season to taste with salt and pepper and set aside.
- Brush the shad with the remaining oil and season with salt and pepper. Broil the shad under high heat until lightly browned and just cooked through, six to eight minutes. Do not turn the fish.
- Put the shad on a serving platter and spoon the rhubarb salsa in a band running the length of the fillet, then serve.

Nutrition Information

- 566: calories;
- 6 grams: saturated fat;
- 14 grams: monounsaturated fat;
- 42 grams: carbohydrates;
- 3 grams: dietary fiber;
- 34 grams: sugars;
- 953 milligrams: sodium;
- 31 grams: protein;
- 0 grams: trans fat;
- 8 grams: polyunsaturated fat;

251. Poached Eggs With Sorrel Sauce

Serving: Four to eight servings | Prep: | Cook: | Ready in: 35mins

Ingredients

- ¼ pound fresh sorrel
- 4 tablespoons butter
- 2 tablespoons flour
- 2 cups fresh or canned chicken broth
- 1 cup heavy cream
- Salt to taste, if desired
- Freshly ground pepper to taste
- ⅛ teaspoon freshly grated nutmeg
- Pinch of cayenne
- 8 cups water
- 2 tablespoons white-wine vinegar
- 8 eggs, at room temperature
- 8 thin slices white sandwich bread

Direction

- Pick over the sorrel. Discard any tough stems and blemished leaves. Rinse the leaves and pat them dry. Pack the leaves closely and cut them crosswise into very thin strips. This is called a chiffonade There should be about two cups or slightly more when loosely packed.
- Heat one tablespoon of the butter in a saucepan and, using a wire whisk, stir in the flour. When blended, add the broth, stirring rapidly with the whisk. Let simmer about 10 minutes or until reduced to about one and one-quarter cups. Stir in the cream, salt and pepper and bring to the boil. Let simmer about five minutes or until reduced to one and three-quarter cups.
- Meanwhile, heat one tablespoon of butter in a saucepan and add the sorrel. Stir until the sorrel is wilted and remove from the heat.
- Scrape the sorrel mixture into the sauce. Stir in the nutmeg and cayenne.
- Bring the water to the boil in a saucepan or deep skillet and add the vinegar. Carefully break the eggs into the simmering liquid,

keeping them separate. Let them simmer until the whites are firm and the yolks remain soft. Carefully scoop out each egg and let drain on absorbent paper toweling.
- Preheat the broiler.
- Using a three-inch biscuit cutter, cut out the center of each bread slice. Or, alternatively, trim the outside crusts from the bread and cut each slice into two triangles. Melt the remaining two tablespoons of butter and butter each piece of bread on both sides and place under the broiler until golden brown on both sides, turning once.
- Arrange one egg on each piece of round toast or two triangles and spoon an equal portion of the sauce over each serving.

Nutrition Information

- 367: calories;
- 3 grams: sugars;
- 16 grams: carbohydrates;
- 8 grams: monounsaturated fat;
- 2 grams: dietary fiber;
- 29 grams: fat;
- 0 grams: trans fat;
- 12 grams: protein;
- 1286 milligrams: sodium;

252. Poireaux Au Gratin (Leeks Au Gratin)

Serving: Six servings | Prep: | Cook: | Ready in: 45mins

Ingredients

- 3 pounds leeks, about 8 small leeks
- 2 tablespoons butter
- Salt, if desired
- Freshly ground pepper
- ⅛ teaspoon freshly grated nutmeg
- 1 cup heavy cream
- ½ cup freshly grated Parmesan cheese

Direction

- Trim off the stem end of each leek. Cut off enough of the green part to leave a main section of about seven inches. Split the leeks lengthwise in half. Cut the split leeks crosswise into one-and-onehalf-inch lengths. There should be about eight cups loosely packed. Rinse thoroughly in cold water. Drain.
- Put the leeks in a heavy skillet and add the butter, salt and pepper to taste and the nutmeg. Cook, stirring, about one minute. Add the cream and bring to the simmer. Cover and cook 15 minutes.
- Preheat broiler.
- Spoon the hot leeks into a baking and serving dish and smooth over the top. Sprinkle the top with cheese and place under the broiler until nicely glazed. Serve hot. If the dish is to be reheated, place it for 20 minutes in an oven that has been preheated to 350 degrees.

Nutrition Information

- 348: calories;
- 6 grams: monounsaturated fat;
- 34 grams: carbohydrates;
- 10 grams: sugars;
- 8 grams: protein;
- 655 milligrams: sodium;
- 22 grams: fat;
- 13 grams: saturated fat;
- 0 grams: trans fat;
- 1 gram: polyunsaturated fat;
- 4 grams: dietary fiber;

253. Polenta With Broccoli Rabe

Serving: 4 servings as main dish or 8 as a side | Prep: | Cook: | Ready in: 35mins

Ingredients

- 1 ½ pounds broccoli rabe
- 1 tablespoon olive oil
- 2 large cloves garlic, chopped fine
- ¼ cup raisins, packed
- ¼ cup pine nuts
- ¼ teaspoon or more crushed red pepper
- 5 cups water
- 1 cup instant polenta
- 6 tablespoons grated Parmigiano Reggiano
- ½ teaspoon salt (optional)

Direction

- Preheat broiler.
- Cut off and discard tough stems from rabe. Wash thoroughly and drain on paper towels. Cut into one-inch pieces.
- Heat oil in a nonstick skillet. Saute the garlic for 30 seconds. Stir in rabe and coat with oil. Cook over medium heat until it begins to soften.
- Stir in raisins, pine nuts and red pepper. Cover and cook 5 to 7 minutes.
- Meanwhile bring water to a boil, then reduce to a simmer. Slowly stir in polenta and stir constantly for several minutes, until mixture begins to thicken. Do not let mixture become so thick that it cannot be stirred.
- Stir in the cheese and salt. Stir in rabe and spoon into a shallow baking dish. Place under broiler for about 2 minutes, just until the top begins to brown. Watch carefully.

Nutrition Information

- 388: calories;
- 17 grams: protein;
- 16 grams: fat;
- 5 grams: saturated fat;
- 6 grams: monounsaturated fat;
- 4 grams: polyunsaturated fat;
- 47 grams: carbohydrates;
- 7 grams: dietary fiber;
- 8 grams: sugars;
- 365 milligrams: sodium;

254. Polenta With Vegetables And Tomato Sauce

Serving: 6 servings | Prep: | Cook: | Ready in: 45mins

Ingredients

- 12 ounces mushrooms
- 4 cloves garlic
- 4 teaspoons olive oil
- ½ pound onion
- 7 or 8 ears corn (2 cups kernels)
- 1 ½ pounds zucchini
- 1 tablespoon fresh oregano leaves
- 2 cups instant polenta
- 2 ½ pounds fully ripe tomatoes
- 6 ounces fresh Parmigiano Reggiano
- ¼ cup chopped parsley

Direction

- Wash, trim, dry and slice mushrooms (use food processor); peel and mince garlic.
- Heat 3 teaspoons of oil in a large nonstick pan. Add the mushrooms and garlic. Saute until the mushrooms begin to brown, stirring occasionally.
- Chop onion in food processor. Heat the remaining oil in a small nonstick pan and saute the onion until it begins to soften and brown.
- Shuck corn and steam for about 3 minutes.
- Scrub, trim and slice zucchini in food processor.
- Wash and chop oregano and add with the zucchini to the mushrooms and continue cooking over medium heat, five or six minutes, until zucchini is crisp but tender.
- Bring water to boil for polenta, following package directions.
- Wash, trim and slice the tomatoes in the food processor and add to onion; simmer until the rest of the dish is ready.
- Coarsely grate the cheese.

- Slowly add polenta to the boiling water and stir until mixture begins to thicken. It is ready when water is almost completely absorbed. Remove from heat and stir in half of the cheese. Then spoon immediately into large shallow baking dish, about 10 by 15 inches, and spread evenly.
- Remove enough corn from cob to make 2 cups and stir into zucchini mixture. Spoon over polenta and top with tomato sauce; sprinkle with remaining cheese. Either serve immediately or run under broiler (do not preheat) for a couple of minutes. Just before serving, sprinkle with parsley.

Nutrition Information

- 460: calories;
- 15 grams: sugars;
- 426 milligrams: sodium;
- 6 grams: saturated fat;
- 0 grams: trans fat;
- 8 grams: dietary fiber;
- 2 grams: polyunsaturated fat;
- 69 grams: carbohydrates;
- 21 grams: protein;
- 13 grams: fat;
- 5 grams: monounsaturated fat;

255. Pomegranate Glazed Lamb Meatballs

Serving: About 2 dozen meatballs, or about 8 servings | Prep: | Cook: | Ready in: 20mins

Ingredients

- 1 pound ground lamb
- 1 small clove garlic, minced
- ¾ teaspoon kosher salt
- ½ teaspoon finely grated orange zest
- ½ teaspoon black pepper
- Olive oil, for brushing
- 3 tablespoons pomegranate molasses
- Chopped fresh mint, as needed

Direction

- In a large bowl, knead together the lamb, garlic, salt, orange zest and pepper until combined. Form into 1-inch meatballs. Transfer to a foil-lined baking sheet and brush with oil.
- Heat the broiler. Run meatballs under the broiler until golden and just cooked through, about 5 minutes. Brush immediately with pomegranate molasses. Spear with toothpicks, sprinkle with mint and serve.

256. Pork Tenderloin With Sweet And Hot Mustard

Serving: 12 servings | Prep: | Cook: | Ready in: 30mins

Ingredients

- 4 pork tenderloins, about 8 ounces each
- 4 tablespoons olive oil
- ¼ tablespoon sherry vinegar
- ½ cup sweet and hot mustard
- 4 cloves garlic, peeled and quartered
- Freshly ground black pepper, to taste

Direction

- Wash and trim excess fat from tenderloins and dry.
- Beat the remaining ingredients together and pour into noncorrosive dish, which will hold the tenderloins.
- Place tenderloins in marinade, turning to coat both sides. Cover and refrigerate at least 2 hours or overnight.
- To cook, heat broiler and cover broiler pan with 2 layers of aluminum foil. Arrange tenderloins on foil and broil for 10 minutes on one side. Baste, turn and baste again and broil for 5 to 10 minutes longer, until tenderloins are barely pink in center.

- Boil remaining marinade. Slice tenderloins and pour marinade and pan juices over slices. Serve with polenta.

Nutrition Information

- 134: calories;
- 7 grams: fat;
- 1 gram: dietary fiber;
- 0 grams: sugars;
- 4 grams: monounsaturated fat;
- 15 grams: protein;
- 152 milligrams: sodium;

257. Pork With Orange Sauce

Serving: 4 servings | Prep: | Cook: |Ready in: 30mins

Ingredients

- 2 pounds country-style pork ribs, or boneless steaks cut from shoulder, about 3/4 to 1 inch thick
- Salt and pepper
- 1 ½ cups freshly squeezed orange juice
- ¼ teaspoon cayenne, or to taste
- 1 teaspoon ground cumin
- 1 shallot, minced
- Vinegar or fresh lemon or lime juice, if necessary
- 1 teaspoon grated orange rind
- ¼ cup chopped fresh parsley leaves

Direction

- Heat oven to 450 degrees or heat broiler, adjusting rack so that it is about 4 inches from heat source. Put an ovenproof skillet large enough to hold pork in one layer on stove top and turn heat to high. Sprinkle meat with salt and pepper. Brown meat quickly on both sides, then transfer skillet to oven or broiler.
- Meanwhile, combine orange juice, cayenne, cumin and shallots in a small saucepan and turn heat to medium. Cook, stirring, until it reduces to about 1/3 cup; taste and add salt as necessary, a touch more cayenne and cumin if you like, and some vinegar or lemon juice if sauce lacks acidity.
- If broiling, turn meat once; if roasting, don't bother. When meat is firm but not tough and a little pink in center (about 10 minutes if broiling, 15 if roasting), remove it to a platter. Combine orange rind with parsley. Spoon sauce over meat, then top with orange rind-parsley mixture. Serve.

258. Pork In Sweet Mustard Marinade

Serving: 2 servings | Prep: | Cook: |Ready in: 20mins

Ingredients

- ½ cup plain nonfat yogurt
- 1 tablespoon hot sweet mustard
- 1 tablespoon lemon juice
- 1 large clove garlic
- Freshly ground black pepper to taste
- 8 ounces pork tenderloin
- ⅛ teaspoon salt, optional

Direction

- Turn on broiler, if using.
- Combine yogurt and mustard in bowl large enough to hold pork.
- Squeeze in lemon juice; mince garlic, and add it and the pepper.
- Wash and dry pork, and cut into four pieces; marinade in mixture, turning to coat both sides well.
- Prepare stove-top grill, if using. Grill or broil pork about 8 to 10 minutes, turning once and basting with yogurt-mustard mixture before turning.
- Cook only until slightly pink inside. Season with salt, if desired.

Nutrition Information

- 191: calories;
- 2 grams: monounsaturated fat;
- 9 grams: carbohydrates;
- 5 grams: sugars;
- 27 grams: protein;
- 4 grams: fat;
- 1 gram: polyunsaturated fat;
- 0 grams: dietary fiber;
- 142 milligrams: sodium;

259. Potato And Onion Frittata

Serving: Serves 10 as a tapa | Prep: | Cook: | Ready in: 8mins

Ingredients

- 1 pound boiling potatoes, peeled if desired and cut in small dice (1/2 to 3/4 inch)
- 2 tablespoons extra virgin olive oil
- 1 medium yellow or red onion, finely chopped
- Salt
- freshly ground pepper to taste (about 3/4 teaspoon)
- 6 large eggs

Direction

- Steam the potatoes until tender, about eight minutes, and set aside.
- Meanwhile, heat 1 tablespoon of the olive oil over medium heat in a heavy 10-inch nonstick skillet, and add the onions and a generous pinch of salt. Cook, stirring, until tender but not browned, about five minutes. Add the potatoes to the pan, and toss together gently so that the potatoes don't break apart. Season generously with salt and pepper. Remove from the heat.
- Beat the eggs in a bowl, and add 1/2 teaspoon salt and a generous amount of freshly ground pepper. Stir in the potatoes and onions.
- Return the pan to the stove, and heat the remaining olive oil over medium-high heat. Drizzle in a drop of egg; when it sizzles and cooks at once, scrape the eggs and vegetables back into the pan. Shake the pan gently while you lift the edges of the frittata, and tilt the pan to let egg run underneath and set. When the bottom of the frittata has set, turn the heat to low and cover the pan. Cook gently for 10 minutes. Meanwhile, heat the broiler.
- Uncover the pan, and slide under the broiler for a minute or two (watch closely) to set the top. Remove from the heat. Let the tortilla set in the pan for a few minutes, then slide out onto a serving plate. Allow to cool to room temperature, and cut into small diamonds to serve as hors d'oeuvres.

Nutrition Information

- 107: calories;
- 5 grams: protein;
- 211 milligrams: sodium;
- 6 grams: fat;
- 1 gram: sugars;
- 0 grams: trans fat;
- 3 grams: monounsaturated fat;
- 9 grams: carbohydrates;

260. Potato Onion Frittata

Serving: 4 to 6 servings | Prep: | Cook: | Ready in: 17mins

Ingredients

- 6 red-skinned new potatoes
- 1 small red onion
- 3 tablespoons olive oil
- 8 eggs
- Coarse salt and freshly ground pepper to taste
- 2 tablespoons Italian parsley, chopped

Direction

- Preheat broiler. Dice the potatoes and chop the onion. In a large skillet (cast iron if available) gently saute the potatoes and the onion in the olive oil until lightly brown.
- Break the eggs into a large bowl and beat with the salt and pepper. Turn the heat up under the skillet and pour in the mixture. Cook until set. Place under broiler until browned and bubbling. Turn out onto a heated platter or serve from the skillet. Sprinkle with parsley before serving.

Nutrition Information

- 213: calories;
- 0 grams: trans fat;
- 7 grams: monounsaturated fat;
- 378 milligrams: sodium;
- 12 grams: fat;
- 3 grams: saturated fat;
- 9 grams: protein;
- 2 grams: dietary fiber;
- 17 grams: carbohydrates;
- 1 gram: sugars;

261. Potatoes Country Style

Serving: 4 servings | Prep: | Cook: | Ready in: 35mins

Ingredients

- 2 pounds Idaho russet potatoes
- ½ cup finely chopped onion
- 1 clove garlic, peeled
- Salt to taste if desired
- 6 tablespoons butter, plus butter for greasing the dish
- Freshly ground pepper to taste
- ⅛ teaspoon freshly grated nutmeg
- 2 tablespoons finely chopped parsley
- 3 tablespoons freshly grated Parmesan cheese

Direction

- Peel the potatoes and cut each into quarters. There should be about 4 cups. Put the potatoes in a large saucepan and add water to a depth of about one-half inch above the potatoes.
- Add the onion, garlic and salt. Bring to a boil and cook 10 to 15 minutes or until tender. Drain the potato mixture and return to the kettle in which it was cooked. Add salt, 4 tablespoons of the butter, pepper, nutmeg and parsley.
- Mash the potatoes to a smooth texture, using the back of a large spoon. Spoon the potato mixture into a buttered baking dish (a dish measuring 6 1/2 by 11 1/2 inches is ideal), and smooth over the top. Sprinkle with Parmesan cheese and dot with the remaining 2 tablespoons butter.
- Meanwhile, preheat the broiler to high.
- Place the potatoes under the broiler 3 or 4 inches from the source of heat. Broil 6 to 8 minutes or until golden brown and slightly bubbling on top.

Nutrition Information

- 413: calories;
- 23 grams: fat;
- 15 grams: saturated fat;
- 6 grams: monounsaturated fat;
- 4 grams: dietary fiber;
- 2 grams: sugars;
- 9 grams: protein;
- 665 milligrams: sodium;
- 1 gram: polyunsaturated fat;
- 44 grams: carbohydrates;

262. Pressure Cooker Spicy Pork Shoulder

Serving: 10 servings | Prep: | Cook: | Ready in: 3hours

Ingredients

- For the pork:

- 5 garlic cloves, grated on a Microplane or minced
- 2 tablespoons brown sugar or honey
- 1 tablespoon Korean chile flakes (gochugaru) or other chile flakes (Maras, Aleppo or crushed red pepper)
- 1 tablespoon kosher salt, more to taste
- 1 teaspoon ground black pepper
- 5 pounds boneless pork shoulder, cut into two or three pieces
- For the sauce:
- 1 tablespoon peanut oil
- 4 garlic cloves, grated on a Microplane
- 2 tablespoons grated fresh ginger root
- ⅓ cup gochujang (Korean chile paste) or other chile paste or sauce such as Sriracha
- ¼ cup soy sauce
- 2 tablespoons ketchup
- 2 tablespoons mirin
- 2 tablespoons honey
- 1 tablespoon rice wine vinegar
- 1 teaspoon Asian fish sauce
- 1 teaspoon sesame oil
- For the sesame pickled cucumbers:
- 6 Persian cucumbers, thinly sliced (or about 4 cups sliced cucumbers)
- 1 ½ tablespoons rice vinegar
- 2 teaspoons sesame oil
- 2 teaspoons brown sugar
- ½ teaspoon fine sea salt
- ¼ cup thinly sliced red onion
- 2 teaspoons sesame seeds
- For serving:
- Cooked rice or toasted slider rolls
- Kimchi (optional)

Direction

- To prepare pork, combine garlic, brown sugar, chile flakes, salt and pepper. Rub marinade all over pork. If you have time, cover and refrigerate for 1 hour to up to 24 hours. Otherwise, proceed with recipe.
- Set electric pressure cooker to sauté (or use a large skillet). Add pork in batches and sear until browned all over, about 2 minutes per side. Add 3/4 cup water to pot (or to skillet to deglaze, then move to pot), cover, and set to cook for 90 minutes on high pressure. Or cook in a slow cooker for 5 to 7 hours until tender.
- While pork cooks, prepare sauce: In a small pot, warm peanut oil over medium heat. Add garlic and ginger, and sauté until fragrant, 1 to 2 minutes. Add remaining ingredients and bring to a simmer. Cook until thickened, 1 to 2 minutes. Set sauce aside. (It can be made up to 1 week ahead and stored in the refrigerator.)
- Manually release steam. Let pork cool until you can handle it, then shred it into bite-size pieces. Pork can be made to this point up to 3 days ahead.
- While pork cools, strain liquid from bottom of pot. Pour off fat (or chill liquid, then scoop off solidified fat with a spoon). Reserve.
- Prepare cucumbers: In a small bowl, combine all ingredients except sesame seeds, and let sit, tossing one or twice, for at least 20 minutes. Stir in sesame seeds.
- When ready to serve, heat broiler. Toss pork with sauce and 1 to 2 tablespoons cooking liquid — just enough so pork is evenly coated but not wet or runny. Spread mixture on a rimmed baking sheet, and broil until crisped on top, 2 to 3 minutes; it will char in places, and that's fine.
- Serve pork over rice or on slider rolls, with cucumbers and kimchi, if desired.

263. Pumpkin Creme Brulee

Serving: 10 servings | Prep: | Cook: |Ready in: 1hours

Ingredients

- 1 5-pound pumpkin
- 2 ½ cups milk
- 1 cup heavy cream
- ½ cup dark molasses
- 1 teaspoon cinnamon
- 6 whole eggs
- 9 egg yolks
- ¾ cup granulated white sugar

- 1 ½ cups brown sugar

Direction

- Preheat the oven to 400 degrees.
- Cut the pumpkin lengthwise into quarters. Scrape out the seeds and membranes from each quarter. Arrange the pumpkin quarters cut-side down on a baking dish. Cover closely with foil. Place in the oven and bake for one hour. Remove the pumpkin pieces and let stand, covered, 15 minutes.
- Scrape the flesh of each quartered pumpkin into the sieve of a food mill or ricer. Press to make a fine puree. There should be about five cups. Of this, you will need one cup for this recipe. The remainder may be frozen or refrigerated to be used later in soups, pies and so on.
- Put one cup of the puree into a saucepan and add the milk, cream, molasses and cinnamon. Stir to blend and bring slowly to the simmer.
- Select a mixing bowl, preferably of stainless steel, that will sit neatly and compactly inside a larger basin of simmering water. Into the mixing bowl put the whole eggs, egg yolks and white sugar. Beat until blended.
- Pour the hot pumpkin mixture into the egg mixture. Sit the custard mixture inside the kettle over barely simmering water and start stirring immediately and constantly with a wire whisk. At this point, great care and caution must be taken to not overheat the mixture, because excess heat will cause it to curdle. Stir rapidly over and around the curves of the mixing bowl. Cook for about 12 minutes, only until the mixture achieves a fairly thick, custardlike texture, then remove the bowl from the bottom basin.
- Spoon equal portions (about five ounces) of the custard into 10 individual six-ounce, heatproof, decorative baking dishes or custard cups. Wipe any spillage off the outside of the baking dishes. Cover with clear plastic wrap, and chill thoroughly.
- Fill a small sieve with the brown sugar. Hold the sieve over each of the dishes and sprinkle with brown sugar. Wipe around the rim of each dish to remove excess sugar.
- Preheat a broiler to high. Arrange the small dishes in a metal pan filled with ice. Place under the broiler until the sugar has formed a nice crust on top. Serve immediately.

Nutrition Information

- 427: calories;
- 64 grams: carbohydrates;
- 57 grams: sugars;
- 9 grams: protein;
- 5 grams: monounsaturated fat;
- 1 gram: dietary fiber;
- 92 milligrams: sodium;
- 17 grams: fat;
- 0 grams: trans fat;

264. Pumpkin And Onion Soup

Serving: 6 servings | Prep: | Cook: | Ready in: 1hours

Ingredients

- 6 cups thinly sliced onions
- 3 tablespoons butter
- 1 teaspoon sugar
- 1 3-pound pumpkin
- 4 cups well-seasoned chicken stock
- Salt and freshly ground black pepper
- 6 to 8 slices French or Italian bread, toasted
- ½ cup grated Swiss cheese

Direction

- In a heavy saucepan, saute the onions in the butter over medium heat until they are golden. Sprinkle with sugar and continue cooking until they just begin to brown.
- While the onions are cooking, peel the pumpkin, remove the seeds and stringy core and cut it into half-inch cubes. Steam the

- pumpkin until it is tender, 10 to 15 minutes. Puree the pumpkin with a little of the stock in a blender or food processor. Better results are obtained in a blender.
- Add the pumpkin puree and the remaining chicken stock to the onions, bring to a simmer and season to taste with salt and pepper.
- Just before serving, preheat a broiler. Top each of the toasted bread croutons with some of the cheese. Divide the soup among six ovenproof ramekins, crocks or bowls and float a cheese-topped crouton on each. Place under the broiler just until the cheese melts, then serve.

Nutrition Information

- 297: calories;
- 3 grams: monounsaturated fat;
- 13 grams: sugars;
- 1262 milligrams: sodium;
- 11 grams: protein;
- 6 grams: saturated fat;
- 0 grams: trans fat;
- 1 gram: polyunsaturated fat;
- 40 grams: carbohydrates;
- 4 grams: dietary fiber;

265. Puree Of Green Beans Au Gratin

Serving: 4 servings | Prep: | Cook: | Ready in: 30mins

Ingredients

- 1 pound fresh green beans
- 1 tablespoon butter
- ¼ cup heavy cream
- Salt to taste if desired
- Freshly ground pepper to taste
- ⅛ teaspoon freshly grated nutmeg
- ⅔ cup freshly grated Gruyere cheese

Direction

- Tear off and discard tips of each green bean. If there are "strings" along the side, strip them off and discard them. Break beans in half or in quarters.
- Bring enough water to a boil to cover beans when they are added. Drop beans into the water and when water returns to the boil let cook 8 to 9 minutes until crisp tender. Drain thoroughly.
- Pour beans into container of a food processor or electric blender and blend until coarsely processed. There should be about two cups.
- Heat butter in a saucepan and add bean puree. Add cream, salt, pepper and nutmeg. Heat, stirring, until piping hot.
- Meanwhile, preheat broiler to high.
- Spoon green bean mixture into a shallow round or oval baking dish and cover evenly with cheese. Place under broiler and cook until cheese is thoroughly melted and nicely browned on top, 3 to 5 minutes.

Nutrition Information

- 204: calories;
- 0 grams: trans fat;
- 1 gram: polyunsaturated fat;
- 16 grams: fat;
- 9 grams: protein;
- 3 grams: dietary fiber;
- 4 grams: sugars;
- 359 milligrams: sodium;
- 5 grams: monounsaturated fat;

266. Quail Roasted In Vine Leaves

Serving: 6 servings | Prep: | Cook: | Ready in: 45mins

Ingredients

- 12 large vine leaves
- 12 quail, about 1/4 pound each
- Salt to taste if desired

- Freshly ground pepper to taste
- 12 thin slices salt fatback, each measuring 2 1/2 by 4 inches
- 6 tablespoons butter
- 2 tablespoons Cognac

Direction

- Preheat oven to 450 degrees.
- If vine leaves have been packed in brine, drain. Add to basin of salt water, rinse, pat dry.
- Sprinkle quail inside and out with salt and pepper. Truss and cover each with vine leaf. Cover with rectangle of fatback. Tie with string.
- Using 4 tablespoons of butter, grease 2 skillets and arrange half of quail, breast side up, in each. Quail should not be too close. Bake in oven 10 minutes. Turn on sides and bake about 3 minutes. Turn to other side and bake 3 to 5 minutes.
- Transfer quail to other skillet and pour fat from empty one. Add 1/2 of Cognac and stir to dissolve particles. Add 1/2 of broth and cook 5 minutes.
- Transfer quail to skillet containing broth. Pour fat from second skillet. Repeat with remaining Cognac and broth. Pour sauce on quail.
- Remove string and fatback, or broil until fatback is crisp.
- Heat remaining 2 tablespoons of butter in skillet and when it is hazelnut brown pour it over quail. Serve hot with wild rice or on toast.

267. Red Beans And Rice, Louisiana Style

Serving: Eight or more servings | Prep: | Cook: | Ready in: 3hours

Ingredients

- 1 pound red kidney beans
- 2 small ham hocks, about 1 1/4 pounds
- 2 tablespoons safflower or corn oil or rendered bacon fat
- 1 tablespoon finely minced garlic
- 2 cups finely chopped onions
- 1 cup finely chopped green peppers
- 1 cup finely chopped celery
- ¼ cup finely chopped parsley
- ¼ teaspoon cayenne pepper
- 1 bay leaf
- ½ teaspoon dried thyme
- 1 teaspoon Tabasco sauce
- 1 teaspoon sugar
- Salt to taste, if desired
- Freshly ground pepper to taste
- 1 cup crushed or chopped canned tomatoes, preferably imported
- 1 pound smoked sausage such as Polish sausage, cut into four pieces
- Cooked rice (see recipe)
- 1 cup finely chopped scallions
- Hot vinegar, optional

Direction

- Put the beans and ham hocks in a large bowl and add cold water to cover, to a level about two inches above the tops of the beans. Cover and let stand overnight.
- Drain the beans and ham hocks, reserving the water in which they soaked. Put the beans and ham hocks in a kettle. Add enough additional water to the soaking water to make eight cups. Add the water to the beans and ham hocks. Bring to the boil and cook, uncovered, two hours, stirring occasionally from the bottom.
- Meanwhile, heat the oil in a skillet and add the garlic, onions, green peppers and celery. Cook, stirring, until the mixture is wilted. Add this to the beans. Add the parsley, cayenne pepper, bay leaf, thyme, Tabasco sauce, sugar, salt, pepper and tomatoes.
- As the beans cook, preheat the broiler to high. Place the sausage pieces on a rack and cook about 10 minutes, turning often. Add the sausage pieces to the beans for the last 30 minutes of cooking.

- Scoop out about one cup of the beans and their liquid and put them in a food processor or electric blender. Blend thoroughly. Return this mixture to the beans. Remove the bay leaf.
- Spoon one serving of rice into each of eight hot soup bowls. Cover with beans. Sprinkle with chopped scallions and serve with a little hot vinegar on the side, to be added, if desired, according to taste.

Nutrition Information

- 522: calories;
- 22 grams: fat;
- 7 grams: saturated fat;
- 11 grams: dietary fiber;
- 6 grams: sugars;
- 0 grams: trans fat;
- 9 grams: monounsaturated fat;
- 5 grams: polyunsaturated fat;
- 45 grams: carbohydrates;
- 37 grams: protein;
- 995 milligrams: sodium;

268. Red Pepper Puree

Serving: 4 servings | Prep: | Cook: | Ready in: 10mins

Ingredients

- 4 sweet red bell peppers
- Salt and freshly ground black pepper, to taste

Direction

- Place peppers under high broiler, 3 inches from heat, turning until they blister and lightly blacken. Or hold over gas flame with long-handled fork, until blistered and lightly blackened.
- Place peppers in a plastic bag for 5 minutes; remove, peel and seed.
- Puree in food processor until smooth. Add salt and pepper

Nutrition Information

- 38: calories;
- 278 milligrams: sodium;
- 0 grams: polyunsaturated fat;
- 7 grams: carbohydrates;
- 3 grams: dietary fiber;
- 5 grams: sugars;
- 1 gram: protein;

269. Red Snapper With Sweet And Hot Pepper Sauce

Serving: 6 servings | Prep: | Cook: | Ready in: 40mins

Ingredients

- 4 tablespoons extra-virgin olive oil
- 2 large sweet red peppers, cored, seeded and chopped
- 1 jalapeno or other hot green chili, seeded and minced
- ½ cup finely chopped onion
- 2 cloves garlic, minced
- 2 cups water
- 1 tablespoon fresh lime juice
- 6 red snapper fillets, each about 6 ounces, skin on
- Salt and freshly ground black pepper
- ¼ teaspoon paprika
- Sprigs of fresh coriander

Direction

- Heat one tablespoon of the oil in a heavy saucepan. Add the red peppers, green chili and onion and saute over low heat until soft, but not brown. Stir in the garlic, cook a few seconds longer, then add the water. Allow to simmer about 20 minutes, until the peppers are very tender.
- Meanwhile, preheat a grill or broiler and oil the rack. Mix the lime juice with two

tablespoons of the olive oil and brush over the fish. Allow to marinate until ready to cook the fish.
- When the peppers are tender, puree the contents of the saucepan in a food processor or blender. Season with the paprika and to taste with salt and pepper. Stir the last tablespoon of the olive oil. Return to saucepan and simmer, then cover to keep warm.
- To grill the fish, place the fish on the grill skin side up. Cook about six minutes, until the fish is lightly seared. Using a large spatula, turn the fish, cook very briefly on the other side, then transfer to warm plates. To broil the fish, broil it skin side down until the fish is cooked through and lightly seared, six to eight minutes. Do not turn it. Transfer the fish to a warm plate.
- To serve, spoon some of the pepper sauce over and around the fish and garnish with coriander.

Nutrition Information

- 280: calories;
- 12 grams: fat;
- 2 grams: dietary fiber;
- 7 grams: carbohydrates;
- 3 grams: sugars;
- 36 grams: protein;
- 788 milligrams: sodium;

270. Restaurant Style Pork Chops

Serving: 4 Servings | Prep: | Cook: | Ready in: 45mins

Ingredients

- ¾ cup maple syrup
- 1 tablespoon balsamic vinegar
- 1 tablespoon dark brown sugar
- ½ teaspoon ground cinnamon
- ½ cup pecans
- 4 (1 1/4-inch thick) pork chops
- Kosher salt
- freshly ground black pepper
- Extra-virgin olive oil
- 2 green apples, cored
- ¼ cup finely chopped candied ginger

Direction

- Preheat a broiler or light a charcoal grill.
- In a small nonreactive bowl, whisk together the syrup, vinegar, sugar and cinnamon.
- Place a small pan over medium heat, add the pecans and about 2 tablespoons of the maple-syrup sauce and cook for a few minutes, until the nuts are glazed and fragrant. Transfer the nuts to a plate and spread them out to cool. Transfer the cooled nuts to a cutting board, chop roughly and set aside.
- Season the pork chops aggressively with salt and pepper, then drizzle with olive oil. When the broiler is hot, or the coals are covered with gray ash and you can hold your hand 5 inches above them for only 1 to 2 seconds, broil or grill the meat for approximately 7 minutes per side. Brush with some of the remaining maple glaze every 2 or 3 minutes, turning them frequently to prevent the sugar from burning.
- When the chops are cooked, remove from the broiler or grill and let them rest for 5 minutes before serving. Meanwhile, slice the cored apples into thick rounds, drizzle with olive oil, season lightly with salt and pepper and place on the broiler pan or grill until tender when pierced with a fork. These, too, should be brushed with the maple glaze and turned frequently.
- Serve chops with the apple slices, sprinkled with pecans and candied ginger.

Nutrition Information

- 735: calories;
- 7 grams: saturated fat;
- 0 grams: trans fat;
- 4 grams: dietary fiber;
- 43 grams: protein;

- 895 milligrams: sodium;
- 59 grams: sugars;
- 32 grams: fat;
- 16 grams: monounsaturated fat;
- 6 grams: polyunsaturated fat;
- 69 grams: carbohydrates;

271. Rib Steaks With Parsley And Crouton Salad

Serving: 4 servings | Prep: | Cook: | Ready in: 20mins

Ingredients

- 4 rib steaks (sometimes called entrecôte or club steaks), about 1 inch thick
- Sea salt and freshly ground black pepper
- 1 ½ tablespoons salt-cured capers, rinsed thoroughly
- 1 tablespoon horseradish, more to taste
- 1 tablespoon freshly squeezed lemon juice
- ½ tablespoon Dijon mustard
- ½ tablespoon coarse-grain mustard
- ¼ cup extra virgin olive oil
- 2 cups day-old bread cut into 1-inch cubes, lightly toasted
- Leaves from 1 large bunch parsley
- Tops from 1 bunch watercress

Direction

- Line a broiler pan with aluminum foil and heat broiler. Season steaks with salt and pepper. Put steaks on broiler pan and broil for 5 minutes on each side for rare.
- Meanwhile, in a salad bowl, whisk together capers, horseradish, lemon juice, mustards and olive oil. Season with salt and pepper. Add toasted bread cubes, parsley and watercress and toss until lightly wilted.
- When steaks are done, let them rest for 5 minutes on a cutting board. Slice and arrange on a platter. Pour about 1 tablespoon of juices on cutting board into salad and toss once more. Pour remaining juices over steak. Serve, passing salad.

272. Rich Red Wine Vegetable Stew

Serving: 5 to 6 cups | Prep: | Cook: | Ready in: 1hours35mins

Ingredients

- ¼ cup plus 2 teaspoons vegetable oil
- 2 medium tomatoes, cored
- 1 onion, peeled and cut in half lengthwise
- 2 cups red wine
- 3 garlic cloves, smashed, peeled and chopped
- 1 ounce dried boletus mushrooms, ground in a spice mill
- 1 bay leaf
- 1 ½ tablespoons tomato paste
- ¼ teaspoon dried marjoram
- ¼ teaspoon dried thyme
- 10 ounces fresh mushrooms, cut in 1/2-inch pieces
- 5 ½ ounces (1 1/2 cups) green beans, tipped and tailed
- ½ pound turnip, peeled and cut into 1/4-inch thick julienne (1 1/2 cups)
- 3 medium carrots, peeled and cut into 1/4-inch thick julienne (1 1/2 cups)
- Black pepper to taste
- 2 tablespoons cornstarch
- 2 tablespoons water
- 1 bunch parsley, chopped
- 4 teaspoons kosher salt

Direction

- Preheat broiler. Coat tomatoes and onion with 2 teaspoons of oil. Place on a cookie sheet and broil for 12 minutes, turning halfway through.
- Remove from the oven. Coarsely chop tomatoes and onion in a food processor. Reserve.

- While tomatoes and onion broil, place wine, garlic, ground mushrooms and bay leaf in a 5-quart dish with a tightly fitted lid. Cook, uncovered, at 100 percent power in a 650- to 700-watt oven for 15 minutes.
- Remove from oven and uncover. Transfer wine mixture to a small bowl. Whisk in tomato paste, marjoram and thyme. Reserve.
- Place mushrooms in the dish and toss with the remaining 1/4 cup oil. Cook, uncovered, for 10 minutes.
- Remove from oven. Scrape tomato mixture over mushrooms and smooth into an even layer. Arrange green beans in a circle around the outer edge of the dish. Arrange turnips in a circle just inside green beans. Place carrots in the center of the dish. Pour the wine mixture over the vegetables. Sprinkle with pepper. Cook, covered, for 30 minutes.
- Combine cornstarch and water in a small bowl and scrape into dish. Add parsley and stir well. Cook, covered, for 3 minutes.
- Remove from oven. Stir in salt.

Nutrition Information

- 241: calories;
- 741 milligrams: sodium;
- 11 grams: fat;
- 1 gram: saturated fat;
- 2 grams: polyunsaturated fat;
- 0 grams: trans fat;
- 8 grams: sugars;
- 19 grams: carbohydrates;
- 4 grams: protein;

273. Ricotta And Spinach Frittata With Mint

Serving: Six servings | Prep: | Cook: | Ready in: 30mins

Ingredients

- 6 ounces fresh spinach, stemmed and washed, or 1/2 6-ounce bag baby spinach
- 6 eggs
- Salt
- freshly ground pepper
- 1 cup fresh ricotta
- 1 tablespoon chopped fresh mint
- 1 garlic clove, minced
- 2 tablespoons olive oil

Direction

- Steam the spinach above 1 inch of boiling water just until it wilts, about two minutes. Rinse with cold water, squeeze out excess moisture and chop fine.
- In a medium bowl, beat together the eggs, salt, pepper, ricotta, garlic, spinach and mint.
- Heat the olive oil over medium-high heat in a heavy 10-inch nonstick skillet. Drop a bit of egg into the pan; if it sizzles and cooks at once, the pan is ready. Pour in the egg mixture. Tilt the pan to distribute the eggs and filling evenly over the surface. Shake the pan gently, tilting it slightly with one hand while lifting up the edges of the frittata with the spatula in your other hand, to let the eggs run underneath during the first few minutes of cooking.
- Turn the heat down to low, cover and cook 10 minutes, shaking the pan gently every once in a while. From time to time, remove the lid, tilt the pan and loosen the bottom of the frittata with a wooden spatula so that the bottom doesn't burn. It should turn a golden color. The eggs should be just about set; cook a few minutes longer if they're not.
- Meanwhile, heat the broiler. Uncover the pan and place under the broiler, not too close to the heat, for one to three minutes, watching very carefully to make sure the top doesn't burn (at most, it should brown very slightly and puff under the broiler). Remove from the heat, shake the pan to make sure the frittata isn't sticking, and allow it to cool for at least five minutes and for as long as 15 minutes. Loosen the edges with a wooden or plastic

spatula. Carefully slide from the pan onto a large round platter. Cut into wedges or into smaller bite-size diamonds. Serve hot, warm, at room temperature or cold.

Nutrition Information

- 182: calories;
- 5 grams: saturated fat;
- 3 grams: carbohydrates;
- 11 grams: protein;
- 14 grams: fat;
- 2 grams: polyunsaturated fat;
- 1 gram: dietary fiber;
- 277 milligrams: sodium;
- 0 grams: sugars;
- 6 grams: monounsaturated fat;

274. Rio's Spicy Chicken Wings

Serving: 4 to 6 servings | Prep: | Cook: | Ready in: 35mins

Ingredients

- For the marinade:
- 3 pounds chicken wings
- 1 large garlic clove, peeled and grated
- 1 1/2-inch piece fresh ginger, peeled and grated
- 2 tablespoons soy sauce
- 1 tablespoon olive oil
- 1 tablespoon nam pla or other Asian fish sauce
- ½ teaspoon mirin
- ½ teaspoon salt
- ½ teaspoon black pepper
- For the glaze:
- 1 cup mirin
- 2 tablespoons soy sauce
- 1 tablespoon nam pla or other Asian fish sauce
- 2 teaspoons red yuzu kosho (see note)
- ½ teaspoon black pepper
- 1 teaspoon grated garlic
- ½ teaspoon shichimi togarashi (optional)
- For serving:
- 1 teaspoon sesame seeds
- Black pepper
- 1 tablespoon chopped scallions

Direction

- In a large bowl, mix together all marinade ingredients except chicken wings. Add the wings and toss to coat. Cover and let chicken marinate overnight in the refrigerator.
- When ready to cook, combine all glaze ingredients in a small saucepan. Simmer over low heat, stirring frequently, until glaze reduces to a saucy consistency, about 20 minutes. Transfer to large mixing bowl and set aside.
- Heat a broiler to high. Set a baking rack on top of a rimmed baking sheet and arrange wings on rack. Broil for 12 minutes, flipping wings halfway through, until they are crisp and golden.
- Transfer wings to the bowl with the glaze and toss to coat. Transfer wings to a serving platter and garnish with sesame seeds, pepper and scallions. Serve hot.

Nutrition Information

- 524: calories;
- 10 grams: saturated fat;
- 0 grams: sugars;
- 7 grams: polyunsaturated fat;
- 41 grams: protein;
- 1249 milligrams: sodium;
- 16 grams: monounsaturated fat;
- 5 grams: carbohydrates;
- 1 gram: dietary fiber;
- 32 grams: fat;

275. Roast Lamb

Serving: 8 to 12 servings | Prep: | Cook: | Ready in: 3hours

Ingredients

- 1 large lamb roast with a cap of fat, 4 to 6 pounds: bone-in leg (these can be as large as 8 pounds), semiboneless leg, bone-in shoulder, boneless butterflied leg or double loin
- 2 ounces (1 can) anchovies packed in olive oil, drained, or 3 tablespoons Dijon mustard
- Leaves from 6 fresh rosemary sprigs (2 heaping tablespoons leaves), plus extra sprigs and branches for garnish
- 6 garlic cloves, smashed and peeled
- 4 ounces unsalted butter, softened at room temperature
- Black pepper
- 1 lemon, cut in half
- 1 ¾ cups white wine, plus extra for gravy

Direction

- Heat oven to 425 degrees. Use a small sharp knife to make about a dozen incisions, each about 2 inches deep, through the fat that covers the top of the meat. Using a mortar and pestle or a blender, blend 2/3 of the anchovies (or 2/3 of the mustard if using), the rosemary leaves and the garlic cloves into a chunky paste. Using your fingers, press paste deeply into incisions.
- Mix remaining anchovies (or mustard) and the butter into a paste. Smear this mixture all over the surface of the roast. Season liberally with black pepper. (Do not add salt; the anchovies are salty enough, and so is the mustard.) Place the lamb on a rack in a roasting pan, fat side up, and squeeze the lemon halves over. Pour the wine around the roast into the pan.
- Roast 15 minutes, then reduce heat to 350 degrees and roast until internal temperature reaches 130 to 135 degrees (for medium-rare or medium meat), about another 60 to 90 minutes. Baste every 20 minutes or so with the wine and drippings in the pan, adding more wine as needed to keep the liquid from scorching. If possible, for the last 15 minutes of cooking, use convection or a broiler to crisp the fat on the roast.
- Remove pan from the oven, remove rack from the pan, and let the roast rest on the rack for at least 15 to 20 minutes in a warm place, tented with foil. The internal temperature will rise to about 140 to 145 degrees.
- To make sauce from the pan drippings, remove a few tablespoons of fat by tipping the pan and spooning off the top layer. Put the pan over medium heat until the liquid simmers. Taste the simmering liquid and whisk in more wine, 1/4 cup at a time, until the consistency and flavor are right. Do not let the mixture become syrupy; it should be a sharp jus, not a thick gravy.
- Carve lamb into 1/2-inch-thick slices and arrange on a heated platter, decorated with rosemary sprigs. Serve with piping hot gravy.

Nutrition Information

- 1047: calories;
- 42 grams: monounsaturated fat;
- 3 grams: carbohydrates;
- 11 grams: protein;
- 258 milligrams: sodium;
- 56 grams: saturated fat;
- 0 grams: dietary fiber;
- 5 grams: polyunsaturated fat;
- 1 gram: sugars;
- 107 grams: fat;

276. Roasted Asparagus Frittata

Serving: 2 servings | Prep: | Cook: | Ready in: 25mins

Ingredients

- 8 to 12 medium to fat asparagus spears, trimmed

- Olive oil
- Salt and black pepper
- 4 eggs
- ¼ to ½ cup chervil, roughly chopped, or parsley
- ½ cup finely grated Parmesan, optional

Direction

- Heat oven to 450 degrees. Spread asparagus on a baking sheet and toss with olive oil, salt and pepper. Roast, shaking the pan occasionally, until the asparagus is lightly charred and tender, about 12 minutes. (You can let the asparagus sit at room temperature for hours, or refrigerate overnight.)
- Beat the eggs with salt, pepper, half the chervil (and half the cheese, if you like). Cut the asparagus into 2-inch lengths and arrange in a single layer in a 10-inch nonstick skillet. Drizzle with more olive oil and set over medium heat.
- Pour the egg mixture over the asparagus. Use a spatula if necessary to make a round frittata. Cook until nearly set, tilting the pan and lifting the edge of the set egg to let the liquid egg flow underneath, about 4 minutes.
- When the top is almost dry, flip the frittata onto a plate, then slide it back into the pan. Let cook for just a few seconds, then flip out onto a plate. Alternatively, use an ovenproof pan and put it in the oven or under the broiler for a few minutes.
- Sprinkle with the remaining chervil (and cheese if you are using it) and serve hot, warm or at room temperature.

Nutrition Information

- 145: calories;
- 0 grams: trans fat;
- 2 grams: carbohydrates;
- 10 grams: fat;
- 3 grams: saturated fat;
- 1 gram: sugars;
- 12 grams: protein;
- 271 milligrams: sodium;
- 4 grams: monounsaturated fat;

277. Roasted Asparagus With Crunchy Parmesan Topping

Serving: 4 servings | Prep: | Cook: | Ready in: 25mins

Ingredients

- 1 thick slice good bread
- 1 small chunk Parmigiano-Reggiano, about 1 ounce
- 1 ½ pounds thin asparagus, more or less
- 3 tablespoons butter, extra virgin olive oil, or a combination
- Salt and freshly ground black pepper

Direction

- Heat oven to 500 degrees; while it heats, put bread in, and check frequently until it is lightly toasted and dry. Coarsely grind or grate bread and cheese together (a small food processor is best), and keep crumbs larger than commercial bread crumbs.
- Rinse asparagus, and break off woody bottoms. Lay stalks in a baking dish that will hold them in two or three layers. Toss with bits of butter or the oil, sprinkle with salt and pepper, and place in oven.
- Roast 5 minutes, then shake dish to redistribute butter or oil. Roast 5 minutes more, then test for doneness by piercing a spear with point of a sharp knife; it should slide in but meet a little resistance. (Up to this point, the recipe can be made as much as two hours before serving; just leave asparagus at room temperature).
- Turn on broiler and place rack as close as possible to heating element. Top asparagus with cheese-crumb mixture and run under broiler to brown, a minute or two. Serve hot or at room temperature.

Nutrition Information

- 186: calories;
- 3 grams: saturated fat;
- 0 grams: trans fat;
- 13 grams: fat;
- 8 grams: protein;
- 1 gram: polyunsaturated fat;
- 11 grams: carbohydrates;
- 4 grams: sugars;
- 462 milligrams: sodium;

278. Roasted Fillet Of Beef With Black Pepper

Serving: 10 to 12 servings | Prep: | Cook: | Ready in: 2hours

Ingredients

- 1 whole fillet of beef, about 5 1/2 pounds
- 1 tablespoon fine sea salt, approximately
- 1 tablespoon crushed black peppercorns
- 2 tablespoons extra virgin olive oil

Direction

- Trim meat, removing excess fat and silver skin. Cut off about 4 inches of narrow end, about 1 pound, and reserve for another use.
- Place fillet on large sheet of parchment paper. Dust all over with salt, using 3/4 teaspoon salt to a pound of meat. Roll in peppercorns. Tie with butcher's string at 2-inch intervals. Wrap meat in parchment loosely, and refrigerate at least 24 hours and up to 48 hours.
- Remove fillet from refrigerator an hour before cooking. Rub all over with oil. Heat oven to 400 degrees. Sear fillet on all sides in a heavy roasting pan over two burners, under broiler or on grill. Or cut in half and sear in two pieces in large, heavy skillet.
- Place in oven in roasting pan. Roast 15 minutes. Test with instant-read meat thermometer: if thickest part registers about 105 degrees, meat will be very rare when finished. For medium rare, roast 20 to 25 minutes, until thermometer registers 115 degrees. For medium, roast longer, to 125 degrees. At these temperatures, meat will be slightly undercooked, but will continue to cook after it is removed from oven. Place meat on cutting board. Allow it to rest 10 to 15 minutes.
- Remove string, cut meat in 1/2-inch thick slices, arrange on a platter, and serve.

Nutrition Information

- 517: calories;
- 2 grams: polyunsaturated fat;
- 0 grams: sugars;
- 40 grams: protein;
- 490 milligrams: sodium;
- 38 grams: fat;
- 15 grams: saturated fat;
- 17 grams: monounsaturated fat;

279. Rosh Ha Shanah Pot Roast

Serving: 6 servings | Prep: | Cook: | Ready in: 3hours30mins

Ingredients

- 3 pound eye-round roast or brisket
- Peanut oil
- Salt, if desired
- Pepper
- 8 cups beef stock
- 12 2-inch new potatoes
- 12 baby carrots
- 18 5-inch batons of celery
- 12 baby turnips
- 3 leeks
- 12 cherry tomatoes
- 11 tablespoons (3/4 cup minus 1 tablespoon) softened unsalted butter or margarine

- 1 cup flour
- Onion confit (see recipe)

Direction

- Rub beef with peanut oil, salt and pepper.
- Add about 2 tablespoons oil to a pot large enough to hold the beef, stock and vegetables. Brown beef on all sides. Add stock to cover; bring to boil, reduce heat, cover and simmer. Eye round should simmer 2 to 2 1/2 hours; brisket must cook longer.
- While beef is cooking, prepare vegetables. Scrub potatoes; trim and scrub carrots; cut celery and trim and scrub turnips. Cut green part from leeks. Trim the root, leaving just a little so leek will hold together. Rinse thoroughly.
- Turn on broiler; rinse and stem tomatoes and arrange on broiler pan.
- Prepare beurre manie by blending butter or margarine with flour to a paste.
- Twenty minutes before beef is ready, add potatoes, carrots, celery, turnips and leeks. Raise heat to return liquid to simmer; cover and finish cooking.
- Remove beef and set aside. Remove 8 cups of stock and bring to boil in separate pot. Keep vegetables warm in remaining stock.
- Gradually beat beurre manie into boiling stock until it has thickened to gravy consistency.
- Broil tomatoes 3 to 5 minutes. Do not let them burst.
- Slice beef. Spoon thin layer of gravy on a platter and top with sliced beef. Arrange vegetables around the meat, using tomatoes to provide spots of color. Place spoonfuls of onion confit down center of meat and pass additional gravy.

280. Rum And Chile Roasted Chicken Thighs With Pineapple

Serving: 3 to 4 servings | Prep: | Cook: | Ready in: 40mins

Ingredients

- 1 tablespoon fresh lemon juice
- ¾ teaspoon kosher salt
- 6 scallions, trimmed and chopped
- 4 garlic cloves, roughly chopped
- 2 tablespoons safflower or canola oil
- 2 tablespoons rum, preferably dark or amber
- 1 tablespoon thyme leaves
- 1 tablespoon brown sugar
- 1 Scotch bonnet or habanero chile pepper, seeded and chopped
- ½ teaspoon ground allspice
- ½ teaspoon freshly grated nutmeg
- 6 chicken thighs, rinsed and patted very dry
- ¾ pound pineapple pieces, diced into 1/4-inch chunks or very roughly chopped
- Lemon wedges, for serving

Direction

- In a blender or food processor, combine lemon juice and salt, and blend for 5 seconds to dissolve salt. Add scallions, garlic, oil, rum, thyme, brown sugar, chili pepper and spices, and blend until mixture forms a paste.
- Rub chili paste all over chicken pieces. If you have time, let marinate for up to 45 minutes at room temperature, or up to 24 hours in refrigerator.
- Preheat oven to 450 degrees. Put chicken in a large baking pan and scatter pineapple around it in one layer. Roast until chicken is cooked through (juices will run clear when pricked with a fork), about 25 minutes.
- Broil chicken and pineapple until chicken skin is crisp and dark brown all over and pineapple is singed in places.
- Serve chicken and pineapple coated with pan drippings, with lemon wedges.

Nutrition Information

- 644: calories;
- 19 grams: carbohydrates;
- 38 grams: protein;
- 541 milligrams: sodium;
- 20 grams: monounsaturated fat;
- 10 grams: polyunsaturated fat;
- 2 grams: dietary fiber;
- 12 grams: sugars;
- 44 grams: fat;
- 11 grams: saturated fat;
- 0 grams: trans fat;

281. Saffron Sweet Potato And Red Pepper Soup

Serving: 8 servings | Prep: | Cook: | Ready in: 45mins

Ingredients

- 2 small red bell peppers, quartered lengthwise, stemmed and seeded
- 2 tablespoons extra virgin olive oil, more for drizzling
- 1 medium onion, chopped
- 5 thyme sprigs
- 1 bay leaf
- Salt to taste
- 2 cups leftover mashed sweet potatoes (from 1 1/2 pounds raw sweet potatoes)
- 4 cups chicken stock
- Pinch of saffron threads
- Freshly ground white pepper to taste

Direction

- Heat broiler to high. Line a baking sheet with foil. Arrange red peppers on sheet skin side up and broil about 4 inches from heat until skin is very charred, 10 to 15 minutes. Remove from oven and wrap peppers in foil to steam skin loose, 10 to 15 minutes. Peel off skin and coarsely chop flesh.
- In a 4-quart saucepan, heat olive oil. Add onion, 3 thyme sprigs, bay leaf and salt. Cover and cook over low heat, stirring occasionally, until soft, about 10 minutes. Add sweet potatoes, bell peppers, stock, 2 cups water and saffron and bring to a boil. Uncover, reduce heat to medium-low and simmer, stirring occasionally, for 15 minutes.
- Discard thyme sprigs and bay leaf. Using an immersion blender, purée soup. Taste and add salt if needed, and white pepper. Ladle soup into bowls and garnish with leaves from remaining thyme sprigs and a drizzle of olive oil.

Nutrition Information

- 87: calories;
- 5 grams: sugars;
- 4 grams: protein;
- 437 milligrams: sodium;
- 2 grams: dietary fiber;
- 0 grams: polyunsaturated fat;
- 1 gram: monounsaturated fat;
- 14 grams: carbohydrates;

282. Salad With Herbs And Warm Goat Cheese

Serving: 4 servings | Prep: | Cook: | Ready in: 25mins

Ingredients

- 4 rounds French bread 1/2-inch thick
- 8 ounces fresh goat cheese, preferably in a log
- 6 tablespoons fruity extra-virgin olive oil
- 1 head Boston lettuce
- 2 tablespoons sherry vinegar
- ½ teaspoon Dijon mustard
- ½ teaspoon fresh rosemary leaves
- ½ teaspoon chopped fresh chervil
- 1 teaspoon minced chives
- Freshly ground black pepper

Direction

- Lightly toast the bread, then arrange the slices on a broiler pan lined with foil. Top each slice of toasted bread with a thick slice of the goat cheese. Brush the portions of cheese with half the olive oil and set aside until just before serving time.
- Rinse and dry the lettuce, tear it into bite-size pieces and arrange it on each of four salad plates.
- Just before serving time mix the vinegar and mustard together, then beat in the remaining three tablespoons of olive oil. Drizzle the dressing over the lettuce on the plates.
- Preheat broiler and broil the goat cheese until it is just beginning to color along the edges. Center a portion of goat cheese on toast on each salad, sprinkle with the herbs and pepper and serve at once.

Nutrition Information

- 1155: calories;
- 13 grams: saturated fat;
- 0 grams: trans fat;
- 19 grams: monounsaturated fat;
- 157 grams: carbohydrates;
- 14 grams: sugars;
- 43 grams: protein;
- 40 grams: fat;
- 5 grams: polyunsaturated fat;
- 7 grams: dietary fiber;
- 2076 milligrams: sodium;

283. Salad Of Spiced Lamb, Rice Vermicelli, Coriander And Holy Basil

Serving: 8 servings | Prep: | Cook: | Ready in: 1hours

Ingredients

- 8 six-ounce lamb medallions
- 5 shallots, finely chopped
- 1 tablespoon coarsely grated ginger
- 1 tablespoon coarsely grated galangal
- 1 bird's-eye chili (tiny, very hot chile), seeded and chopped
- ½ green pepper, seeded and cut in chunks
- ⅓ cup palm sugar
- 3 tablespoons fish sauce (nam pla or nuoc mam)
- 3 tablespoons peanut oil
- 1 tablespoon hoisin sauce
- Dressing (recipe follows)
- Salad (recipe follows)

Direction

- Ask the butcher to make lamb medallions from a boneless leg of lamb; separate top round, the tip and bottom round, and trim the fat and cut medallions from each part.
- Combine the remaining ingredients in a food processor, and puree.
- Preheat the broiler. Coat one side of each medallion with some of the puree. Broil medallions for 10 minutes. Turn and coat with more of the puree, reserving the remainder, and continue broiling until medallions are medium rare, about 5 minutes, or to your taste.
- Cut lamb into 1/4-inch-wide strips; mix with salad and dressing.

Nutrition Information

- 1208: calories;
- 50 grams: monounsaturated fat;
- 7 grams: polyunsaturated fat;
- 1 gram: dietary fiber;
- 625 milligrams: sodium;
- 122 grams: fat;
- 61 grams: saturated fat;
- 14 grams: carbohydrates;
- 10 grams: sugars;
- 12 grams: protein;

284. Salmon Fillet With Thyme And Roasted Tomatoes

Serving: 2 servings | Prep: | Cook: | Ready in: 35mins

Ingredients

- 4 ripe tomatoes
- 1 salmon fillet (about 1 pound)
- Juice of 1/2 lemon
- 2 tablespoons olive oil
- Coarse salt and freshly ground pepper to taste
- 1 teaspoon fresh thyme leaves

Direction

- Preheat oven to 300 degrees. Slice the tomatoes very thin and place them on an oiled roasting dish. Roast for 30 minutes to an hour, or until they begin to shrivel and get brown around the edges. Remove from the oven, scrape up with a spatula and set aside. They will not hold their shape but this does not matter.
- Preheat broiler. Sprinkle the salmon fillet with the lemon juice and olive oil and season to taste. Broil for six minutes on each side or until the fish is done as you like it. Sprinkle with thyme and tomato pieces and serve.

Nutrition Information

- 644: calories;
- 9 grams: saturated fat;
- 10 grams: polyunsaturated fat;
- 49 grams: protein;
- 1169 milligrams: sodium;
- 45 grams: fat;
- 18 grams: monounsaturated fat;
- 12 grams: carbohydrates;
- 4 grams: dietary fiber;
- 7 grams: sugars;

285. Salmon Fillets With Sorrel Sauce

Serving: 4 servings | Prep: | Cook: | Ready in: 15mins

Ingredients

- 2 salmon fillets (about 1 1/2 to 2 pounds)
- 1 to 2 tablespoons olive oil
- Juice 1/2 lemon
- 2 tablespoons unsalted butter
- 1 ½ pounds sorrel, trimmed of stalks
- ¾ cup fish or chicken stock, preferably homemade
- ½ to ¾ cup heavy cream
- Coarse salt and freshly ground pepper to taste

Direction

- Wipe the fillets dry with paper towels and sprinkle with oil and lemon juice. Preheat broiler.
- Heat the butter in a small saucepan and saute the sorrel leaves until they are limp. Add the stock and cream. Bring to boil, season, simmer until thickened slightly.
- Pure sauce in a food processor and return it to pan. Heat through.
- Broil the fillets for about five minutes on each side or until they are cooked. Arrange them on a serving platter. Serve the sauce separately.

Nutrition Information

- 735: calories;
- 53 grams: fat;
- 17 grams: monounsaturated fat;
- 20 grams: carbohydrates;
- 3 grams: sugars;
- 7 grams: dietary fiber;
- 47 grams: protein;
- 1097 milligrams: sodium;
- 19 grams: saturated fat;
- 0 grams: trans fat;
- 10 grams: polyunsaturated fat;

286. Salmon Fillets With Horseradish Crust, Cucumbers And Salmon Caviar

Serving: 6 servings | Prep: | Cook: | Ready in: 20mins

Ingredients

- 3 medium cucumbers, peeled
- 2 tablespoons plus 1 teaspoon sea salt
- 8 ounces smoked salmon, cut crosswise into 3-inch sections
- 1 cup finely grated fresh horseradish
- ½ pound unsalted butter at room temperature, cut into chunks
- 4 cups freshly grated bread crumbs
- 3 tablespoons Dijon-style mustard
- ½ tablespoon cayenne
- 6 salmon fillets, skinless, about 8 ounces each
- Salt and freshly ground pepper
- 1 tablespoon olive oil
- 6 tablespoons creme fraiche or sour cream
- 3 tablespoons chopped parsley
- 2 tablespoons chopped dill
- 2 tablespoons chopped chives
- 6 tablespoons salmon roe

Direction

- Slice the cucumbers on a bias, about 1/4-inch thick. In a bowl, toss the cucumbers with 1 teaspoon of sea salt; then, transfer to a colander. Let drain for 2 hours.
- Place the smoked salmon and horseradish in the bowl of a food processor, and blend until smooth. Add the butter, bread crumbs, the remaining sea salt, mustard and cayenne. Blend well.
- Season the salmon fillets with salt and pepper.
- Turn on broiler. Place 1 tablespoon olive oil in a nonstick saute pan over medium high heat. Cook the salmon for about 45 seconds a side. Remove pan from heat. Carefully cover the fillets with the smoked salmon and horseradish mixture.
- Place the fillets in the broiler, and cook until nicely browned. Remove from the oven and keep warm.
- Quickly heat the cucumbers in the creme fraiche. Distribute the cucumbers evenly over six plates. Sprinkle with parsley, dill and chives. Sprinkle some salmon roe around the cucumbers. Arrange salmon over the cucumbers, and serve immediately.

Nutrition Information

- 1187: calories;
- 30 grams: saturated fat;
- 21 grams: monounsaturated fat;
- 13 grams: polyunsaturated fat;
- 68 grams: protein;
- 1345 milligrams: sodium;
- 73 grams: fat;
- 1 gram: trans fat;
- 63 grams: carbohydrates;
- 6 grams: dietary fiber;
- 10 grams: sugars;

287. Salmon Steaks With Orange And Tarragon Sauce

Serving: 4 servings | Prep: | Cook: | Ready in: 1hours15mins

Ingredients

- 4 salmon steaks (a total of about 2 pounds)
- 2 tablespoons olive oil
- 3 tablespoons fresh tarragon leaves
- Freshly ground pepper
- 2 tablespoons unsalted butter
- 2 shallots, minced
- 2 ripe tomatoes, peeled, seeded and diced
- ½ cup freshly squeezed orange juice
- ½ cup dry white wine
- Coarse salt to taste

Direction

- Wipe the steaks dry with paper towels and sprinkle with olive oil, one tablespoon tarragon leaves and pepper. Leave to marinate for one hour.
- Meanwhile, preheat broiler to high.
- Melt the butter and soften the shallots without browning. Add the tomatoes, orange juice and white wine and reduce by half, over high heat. Season to taste with salt and pepper and set aside.
- Broil the fish for three to five minutes on each side. Place on a heated platter and pour the sauce on top. Sprinkle with remaining tarragon and serve.

Nutrition Information

- 599: calories;
- 39 grams: fat;
- 11 grams: saturated fat;
- 0 grams: trans fat;
- 14 grams: monounsaturated fat;
- 9 grams: polyunsaturated fat;
- 2 grams: dietary fiber;
- 13 grams: carbohydrates;
- 7 grams: sugars;
- 42 grams: protein;
- 848 milligrams: sodium;

288. Salmon With Lemon Herb Marinade

Serving: 6 servings | Prep: | Cook: | Ready in: 1hours20mins

Ingredients

- 1 3-pound salmon fillet, in one piece
- 1 clove garlic, minced
- 2 tablespoons dark brown sugar
- 2 tablespoons soy sauce
- 1 tablespoon grated lemon peel
- 2 tablespoons parsley, chopped fine
- 2 tablespoons fresh thyme leaves
- 1 tablespoon fresh rosemary leaves
- Juice of 1/2 lemon
- 2 tablespoons sesame oil
- ¼ cup extra-virgin olive oil
- Coarse salt and freshly ground pepper to taste
- 1 lemon, cut into 6 wedges
- Sprigs of rosemary, for garnish

Direction

- Wipe salmon fillet dry with paper towels. Combine remaining ingredients (except lemon wedges and rosemary sprigs) in small bowl and mix well. Pour mixture over salmon, making sure it is coated on both sides. Marinate for at least an hour before cooking.
- Preheat broiler or grill. Cook salmon, turning once — five to six minutes each side for medium rare.
- Place salmon on serving platter and garnish with lemon wedges and sprigs of rosemary.

Nutrition Information

- 616: calories;
- 44 grams: fat;
- 9 grams: saturated fat;
- 17 grams: monounsaturated fat;
- 627 milligrams: sodium;
- 12 grams: polyunsaturated fat;
- 6 grams: carbohydrates;
- 1 gram: dietary fiber;
- 3 grams: sugars;
- 47 grams: protein;

289. Salmon And Olives With Linguine

Serving: 2 to 3 servings | Prep: | Cook: | Ready in: 15mins

Ingredients

- 1 pound salmon fillets, skinned

- 2 tablespoons olive oil
- 2 medium onions, chopped
- 2 cloves garlic, minced
- 4 tablespoons chopped Greek olives, or other olives packed in brine
- 2 teaspoons dried oregano
- ½ pound linguine
- Freshly ground black pepper to taste

Direction

- Broil fillets 5 to 7 minutes, depending on thickness.
- In hot oil, saute onion and garlic until onion is soft. Add olives and oregano and stir; cook 2 minutes over low heat.
- Meanwhile, cook linguine in 4 quarts boiling water until it is al dente. Drain.
- Cut salmon into small pieces and add to onion. Reheat and serve mixed with pasta.
- Sprinkle with freshly ground black pepper.

Nutrition Information

- 724: calories;
- 6 grams: saturated fat;
- 13 grams: monounsaturated fat;
- 5 grams: sugars;
- 32 grams: fat;
- 7 grams: polyunsaturated fat;
- 66 grams: carbohydrates;
- 42 grams: protein;
- 180 milligrams: sodium;

---

290. Salsa Fresca With Kohlrabi

Serving: About 2 1/4 cups | Prep: | Cook: | Ready in: 15mins

Ingredients

- ¼ cup finely chopped red or white onion
- ½ medium kohlrabi (about 1/2 pound), cut in small dice (1 cup)
- 1 pound ripe tomatoes, diced (2 cups)
- 1 to 2 serrano or jalepeño chiles (or more, to taste), minced
- ¼ to ½ cup chopped cilantro (to taste)
- 1 to 2 tablespoons fresh lime juice (to taste)
- Salt to taste

Direction

- Place onion in a small bowl and cover with cold water. Let sit for 5 minutes. Drain and rinse with cold water. Drain on paper towels.
- Combine kohlrabi and tomatoes in a medium bowl. Add onions, chiles, cilantro, lime juice and salt to taste and stir together. Let sit for 15 to 30 minutes before serving.

Nutrition Information

- 27: calories;
- 1 gram: protein;
- 294 milligrams: sodium;
- 0 grams: polyunsaturated fat;
- 6 grams: carbohydrates;
- 2 grams: dietary fiber;
- 3 grams: sugars;

---

291. Sausages With Ginger, Star Anise And Soy Sauce

Serving: About 1 pound of sausages | Prep: | Cook: | Ready in: 10mins

Ingredients

- 1 teaspoon fennel seeds
- 1 star anise, broken into pieces
- 1 pound ground dark-meat chicken or pork
- 2 tablespoons soy sauce
- 1 ½ tablespoons grated fresh ginger
- 1 tablespoon minced garlic
- 2 teaspoons light brown sugar

- Olive oil for cooking

Direction

- In a small skillet over medium-low heat, toast fennel seeds until fragrant, 1 to 2 minutes. Transfer fennel and star anise to a spice grinder and grind well.
- In a large bowl, combine all ingredients. Form sausage mixture into desired shape: cylinders or patties. Chill for up to 5 days, freeze for up to 3 months, or use immediately.
- Brush sausages with oil and grill or broil them until browned and cooked through. Or fry them in a little oil until well browned all over.

Nutrition Information

- 185: calories;
- 2 grams: carbohydrates;
- 347 milligrams: sodium;
- 13 grams: fat;
- 3 grams: polyunsaturated fat;
- 0 grams: dietary fiber;
- 6 grams: monounsaturated fat;
- 1 gram: sugars;
- 15 grams: protein;

292. Sausages With Peppers

Serving: 4 servings | Prep: | Cook: | Ready in: 30mins

Ingredients

- 8 pork sausages (Italian, sweet or country)
- 2 tablespoons olive oil
- 1 tablespoon butter
- 1 large onion, chopped
- 1 clove garlic, minced
- 1 pound sweet peppers (green, red and yellow, if available) seeded and cut into thick strips
- ½ cup dry white wine
- ½ to ¾ cup chicken stock
- 1 teaspoon arrowroot dissolved in 1 tablespoon water
- Coarse salt and freshly ground pepper to taste

Direction

- Prick the sausages all over with a fork and place on a broiling rack. Sprinkle with one tablespoon olive oil and broil slowly until browned on all sides, and cooked through. Keep warm.
- Meanwhile, heat the butter with remaining oil in a skillet and saute the onion, garlic and peppers until the onions are soft.
- Add the wine and chicken stock and simmer gently for five minutes. Stir in the arrowroot mixture and bring to boil. Season to taste with salt and pepper. Turn down heat and add the sausages. Cover the pan and cook for five to 10 more minutes.

Nutrition Information

- 319: calories;
- 0 grams: trans fat;
- 8 grams: sugars;
- 10 grams: protein;
- 7 grams: saturated fat;
- 23 grams: fat;
- 11 grams: monounsaturated fat;
- 3 grams: dietary fiber;
- 14 grams: carbohydrates;
- 649 milligrams: sodium;

293. Savory Bread Pudding

Serving: 8 servings | Prep: | Cook: | Ready in: 45mins

Ingredients

- 8 ounces sourdough bread, cut into 1-inch cubes
- 4 ounces Swiss cheese, grated
- 2 ounces Parmesan cheese, grated

- 3 tablespoons butter
- 4 ounces mixed wild mushrooms (shiitake, oyster, black trumpet or others), sliced
- 2 cups roughly chopped fresh spinach
- 1 cup chopped Swiss chard leaves
- 1 leek, white and light green parts only, rinsed well and very thinly sliced
- ⅓ cup Swiss chard stems, diced
- 1 large egg
- ¾ cup whole milk
- ¾ cup heavy cream
- Salt and freshly ground black pepper

Direction

- In a large mixing bowl, combine the bread, Swiss cheese and half of the Parmesan cheese.
- In a large skillet over medium-low heat, melt 1 tablespoon of the butter. Add mushrooms, and saute until tender, 2 to 3 minutes. Transfer mushrooms to the mixing bowl. Add 1 tablespoon of the butter to the skillet, and add the spinach and Swiss chard leaves. Saute until wilted, about 2 minutes, and transfer to the mixing bowl.
- Bring a small pan of water to a boil, and add the leeks and Swiss chard stems. Blanch for 1 minute, remove from heat and drain well. Add to bread mixture.
- Preheat oven to 400 degrees. Rub the inside of an 8-inch-square baking pan with the remaining 1 tablespoon butter. In a medium bowl, beat egg just until blended.
- In a saucepan over medium-low heat, combine milk and heavy cream. Bring to a boil, and remove from heat. While whisking vigorously, add about 1/2 cup of the hot milk mixture to the egg, then return the egg mixture to the pan and whisk until blended. Add milk mixture to the bowl of dry ingredients, and stir. Season with salt and pepper to taste. Transfer mixture to the baking pan, pressing gently on surface. Bake pudding until set, about 15 minutes.
- Remove pan from oven. Preheat a broiler with a rack about 6 inches from the heat. Unmold pudding onto a cookie sheet or other flat pan. Sprinkle remaining Parmesan cheese on top of the pudding, and place under broiler until golden brown, about 20 seconds. Serve while hot.

Nutrition Information

- 313: calories;
- 21 grams: carbohydrates;
- 12 grams: protein;
- 6 grams: monounsaturated fat;
- 2 grams: dietary fiber;
- 4 grams: sugars;
- 0 grams: trans fat;
- 1 gram: polyunsaturated fat;
- 339 milligrams: sodium;

294. Serious Potato Skins

Serving: Serves 4 | Prep: | Cook: | Ready in: 1hours30mins

Ingredients

- 4 Idaho baking potatoes
- Extra-virgin olive oil
- 8 ounces thick-cut bacon, diced
- 6 ounces cheddar cheese
- 1 bunch scallions
- Kosher salt
- freshly ground black pepper
- 1 cup sour cream
- Hot sauce, to taste

Direction

- Preheat the oven to 400 degrees. Rub the potatoes lightly with olive oil and bake them on a foil-lined baking sheet until their skins are crisp and a fork easily slides into their flesh, about 1 hour. Transfer the potatoes to a wire rack and let cool for 10 minutes.
- While the potatoes are cooking, assemble the toppings. Cook the bacon in a large skillet over medium heat until crisp, then transfer to a

small bowl. Reserve the bacon fat. Grate the cheese into a small bowl; you should have about 2 cups. Trim and thinly slice the scallions. (Feeling frisky? Caramelize some onions. Shred some ham or grate some Gruyère.)

- Using an oven mitt or a folded kitchen towel to handle the hot potatoes, cut each into quarters lengthwise to create four wedges. Using a small spoon, scoop the flesh from each wedge, leaving 1/4 inch or more of the flesh. (Save the scooped potatoes for another use, like potato pancakes or soup.)
- Set the oven to broil. Return the wedges to the foil-lined baking sheet. Paint a bit of bacon fat on each, then top with cheese and bacon. Place under the broiler until the cheese is bubbling. Place the skins on a serving plate. Season with salt and pepper. Spoon a teaspoon or so of sour cream on each and scatter the scallions over the plate. Serve with hot sauce.

295. Sesame Chicken Kebabs With Orange Hoisin Sauce

Serving: 4 to 6 servings | Prep: | Cook: | Ready in: 2hours30mins

Ingredients

- 3 whole chicken breasts, cut in 2-inch cubes
- For marinade:
- ½ cup soy sauce
- 2 tablespoons sesame oil
- 2 tablespoons olive oil
- Juice of 1/2 lemon
- 2 cloves garlic, minced
- 1 teaspoon fresh ginger, minced
- ¼ teaspoon ground chilies
- 1 teaspoon rosemary leaves
- For the sauce:
- ¾ cup hoisin sauce (available in Oriental groceries)
- 3 tablespoons rice vinegar
- ½ cup freshly squeezed orange juice
- 2 minced scallions
- 2 tablespoons sesame oil
- Coarse salt and freshly ground pepper to taste
- Sprigs of rosemary for garnishing

Direction

- Marinate chicken in mixture of soy sauce, sesame oil, olive oil, lemon juice, garlic, ginger, chilies and rosemary leaves for at least two hours. Thread chicken on skewers.
- Combine hoisin sauce, vinegar, orange juice, scallions and sesame oil. Season to taste with salt and pepper.
- Preheat grill or broiler. Cook chicken for about five minutes on each side, or until done, basting with marinade. Garnish plates with rosemary sprigs. Serve sauce separately in small bowl.

Nutrition Information

- 368: calories;
- 4 grams: saturated fat;
- 11 grams: sugars;
- 19 grams: carbohydrates;
- 1741 milligrams: sodium;
- 23 grams: fat;
- 0 grams: trans fat;
- 7 grams: polyunsaturated fat;
- 2 grams: dietary fiber;
- 21 grams: protein;

296. Sheet Pan Chicken With Apple, Fennel And Onion

Serving: None | Prep: | Cook: | Ready in:

Ingredients

- 2 teaspoons fennel seeds
- 2 ½ to 3 pounds bone-in, skin-on chicken thighs, patted dry

- 3 tablespoons olive oil
- Kosher salt and black pepper
- 1 medium yellow onion, thinly sliced (about 1 1/2 cups)
- 1 medium fennel bulb, tough outer leaves removed, cored and thinly sliced (about 1 cup)
- 1 tart apple, such as Mutsu (Crispin) or Granny Smith, halved, cored and cut into 8 wedges
- 4 sprigs rosemary
- Flaky salt, for serving

Direction

- Heat oven to 425 degrees. In a small skillet, toast the fennel seeds over medium-low heat, stirring frequently until fragrant, about 2 to 3 minutes. Pound into a coarse powder with a mortar and pestle or, alternatively, roughly chop. In a large bowl, toss together the chicken with 1 tablespoon olive oil and the fennel seeds and season well with salt and pepper.
- Place the onion, fennel and apple slices on the sheet pan. Toss with the remaining olive oil and season well with salt. Spread in an even layer. Add the chicken skin side up on top of the vegetables and lay the rosemary (distributing evenly) on top of the chicken. Roast for 25 to 30 minutes until the chicken is cooked through and the onions, fennel and apples are softened and have begun to caramelize at the edge of the pan.
- Turn the oven to broil and move the oven rack to sit right below it. Remove and discard the rosemary sprigs and broil the chicken for 1 to 2 minutes until the skin of the chicken is crispy and golden. Season with flaky salt.

297. Sheet Pan Chicken With Shallots And Grapes

Serving: 4 to 6 servings | Prep: | Cook: | Ready in: 35mins

Ingredients

- 2 ½ to 3 pounds bone-in, skin-on chicken thighs, patted dry
- 3 tablespoons olive oil
- 2 garlic cloves, finely chopped
- 1 tablespoon za'atar (optional)
- Kosher salt and black pepper
- 6 medium to large shallots, peeled and quartered root to stem
- 8 ounces seedless red or green grapes, or a combination, broken into small clusters on the vine
- 4 to 5 thyme sprigs, plus 2 teaspoons finely chopped thyme
- Flaky sea salt, for serving

Direction

- Heat oven to 425 degrees. In a large bowl, toss together the chicken with 1 tablespoon olive oil, garlic and za'atar, if using. Season well with salt and pepper. Place the shallots and the grapes on the sheet pan and gently toss with the remaining olive oil and season well with salt.
- Nestle the chicken skin-side up in between the shallots and grapes and lay the thyme sprigs on top of the mixture. Roast for 25 to 30 minutes until the chicken is cooked through and the shallots and grapes at the edges of the pan begin to soften and caramelize.
- Turn the oven to broil and move the oven rack to sit right below it. Remove and discard the thyme sprigs and broil the chicken for 1 to 2 minutes until the skin of the chicken is crispy and golden. Scatter with chopped thyme and season with flaky salt.

Nutrition Information

- 609: calories;
- 41 grams: fat;
- 19 grams: monounsaturated fat;
- 8 grams: polyunsaturated fat;
- 22 grams: carbohydrates;
- 12 grams: sugars;
- 37 grams: protein;
- 10 grams: saturated fat;

- 0 grams: trans fat;
- 3 grams: dietary fiber;
- 783 milligrams: sodium;

298. Sheet Pan Gochujang Shrimp And Green Beans

Serving: 4 servings | Prep: | Cook: | Ready in: 10mins

Ingredients

- 2 tablespoons plus 2 teaspoons gochujang
- 2 tablespoons extra-virgin olive oil
- 1 tablespoon soy sauce
- 2 teaspoons honey
- 1 pound large shrimp, peeled and deveined
- 1 pound green beans, trimmed

Direction

- Place an oven rack as close to the broiler as possible. (If your broiler is in a drawer below the oven, skip this step.) Heat broiler for at least 5 minutes.
- Meanwhile, in a large bowl, whisk together the gochujang, olive oil, soy sauce and honey until smooth and emulsified. Add the shrimp and green beans and stir to coat.
- On a foil-lined baking sheet, spread the shrimp and string beans evenly in a single layer, leaving behind any excess marinade. Broil until the beans are charred in spots and the shrimp is cooked through, about 5 minutes. (Depending on your broiler, you may need to rotate the pan after 2 or 3 minutes so all the food gets exposure under the heat source.)

Nutrition Information

- 211: calories;
- 1 gram: saturated fat;
- 5 grams: monounsaturated fat;
- 7 grams: sugars;

- 19 grams: protein;
- 1296 milligrams: sodium;
- 4 grams: dietary fiber;
- 9 grams: fat;
- 0 grams: trans fat;
- 2 grams: polyunsaturated fat;
- 15 grams: carbohydrates;

299. Sheet Pan Shrimp With Tomatoes, Feta And Oregano

Serving: 4 servings | Prep: | Cook: | Ready in: 10mins

Ingredients

- 1 garlic clove
- 1 teaspoon salt
- 1 tablespoon chopped fresh oregano
- 1 tablespoon lemon juice
- 2 tablespoons olive oil
- Black pepper
- 1 ½ pounds peeled shrimp
- Chopped tomatoes, for serving
- Crumbled feta, for serving

Direction

- Turn on the broiler, and position the oven rack close to the heat.
- Mash garlic clove with salt until it forms a paste. Add chopped oregano, lemon juice, olive oil and lots of black pepper. Rub paste all over 1 1/2 pounds peeled shrimp.
- Spread shrimp out on a pan and broil, 2 to 3 minutes per side. Served topped with chopped tomatoes and crumbled feta.

Nutrition Information

- 188: calories;
- 1 gram: dietary fiber;
- 0 grams: sugars;
- 5 grams: monounsaturated fat;
- 3 grams: carbohydrates;

- 23 grams: protein;
- 964 milligrams: sodium;
- 9 grams: fat;

300. Shiitake Crusted Chicken With Spinach Sauce

Serving: 6 servings | Prep: | Cook: | Ready in: 2hours

Ingredients

- For the sauce:
- 8 cups stemmed and coarsely chopped spinach (about 10 ounces)
- 2 tablespoons unsalted butter
- 1 small Spanish onion, chopped
- 2 cloves garlic, finely chopped
- 1 tablespoon Champagne vinegar
- 1 cup homemade or low-sodium chicken broth
- 1 teaspoon granulated sugar
- ¼ teaspoon curry powder
- Kosher salt and freshly ground pepper to taste
- For the chicken:
- 3 tablespoons olive oil
- 1 ½ pounds shiitake mushrooms
- 2 large shallots, coarsely chopped
- 2 large cloves garlic, finely chopped
- Kosher salt and pepper to taste
- 6 large boned and skinned chicken breast halves, tenderloins removed and reserved (about 2 1/4 pounds)
- 2 tablespoons plain bread crumbs

Direction

- To make the sauce, in a large pot of salted boiling water, cook the spinach until deep green, about 45 seconds. Drain it and transfer to a plate to cool. When cool enough to handle, squeeze out the excess liquid and set aside.
- In a medium saucepan over medium heat, heat the butter. Add the onion and cook, stirring occasionally, until soft, about 5 minutes. Add the garlic, vinegar, broth, sugar and curry and bring to a boil. Boil until reduced by a third, about 1 1/2 minutes. Stir in the spinach and return to a boil. Remove from the heat and set aside.
- When the spinach mixture has cooled, transfer to a blender and puree until smooth. Season with salt and pepper and set aside.
- To make the chicken, in a large skillet over high heat, heat 2 tablespoons of the oil. Add the mushrooms, shallots and garlic and cook, stirring occasionally, until lightly browned and soft, about 6 minutes. Season with salt and pepper. Transfer the mushroom mixture to a baking sheet in an even layer and set aside to cool.
- Preheat the oven to 300 degrees. When the mushroom mixture is cool, transfer to a food processor with the chicken tenderloins and pulse until a paste forms. Divide the paste into 6 equal portions. Season the chicken breasts with salt and pepper. On a work surface, lay out a 12-inch length of heavy-duty plastic wrap and place 1 portion of the paste in the center. Fold the plastic in half and, using a rolling pin, flatten the paste until slightly larger than half a chicken breast. Unfold the plastic and place a piece of chicken, smooth-side down, on the paste and gather the plastic up and around the breast. Cut the excess plastic and discard. Transfer the wrapped chicken, paste-side up, to a parchment-lined baking sheet. Repeat with the remaining paste and chicken breasts. Bake until firm and cooked through, about 25 minutes. (The plastic will not melt.)
- Remove the chicken from the oven and preheat the broiler. Carefully unwrap the plastic and return the breasts, paste-side up, to the baking sheet relined with foil. Brush with the remaining tablespoon of oil and lightly sprinkle with bread crumbs. Broil until golden brown, about 3 minutes. Set aside for 5 minutes.
- Reheat the sauce. Slice the breast halves on the diagonal and arrange each one on a plate, fanning out the slices. Ladle the sauce alongside each breast and serve.

Nutrition Information

- 344: calories;
- 809 milligrams: sodium;
- 20 grams: carbohydrates;
- 6 grams: sugars;
- 0 grams: trans fat;
- 9 grams: monounsaturated fat;
- 3 grams: polyunsaturated fat;
- 24 grams: protein;

301. Shirley Savis's Amendoa Cake

Serving: Eight to 10 servings | Prep: | Cook: | Ready in: 50mins

Ingredients

- ⅓ cup unsalted butter, melted and cooled to room temperature, plus some for greasing the pan
- 1 cup sifted all-purpose flour
- 1 ½ cups plus 2 tablespoons sugar
- ½ teaspoon baking powder
- ½ teaspoon baking soda
- ¼ teaspoon salt
- 1 egg, cold
- ½ cup cold buttermilk
- ½ teaspoon vanilla extract
- ⅔ cup sliced almonds
- ½ teaspoon almond extract

Direction

- Preheat the oven to 350 degrees. Grease a 9-inch round springform cake pan.
- Sift together the flour, 3/4 cup plus 2 tablespoons sugar, baking powder, baking soda and salt. Beat together the egg, buttermilk and vanilla until smooth. Stir in the butter. Pour into the flour mixture and beat with a spoon until nearly smooth. Pour into the pan.
- Bake until the center of the cake springs back when lightly touched, 25 to 35 minutes. Immediately sprinkle the top evenly with almonds. Turn on the broiler.
- Meanwhile, combine the remaining 3/4 cup sugar with 6 tablespoons water in a pot and boil until the mixture reaches 220 degrees on a candy thermometer. Remove from the heat and stir in the almond extract.
- Slowly pour the hot almond syrup evenly over the cake, letting it soak in. Broil about 6 inches from the heat until the almonds are lightly toasted, about 1 1/2 minutes. Unmold and cool.

Nutrition Information

- 273: calories;
- 4 grams: protein;
- 0 grams: trans fat;
- 1 gram: dietary fiber;
- 44 grams: carbohydrates;
- 33 grams: sugars;
- 170 milligrams: sodium;
- 10 grams: fat;

302. Shortcut Tortilla Soup

Serving: 4 to 6 servings | Prep: | Cook: | Ready in: 1hours

Ingredients

- 2 fresh chiles, preferably pasilla
- 1 ½ pounds tomatoes, each cut in half
- 2 tablespoons neutral oil, like grapeseed or corn
- 3 cloves garlic, sliced
- 1 large onion, sliced
- Salt and freshly ground pepper
- Pinch dried oregano
- 4 cups any stock or water
- 1 to 2 cups tortilla chips
- 1 cup fresh cilantro leaves, chopped, optional
- 1 ripe avocado, peeled and sliced, optional

- 1 or 2 radishes, thinly sliced, optional
- 1 lime, juiced, plus one cut into wedges

Direction

- Heat broiler. Arrange chilies and tomatoes in a single layer on a rimmed baking sheet and place a few inches away from broiling element. Cook until charred on one side, then flip them with tongs and char other side, about 5 to 8 minutes total. When cool, skin, stem and seed chilies, then chop them.
- Put oil in a large saucepan over medium heat; a minute later add garlic and onion and cook, stirring occasionally, until golden and softened, about 10 minutes. Add tomatoes and chilies, crushing tomatoes with back of a wooden spoon. Season with salt, pepper and a pinch of oregano; add stock or water and adjust heat so mixture simmers gently. Cook for 20 to 30 minutes, crushing tomatoes from time to time. (You can prepare soup up to this point in advance. Let it sit for a few hours, or cover and refrigerate for up to a day before reheating and finishing.)
- Stir in tortilla chips and simmer another three to five minutes. Season to taste with lime juice, salt and pepper, then garnish if desired and serve with lime wedges.

Nutrition Information

- 181: calories;
- 0 grams: trans fat;
- 27 grams: carbohydrates;
- 4 grams: dietary fiber;
- 6 grams: fat;
- 1 gram: saturated fat;
- 2 grams: polyunsaturated fat;
- 7 grams: protein;
- 773 milligrams: sodium;

303. Shredded Potato Cake With Egg And Cheese And Bacon

Serving: 4 to 8 servings | Prep: | Cook: | Ready in: 40mins

Ingredients

- ½ pound slab or other good bacon, cut into 1/4-inch chunks
- 3 or 4 potatoes, about 1 1/2 pounds
- Salt and pepper to taste
- At least 1 cup shredded cheese, like Gruyère, Emmenthal or Cheddar
- 6 to 8 eggs

Direction

- Put bacon in large nonstick skillet over medium heat; while fat is rendering, peel and grate potatoes (shredding disk of a food processor works great).
- When bacon is about halfway crisp, spread it evenly in pan, and put potatoes over it; sprinkle with salt and pepper. Press the potatoes down with a plate almost as big as pan, and leave plate in place for about 5 minutes. Remove plate, and continue to cook, undisturbed, so potatoes form a cake, and adjusting heat so potatoes brown without burning. When potatoes are brown, slide cake out onto a plate, invert it onto another plate, and slide it back in, cooked side up.
- Turn on broiler while potatoes brown on the bottom, about 5 minutes. Sprinkle cheese on potatoes and carefully break eggs into the cheese (if you like softer eggs, put eggs on first, followed by cheese). Broil until cheese melts and eggs are set, about 5 minutes. Serve hot.

Nutrition Information

- 387: calories;
- 1 gram: sugars;
- 19 grams: protein;

- 4 grams: polyunsaturated fat;
- 27 grams: fat;
- 11 grams: monounsaturated fat;
- 0 grams: trans fat;
- 16 grams: carbohydrates;
- 2 grams: dietary fiber;
- 521 milligrams: sodium;

304. Shu Mai Style Burgers

Serving: 8 burgers | Prep: | Cook: | Ready in: 30mins

Ingredients

- ½ pound shrimp, peeled
- 2 medium cloves garlic
- 1 ½ pounds boneless pork shoulder, with the fat, cut into 1-inch cubes
- 2 teaspoons soy sauce
- ¼ cup chopped scallion plus more for garnish
- ¼ cup chopped cilantro plus more for garnish
- 1 small fresh chili, seeded and minced
- 1 tablespoon minced fresh ginger
- Salt
- freshly ground black pepper to taste
- Shredded cabbage to garnish (optional)
- pickled pepper, to garnish (optional)

Direction

- If grilling or broiling, heat should be medium-high and rack about 4 inches from fire. Put shrimp and garlic in a food processor and pulse until just chopped; remove to a large bowl. Working in batches, grind pork fat until just chopped (be careful not to over-process). Add to bowl. Then grind meat until just chopped, again being careful not to over-process; add to bowl.
- Mix shrimp, pork fat and meat with the soy sauce, scallion, cilantro, chili and ginger; sprinkle with salt and pepper. Shape into 8 patties.
- To broil or grill, cook about 4 minutes, then turn and cook for a total of 8 to 10 minutes, or until nicely browned and cooked through. For stovetop, heat a large skillet over medium heat for 2 or 3 minutes, then add the patties; cook undisturbed, for about 4 minutes, then turn and cook for a total of 8 to 10 minutes, or until nicely browned and cooked through.
- Garnish with scallion, cilantro, cabbage and pickled pepper, to taste.

Nutrition Information

- 226: calories;
- 16 grams: fat;
- 19 grams: protein;
- 0 grams: sugars;
- 7 grams: monounsaturated fat;
- 2 grams: polyunsaturated fat;
- 1 gram: carbohydrates;
- 289 milligrams: sodium;
- 5 grams: saturated fat;

305. Skillet Macaroni And Broccoli And Mushrooms And Cheese

Serving: Makes six side-dish servings. | Prep: | Cook: | Ready in: 30mins

Ingredients

- 4 ounces grated Cheddar
- 2 ounces finely grated Parmigiano-Reggiano or other hard cheese
- 1 tablespoon unsalted butter
- 1 small yellow onion, chopped
- 6 ounces cremini or white button mushrooms, sliced
- 3 tablespoons unbleached all-purpose flour
- 3 cups low-fat or fat-free milk
- 1 tablespoon Dijon mustard
- 1 tablespoon minced tarragon leaves or 2 teaspoons dried tarragon
- ½ teaspoon salt

- ½ teaspoon freshly ground black pepper
- 8 ounces dried whole-wheat pasta shells (not the large ones for stuffing), cooked and drained according to the package instructions
- 4 cups small broccoli florets, cooked in boiling water for 1 minute (broccoli can be added to the pasta during the last minute of cooking, then drained with the pasta in a colander)

Direction

- Mix the Cheddar and Parmigiano-Reggiano in a medium bowl. Set aside.
- Melt the butter in a large, high-sided, oven-safe skillet. Add the onion and cook, stirring often, until softened, about 3 minutes.
- Add the mushrooms and cook until they release their liquid and it comes to a simmer, and then reduces by about two-thirds, about 5 minutes.
- Sprinkle the flour over the vegetables in the skillet. Stir well to coat.
- Whisk in the milk in a steady, thin stream until creamy. Then whisk in the mustard, tarragon, salt and pepper. Continue whisking until the mixture starts to bubble and the liquid thickens, about 3 minutes
- Remove the skillet from the heat. Stir in three-quarters of the mixed cheeses until smooth. Then stir in the cooked pasta and broccoli.
- Preheat the broiler after setting the rack 4 to 6 inches from the heat source. Meanwhile, sprinkle the remaining cheese over the ingredients in the skillet. Set the skillet on the rack and broil until light browned and bubbling, about 5 minutes. (If your skillet has a plastic or wooden handle, make sure it sticks outside the oven, out from under the broiler, so the handle doesn't melt.) Cool for 5 to 10 minutes before dishing up.

Nutrition Information

- 353: calories;
- 0 grams: trans fat;
- 1 gram: polyunsaturated fat;
- 42 grams: carbohydrates;
- 8 grams: sugars;
- 13 grams: fat;
- 7 grams: saturated fat;
- 3 grams: monounsaturated fat;
- 2 grams: dietary fiber;
- 19 grams: protein;
- 482 milligrams: sodium;

306. Smoky Eggplant Spread

Serving: about 2 cups | Prep: | Cook: |Ready in: 40mins

Ingredients

- 3 medium eggplants, about 2 pounds
- Salt
- ¼ cup tahini paste
- ¼ cup lemon juice
- 4 garlic cloves, mashed to a paste
- ⅛ teaspoon cayenne
- ½ teaspoon cumin seed, toasted until fragrant and coarsely ground
- 3 tablespoons olive oil
- ½ teaspoon paprika
- 1 tablespoon finely chopped parsley
- 1 tablespoon finely chopped mint
- Pita or other flatbread, for serving (optional)

Direction

- Prepare a charcoal fire or heat the broiler. Pierce eggplants here and there with the point of a paring knife. Place eggplants 2 inches from heat source. Allow skins to blister and char, turning with tongs until entire surface is blackened and eggplants are completely soft, about 10 to 12 minutes. Set aside until cool enough to handle.
- Slice eggplants in half lengthwise and lay skin side down on a cutting board. Carefully scrape away flesh with a knife and put it in a colander. Discard burned skins. Do not rinse eggplant flesh — a few bits of remaining char is fine. Salt flesh lightly and leave for 5 to 10

minutes, then squeeze into a ball to remove liquid.
- Blitz eggplant, 1/2 teaspoon salt, tahini, lemon juice, garlic and cayenne in a food processor or blender to obtain a creamy purée. (For a more rustic spread, beat with a whisk instead.) Taste and adjust salt and lemon juice if necessary. Transfer mixture to a shallow serving bowl.
- Just before serving, stir together cumin and olive oil, and spoon over the mixture's surface. Sprinkle with paprika, parsley and mint. Serve with warm pita cut into triangles if desired.

Nutrition Information

- 157: calories;
- 12 grams: fat;
- 2 grams: saturated fat;
- 7 grams: monounsaturated fat;
- 3 grams: protein;
- 11 grams: carbohydrates;
- 5 grams: sugars;
- 423 milligrams: sodium;

307. Soft Tacos With Roasted Or Grilled Tomatoes And Squash

Serving: Enough for 10 tacos | Prep: | Cook: | Ready in: 40mins

Ingredients

- 1 pound tomatoes
- 2 tablespoons extra virgin olive oil
- ½ medium onion, chopped (about 1 cup chopped)
- 2 large garlic cloves, minced
- 2 serrano chiles or 1 large jalapeño, minced
- 1 ½ pounds summer squash, cut in 1/4-inch dice
- Salt and freshly ground pepper
- 1 cup cooked black beans, rinsed if using canned
- 2 to 3 tablespoons chopped cilantro
- 10 corn tortillas
- 2 to 3 ounces goat cheese

Direction

- Preheat the broiler. Line a baking sheet with foil and place the tomatoes on the foil. Place under the broiler, about 2 inches from the heat, and broil until charred black. Turn over and broil on the other side until charred black. This takes about 3 minutes on each side in my oven but all broilers/ovens are different. Remove from the heat and allow to cool until you can handle them, then remove the skins, core and cut in half along the equator. Set a strainer over a bowl and squeeze out the seeds (make sure they have cooled before you do this!), then rub the gelatinous pulp that surrounds the seeds through the strainer. Chop the tomatoes and combine with the juice in the bowl.
- Heat the olive oil in a large, heavy skillet over medium heat and add the onion. Cook, stirring often, until tender, about 5 minutes, and add the garlic, chiles, summer squash, and a generous pinch of salt. Turn the heat to medium-high and cook, stirring often, for about 5 minutes, until the squash is tender. Add the chopped tomatoes and their juices and cook, stirring often, until the tomatoes have cooked down and the mixture is fragrant, 5 to 10 more minutes. Add more salt to taste, and freshly ground pepper. Stir in the black beans, add the cilantro, taste, adjust seasonings, and remove from the heat.
- Pile onto warm corn tortillas, sprinkle on a little goat cheese, fold the tortillas over and serve.

Nutrition Information

- 142: calories;
- 3 grams: sugars;
- 1 gram: polyunsaturated fat;
- 20 grams: carbohydrates;
- 6 grams: protein;

- 403 milligrams: sodium;
- 5 grams: dietary fiber;
- 2 grams: saturated fat;

308. Soft Shell Crab Crostini With Arugula Butter

Serving: 4 servings as an appetizer, 2 as a main course | Prep: | Cook: | Ready in: 25mins

Ingredients

- ¾ cup arugula leaves, stems trimmed
- 8 tablespoons (1 stick) unsalted butter, at room temperature
- 1 tablespoon finely chopped chives
- 2 garlic cloves, minced
- ½ teaspoon kosher salt, more as needed
- ¼ teaspoon black pepper
- 4 soft-shell crabs, cleaned and patted dry
- 4 half-inch-thick slices country-style bread

Direction

- Finely chop 1/4 cup of the arugula. Combine in a bowl with the butter, chives, garlic, salt and pepper.
- Heat 4 tablespoons of the arugula butter mixture in a large skillet over medium-high heat. Add the crabs and cook, without moving, until crisp and golden, 2 to 3 minutes a side. Transfer to a paper-towel-lined plate and sprinkle with salt.
- Preheat the broiler. Place the bread on a baking sheet and run under the broiler until golden, 1 to 2 minutes. (Watch carefully to see that they don't burn.) Spread the toasted bread with the remaining butter and each slice with a crab. Thinly slice the remaining arugula and sprinkle on top of each serving.

Nutrition Information

- 303: calories;

- 213 milligrams: sodium;
- 24 grams: fat;
- 15 grams: carbohydrates;
- 1 gram: dietary fiber;
- 6 grams: monounsaturated fat;
- 2 grams: sugars;
- 7 grams: protein;

309. Souffléed Horseradish Oysters

Serving: 6 servings as a first course, 12 or more with drinks | Prep: | Cook: | Ready in: 20mins

Ingredients

- 6 tablespoons crème fraîche
- 2 tablespoons prepared horseradish
- 1 teaspoon ketchup
- 2 tablespoons minced chives
- Ground white pepper
- 2 large egg whites
- 3 dozen oysters on the half-shell

Direction

- Heat broiler. Place crème fraîche in a medium-size bowl and mix in horseradish, ketchup and chives. Season with pepper. Beat egg whites until they hold peaks. Fold into crème fraîche mixture.
- Arrange oysters on a baking pan lined with crumpled aluminum foil to hold them steady, or place them in madeleine pans. Spoon about a tablespoon of the crème fraîche mixture on each. Broil about 3 inches from the source of heat, a minute or so, until lightly dappled with brown on top. Arrange on a platter or on individual plates and serve.

310. Spanish Tortilla With Mushrooms And Kale

Serving: 4 to 6 servings | Prep: | Cook: |Ready in: 45mins

Ingredients

- 7 tablespoons extra-virgin olive oil
- 1 medium-large Yukon Gold potato, about 6 ounces, peeled and diced
- Salt and ground black pepper
- ⅔ cup diced onion
- 4 ounces shiitake mushrooms, stemmed and diced
- Leaves from 5 branches fresh thyme
- ½ cup finely chopped kale
- 6 large eggs, beaten
- Large pinch ground espelette pepper or cayenne, or to taste

Direction

- Heat 3 1/2 tablespoons of the olive oil at medium low in a heavy 8- to 9-inch skillet, preferably nonstick. Add potatoes, spreading them in the pan, and cook 10 minutes, stirring from time to time to prevent sticking. Do not let them brown. Season with salt and pepper.
- Add onions, mushrooms, thyme and another tablespoon of oil and continue cooking, stirring from time to time, another 10 minutes or so, until mushrooms and onions have softened and potatoes are tender. Add the kale and cook 5 minutes more. Check seasoning. Turn off heat and remove the vegetables to a bowl. Fold in the eggs.
- Wipe out the pan, removing any clinging bits. To flip the tortilla, have ready a plate that's larger than the pan, the lid of the pan or a plastic cutting board wrapped in foil. Alternatively, you can finish the tortilla under the broiler; if so, heat the broiler.
- Return pan to the stove on medium-high heat. Add 2 tablespoons oil. When oil is hot, add the eggs and vegetables. Reduce heat to medium low. Slide the pan back and forth to prevent the tortilla from sticking and run a spatula around the edges to loosen the eggs. When the eggs are nearly set on top, finish under the broiler for a minute or two, until very lightly browned, or flip the tortilla.
- To flip, place the plate, lid or cutting board over the pan. Using towels or mitts, grasp the plate, lid or board and the skillet together and turn them over so the tortilla comes out. Return the skillet to the stove on medium heat, add the remaining half-tablespoon of oil, slide the tortilla back into the pan to cook the second side for 1 to 2 minutes. Transfer to a platter, dust with espelette or cayenne and serve at once or set aside to serve warm.

311. Spice Rubbed Lamb Skewers With Herb Yogurt Sauce

Serving: 6 servings | Prep: | Cook: |Ready in: 4hours40mins

Ingredients

- 2 pounds boneless leg of lamb in one piece
- 4 tablespoons extra virgin olive oil
- 2 teaspoons Hungarian sweet paprika
- 2 teaspoons ground cumin
- 1 teaspoon ground black pepper
- Salt
- 1 clove garlic
- 1 cup loosely packed flat-leaf parsley leaves
- 1 cup loosely packed cilantro leaves
- 1 cup loosely packed mint leaves
- 1 ½ cups plain yogurt
- 1 large red onion, sliced
- 6 pita breads, split horizontally

Direction

- Slice lamb into 12 strips, each 1/2-inch thick, about 2 inches wide and 4 to 6 inches long. Place in a dish and rub with 1 tablespoon oil. Mix paprika, cumin, 3/4 teaspoon pepper and

1/2 teaspoon salt together and rub over meat. Cover and set aside for 4 hours at room temperature. Place 12 8-inch bamboo skewers in water.
- Mince garlic and herbs by hand or machine. Place in a serving bowl and add yogurt and 2 tablespoons oil. Add 2 to 4 tablespoons cold water to thin to saucelike consistency. Stir in remaining 1/4 teaspoon pepper and add salt to taste. Refrigerate.
- About 30 minutes before serving, heat grill or broiler. Heat remaining oil in a skillet, add onion and sauté over medium heat until just starting to brown. Place in a serving dish.
- Thread meat on skewers and sear quickly on grill or broiler, 1 1/2 to 3 minutes a side for medium-rare to medium. Arrange on a platter, lightly toast cut sides of pita breads on grill or under broiler. Arrange in a basket. Serve kebabs with pita, onions and sauce.

Nutrition Information

- 583: calories;
- 36 grams: protein;
- 34 grams: carbohydrates;
- 12 grams: saturated fat;
- 16 grams: monounsaturated fat;
- 3 grams: polyunsaturated fat;
- 6 grams: dietary fiber;
- 5 grams: sugars;
- 750 milligrams: sodium;

312. Spiced Pasta, Avocado And Onion Feta Salad

Serving: Six servings | Prep: | Cook: | Ready in: 20mins

Ingredients

- The pasta:
- 1 pound fusilli
- 2 jalapenos, seeded and minced
- 2 teaspoons olive oil
- 3 tablespoons chopped fresh cilantro
- 1 ½ teaspoons kosher salt
- Freshly ground pepper to taste
- The onions:
- 6 medium red onions, peeled and cut into 1/8-inch slices
- 1 tablespoon olive oil
- ½ cup crumbled feta
- Kosher salt and freshly ground pepper to taste
- The peppers:
- 3 red and 3 yellow bell peppers, roasted, peeled, seeded and cut into 1/4-inch strips
- 1 tablespoon olive oil
- 1 tablespoon fresh lemon juice
- 1 teaspoon kosher salt
- Freshly ground pepper to taste
- The avocados:
- 3 avocados, peeled, pitted and cubed
- 1 tablespoon fresh lime juice
- 3 cloves garlic, peeled and minced
- ¾ teaspoon kosher salt
- ¾ teaspoon Tabasco sauce
- The greens:
- 12 cups salad greens
- 2 tablespoons olive oil
- 1 tablespoon lime juice
- 1 teaspoon kosher salt
- Freshly ground pepper to taste

Direction

- Cook the fusilli in boiling salted water until al dente. Drain, rinse and drain well. Place in a bowl and toss with the jalapenos, olive oil, cilantro, salt and pepper.
- Meanwhile, preheat the broiler. Place the onions on baking sheets and brush with oil. Broil until browned, about 5 minutes. Cool and coarsely chop. Place in a bowl and toss with the feta, salt and pepper.
- Place the roasted peppers in a bowl and toss with the olive oil, lemon juice, salt and pepper. Place the avocados in a bowl and toss with the lime juice, garlic, salt and Tabasco.
- Place the salad greens in a large bowl and toss with the olive oil, lime juice, salt and pepper.

Pass the dishes separately, letting guests build their own salads.

313. Spicy Ecuadorean Shrimp

Serving: 6 to 8 appetizers or 4 entrees | Prep: | Cook: | Ready in: 12hours10mins

Ingredients

- 1 cup olive oil
- 2 tablespoons black peppercorns
- 2 tablespoons pink peppercorns
- 2 teaspoons salt
- ½ teaspoon cayenne pepper
- 1 roasted poblano chili pepper, skinned, seeded and chopped
- 2 tablespoons sherry vinegar
- 1 ½ pounds large shrimp, preferably Ecuadorean, with shells on

Direction

- Combine all the ingredients except the shrimp in a blender and process until smooth. Place the shrimp in a large plastic bag or in a nonreactive bowl and pour the marinade over them, turning or stirring to coat. Refrigerate, stirring occasionally, for at least 2 hours and up to 12.
- When ready to cook, preheat the broiler or prepare a charcoal grill. Thread the shrimp on metal skewers and broil or grill, turning and basting with some of the leftover marinade, until nicely browned and cooked through, about 5 to 6 minutes. Serve immediately.

Nutrition Information

- 311: calories;
- 20 grams: monounsaturated fat;
- 28 grams: fat;
- 0 grams: sugars;
- 12 grams: protein;
- 483 milligrams: sodium;

- 4 grams: carbohydrates;
- 3 grams: polyunsaturated fat;
- 1 gram: dietary fiber;

314. Spicy Marinated Chicken

Serving: 4 servings | Prep: | Cook: | Ready in: 20mins

Ingredients

- 1 3 1/2-pound chicken
- 1 medium onion chopped coarse
- Juice of 1 lemon
- A 1-inch piece of fresh ginger, grated
- 3 tablespoons sun-dried tomato paste
- 1 ½ tablespoons medium-hot curry powder
- ½ teaspoon red pepper flakes (or to taste)
- 1 to 2 tablespoons peanut or vegetable oil

Direction

- Cut the chicken into eighths and remove the skin, except from the wings. Set aside.
- Combine the remaining ingredients in a food processor and puree. Coat the chicken pieces thoroughly with the mixture and allow them to marinate for two to three hours, or overnight.
- Preheat broiler or grill. Place the chicken pieces on a rack and cook until done (about 20 minutes), turning occasionally.

Nutrition Information

- 663: calories;
- 21 grams: monounsaturated fat;
- 287 milligrams: sodium;
- 52 grams: protein;
- 46 grams: fat;
- 12 grams: saturated fat;
- 0 grams: trans fat;
- 10 grams: polyunsaturated fat;
- 8 grams: carbohydrates;
- 3 grams: sugars;

shrimp on top or around them; garnish shrimp with the remaining minced mint.

315. Spicy Shrimp Salad With Mint

Serving: 4 to 6 servings | Prep: | Cook: | Ready in: 20mins

Ingredients

- 2 pounds shrimp in the 15-to-30-a-pound range, peeled (deveined, if you like)
- 1 teaspoon minced garlic, or more to taste
- 1 teaspoon salt
- ½ teaspoon cayenne, or to taste
- 1 teaspoon paprika
- 4 tablespoons olive oil
- 2 tablespoons plus 2 teaspoons lemon juice
- 30 to 40 mint leaves
- 6 cups arugula and other greens

Direction

- Preheat broiler; adjust the rack, moving it as close to the heat source as possible. Place a large ovenproof skillet or thick-bottomed roasting pan on the stove over low heat.
- Combine the shrimp with garlic, salt, cayenne, paprika, half the olive oil and the 2 teaspoons of lemon juice; stir to blend. Turn heat under the skillet to high.
- When skillet smokes, toss in shrimp. Shake the pan once or twice to distribute them evenly, then immediately place skillet in the broiler.
- Mince about one-third of the mint, and set aside. Tear remaining leaves, and toss them with the arugula. Stir remaining olive oil and lemon juice together in a bowl.
- The shrimp are done when opaque, usually 3 to 4 minutes. Use a slotted spoon to transfer them to a plate; it is fine if they cool for a moment. Add shrimp juices to olive oil-lemon juice mixture, and stir. Dress the greens with this mixture, and toss; if the greens seem dry, add a little more olive oil or lemon juice, or both. Place greens on a platter, and arrange

Nutrition Information

- 196: calories;
- 0 grams: trans fat;
- 7 grams: monounsaturated fat;
- 1 gram: sugars;
- 21 grams: protein;
- 862 milligrams: sodium;
- 11 grams: fat;
- 2 grams: polyunsaturated fat;
- 3 grams: carbohydrates;

316. Spinach And Red Pepper Frittata

Serving: Six servings | Prep: | Cook: | Ready in: 1hours

Ingredients

- 1 6-ounce bag baby spinach, or 1 bunch spinach, washed and stemmed
- 2 tablespoons extra virgin olive oil
- 2 red bell peppers, seeded and cut in small dice
- 1 to 2 garlic cloves (to taste), minced
- 10 fresh marjoram leaves, chopped
- Salt
- 8 eggs
- Freshly ground pepper
- 2 tablespoons low-fat milk

Direction

- Steam the spinach above an inch boiling water until just wilted, about two minutes; or wilt in a large frying pan with the water left on the leaves after washing. Remove from the heat, rinse with cold water and squeeze out excess water. Chop fine, and set aside.
- Heat 1 tablespoon of the olive oil over medium heat in a heavy 10-inch nonstick skillet. Add

the bell peppers. Cook, stirring often, until tender, five to eight minutes. Add the garlic and salt to taste, stir for about half a minute, and stir in the chopped spinach and the marjoram. Stir together for a few seconds, then remove from the heat and set aside.
- Beat the eggs in a large bowl. Stir in the salt (about 1/2 teaspoon), pepper, milk, spinach and red peppers. Clean and dry the pan, and return to the burner, set on medium-high. Heat the remaining tablespoon of olive oil in the skillet. Drop a bit of egg into the pan; if it sizzles and cooks at once, the pan is ready. Pour in the egg mixture. Tilt the pan to distribute the eggs and filling evenly over the surface. Shake the pan gently, tilting it slightly with one hand while lifting up the edges of the frittata with a spatula in your other hand, to let the eggs run underneath during the first few minutes of cooking.
- Turn the heat to low, cover and cook 10 minutes, shaking the pan gently every once in a while. From time to time, remove the lid, tilt the pan, and loosen the bottom of the frittata with a wooden spatula so that it doesn't burn. The bottom should turn a golden color. The eggs should be just about set; cook a few minutes longer if they're not.
- Meanwhile, heat the broiler. Uncover the pan and place under the broiler, not too close to the heat, for one to three minutes, watching very carefully to make sure the top doesn't burn (at most, it should brown very slightly and puff under the broiler). Remove from the heat, shake the pan to make sure the frittata isn't sticking, and allow it to cool for at least five minutes and for as long as 15 minutes. Loosen the edges with a wooden or plastic spatula. Carefully slide from the pan onto a large round platter. Cut into wedges or into smaller bite-size diamonds. Serve hot, warm, at room temperature or cold.

Nutrition Information

- 148: calories;
- 10 grams: fat;
- 2 grams: sugars;
- 0 grams: trans fat;
- 5 grams: carbohydrates;
- 9 grams: protein;
- 319 milligrams: sodium;

317. Spring Quiche

Serving: 6 to 8 servings | Prep: | Cook: | Ready in: 42mins

Ingredients

- 2 tablespoons unsalted butter
- ½ pound new potatoes, scrubbed and sliced 1/4 inch thick
- ½ pound chanterelles, cleaned and halved lengthwise, or sliced domestic mushrooms
- ½ cup sliced scallion greens
- 1 ½ teaspoons coarse kosher salt
- Freshly ground pepper to taste
- ¼ cup dry bread crumbs
- ¾ cup small peas
- 4 eggs
- 2 egg yolks
- 1 cup milk
- 1 cup heavy cream
- Pinch nutmeg
- 4 ounces Gruyere, grated
- ⅓ cup fresh chervil leaves

Direction

- Preheat broiler. Position rack 6 inches from heat source.
- In a 2-quart oval or 2 1/2-quart round souffle dish, melt butter at 100 percent power for 2 minutes. Stir in potatoes and mushrooms. Cook, uncovered, at 100 percent for 5 minutes. Add scallions, 1/2 teaspoon salt, pepper, bread crumbs and peas. Cook, uncovered, for 5 minutes.
- Whisk together remaining ingredients including 1 teaspoon salt and pepper to taste.

Pour over vegetables; stir. Cover tightly with microwave plastic wrap. Cook at 100 percent for 5 minutes. Slash plastic with a sharp knife. Placing wooden spoon through slit, stir thoroughly. Patch split in plastic with small piece of plastic. Cook 5 minutes longer. Prick plastic to release steam. Uncover and cook 2 minutes.
- Brown under broiler. Allow to stand 10 minutes before serving.

Nutrition Information

- 300: calories;
- 13 grams: carbohydrates;
- 4 grams: sugars;
- 2 grams: dietary fiber;
- 12 grams: protein;
- 420 milligrams: sodium;
- 23 grams: fat;
- 0 grams: trans fat;
- 7 grams: monounsaturated fat;

318. Squid And Arugula Salad With Sesame Seeds

Serving: 4 servings | Prep: | Cook: | Ready in: 25mins

Ingredients

- 1 sprig thyme
- 1 bay leaf
- 10 coriander seeds
- Juice of 2 lemons
- ½ pound squid, cleaned, washed and drained
- 2 sweet red peppers, split and seeded
- 3 tablespoons olive oil
- 1 small clove garlic, peeled and chopped
- 2 sprigs fresh coriander, leaves only, chopped
- ½ tablespoon sesame oil
- 1 tablespoon shallots, peeled and finely chopped
- 1 sprig fresh mint, leaves only, half of them chopped
- 2 bunches arugula, leaves only
- 1 tablespoon chives, minced
- 1 tablespoon sesame seeds
- Coarse salt and freshly ground pepper to taste

Direction

- In a large pot over high heat, combine one quart water with one teaspoon salt, thyme, bay leaf, coriander seeds, the juice of half a lemon and freshly ground pepper. Bring to boil and cook for three minutes. Add the squid and boil again for another two to three minutes. Drain the squid and set aside to cool. Discard the cooking liquid with the herbs and condiments. Slice the squid into fourth-inch pieces and set aside.
- Preheat the broiler. Brush the skin of the sweet red peppers with a half tablespoon of the oil and place on a baking sheet. Cook under the broiler until the skin turns black, about five to seven minutes. Remove from heat, let cool and wash the burned skin off under running water. Pat dry and cut the roasted pepper into thin strips. Set aside.
- In a bowl, mix the squid, the red pepper strips, the juice of one lemon, one-and-a-half tablespoons of the olive oil, the garlic, half of the chopped coriander leaves, the sesame oil, the shallots, the chopped mint leaves and salt and pepper to taste.
- In a separate bowl, mix the arugula with half of the chives, half of the sesame seeds, juice from one-half lemon, the remaining tablespoon olive oil and salt and pepper to taste.
- Toast the remaining sesame seeds in a dry pan over medium heat or under the broiler, tossing often for one to two minutes or until golden, and set aside. Divide the arugula among four plates and spoon even amounts of squid on top of each bed of leaves. Sprinkle with the remaining minced chives, toasted sesame seeds, coriander leaves and mint leaves.

Nutrition Information

- 245: calories;
- 2 grams: saturated fat;
- 17 grams: carbohydrates;
- 14 grams: protein;
- 16 grams: fat;
- 7 grams: dietary fiber;
- 6 grams: sugars;
- 660 milligrams: sodium;
- 9 grams: monounsaturated fat;
- 3 grams: polyunsaturated fat;

319. Steven Raichlen's Romesco Sauce

Serving: 2 cups | Prep: | Cook: | Ready in: 35mins

Ingredients

- 1 dried ancho chili (or 3 dried anorra chilies), stemmed
- 2 tablespoons blanched almonds
- 2 tablespoons hazelnuts
- 3 ripe tomatoes (about 1 1/4 pounds), cut in half
- 1 small onion, peeled and quartered
- ½ red bell pepper, seeded
- 1 jalapeno pepper, halved and seeded
- 5 cloves garlic, peeled
- 1 slice country-style white bread
- ¼ cup finely chopped flatleaf parsley
- ½ cup extra virgin olive oil (preferably Spanish)
- 2 tablespoons red wine vinegar, or more, to taste
- ¼ teaspoon sugar, or more, to taste
- Salt and freshly ground black pepper

Direction

- Soak chilies in hot water until soft and pliable, 30 minutes. Drain, reserving the soaking liquid, and blot dry.
- Meanwhile, preheat broiler. Arrange nuts on a foil-lined baking sheet, and broil until toasted and fragrant, 4 to 6 minutes, shaking the pan two or three times to insure even browning. Transfer nuts to a plate. When they have cooled a bit, rub hazelnuts between the palms of your hands to remove skin. (Don't worry about removing every last bit.)
- Arrange tomatoes, onion, bell pepper, jalapeno pepper and garlic on the baking sheet, and broil until darkly browned, turning to insure browning is even. This will take 4 to 6 minutes a side: remove vegetables as they are ready. Transfer vegetables to a plate and let cool.
- Place bread on baking sheet, and toast under the broiler, 2 minutes a side, until dark. Break toast into several pieces.
- Place nuts and toast in food processor, and grind to a fine powder. Add vegetables and parsley, and puree to a coarse paste. Add oil, vinegar, sugar, salt and pepper, and process to mix. The sauce should be thick but pourable: if it is too thick, add a little soaking liquid from the chili. If desired, add salt, sugar or vinegar to taste.

Nutrition Information

- 366: calories;
- 4 grams: polyunsaturated fat;
- 5 grams: protein;
- 559 milligrams: sodium;
- 33 grams: fat;
- 0 grams: trans fat;
- 23 grams: monounsaturated fat;
- 17 grams: carbohydrates;
- 6 grams: sugars;

320. Stuffed Clams

Serving: 10 servings | Prep: | Cook: | Ready in: 22mins

Ingredients

- 24 littleneck clams
- 1 cup fine fresh bread crumbs

- 1 teaspoon finely minced garlic
- 1 tablespoon finely chopped Italian parsley
- 1 teaspoon dried oregano
- Salt to taste, if desired
- Freshly ground pepper to taste

Direction

- Rinse the clams, and set aside.
- In a mixing bowl combine the bread crumbs, garlic, parsley, oregano, salt and pepper. If salt is used, use a small amount because the clams themselves are salty.
- Open the clams or have them opened at the seafood shop. If desired, you may cut the meat of each clam in half and fill each half of the shell. Or you may leave the clams whole and fill only half the shells. Sprinkle the clams with equal portions of the bread-crumb mixture.
- Preheat the broiler to high. Place the clams under it, about four or five inches from the source of heat. Broil the clams for 1 to 2 minutes or until the crumbs are golden brown on top.

Nutrition Information

- 74: calories;
- 1 gram: sugars;
- 0 grams: polyunsaturated fat;
- 9 grams: carbohydrates;
- 7 grams: protein;
- 289 milligrams: sodium;

321. Stuffed Peppers (Chiles Rellenos)

Serving: 3 or 4 servings | Prep: | Cook: | Ready in: 40mins

Ingredients

- 6-8 fresh Anaheim chiles, peeled
- ½ pound Monterey Jack cheese
- ½ cup flour
- 5 eggs, separated
- Salt to taste
- Vegetable oil for frying
- Tomato sauce (see recipe)

Direction

- Wash chiles, dry and place on broiler rack about an inch from heat. Turn chiles frequently until they are blistered and lightly brown. Watch carefully. As each chile is done, place it in a plastic bag and keep bag closed. As each chile cools, remove from bag and peel. Use a paring knife and your fingers. (Chiles can be peeled a day ahead and refrigerated in a plastic bag.)
- Cut a slit down the side of each chile. Carefully remove seeds and white membrane. Be careful not to weaken stem.
- Stuff each chile with a piece of cheese about 1/2 inch wide and 1/2 inch thick and a little shorter than the length of the chile. Lap the cut edges over a little to encase the filling.
- Roll chiles in flour to coat evenly; shake off excess.
- Beat egg whites with salt until soft peaks form. Beat yolks until thick. Fold whites into yolks.
- Heat enough oil in large frying pan to the depth of 1/4 inch.
- Hold each chile by stem end and dip into batter. Fry in hot oil, only as many as the skillet can hold without crowding. When golden brown, turn and fry until golden brown on second side. Remove and drain thoroughly on paper towels. Serve immediately with the following tomato sauce, if desired.

322. Sugar Glazed Duck And Exotic Fruit

Serving: 4 servings | Prep: | Cook: | Ready in: 1hours

Ingredients

- For the duck:
- 8 small boneless half-breasts of duck (about 6 ounces each), skinned
- ½ cup plus 4 teaspoons sugar
- ½ cup soy sauce
- ½ tablespoon unsalted butter
- 2 tablespoons orange juice
- 1 tablespoon rice vinegar
- ¼ cup chicken broth, homemade or low-sodium canned
- For the fruit:
- 1 ripe pineapple, peeled, cored and cut into 1/4-inch-thick rings
- 1 ripe mango, peeled and cut lengthwise into 1/4-inch-thick slices
- 5 tablespoons sugar
- Juice of 1/2 lemon

Direction

- To prepare the duck, place the breasts in a shallow dish just large enough to hold them in a single layer. Sprinkle with 4 teaspoons of sugar. Pour 1/4 cup of soy sauce over the duck. Marinate for 30 minutes, turning the breasts once.
- Preheat the broiler. Line 2 baking sheets with aluminum foil. Arrange the pineapple in a single layer on 1 sheet and sprinkle with 3 tablespoons of sugar. Arrange the mango on the other sheet and sprinkle with 2 tablespoons of sugar. Place the pineapple under the broiler until it begins to brown, about 5 minutes. Turn the pineapple over and broil 1 more minute.
- Meanwhile, place the remaining 1/2 cup sugar in a shallow bowl. Remove the duck from the marinade and coat well on both sides with the sugar.
- When the pineapple is done, remove it from the oven and place the mango under the broiler until browned, about 3 minutes. Turn off the broiler and set the baking sheets with pineapple and mango in the oven to keep warm.
- Melt the butter in a large cast-iron skillet over medium-high heat. Add the duck breasts, lower the heat and cook until the sugar glaze turns a deep brown and the duck is cooked to medium rare, about 2 to 3 minutes per side, being very careful not to let the sugar burn.
- Remove the duck from the skillet and keep warm. Add 1/4 cup of soy sauce, the orange juice, vinegar and chicken broth to the skillet and simmer over medium heat for about 2 minutes, scraping the bottom of the skillet with a wooden spoon.
- Slice the duck on the diagonal into thin slices. Remove the fruit from the oven. Squeeze the lemon juice over the fruit and divide the pineapple among 4 plates. Cross the mango slices over the pineapple. Fan the duck slices beside the fruit and spoon the sauce over the duck. Serve immediately.

323. Suzanne Hart's Bluefish With Garlic Mayonnaise

Serving: Four servings | Prep: | Cook: | Ready in: 20mins

Ingredients

- 4 cloves garlic
- 2 tablespoons dry vermouth
- 2 tablespoons horseradish
- ¾ cup mayonnaise, preferably homemade
- ¼ cup heavy cream if available, or evaporated milk
- 4 boneless bluefish fillets, about 1 1/4 pounds
- 2 tablespoons fresh tarragon, if available, or 1/2 teaspoon dried

Direction

- Preheat the broiler to high.
- Broil the garlic cloves until they are tender, peel the skins and mash to a paste.
- Add the paste, vermouth and horseradish to the mayonnaise. Stir in the cream and blend well.

- Select a flame-proof baking dish large enough to hold fish in one layer. Coat both sides of the fillets with the garlic mayonnaise and place in the dish, skin side down. Place under broiler about 5 inches from the heat. Cook 5 to 7 minutes, depending on the thickness of the fillet. The fish is done when it flakes easily with a fork.
- Sprinkle with tarragon and serve immediately. Serve additional garlic mayonnaise on the side.

Nutrition Information

- 513: calories;
- 11 grams: monounsaturated fat;
- 30 grams: protein;
- 41 grams: fat;
- 7 grams: saturated fat;
- 4 grams: carbohydrates;
- 0 grams: dietary fiber;
- 2 grams: sugars;
- 385 milligrams: sodium;
- 22 grams: polyunsaturated fat;

324. Sweet Peppers Conserved In Oil

Serving: About 2 cups marinated peppers | Prep: | Cook: | Ready in: 15mins

Ingredients

- 2 pounds firm red sweet peppers
- 1 bay leaf
- A few peppercorns
- 1 garlic clove, peeled
- 2 sprigs thyme
- Salt
- Extra virgin olive oil

Direction

- Roast the peppers over a grill or burner, under the broiler, or in the oven. When they are charred, remove them from the heat and place them in a bowl. Cover the bowl tightly with plastic, or set a lid or plate on top and allow the peppers to cool. Skin and seed. Cut or pull the peppers apart into 3 or 4 wide pieces. Wipe dry with paper towels or a damp kitchen towel. Season with salt.
- Pour a little olive oil into the bottom of two clean, sterilized 1-cup jars or one 1-pint wide-mouth jar. Place the bay leaf and garlic in the jar, then a layer of pepper pieces. Drizzle olive oil over the peppers and repeat with another layer, drizzling each layer with oil until you have filled the jar. Stick a thyme sprig into the jar, cover the peppers completely with oil, and screw on the top. Leave at room temperature for a day, then refrigerate.

Nutrition Information

- 101: calories;
- 2 grams: protein;
- 14 grams: carbohydrates;
- 5 grams: dietary fiber;
- 10 grams: sugars;
- 540 milligrams: sodium;
- 4 grams: fat;
- 1 gram: polyunsaturated fat;

325. Sweet Potato Tian With Spiced Shrimp And Prosciutto

Serving: Six servings | Prep: | Cook: | Ready in: 1hours35mins

Ingredients

- ¼ cup plus 1 tablespoon olive oil
- 4 pounds sweet potatoes (about 6 medium), peeled and cut into 1/8-inch-thick slices
- 3 ½ teaspoons kosher salt
- Freshly ground pepper to taste

- 3 medium red onions, peeled and thinly sliced
- 1 ½ cups white wine
- ¼ cup Sherry
- ¼ cup fresh lemon juice
- 1 teaspoon crushed pepper flakes
- ¼ teaspoon cayenne pepper
- 2 ½ pounds jumbo shrimp, shelled and deveined
- ½ pound thinly sliced prosciutto, trimmed of excess fat, cut across into thirds
- 1 cup coarse fresh bread crumbs
- 1 tablespoon chopped Italian parsley

Direction

- Preheat the oven to 350 degrees. Brush 1 tablespoon of olive oil over the bottom of a 12-by-3 1/2-inch round clay casserole dish. Layer 1/3 of the sweet potatoes in the dish, overlapping the slices slightly. Season with 3/4 teaspoon of salt and pepper. Scatter 1/3 of the onions over the sweet potatoes.
- Repeat with the remaining sweet potatoes and onions, seasoning each layer of potatoes with 3/4 teaspoon of salt and pepper. Combine the wine and Sherry and pour over the top. Cover with aluminum foil and bake until the potatoes are tender, about 1 hour.
- Meanwhile, in a bowl, combine the lemon juice, 1/4 cup of olive oil, 1/2 teaspoons of salt, pepper, pepper flakes and cayenne. Add the shrimp and toss to coat. Refrigerate until ready to use.
- Scatter the prosciutto strips over the sweet-potato mixture. Top with the shrimp. Bake, uncovered, until the shrimp is just cooked through, about 16 minutes. Combine the bread crumbs with the parsley, 1/2 teaspoon of salt and pepper. Sprinkle the crumbs over the shrimp and place under the broiler until lightly browned, about 2 minutes. Serve immediately.

Nutrition Information

- 722: calories;
- 18 grams: fat;
- 10 grams: monounsaturated fat;
- 12 grams: dietary fiber;
- 17 grams: sugars;
- 44 grams: protein;
- 3 grams: polyunsaturated fat;
- 0 grams: trans fat;
- 85 grams: carbohydrates;
- 2393 milligrams: sodium;

326. Swordfish Nicoise

Serving: 2 servings | Prep: | Cook: | Ready in: 1hours30mins

Ingredients

- 1 swordfish steak
- 2 tablespoons olive oil
- 1 teaspoon fresh thyme (or 1/2 dried)
- 1 teaspoon fresh rosemary leaves (or 1/2 teaspoon dried)
- 1 shallot, chopped
- 1 clove garlic, minced
- ¼ cup chopped black oil-cured olives, pitted
- 2 anchovies, chopped
- 2 tablespoons capers, chopped
- 2 tomatoes, peeled and chopped (see note)
- ½ cup dry red wine
- Coarse salt and freshly ground pepper to taste

Direction

- Sprinkle the swordfish steak with one tablespoon olive oil, thyme and rosemary. Marinate at room temperature for an hour.
- Heat remaining olive oil in a frying pan. Soften the shallot with the garlic. Add the olives, anchovies, capers and tomatoes. Add the wine, bring to boil, turn down heat, cover and simmer gently for 10 minutes or until thickened. Season with salt and pepper.
- Preheat broiler.
- Broil the swordfish steak until medium rare, about four to six minutes on each side. Place

on individual plates and put the sauce on top. Serve immediately.

Nutrition Information

- 342: calories;
- 13 grams: monounsaturated fat;
- 6 grams: sugars;
- 17 grams: protein;
- 747 milligrams: sodium;
- 20 grams: fat;
- 3 grams: polyunsaturated fat;
- 0 grams: trans fat;
- 14 grams: carbohydrates;
- 4 grams: dietary fiber;

327. Swordfish Roll Ups As Prepared In Messina

Serving: 6 servings | Prep: | Cook: | Ready in: 30mins

Ingredients

- 6 or 12 metal or bamboo skewers
- 2 ¼ pounds swordfish, cut into 3/4-inch steaks, untrimmed (see notes)
- Caper stuffing
- 5 tablespoons olive oil
- 1 tablespoon minced onions
- 1 tablespoon minced carrot
- ½ tablespoon crushed garlic
- 2 cups grated fresh bread crumbs, preferably Italian semolina
- 3 heaping tablespoons salted capers, rinsed, plumped and drained (see notes)
- 5 tablespoons grated pecorino cheese
- 1 teaspoon finely grated lemon rind
- 1 teaspoon finely chopped parsley leaves
- Salt and pepper to taste
- Lemon juice to taste
- 12 imported bay leaves, cut into halves or quarters
- 1 small onion, quartered, separated into 1-inch segments
- Pinches of granulated sugar
- Salmoriglio sauce
- ⅓ cup extra-virgin olive oil
- 2 tablespoons hot water
- 2 ½ tablespoons lemon juice
- 1 teaspoon grated lemon rind
- ½ teaspoon fresh oregano or thyme
- ¾ teaspoon salt
- ½ teaspoon pepper
- ¼ teaspoon sugar
- 1 tablespoon chopped fresh Italian flat parsley

Direction

- Cut off and discard swordfish skin and center bone. Cut each fish steak into pieces approximately three by three by three-quarter inches thick. Cut each piece horizontally into three even slices, making 24 swordfish slices.
- Reserve and chop any trimmings for the stuffing. Place each slice between sheets of oiled waxed paper. Use a flat mallet to gently pound them (see notes). They should become about one-third larger in size. Avoid breaking the flesh. Keep fish refrigerated between sheets of waxed paper or plastic wrap.
- To make the caper stuffing, place oil, swordfish trimmings, vegetables and garlic in a large skillet and cook one minute or until the vegetables are soft but not brown. Add bread crumbs to the skillet and mix well over low heat, 30 seconds. Scrape into a clean bowl; add the remaining ingredients and, if necessary, one to two tablespoons water to help bind the mixture.
- Place slices on work surface. Evenly divide stuffing and place a portion of the filling on each slice. Roll up one slice, press in sides, then squeeze gently to form the shape of a stuffed grape leaf (see notes). Repeat with the remaining slices. Slip a small piece of bay leaf and an onion segment on either side of each roll. Thread rolls onto skewers. If necessary, fasten any openings with toothpicks. Brush rolls with olive oil and sprinkle lightly with

granulated sugar (to develop a good color when broiled). Refrigerate until ready to cook.
- To make the salmoriglio sauce, combine the first eight ingredients in a blender jar and blend until smooth and creamy. Pour into a sauce boat. Stir in the parsley. Adjust seasoning. Can be prepared in advance to this point.
- Cook over charcoal or very close to heated broiler about one and one-half minutes to a side. Baste with the salmoriglio sauce and serve at once.

328. Swordfish With Bread Crumb Salsa

Serving: 6 servings | Prep: | Cook: | Ready in: 2hours

Ingredients

- 2 cups fresh crumbs from a dense white bread like Tuscan bread
- 1 ½ cups extra-virgin olive oil
- 2 tablespoons white-wine vinegar or champagne vinegar
- 1 teaspoon finely chopped anchovy fillets or anchovy paste
- 1 tablespoon fresh thyme leaves
- 1 tablespoon capers, rinsed and coarsely chopped
- 1 tablespoon minced shallots
- 1 tablespoon cracked black pepper
- 2 pounds swordfish steaks
- Freshly ground black pepper to taste

Direction

- Preheat oven to 300 degrees.
- Knead the bread crumbs with 2 tablespoons of the oil and spread them evenly in a sheet pan. Bake about one hour, until the crumbs are amber colored and very crisp. Allow them to cool to room temperature.
- Mix the vinegar, anchovies, thyme, capers, shallots and cracked pepper in a bowl. Add the crumbs, mix, then add all but 4 tablespoons of remaining olive oil. Mix again. Set aside.
- Preheat a grill or broiler. Pat the fish dry and cut into six equal size pieces. Brush on both sides with the remaining oil. Season generously with ground pepper. Grill or broil the fish to desired degree of doneness, about four minutes on the first side, two to three on the other.
- Transfer the fish to a platter or individual plates. Sprinkle each portion with some of the bread-crumb mixture and serve.

Nutrition Information

- 740: calories;
- 65 grams: fat;
- 10 grams: saturated fat;
- 44 grams: monounsaturated fat;
- 32 grams: protein;
- 0 grams: trans fat;
- 8 grams: carbohydrates;
- 1 gram: sugars;
- 250 milligrams: sodium;

329. Swordfish With Scallions And Cracked Peppercorns

Serving: 4 servings | Prep: | Cook: | Ready in: 45mins

Ingredients

- 1 cup fish stock
- 1 cup dry white wine
- 1 ½ cups heavy cream
- 1 bunch scallions, green part only, chopped
- 1 tablespoon whole black peppercorns, cracked
- 1 tablespoon whole white peppercorns, cracked
- ¼ cup Sichuan peppercorns, cracked
- 4 swordfish steaks, 6 to 8 ounces each, trimmed of skin and fat

- Salt to taste
- ¼ cup snipped fresh chives
- 4 red radishes, thinly sliced

Direction

- Preheat broiler.
- In a medium-sized saucepan, combine the stock and the wine. Bring to a simmer over high heat and cook until reduced to one-half cup, about eight minutes. Add the cream and cook until reduced to one cup, about 10 minutes longer. Remove from heat, add the scallion greens and set aside for five minutes.
- Transfer the cooled mixture to a blender and purée until smooth. Strain into a clean saucepan.
- Mix the peppercorns together in a small bowl, then divide them among the swordfish steaks, pressing them into the surface of the fish on one side. Place the fish, pepper side up, on a lightly oiled broiling pan and broil it to the desired degree of doneness, about four to six minutes, or longer, depending on the thickness of the fish and the heat of the broiler. Do not turn the fish.
- While the fish is cooking, return the sauce to a simmer and reduce it for about two minutes, until it is thick enough to coat the back of a spoon. Add salt to taste.
- To serve, spoon some of the sauce on each four warm plates. Sprinkle the chives and radish slices over the sauce, then place a swordfish steak on top. Serve immediately.

Nutrition Information

- 688: calories;
- 1061 milligrams: sodium;
- 47 grams: fat;
- 0 grams: trans fat;
- 4 grams: sugars;
- 13 grams: carbohydrates;
- 44 grams: protein;
- 24 grams: saturated fat;
- 16 grams: monounsaturated fat;

330. Swordfish On Black Bean And Pineapple Salsa

Serving: 2 servings | Prep: | Cook: | Ready in: 30mins

Ingredients

- 1 swordfish steak, 3/4 to 1 pound
- A little oil for brushing
- 1 15- or 16-ounce can black beans
- ½ small fresh pineapple, diced
- ½ small onion, diced
- ½ medium red pepper, cored, seeded and diced
- ½ medium yellow, orange or purple pepper, cored, seeded and diced
- ¼ to ½ jalapeno or Serrano chili, finely minced
- 1 teaspoon ground coriander
- 1 teaspoon ground cumin
- 1 tablespoon rice vinegar
- ¼ cup chopped fresh cilantro

Direction

- Wash and dry the fish.
- If broiling, heat broiler and cover broiler pan with aluminum foil. If using a stovetop grill, lightly brush it with oil.
- Drain beans and rinse under cold water. Set aside.
- Combine pineapple, onion, peppers, chili, coriander, cumin and vinegar. Stir in beans.
- Grill or broil the fish for 10 minutes for each inch at the thickest part.
- Just before serving, stir cilantro into the salsa and arrange on serving plates. Place fish on top, then top it with additional salsa.

Nutrition Information

- 458: calories;
- 20 grams: sugars;
- 4 grams: dietary fiber;
- 0 grams: trans fat;
- 10 grams: monounsaturated fat;

- 28 grams: carbohydrates;
- 41 grams: protein;
- 169 milligrams: sodium;

- 4 grams: protein;
- 1 gram: polyunsaturated fat;
- 3 grams: sugars;
- 25 grams: carbohydrates;
- 6 grams: dietary fiber;

331. Tabbouleh Salad With Grilled Eggplant

Serving: 6 servings | Prep: | Cook: | Ready in: 1hours

Ingredients

- 1 cup bulgur
- 1 ½ cups boiling water
- Juice of 1 1/2 lemons
- A 1-pound eggplant, sliced 1/2-inch thick
- 3 tablespoons minced scallions
- 1 medium-size tomato, peeled, seeded, juiced and chopped
- 1 garlic clove, minced
- 3 tablespoons minced fresh flat-leaf parsley
- 2 tablespoons minced fresh mint
- 1 ½ to 2 tablespoons extra-virgin olive oil
- Salt and freshly ground black pepper

Direction

- Place the bulgur in a bowl, pour the boiling water over it and stir in the lemon juice. Cover and set it aside.
- Preheat a grill or broiler. Grill or broil the eggplant slices until they are nicely browned, turning them once to brown both sides. Coarsely chop the eggplant and set it aside.
- After about 30 minutes, when the bulgur has softened and is cool enough to handle, transfer it to a fine-mesh sieve and press out any excess liquid. Return the bulgur to a bowl.
- Fold in the eggplant and all the remaining ingredients. Serve at room temperature.

Nutrition Information

- 143: calories;
- 477 milligrams: sodium;

332. Tagliata With Radicchio And Parmesan

Serving: 4 to 6 servings | Prep: | Cook: | Ready in: 15mins

Ingredients

- 3 pounds sirloin or other cut of steak, 1 1/2 to 2 inches thick, at room temperature
- 1 cup shredded radicchio
- 1 ounce Parmesan cheese, shaved with a vegetable peeler

Direction

- Grill, sauté or broil steak to taste. Allow to rest on a carving board for 10 minutes. Slice thinly, diagonally against the grain, and arrange on a large warmed plate.
- Pour pan juices over meat, and cover with shredded radicchio. Top with shredded Parmesan, and serve.

Nutrition Information

- 537: calories;
- 2 grams: polyunsaturated fat;
- 17 grams: monounsaturated fat;
- 0 grams: sugars;
- 47 grams: protein;
- 146 milligrams: sodium;
- 37 grams: fat;
- 16 grams: saturated fat;

333. Tamarind Glazed Pork Chops

Serving: Four servings | Prep: | Cook: | Ready in: 45mins

Ingredients

- ½ cup red wine vinegar
- ½ cup dark brown sugar
- ½ cup chicken broth, homemade or low-sodium canned
- 1 plum tomato, chopped
- 1 tablespoon tamarind paste
- 4 center-cut pork chops, 6 to 7 ounces each
- Salt to taste

Direction

- In a small saucepan, combine the vinegar, brown sugar, chicken broth, tomato and tamarind paste. Cook over medium heat until thickened, about 30 minutes. Strain through a coarse strainer into a mixing bowl and let cool.
- Preheat broiler. Sprinkle the pork chops on both sides with the salt and brush generously with the tamarind glaze. Place the chops on a broiler pan and broil until deep brown on the outside and just cooked through but still moist in the center, about 5 minutes per side. Serve immediately, spooning any remaining glaze over the top.

Nutrition Information

- 328: calories;
- 0 grams: dietary fiber;
- 2 grams: polyunsaturated fat;
- 21 grams: carbohydrates;
- 19 grams: sugars;
- 13 grams: fat;
- 4 grams: saturated fat;
- 5 grams: monounsaturated fat;
- 30 grams: protein;
- 650 milligrams: sodium;

334. Tandoori Mushrooms

Serving: 4 servings | Prep: | Cook: | Ready in: 30mins

Ingredients

- 1 2-inch piece peeled ginger, roughly chopped
- 2 cloves garlic, peeled and roughly chopped
- 1 teaspoon salt, more to taste
- 1 teaspoon ground cumin
- 1 teaspoon red chili powder or hot paprika
- ½ teaspoon ground turmeric
- ½ teaspoon white pepper
- ¼ cup fresh lemon juice (from 2 lemons)
- 2 tablespoons vegetable oil
- ¾ cup sour cream
- 3 tablespoons plain Greek yogurt
- 12 ounces cremini, portobello or other mushrooms, trimmed

Direction

- Place the ginger, garlic, salt, cumin, chili powder, turmeric and white pepper in a food processor. Finely chop, scraping down the sides of the bowl with a rubber spatula. Add the lemon juice and 1 tablespoon vegetable oil, and purée. Add the sour cream and yogurt, and pulse processor in short bursts, just to mix. Transfer marinade to a glass, ceramic or stainless steel mixing bowl.
- Wipe mushrooms clean with damp paper towels. Stir mushrooms into the marinade. Cover and refrigerate for 30 minutes.
- If using a tandoor, heat it to 500 degrees. If using a grill or broiler, heat to high.
- Thread mushrooms on bamboo or metal skewers. In tandoor, cook mushrooms until lightly browned on outside, 2 to 3 minutes. Baste with 1 tablespoon oil and continue cooking until golden brown and tender, 1 to 2 minutes more. If grilling or broiling, cook mushrooms until golden and tender, 3 to 4 minutes a side, 6 to 8 minutes total, basting with oil.

Nutrition Information

- 190: calories;
- 0 grams: trans fat;
- 2 grams: polyunsaturated fat;
- 9 grams: carbohydrates;
- 4 grams: protein;
- 17 grams: fat;
- 6 grams: saturated fat;
- 1 gram: dietary fiber;
- 398 milligrams: sodium;
- 7 grams: monounsaturated fat;

335. Tandoori Steak

Serving: 4 servings | Prep: | Cook: |Ready in: 30mins

Ingredients

- 2 tablespoons mustard seeds
- 2 tablespoons fennel seeds
- 2 tablespoons cracked black peppercorns
- 1 tablespoon grains of paradise (see note)
- 1 ½ tablespoons coarse sea salt
- 1 teaspoon hot pepper flakes
- ¼ teaspoon cayenne pepper
- 2 pounds New York strip steak (about 1 1/4 inches thick)
- 1 tablespoon extra virgin olive oil

Direction

- Heat a dry cast-iron skillet over a medium flame. Add mustard seeds, fennel seeds, peppercorns and grains of paradise, and cook until fragrant and lightly toasted, 1 to 3 minutes, stirring with a wooden spoon. Do not let burn. Transfer spices to a heatproof bowl to cool, then place in a spice grinder; grind in short bursts until a coarse powder forms. Add the salt, pepper flakes and cayenne.
- Cut steak into pieces about 1 1/2 inches wide and 3 1/2 inches long. Spray or brush meat on all sides with the olive oil and generously season with the spice rub. Refrigerate excess rub for later use. Pierce the steak pieces through the narrow end with tandoor or shish kebab skewers, about 3 pieces per skewer.
- If using a tandoor, heat it to about 500 degrees. If using a grill or broiler, heat to high. In tandoor, cook kebabs until browned all around, about 5 minutes total for medium-rare. If grilling or broiling, cook for 3 to 4 minutes a side, 6 to 8 minutes total.

336. Thai Beef Salad

Serving: 2 servings | Prep: | Cook: |Ready in: 25mins

Ingredients

- 8 ounces flank steak
- 1 large clove garlic
- 10 sprigs cilantro, to yield 2 tablespoons, finely chopped
- 6 or 7 large mint leaves to yield 1 tablespoon, chopped
- 1 large green onion
- 1 stalk lemon grass
- 1 tablespoon fish sauce (nam pla)
- 1 ½ tablespoons lime juice
- 2 teaspoons sugar
- ¼ teaspoon red pepper flakes
- 8 ounces whole red bell pepper or 7 ounces chopped ready-cut pepper (1 1/2 cups)
- 6 or 8 soft lettuce leaves

Direction

- Turn on broiler, if using, and cover broiler pan with aluminum foil.
- Wash, dry and slice beef very thinly, less than 1/8 inch thick.
- Prepare stove-top grill, if using. Broil or grill beef about 3 minutes, turning once.
- Crush or finely mince garlic; wash, dry and finely chop cilantro; wash, dry and chop mint.
- Wash, trim and thinly slice green onion; wash, trim, remove tough outer sheath of lemon grass and thinly slice bulb part.

- Combine garlic, cilantro, mint, onion, lemon grass, fish sauce, lime juice, sugar and red pepper flakes.
- When beef is cooked, cut into bite-size pieces and stir into fish-sauce mixture.
- Wash, dry and finely slice or chop red pepper; stir into beef mixture.
- Wash and dry lettuce and arrange on serving plate. Spoon beef-pepper mixture into center.

Nutrition Information

- 268: calories;
- 27 grams: protein;
- 782 milligrams: sodium;
- 10 grams: sugars;
- 4 grams: monounsaturated fat;
- 1 gram: polyunsaturated fat;
- 18 grams: carbohydrates;
- 3 grams: dietary fiber;

337. Thai Beef Salad With Mint

Serving: 4 servings | Prep: | Cook: | Ready in: 25mins

Ingredients

- 8 ounces beef tenderloin or sirloin
- 4 cups torn Boston or romaine lettuce, mesclun or any salad greens mixture (trimmed, washed and dried)
- 1 cup torn fresh mint leaves (trimmed, washed and dried)
- ¼ cup minced red onion
- 1 medium cucumber, peeled, cut in half lengthwise, seeded and diced
- Juice of 2 limes
- 1 tablespoon fish sauce (nam pla, available at Asian markets) or soy sauce
- ⅛ teaspoon cayenne, or to taste
- ½ teaspoon sugar

Direction

- Start a charcoal or wood fire or heat a gas grill or broiler. Rack should be about 4 inches from heat source. Grill or broil beef until medium rare, 5 to 10 minutes. Set aside to cool.
- Toss greens with mint, onion and cucumber. Combine all remaining ingredients with 1 tablespoon water -- mixture will be thin -- and toss greens with this dressing. Remove greens to a platter, reserving dressing remaining at bottom of bowl.
- Slice cooled beef thinly, reserving its juice. Combine juice with leftover dressing. Lay slices of beef over salad, drizzle dressing all over, and serve.

Nutrition Information

- 184: calories;
- 3 grams: sugars;
- 14 grams: protein;
- 395 milligrams: sodium;
- 11 grams: carbohydrates;
- 4 grams: dietary fiber;
- 1 gram: polyunsaturated fat;

338. Thai Style Broiled Shrimp

Serving: | Prep: | Cook: | Ready in: 10mins

Ingredients

- 1 garlic clove
- minced Thai chiles
- 1 teaspoon salt
- 1 teaspoon sugar
- 1 tablespoon fish sauce
- 2 tablespoons lime juice
- black pepper
- 1 ½ pounds peeled shrimp
- Cilantro and mint

Direction

- Turn on the broiler, and put the rack close to heat. Mash 1 garlic clove and a few minced Thai chiles with 1 teaspoon salt until it forms a paste. Add to it 1 teaspoon sugar, 1 tablespoon fish sauce, 2 tablespoons lime juice and a little black pepper. Rub paste all over 1 1/2 pounds peeled shrimp. Broil, 2 to 3 minutes per side. Garnish: Cilantro and mint.

Nutrition Information

- 134: calories;
- 5 grams: carbohydrates;
- 24 grams: protein;
- 1318 milligrams: sodium;
- 2 grams: sugars;
- 0 grams: dietary fiber;
- 1 gram: polyunsaturated fat;

339. The Four Seasons Chopped Lamb Steak With Pine Nuts

Serving: Two to four servings | Prep: | Cook: | Ready in: 2hours25mins

Ingredients

- 1 pound ground lean lamb
- 6 tablespoons pine nuts
- 1 teaspoon curry powder
- ¼ teaspoon ground coriander
- Salt, if desired
- ½ teaspoon Hungarian sweet paprika
- ⅓ cup ice water

Direction

- Combine the lamb, pine nuts, curry powder, coriander, salt to taste and paprika in a mixing bowl.
- Start blending, gradually adding the ice water. Take care not to overwork the mixture or it will become pastelike and toughen when cooked.
- Divide the mixture into four portions of equal weight. Shape each portion into a five-inch-long, egg-shaped patty.
- Place the patties on a plate. Cover and let chill for two hours before cooking. This will bring out the flavor and set the shape.
- Preheat the broiler to high.
- Place the patties under the broiler. Cook five minutes on one side for rare. Turn and cook five minutes on the other side. Cook longer on each side if more well-done meat is desired. Serve with chutney.

Nutrition Information

- 822: calories;
- 8 grams: polyunsaturated fat;
- 1 gram: dietary fiber;
- 0 grams: sugars;
- 341 milligrams: sodium;
- 41 grams: saturated fat;
- 34 grams: monounsaturated fat;
- 2 grams: carbohydrates;
- 9 grams: protein;
- 87 grams: fat;

340. Tiger Shrimp With Pineapple And Smoked Bacon

Serving: 4 first-course servings | Prep: | Cook: | Ready in: 45mins

Ingredients

- 16 large tiger shrimp (about 1 pound), shelled, deveined and slit length-wise
- 1 tablespoon lime juice
- 2 teaspoons hot chili oil
- 16 thin slices pineapple, each 1 inch by 2 inch
- 8 strips thickly cut smoked bacon, halved crosswise

Direction

- Soak 16 6-inch bamboo skewers in water to cover for 30 minutes. Meanwhile, preheat broiler, or prepare a grill. Toss the shrimp, lime juice and chili oil and allow to sit for 5 minutes.
- Take a shrimp and place a piece of pineapple in the slit. Wrap a piece of bacon around it and secure with a skewer. Repeat with all the shrimp. Broil or grill, turning once, until bacon is crispy and shrimp are cooked through, 2 to 3 minutes per side. Serve.

Nutrition Information

- 455: calories;
- 24 grams: protein;
- 1028 milligrams: sodium;
- 5 grams: polyunsaturated fat;
- 31 grams: carbohydrates;
- 23 grams: sugars;
- 3 grams: dietary fiber;
- 27 grams: fat;
- 8 grams: saturated fat;
- 0 grams: trans fat;
- 12 grams: monounsaturated fat;

341. Toasted Rhubarb Pudding (Hambleton Hall)

Serving: 6 to 8 servings | Prep: | Cook: | Ready in: 1hours

Ingredients

- The pudding:
- ½ pound rhubarb
- 2 packages gelatin
- ½ cup heavy cream
- 7 eggs, separated
- 1 cup sugar
- 3 tablespoons flour, sifted
- The sauce:
- 1 pound rhubarb, cooked, pureed, sieved and sweetened to taste
- Granulated sugar for topping

Direction

- Cut the rhubarb into 1/2-inch slices; cover with cold water and poach until tender. Strain rhubarb and conserve the cooking liquid.
- Soak the gelatin in 3 tablespoons cold water.
- Add 2 cups of rhubarb juice to the heavy cream and bring to boil. Remove from heat and set aside.
- Whisk the egg yolks with 1/4 cup of sugar and the flour.
- Stir the hot cream-rhubarb mixture slowly into the yolk mixture and bring to a boil, stirring with wooden spoon. Cook until mixture thickens to the consistency of custard. Stir in dissolved gelatin; cool.
- Combine remaining sugar with 6 tablespoons water and boil until it reaches 235 degrees.
- Beat the whites until soft peaks form; slowly beat in hot syrup. After all syrup is beaten in continue beating for about 1 minute, to cool mixture. Fold whites into rhubarb-cream.
- Spoon half of the rhubarb-cream mixture into an 8- or 9-inch spring form; add rhubarb chunks; top with remaining rhubarb-cream mixture and smooth. Refrigerate for a few hours.
- Just before serving remove ring and place spring form in freezer for 10 to 15 minutes. Sprinkle the top of the pudding generously and evenly with sugar. Run under very hot broiler until sugar caramelizes, less than 2 minutes. sugar. Watch carefully or it will burn (the edges may melt slightly).
- Serve pudding with pureed rhubarb.

Nutrition Information

- 254: calories;
- 77 milligrams: sodium;
- 9 grams: fat;
- 3 grams: monounsaturated fat;
- 32 grams: carbohydrates;

- 1 gram: polyunsaturated fat;
- 2 grams: dietary fiber;
- 26 grams: sugars;
- 12 grams: protein;
- 5 grams: saturated fat;
- 0 grams: trans fat;

342. Tomates Grillees (Broiled Tomatoes)

Serving: 4 servings | Prep: | Cook: | Ready in: 15mins

Ingredients

- 4 red, ripe, firm tomatoes
- Salt to taste, if desired
- Freshly ground pepper to taste
- ¼ cup fine fresh bread crumbs
- 1 teaspoon finely minced garlic
- 2 tablespoons finely chopped parsley
- 2 teaspoons olive oil

Direction

- Preheat the broiler to high.
- Split the tomatoes in half. Arrange the tomatoes cut side up on a baking dish. Sprinkle the cut halves with salt and pepper.
- Blend the bread crumbs, garlic, parsley and oil. Sprinkle equal portions over the tops of the tomatoes.
- Place the tomatoes about six inches from the source of heat and broil about five minutes.

Nutrition Information

- 71: calories;
- 3 grams: fat;
- 0 grams: polyunsaturated fat;
- 2 grams: protein;
- 10 grams: carbohydrates;
- 4 grams: sugars;
- 314 milligrams: sodium;

343. Tomatillo Guacamole

Serving: 1 1/2 cups, serving six | Prep: | Cook: | Ready in: 20mins

Ingredients

- ½ pound fresh tomatillos, husked
- 1 jalapeño or 2 to 3 serrano chilies, seeded if desired and roughly chopped
- 10 cilantro sprigs, plus additional leaves for garnish
- Salt to taste
- 2 small or 1 1/2 large ripe avocados
- 1 tablespoon freshly squeezed lime juice

Direction

- Preheat the broiler. Cover a baking sheet with foil and place the tomatillos on top, stem side down. Place under the broiler at the highest rack setting and broil two to five minutes, until charred on one side. Turn over and broil on the other side for two to five minutes, until charred on the other side. Remove from the heat and transfer to a blender, tipping in any juice that has accumulated on the baking sheet. Add the chilies, cilantro sprigs and salt to the blender and blend to a coarse purée.
- Cut the avocados in half and twist the two halves apart. Scoop out the flesh into a bowl or the bowl of a mortar and pestle. Mash with a fork or pestle. Do not use a food processor or a blender, as you want to retain some texture. Stir in the lime juice, the tomatillo mixture and salt to taste and combine well. Transfer to a bowl and serve with baked or microwaved tortilla chips or crudités, or use for tacos or avocado sandwiches.

Nutrition Information

- 147: calories;
- 13 grams: fat;
- 2 grams: protein;

- 8 grams: monounsaturated fat;
- 10 grams: carbohydrates;
- 6 grams: dietary fiber;
- 291 milligrams: sodium;

344. Tomato Bread Salad With Chorizo And Herbs

Serving: 4 to 6 servings | Prep: | Cook: | Ready in: 20mins

Ingredients

- 3 ounces day-old country bread, torn into bite-size pieces, about 3 cups
- 5 tablespoons extra-virgin olive oil
- ½ pound dried (cured) chorizo, cut into 1/2-inch pieces
- ½ cup Spanish onion, finely chopped
- ½ teaspoon chopped fresh oregano leaves
- 1 tablespoon sherry vinegar
- ¾ teaspoon fine sea salt, more to taste
- Black pepper, as needed
- 2 ripe, juicy tomatoes, about 1 pound, cut into 1-inch chunks, about 3 cups
- ⅓ cup basil leaves, torn into pieces
- ⅓ cup packed cilantro leaves

Direction

- Heat broiler. Spread bread on large baking sheet and toast until just golden, about 1 minute.
- In a large skillet, heat 1 tablespoon oil over medium-high heat. Add chorizo and onion; cook until sausage is golden and onion soft, about 5 minutes. Stir in oregano and remove from heat.
- In a small bowl, whisk together vinegar, salt and pepper. Whisk in remaining oil. In a large bowl, combine bread, tomato, and chorizo mixture. Toss in dressing, basil and cilantro. Let stand at least 15 minutes before serving.

Nutrition Information

- 324: calories;
- 26 grams: fat;
- 7 grams: saturated fat;
- 542 milligrams: sodium;
- 0 grams: trans fat;
- 15 grams: monounsaturated fat;
- 3 grams: polyunsaturated fat;
- 11 grams: protein;
- 1 gram: dietary fiber;
- 2 grams: sugars;

345. Tomatoes And Gorgonzola

Serving: 2 servings | Prep: | Cook: | Ready in: 15mins

Ingredients

- 1 very large tomato or 2 small tomatoes
- 2 teaspoons chopped fresh basil
- 4 teaspoons Gorgonzola
- Freshly ground black pepper to taste

Direction

- Core tomato and slice in half. If necessary cut a thin slice off bottom so the halves will stand upright.
- Sprinkle basil and pepper on tomato halves. Top with cheese.
- Broil 8 to 12 minutes, depending on the size of the halves, until cheese melts and tomato is beginning to soften.

Nutrition Information

- 47: calories;
- 120 milligrams: sodium;
- 3 grams: protein;
- 2 grams: sugars;
- 1 gram: dietary fiber;
- 0 grams: polyunsaturated fat;

346. Troisgros Potatoes Gratin

Serving: 4 servings | Prep: | Cook: | Ready in: 30mins

Ingredients

- 4 medium-size Idaho or Washington potatoes, peeled and halved
- 1 ½ cups whole milk
- 1 ½ cups heavy cream
- 2 garlic cloves, peeled
- Salt to taste

Direction

- Slice each potato section into disks about a quarter-inch thick. Slice each disk in half widthwise. Do not wash.
- In a saucepan over medium-high heat, combine milk, cream, garlic and salt. Bring to a boil, add potatoes, reduce heat to medium and cook for about 10 to 15 minutes or until they are semifirm but not too soft. Remove with a slotted spoon and set aside.
- Over medium heat, reduce milk mixture to about a cup. Discard garlic.
- Arrange potatoes in individual gratin dishes. Evenly distribute milk mixture over them. Before serving, place under a broiler until potatoes are golden brown.

Nutrition Information

- 530: calories;
- 919 milligrams: sodium;
- 22 grams: saturated fat;
- 45 grams: carbohydrates;
- 5 grams: dietary fiber;
- 36 grams: fat;
- 10 grams: monounsaturated fat;
- 2 grams: polyunsaturated fat;
- 9 grams: protein;

347. Tuna Steaks Moroccan Style

Serving: 4 servings | Prep: | Cook: | Ready in: 30mins

Ingredients

- 1 teaspoon paprika
- ½ teaspoon ground cumin
- 1 teaspoon turmeric
- ¼ teaspoon ground anise seed
- ½ teaspoon ground ginger
- ⅛ teaspoon ground cinnamon
- ¼ teaspoon red hot pepper flakes
- Salt and freshly ground white pepper to taste
- 4 tuna steaks, about 1 1/2 pounds total weight, about 1 1/2 inches thick
- 1 tablespoon fresh lemon juice
- 2 tablespoons olive oil
- 2 tablespoons melted butter
- 4 tablespoons coarsely chopped coriander

Direction

- In a small mixing bowl, combine paprika, cumin, turmeric, anise, ginger, cinnamon, red pepper flakes, salt and and pepper, and blend well.
- Place the tuna steaks on a large platter and sprinkle and rub each side with the spice mixture. Sprinkle evenly with the lemon juice and oil. Cover with plastic wrap. Let stand until ready to cook.
- If broiling, arrange the steaks on a rack and place under a very hot broiler about 4 inches from the heat. Broil 4 minutes with the door partly open. Turn, continue cooking or broiling leaving the door open for about 3 to 4 minutes for pink inside. For rare, cook less. The steaks should be well browned.
- For pan frying, heat a heavy cast-iron skillet, large enough to hold the steaks in one layer. Do not add fat. When the skillet is quite hot, add the tuna steaks, cook until well browned on one side, about 3 minutes. Turn and cook 3

minutes more on the second side for rare. If desired, cook longer.
- Place the steaks on warm plates, brush them with the melted butter, sprinkle with coriander. Serve with couscous.

Nutrition Information

- 318: calories;
- 7 grams: monounsaturated fat;
- 1 gram: polyunsaturated fat;
- 4 grams: carbohydrates;
- 42 grams: protein;
- 453 milligrams: sodium;
- 0 grams: sugars;
- 3 grams: dietary fiber;
- 14 grams: fat;
- 5 grams: saturated fat;

348. Turkey Cutlets With Prosciutto And Cheese

Serving: 4 servings | Prep: | Cook: | Ready in: 25mins

Ingredients

- 4 turkey breast tenderloin steaks, about 1 1/2 pounds
- Salt to taste, if desired
- Freshly ground pepper to taste
- ¼ pound Fontina, Gruyere or Cheddar cheese
- 3 tablespoons butter
- 4 thin slices prosciutto or other ham, about 2 ounces
- 2 teaspoons dried rosemary
- 1 tablespoon chopped shallots
- ¼ pound mushrooms, thinly sliced
- ¼ cup chicken broth

Direction

- Preheat grill to high.
- Sprinkle turkey pieces with salt and pepper.
- Cut cheese into thin slices to fit neatly in one layer, slightly overlapping, on turkey steaks. Set aside.
- Heat 2 tablespoons butter in a heavy skillet large enough to hold the turkey steaks in one layer. Add the steaks and cook about 4 minutes or until nicely browned on one side. Turn the steaks and top each with one slice of prosciutto. Sprinkle evenly with rosemary and cover closely. Cook about 3 minutes.
- Transfer prosciutto-topped steaks to a serving dish. Add remaining 1 tablespoon butter to the skillet and when it melts add shallots. Cook briefly, stirring, and add mushrooms. Cook, stirring, about 2 minutes.
- Add chicken broth and stir. Cook about 1 minute over relatively high heat.
- Meanwhile, cover prosciutto-topped steaks with equal portions, and in one layer, of cheese. Run briefly under the broiler until cheese melts. Pour mushroom mixture over the cheese and serve hot.

Nutrition Information

- 659: calories;
- 24 grams: saturated fat;
- 1 gram: sugars;
- 19 grams: monounsaturated fat;
- 2 grams: polyunsaturated fat;
- 3 grams: carbohydrates;
- 46 grams: protein;
- 51 grams: fat;
- 630 milligrams: sodium;

349. Turkey Hash With Lemon Chili Mayonnaise

Serving: 4 servings | Prep: | Cook: | Ready in: 45mins

Ingredients

- For the mayonnaise:
- 1 egg yolk (see note)

- 1 teaspoon Dijon mustard
- 2 tablespoons fresh lemon juice
- ¾ cup vegetable oil
- 1 tablespoon grated lemon zest
- 1 teaspoon pure ground chili powder
- Salt and freshly ground pepper to taste
- For the hash:
- ¾ cup slab bacon, cut into 1/4-inch pieces
- 1 cup yellow onion, peeled and cut into 1/4-inch cubes
- 1 ½ tablespoons minced garlic
- 2 cups julienned baking potatoes, in 1 1/2-inch-long strips
- 1 ½ tablespoons finely chopped fresh thyme
- 2 tablespoons finely chopped fresh sage
- 1 teaspoon ground cumin
- 4 cups diced cooked turkey
- 1 teaspoon salt, or more to taste
- Freshly ground pepper to taste
- 2 tablespoons fresh lemon juice
- ¼ cup coarsely chopped Italian parsley

Direction

- To make the mayonnaise, place the egg yolk, mustard and lemon juice in a blender and process to combine. With the motor running, add the oil by drops until the mixture begins to emulsify. Continue by adding the oil slowly in a thin, steady stream, until the mayonnaise is thick. Place in a bowl and stir in the lemon zest, chili powder, salt and pepper. Cover and refrigerate at least 1 hour.
- To make the hash, preheat broiler. Heat a large nonstick skillet over medium heat until hot. Add the bacon and onion, and saute until the onion is translucent, about 5 minutes. Add the garlic and cook, stirring constantly, for 1 minute. Add the potatoes and saute until tender, about 10 minutes. Stir in the thyme, sage, cumin and turkey and cook until the turkey is just heated through. Remove from heat and stir in salt, pepper, lemon juice and parsley.
- Place the hash in a baking dish and place under the broiler until nicely browned, about 2 minutes. Serve with a dollop of the mayonnaise.

Nutrition Information

- 804: calories;
- 8 grams: saturated fat;
- 36 grams: monounsaturated fat;
- 25 grams: carbohydrates;
- 3 grams: sugars;
- 58 grams: fat;
- 0 grams: trans fat;
- 10 grams: polyunsaturated fat;
- 5 grams: dietary fiber;
- 47 grams: protein;
- 826 milligrams: sodium;

350. Turkey Scaloppine With Prosciutto And Cheese

Serving: 4 servings | Prep: | Cook: | Ready in: 20mins

Ingredients

- 4 turkey breast "steaks" sometimes referred to as turkey breast tenderloin steaks, about 1 1/4 pounds
- Salt to taste, if desired
- Freshly ground pepper to taste
- 2 tablespoons flour
- 2 tablespoons olive oil
- 2 tablespoons butter
- 1 tablespoon finely chopped shallots
- ¼ cup dry Marsala or sherry wine
- 4 very thin slices prosciutto, about 2 ounces
- 4 very thin slices Gruyere or Swiss cheese, about 2 ounces

Direction

- Put the turkey slices on a flat surface and pound lightly with a flat mallet. Each should be about 1/4-inch thick.

- Sprinkle the turkey pieces on both sides with salt and pepper.
- Dip the pieces in flour to coat well on both sides. Shake off excess.
- Preheat the broiler to high.
- Heat the oil and butter in a skillet and add the turkey pieces. Cook about 1 1/2 minutes or until lightly browned on one side. Turn and cook about 2 minutes longer, turning the pieces occasionally. Scatter the shallots around the turkey pieces. Cook briefly and add the Marsala. Cook about 1 minute.
- Transfer the turkey pieces to a heatproof dish and pour the wine sauce over all. Cover each piece with a slice of prosciutto. Cover the prosciutto neatly with a slice of cheese.
- Place the covered turkey pieces under the broiler, about 3 inches from the source of heat. Cook until cheese melts, 45 seconds to 1 minute. Serve immediately.

Nutrition Information

- 644: calories;
- 2 grams: polyunsaturated fat;
- 5 grams: carbohydrates;
- 1 gram: sugars;
- 49 grams: fat;
- 0 grams: dietary fiber;
- 21 grams: monounsaturated fat;
- 20 grams: saturated fat;
- 42 grams: protein;
- 545 milligrams: sodium;

351. Vegetables Au Gratin

Serving: 4 or more servings | Prep: | Cook: | Ready in: 30mins

Ingredients

- 1 small eggplant, about 3/4 pound
- 1 yellow squash, about 1/4 pound
- 1 small zucchini, about 1/4 pound
- 7 tablespoons olive oil
- 1 cup finely chopped onions
- 1 teaspoon finely minced garlic
- 1 bay leaf
- Salt to taste if desired
- Fresh pepper to taste
- 3 red ripe plum tomatoes, about 1/2 pound
- ¼ cup freshly grated Parmesan cheese

Direction

- Preheat broiler to high.
- Cut off and discard ends of the eggplant, squash and zucchini. Cut squash and eggplant into very thin rounds. There should be about 2 cups of each. Cut eggplant lengthwise into quarters and cut each quarter into thin slices. There should be about 4 cups.
- Heat 6 tablespoons of oil in a skillet and add eggplant, zucchini and squash slices. Cook, shaking skillet and stirring so slices cook evenly, about 8 minutes. Add onions and garlic and stir to blend. Add bay leaf, salt and pepper. Cover and cook, stirring occasionally, about 3 minutes.
- Meanwhile, cut away and discard core of each tomato. Cut tomatoes crosswise into thin slices.
- Remove and discard bay leaf. Pour cooked vegetables into a baking dish and arrange tomato slices on top to cover. Brush tomatoes with remaining 1 tablespoon oil and sprinkle evenly with cheese.
- Place dish under broiler about 4 inches from heat. Leave broiler door partly open and cook 5 minutes.

Nutrition Information

- 296: calories;
- 26 grams: fat;
- 5 grams: protein;
- 18 grams: monounsaturated fat;
- 14 grams: carbohydrates;
- 4 grams: dietary fiber;
- 6 grams: sugars;

- 3 grams: polyunsaturated fat;
- 630 milligrams: sodium;

352. Warm Barley And Mushroom Salad Over Portobellos

Serving: 4 servings | Prep: | Cook: | Ready in: 1hours40mins

Ingredients

- 3 cups water
- ¾ cup medium pearl barley
- 1 ¾ cups chicken broth
- 2 large shallots, peeled and minced
- 8 cups mixed wild mushrooms, like portobellos and shiitakes, cut into large cubes
- 2 teaspoons chopped fresh sage
- 1 tablespoon chopped fresh rosemary
- 1 ½ teaspoons salt, plus more to taste
- Freshly ground pepper to taste
- 4 large portobello mushrooms
- 1 tablespoon chopped Italian parsley

Direction

- Bring the water to a boil in a medium-size saucepan. Stir in the barley, lower the heat, cover and simmer until tender, about 50 minutes.
- Meanwhile, heat 1/4 cup broth in a large skillet over medium heat until it simmers. Add the shallots and stir until most of the liquid has evaporated, about 2 minutes. Add the mushroom cubes and 1/4 cup of broth. Cook, stirring often, for 5 minutes. Pour in 1 cup of broth and stir, scraping the bottom of the skillet. Bring to a boil. Reduce heat and simmer until the liquid is reduced to a sauce consistency, about 15 minutes. Stir in the sage, rosemary, salt and pepper. Stir in the barley. Keep warm.
- Preheat the broiler. Brush both sides of the portobellos with the remaining 1/4 cup chicken broth. Season the underside lightly with salt and pepper to taste. Broil until softened, about 2 minutes per side. Place 1 mushroom on each of 4 plates and spoon the barley mixture over them. Garnish with parsley and serve immediately.

Nutrition Information

- 270: calories;
- 13 grams: dietary fiber;
- 1062 milligrams: sodium;
- 14 grams: protein;
- 3 grams: fat;
- 1 gram: polyunsaturated fat;
- 0 grams: trans fat;
- 52 grams: carbohydrates;
- 11 grams: sugars;

353. Warm Bread Salad

Serving: 4 servings | Prep: | Cook: | Ready in: 1hours

Ingredients

- 1 tablespoon dried currants
- 1 tablespoon red wine vinegar
- 2 tablespoons pine nuts
- 8 to 10 ounces slightly stale ciabatta or other open-textured white bread
- 8 tablespoons extra virgin olive oil
- 1 ½ tablespoons Champagne vinegar or white wine vinegar, approximately
- Salt and coarsely ground black pepper
- 3 garlic cloves, slivered
- ¼ cup thinly sliced scallions
- 4 tablespoons lightly salted chicken stock or lightly salted water
- 4 cups arugula leaves or mustard greens, rinsed and dried

Direction

- Place currants in a small dish, add red wine vinegar and 1 tablespoon warm water, and set aside. Heat broiler. Place pine nuts in small baking dish, and toast under broiler until very lightly colored. Set aside.
- Cut bread into three or four large chunks. Closely trim off most of the crust and reserve, if desired, to toast and use for bread crumbs or to float in soup. Brush bread all over with 2 tablespoons olive oil. Briefly broil bread chunks, turning until crisp and golden on surface. Remove from oven, trim off any charred tips, and tear chunks into irregular pieces, from 2-inch wads to large crumbs. You should have 4 cups. Place in wide metal, glass or ceramic salad bowl.
- Whisk 1/4 cup olive oil with 1 1/2 tablespoons Champagne vinegar. Season with salt and pepper. Drizzle 1 1/2 tablespoons of this dressing over bread and toss.
- Place one tablespoon olive oil in a small skillet. Add garlic and scallions, and cook, stirring constantly, over low heat until softened but not colored. Add to bread and fold in. Drain currants and fold in. Add pine nuts and fold in. Drizzle salad with stock or water, and fold in. Taste a couple of pieces of bread. Add a little more vinegar, salt and pepper if necessary. Toss well, and transfer to a 4-cup baking dish. Tent lightly with foil. Do not wash salad bowl. Set salad aside until about 30 minutes before serving time.
- Heat oven to 450 degrees. Place bread salad in oven, turn off heat, and leave for 15 minutes. Return salad to bowl. Add greens, remaining vinaigrette, and enough of remaining olive oil so bread is not dry. Toss again. Serve with grilled or roasted meat.

Nutrition Information

- 473: calories;
- 21 grams: monounsaturated fat;
- 38 grams: carbohydrates;
- 32 grams: fat;
- 5 grams: dietary fiber;
- 7 grams: sugars;
- 10 grams: protein;
- 434 milligrams: sodium;
- 4 grams: saturated fat;
- 0 grams: trans fat;

354. Warm Passion Fruit Gratin With Raspberries

Serving: 4 servings | Prep: | Cook: | Ready in: 1hours

Ingredients

- 2 tablespoons unsalted butter at room temperature
- 2 teaspoons arrowroot
- 6 egg yolks
- 2 teaspoons unflavored gelatin
- 8 tablespoons cold water
- 5 ounces passion-fruit juice
- 4 tablespoons heavy cream
- ¾ cup granulated sugar
- 4 egg whites
- 1 pint fresh raspberries
- 1 tablespoon confectioners' sugar for dusting

Direction

- Butter the insides of eight 3 1/2-inch flan rings.
- Line a cookie sheet with parchment paper or wax paper; place rings on top and refrigerate.
- Whisk arrowroot gradually into yolks, beating until smooth.
- Soften gelatin in 2 tablespoons of the water.
- Combine passion-fruit juice and cream in saucepan and bring to boil; remove from heat. Stir a little of the juice mixture into the yolk mixture; then stir all the yolk mixture into the juice mixture. Bring to boil over low heat, stirring constantly. Add gelatin and simmer gently at least 5 minutes, stirring constantly. Mixture will be smooth and as thick as a light pastry cream. Set aside and cover with wax

paper or plastic wrap to keep film from forming.
- Combine sugar and remaining 6 tablespoons water in a small saucepan. Bring to boil; cover and cook 3 minutes. Remove lid and cook to 275 degrees on a candy thermometer.
- In a large bowl, beat egg whites to soft peaks. Slowly beat sugar syrup into whites and continue beating until mixture is barely warm and glossy.
- Fold warm cream mixture into meringue mixture. Half-fill each ring mold with this mixture, burying 8 to 10 raspberries inside; then completely cover berries with the remaining mixture. Reserve some berries for garnish if desired.
- Refrigerate at least 4 hours in advance, and as long as 24 hours.
- To prepare for serving, preheat broiler. Dust each ring with confectioners' sugar. Arrange rings on oven-proof tray. Glaze briefly under broiler. Watch carefully.
- Slip the molds onto serving plates and serve immediately.

Nutrition Information

- 393: calories;
- 47 grams: sugars;
- 9 grams: protein;
- 0 grams: trans fat;
- 6 grams: monounsaturated fat;
- 53 grams: carbohydrates;
- 67 milligrams: sodium;
- 17 grams: fat;
- 2 grams: polyunsaturated fat;
- 5 grams: dietary fiber;

355. Warm Plums With Cinnamon Toast And Red Plum Sorbet

Serving: 4 servings | Prep: | Cook: |Ready in: 1hours30mins

Ingredients

- For the sorbet:
- ¾ pound ripe red plums, pitted and chopped
- ⅓ cup plus 2 tablespoons water
- ½ cup sugar
- ½ teaspoon vanilla extract
- 1 teaspoon fresh lemon juice
- For the plums and cinnamon toast:
- 6 large plums, underripe, halved and pitted
- ½ cup sugar
- ⅓ cup water
- ¾ teaspoon ground cinnamon
- 4 large slices white bread, toasted, crusts removed
- 2 tablespoons unsalted butter, softened

Direction

- Make the sorbet: Combine chopped plums and 2 tablespoons of the water in a heavy saucepan. Cook over medium-low heat until soft, about 15 minutes. Transfer to a blender and puree until smooth, set aside.
- Place the remaining water and sugar in a clean saucepan and boil for 4 minutes. Combine plum puree, sugar syrup, vanilla extract and lemon juice in a glass or ceramic bowl. Refrigerate until chilled. Pour the mixture into an ice-cream maker and proceed according to manufacturer's directions.
- Prepare the plums: preheat the oven to 350 degrees. Place the halved plums, cut side up, in an earthenware dish or heavy skillet. Sprinkle with the sugar and water, and dust with 1/2 teaspoon of the cinnamon. Bake until tender, about 25 minutes. Remove from oven and keep warm.
- Meanwhile, make the cinnamon toast. Preheat the broiler. Place the toast on a baking sheet.

Spread with butter and dust with the remaining cinnamon. Broil just until the butter starts to bubble, about 2 minutes. Remove and set aside.
- To assemble the dessert, arrange 3 plum halves like flower petals on each of four dessert plates. Place a small scoop of sorbet in the middle, drizzle with a spoonful of the plum juices and serve with cinnamon toast.

Nutrition Information

- 440: calories;
- 4 grams: saturated fat;
- 2 grams: monounsaturated fat;
- 1 gram: polyunsaturated fat;
- 5 grams: protein;
- 8 grams: fat;
- 0 grams: trans fat;
- 92 grams: carbohydrates;
- 73 grams: sugars;
- 187 milligrams: sodium;

356. Warm White Bean And Shrimp Salad With Lime Vinaigrette

Serving: Four servings | Prep: | Cook: | Ready in: 1hours10mins

Ingredients

- The beans:
- 1 teaspoon olive oil
- 1 medium onion, peeled and diced
- 1 cup Great Northern beans, soaked overnight and drained
- 7 cups water
- 1 medium-size ancho chili
- 1 teaspoon salt, plus more to taste
- Freshly ground pepper to taste
- 2 teaspoons chopped cilantro
- The vinaigrette:
- 1 large clove garlic, peeled and minced
- 2 tablespoons fresh lime juice
- 3 tablespoons olive oil
- 1/8 teaspoon salt
- Freshly ground pepper to taste
- The shrimp:
- 1/2 cup sesame seeds
- 1/4 cup cumin seeds
- 1/2 teaspoon salt, plus more to taste
- Olive oil spray
- 1 pound large shrimp, peeled and deveined
- 2 egg whites, lightly beaten
- 1 lime, halved

Direction

- To make the beans, heat the olive oil in a large saucepan over medium heat. Add the onion and cook until soft, about 5 minutes. Add the beans and water and bring to a boil. Reduce heat so the liquid simmers and cook until the beans are tender, about 1 hour. Drain and season with the salt and pepper to taste.
- Meanwhile, place the chili in a saucepan and cover with water. Simmer until the chili is soft, about 5 minutes. Stem and seed the chili. Cut into small dice and set aside.
- To make the dressing, whisk together the garlic, lime juice, olive oil, salt and pepper. Set aside.
- To make the shrimp, heat a small skillet over medium heat. Add sesame seeds and shake pan until seeds are toasted, about 20 seconds. Place in a bowl. Place cumin seeds in the skillet and toast for about 15 seconds. Place in a spice grinder and pulse until cracked but not ground. Stir together sesame and cumin seeds and 1/2 teaspoon salt.
- Preheat broiler. Spray a baking sheet with the olive oil. One at a time, dip the shrimp into the egg whites and then coat with the sesame seed mixture. Place on the prepared baking sheet. Broil the shrimp until cooked through and nicely browned, about 3 minutes per side. Season with additional salt and squeeze the lime juice over the shrimp.

- Place the warm beans in a large bowl. Stir in the chili and toss with the vinaigrette. Season with additional salt if needed. Divide the salad among 4 plates and top with shrimp. Garnish with the cilantro and serve.

Nutrition Information

- 440: calories;
- 1640 milligrams: sodium;
- 25 grams: fat;
- 6 grams: polyunsaturated fat;
- 32 grams: carbohydrates;
- 3 grams: sugars;
- 9 grams: dietary fiber;
- 27 grams: protein;
- 4 grams: saturated fat;
- 0 grams: trans fat;
- 14 grams: monounsaturated fat;

357. Watermelon & Tomato Salsa

Serving: Makes 3 cups | Prep: | Cook: | Ready in: 30mins

Ingredients

- 2 cups finely diced watermelon (about 6 ounces)
- 1 cup finely chopped tomatoes (about 1/2 pound)
- ¾ cup finely diced jicama
- 1 to 2 serrano chiles, minced (to taste)
- Salt to taste
- 1 to 2 tablespoons fresh lime juice (to taste)
- 1 to 2 tablespoons fresh lime juice (to taste)

Direction

- Combine all the ingredients in a medium bowl and stir together. Let sit for 15 to 30 minutes before serving.

Nutrition Information

- 23: calories;
- 6 grams: carbohydrates;
- 1 gram: protein;
- 3 grams: sugars;
- 210 milligrams: sodium;
- 0 grams: polyunsaturated fat;

358. Welsh Rabbit

Serving: Four servings | Prep: | Cook: | Ready in: 15mins

Ingredients

- 1 pound Cheddar cheese
- 2 tablespoons butter
- 2 tablespoons light ale
- 1 teaspoon English mustard (see recipe)
- ½ teaspoon Worcestershire sauce
- Salt to taste, if desired
- Freshly ground pepper to taste
- 4 slices buttered toast (see recipe)

Direction

- Preheat the broiler to high.
- Grate the cheese coarsely. There should be about two cups.
- Melt the butter in a heavy saucepan and add the cheese. Stir briefly and add the ale. Continue cooking over low heat, stirring, until the cheese is thoroughly melted and smooth. Add the mustard, Worcestershire sauce, salt and pepper.
- Arrange the toast slices in four fairly shallow ramekins. Spoon an equal amount of the rabbit on top of each. Place under the broiler, and broil until bubbling and lightly browned. Serve immediately.

Nutrition Information

- 592: calories;
- 1 gram: dietary fiber;

- 897 milligrams: sodium;
- 45 grams: fat;
- 2 grams: sugars;
- 11 grams: monounsaturated fat;
- 16 grams: carbohydrates;
- 31 grams: protein;
- 26 grams: saturated fat;

- 358: calories;
- 4 grams: monounsaturated fat;
- 3 grams: carbohydrates;
- 63 grams: protein;
- 1 gram: dietary fiber;
- 0 grams: sugars;
- 773 milligrams: sodium;
- 9 grams: fat;
- 2 grams: polyunsaturated fat;

359. Whole Baked Fish, Moroccan Style

Serving: 4-6 servings | Prep: | Cook: | Ready in: 2hours30mins

Ingredients

- 1 bunch fresh coriander
- 2 cloves garlic
- 2 tablespoons vinegar
- Juice of 1 lemon or lime
- 1 tablespoon paprika
- 1 tablespoon cumin
- ½ teaspoon crushed chili
- Coarse salt and freshly ground pepper to taste
- 2 tablespoons olive oil
- 1 4-pound whole fish such as striped bass, sea bass, red snapper, head and tail intact

Direction

- Reserving a few sprigs of coriander for garnishing, combine all the ingredients except the fish in an electric blender and mix until smooth. With a sharp knife, make three slashes in the skin. Smear the mixture in the fish cavity and over the skin. Leave to marinate at room temperature for about 2 hours.
- Broil the fish for about 10 minutes on each side, depending on the thickness of the fish, or until cooked. Arrange on a serving platter, garnish with coriander and lemon slices.

Nutrition Information

360. Whole Roasted Cauliflower With Romesco

Serving: 4 servings | Prep: | Cook: | Ready in: 1hours45mins

Ingredients

- 3 red bell peppers
- 1 medium-to-large head cauliflower
- Olive oil
- Salt and pepper
- ½ cup Marcona almonds
- 1 small garlic clove, peeled
- 1 tablespoon sherry vinegar

Direction

- Fill a large pot 2/3 of the way with water, and set to boil; turn on the broiler, and put the rack about 4 inches from the heat source. Put the peppers on a foil-lined baking sheet, and broil, turning as each side browns, until they have darkened and collapsed, 15 to 20 minutes. Wrap the peppers in the same foil that lined the pan; when they are cool enough to handle, remove the skins, seeds and stems (this is easiest under running water). Set aside.
- Move oven rack to the lowest setting. Heat the oven to 450. Remove the leaves from the cauliflower. When the water boils, salt it generously. Submerge the head of cauliflower in the water, reduce the heat to a simmer and cook until you can easily insert a knife into the center, 15 minutes or more. Don't overcook.

- Using two spoons or a shallow strainer, transfer the cauliflower to a rimmed baking sheet, and pat dry with paper towels. Drizzle all over with olive oil, sprinkle with salt and roast until it's nicely browned all over, 40 to 50 minutes.
- Meanwhile, combine the roasted red peppers, almonds, garlic, vinegar and a sprinkle of salt and pepper in a food processor. Turn the machine on and stream in 1/4 cup olive oil; purée into a thick paste. Taste, and adjust the seasoning.
- When the cauliflower is browned, transfer it to a serving platter. Cut it into slices or wedges, and serve the romesco on the side for dipping.

Nutrition Information

- 202: calories;
- 13 grams: fat;
- 1 gram: saturated fat;
- 0 grams: trans fat;
- 8 grams: protein;
- 3 grams: polyunsaturated fat;
- 17 grams: carbohydrates;
- 611 milligrams: sodium;
- 7 grams: sugars;

361. Wolfgang Puck's Salmon With Celery Root Puree

Serving: Four servings | Prep: | Cook: | Ready in: 50mins

Ingredients

- The sauce:
- 6 tablespoons unsalted butter
- 1 shallot, chopped
- 1 clove garlic, minced
- 1 tomato, peeled, seeded and chopped
- ½ bottle cabernet sauvignon
- 2 tablespoons balsamic vinegar
- 1 cup chicken stock
- Salt and freshly ground pepper to taste
- The celery-root puree:
- 1 medium-sized baking potato, peeled
- 1 celery root, peeled
- ½ cup heavy cream
- 2 tablespoons butter
- Salt and freshly ground pepper to taste
- The salmon:
- 1 ½ tablespoons fresh ginger, finely minced
- 1 ½ tablespoons black pepper, chopped or roughly cracked
- 4 salmon fillets, Alaskan King or other, each about 6 ounces
- Olive oil for grilling or sauteing

Direction

- To make the sauce, heat two tablespoons of the butter in a large saute pan until the butter is foamy. Add the shallot, garlic and tomato and saute at medium-low heat for about five minutes, or until the shallot is translucent.
- Add the wine and vinegar and cook over medium-high heat until reduced by half. Add the chicken stock and reduce again by half. Finish the sauce by stirring in the remaining four tablespoons of butter, one tablespoon at a time. Season with salt and freshly round pepper to taste. Keep warm.
- Prepare the celery-root puree by chopping the potato and celery root into one-inch cubes. Put in a medium-sized pot and cover with lightly salted cold water. When the water comes to a boil, cook for 15 to 20 minutes, or until soft. Drain and return the potato and celery root to the pot. Heat briefly until the excess moisture evaporates.
- Pass the celery Root-potato mixture through the small disk of a food mill or a ricer. (Do not use a food processor; it will make a gluey puree.) Return to the pot.
- Stir in the cream and cook, stirring, over medium heat for about three minutes, or until thickened.
- Remove from the heat. Stir in the butter and the salt and pepper to taste.
- In a small bowl, combine the ginger and black pepper. Season the salmon with salt and coat

with the ginger-pepper mixture. If grilling or broiling the salmon, sprinkle the fillets with olive oil and cook two minutes on each side. If sauteing the salmon, heat one tablespoon of olive oil in a large saute pan. When the pan is very hot, add the salmon and cook two minutes on each side.
- Divide the sauce among four warm dinner plates. Spoon equal amounts of celery-root puree on the center of each plate. Place salmon on top.

362. Yakitori Chicken With Ginger, Garlic And Soy Sauce

Serving: 6 appetizer servings | Prep: | Cook: | Ready in: 15mins

Ingredients

- 1 pound chicken livers, gizzards or boneless thigh meat
- ½ cup dark soy sauce or tamari
- ¼ cup mirin
- 2 tablespoons sake or dry sherry
- 1 tablespoon brown sugar
- 2 garlic cloves, peeled and smashed
- ½ teaspoon grated fresh ginger
- Scallions, thinly sliced, for garnish

Direction

- Cut chicken into one-inch pieces and place in a shallow dish.
- In a small saucepan, combine soy sauce or tamari, mirin, sake or sherry, brown sugar, garlic and ginger. Bring to a simmer and cook for 7 minutes, until thickened. Reserve 2 tablespoons sauce for serving. Pour remaining sauce over chicken, cover, and chill for at least one hour (and up to 4 hours).
- If using wooden or bamboo skewers, soak them in water for one hour. Preheat grill or broiler. Thread chicken pieces onto skewers, and grill or broil, turning halfway, for about 3 minutes for livers, 10 minutes for gizzards and 6 minutes for thighs. Serve drizzled with reserved sauce and garnished with scallions.

Nutrition Information

- 136: calories;
- 4 grams: carbohydrates;
- 2 grams: sugars;
- 0 grams: dietary fiber;
- 18 grams: protein;
- 1228 milligrams: sodium;

363. Yellow Fruited Rice With Fish

Serving: 2 servings | Prep: | Cook: | Ready in: 35mins

Ingredients

- 4 ounces whole onion or 3 ounces chopped ready-cut onion (1 cup)
- 1 teaspoon olive oil
- ¾ cup long-grain rice
- 1 ½ cups no-salt-added chicken stock
- ½ teaspoon turmeric or 1/4 teaspoon saffron threads
- 10-ounce piece of salmon, swordfish or tuna
- 1 tablespoon lime juice
- ¼ cup dried cherries
- 1 ½ scallions
- 1 ripe banana
- ¼ teaspoon salt
- Pinch nutmeg

Direction

- Insert a double thickness of aluminum foil in broiler, and preheat.
- Chop whole onion.
- In a very hot nonstick pan, heat oil; saute onion over medium-high heat until it begins to soften and brown. Stir in rice, stock and turmeric; bring to boil, reduce heat, cover, and

- cook 17 minutes, until rice is tender and liquid has been absorbed.
- After the rice has been cooking for about 5 minutes, wash and dry the fish, and place it in the broiler. Measure the fish at the thickest part and cook 8 to 10 minutes to the inch. For thick cuts, like swordfish or tuna, turn fish halfway through broiling.
- Squeeze lime juice over cherries; set aside.
- Wash, trim and slice scallions; cut banana into small cubes.
- When rice is cooked, stir in cherries with the lime juice, scallions, banana, salt and nutmeg, and serve with fish.

Nutrition Information

- 782: calories;
- 5 grams: saturated fat;
- 0 grams: trans fat;
- 8 grams: monounsaturated fat;
- 6 grams: polyunsaturated fat;
- 98 grams: carbohydrates;
- 40 grams: protein;
- 24 grams: fat;
- 4 grams: dietary fiber;
- 26 grams: sugars;
- 643 milligrams: sodium;

364. Yellow Tomato Gazpacho With Goat Cheese Croutons

Serving: 6 servings | Prep: | Cook: | Ready in: 30mins

Ingredients

- 1 clove garlic
- 2 pounds yellow tomatoes, peeled, seeded and coarsely chopped
- 1 yellow bell pepper, cored, seeded and coarsely chopped
- 1 cucumber, peeled, seeded and coarsely chopped
- 1 bunch scallions (about 6), trimmed, white part only, chopped
- ¼ cup extra virgin olive oil
- ¼ teaspoon ground cumin
- 1 tablespoon mayonnaise
- Juice of 1 lemon
- ¼ cup Champagne vinegar
- 12-inch piece baguette
- Salt
- 3 ounces fresh goat-cheese log
- 1 cup cooked fresh yellow corn kernels (1 ear of corn)

Direction

- Turn on food processor. Drop in garlic and process to chop fine. Add tomatoes, bell pepper, cucumber, scallions, oil, cumin, mayonnaise, lemon juice and vinegar. Cut 6 thin slices from baguette and set aside. Remove crusts from the rest. Crumble the insides and add to food processor. Add 1 cup cold water. Pulse to chop very fine.
- Transfer to a blender and purée. You will probably have to do this in two or three shifts. Place purée in a metal bowl. Cover and refrigerate until very cold. Season with salt.
- Toast one side of reserved bread slices under a broiler. Turn slices over and top each with a slice of goat cheese. Place under broiler until cheese is very lightly browned. To serve, place soup in bowls, top each with a goat cheese crouton and a scattering of corn.

Nutrition Information

- 219: calories;
- 749 milligrams: sodium;
- 4 grams: saturated fat;
- 0 grams: trans fat;
- 2 grams: sugars;
- 18 grams: carbohydrates;
- 6 grams: protein;
- 15 grams: fat;
- 8 grams: monounsaturated fat;
- 3 grams: dietary fiber;

365. Zucchini With Parmesan Cheese

Serving: 4 servings | Prep: | Cook: | Ready in: 10mins

Ingredients

- 4 medium-size zucchini, trimmed, about 1 1/4 pounds
- 2 tablespoons olive oil
- ¼ cup sliced white onions
- Salt and freshly ground pepper to taste
- 2 teaspoons finely chopped garlic
- 4 tablespoons coarsely chopped basil
- 4 tablespoons grated Parmesan cheese, or Gruyere

Direction

- Preheat broiler.
- Cut the zucchini into even slices about 1/8 inch thick.
- Heat the olive oil in a large nonstick skillet over high heat. Add the zucchini, onions, salt and pepper. Cook, stirring, for 3 to 4 minutes or until wilted.
- Add the garlic and the basil. Blend well and cook for a few minutes, but do not brown the garlic.
- Transfer to an ovenproof dish. Smooth the top and sprinkle evenly with the cheese. Place under broiler until brown. Serve with the chicken.

Nutrition Information

- 145: calories;
- 7 grams: protein;
- 3 grams: saturated fat;
- 1 gram: polyunsaturated fat;
- 4 grams: sugars;
- 406 milligrams: sodium;
- 11 grams: fat;
- 6 grams: carbohydrates;
- 2 grams: dietary fiber;

Index

A
Ale 172
Almond 6,150
Anise 7,190
Apple 7,193
Apricot 3,5,30,130
Artichoke 3,5,11,42,125
Asparagus 3,6,12,46,181,182
Avocado 4,6,7,60,164,204

B
Bacon 6,7,154,198,221
Balsamic vinegar 12,149
Barley 8,229
Basil 5,7,111,186
Beans 6,7,163,174,175,195
Beef 3,4,5,6,7,19,68,73,132,183,219,220
Black pepper 32,34,65,67,136,151,178,180,181,195,224
Bratwurst 3,23
Bread 4,6,7,8,48,69,92,146,191,215,224,229
Brie 72,144,230
Brisket 5,126
Broccoli 3,6,7,23,166,199
Burger 3,4,7,9,68,118,199
Butter 3,4,5,7,35,38,53,64,65,69,76,77,98,117,122,141,150,202,230

C
Cake 3,5,7,29,127,197,198
Capers 4,58,133
Caramel 193
Carrot 3,4,44,86
Cauliflower 8,234
Caviar 7,188
Cayenne pepper 47,81,119,132
Celery 3,8,40,45,235
Champ 4,5,80,137,196,229,230,237
Chard 4,78
Cheddar 4,40,47,76,132,198,199,200,226,233
Cheese 3,4,5,6,7,8,13,14,15,28,47,56,64,84,93,98,117,120,131,146,157,158,185,198,199,226,227,237,238
Cherry 4,48
Chicken 3,4,5,6,7,8,16,24,25,26,33,39,49,50,51,52,53,54,66,70,93,94,95,102,120,138,146,180,184,193,194,196,205,236
Chipotle 4,54
Chips 4,82
Chopped tomatoes 195
Chorizo 7,224
Chutney 4,46
Cinnamon 3,8,16,231
Clams 5,7,118,209
Coconut 3,33
Cod 3,4,5,13,20,65,126
Cognac 175
Coriander 3,5,7,19,110,112,186
Couscous 3,4,37,81
Crab 4,6,7,61,62,161,202
Cream 3,4,6,9,63,77,119,161
Crostini 4,7,47,65,202
Crumble 58,195,237
Cucumber 7,188
Cumin 4,66,67
Curd 3,40
Curry 3,4,5,24,68,128

Custard 6,159

D

Dab 118

Date 3,46

Demerara sugar 16

Dijon mustard 18,19,38,47,55,64,70,93,96,107,130,133,146,149,178,181,185,199,227

Dill 4,84,86

Duck 3,5,7,27,41,96,124,210

E

Egg 3,4,5,6,7,46,57,72,73,74,75,76,85,98,136,139,140,142,157,165,198,200,217

English muffin 140

English mustard 233

F

Fennel 3,4,7,28,63,193

Feta 4,7,73,195,204

Fig 4,77

Fish 3,4,5,6,8,29,79,82,97,140,234,236

Flank 5,98

Flatbread 6,147

Flour 143

French bread 65,86,96,185

Fruit 3,7,8,40,210,230,236

Fusilli 4,73

G

Garlic 3,4,5,6,7,8,46,52,57,79,86,90,117,138,151,211,236

Gin 3,4,7,8,25,29,44,87,190,236

Gorgonzola 7,224

Grapes 7,194

Gratin 3,4,5,6,8,10,39,45,61,74,77,89,90,125,144,145,159,166,174,225,228,230

Guacamole 4,7,91,223

H

Halibut 5,6,116,149

Halloumi 5,116

Ham 4,5,7,9,88,117,134,222

Harissa 5,118,121

Hazelnut 3,23

Heart 3,11

Herbs 5,7,113,185,224

Horseradish 6,7,154,188,202

J

Jerusalem artichoke 125

Jus 88,119,168,174,186,201,216,222

K

Kale 7,203

Ketchup 76

Kohlrabi 7,190

L

Lamb 3,4,5,6,7,21,30,46,67,68,87,88,99,101,102,103,109,127,128,129,130,136,142,158,168,181,186,203,221

Leek 3,5,6,44,100,166

Lemon 3,4,7,8,26,34,63,71,78,151,184,189,214,226

Lettuce 59,150

Lime 3,5,8,21,29,33,35,51,92,94,232

Ling 7,189

Lobster 3,5,31,132

M

Macaroni 5,7,131,132,199

Mackerel 3,32

Madeira 96,125

Manchego 56

Mango 5,112,133

Mascarpone 6,159

Mayonnaise 3,7,8,18,211,226

Meat 4,5,6,61,67,124,150,168

Melon 3,5,32,95

Meringue 6,160

Mesclun 5,137

Mince 33,53,55,70,73,79,204,206

Mint 6,7,179,206,220

Miso 3,6,20,139,140,149,154

Monkfish 6,141

Morel 5,115

Mushroom 3,6,7,8,34,144,155,199,203,218,229

Mustard 3,5,6,18,101,133,146,168,169

N

Nut 4,5,7,9,10,11,12,13,14,16,17,18,19,20,21,22,23,24,25,26,27,28,29,30,31,32,33,34,35,36,37,38,39,40,41,43,44,45,46,47,48,49,51,52,53,54,55,56,57,58,59,60,61,62,63,64,65,66,67,68,69,70,72,73,74,75,76,77,78,79,80,81,82,83,84,85,86,87,88,89,90,91,92,93,94,95,96,97,99,101,102,103,104,105,106,107,108,109,110,111,113,114,115,116,117,118,119,120,121,122,123,124,125,126,127,128,129,130,131,132,133,134,135,136,137,138,139,140,141,142,143,144,145,146,147,148,149,151,152,153,154,155,157,158,159,160,161,162,163,164,165,166,167,168,169,170,171,173,174,176,177,179,180,181,182,183,185,186,187,188,189,190,191,192,193,194,195,197,198,199,200,201,202,204,205,206,207,208,209,210,212,213,214,215,216,217,218,220,221,222,223,224,225,226,227,228,229,230,231,232,233,234,235,236,237,238

O

Oatmeal 6,150

Oil 5,7,42,50,97,111,122,212

Olive 4,7,54,55,57,67,72,83,109,121,146,168,182,189,191,232,234,235

Onion 3,4,6,7,36,75,151,170,173,184,193,204

Orange 3,4,6,7,27,35,79,150,152,169,188,193

Oregano 7,195

Oyster 3,4,5,6,7,33,80,106,154,202

P

Paella 4,70

Papaya 4,91

Paprika 133

Parmesan 3,4,6,7,8,11,13,14,15,22,28,37,42,45,49,56,62,63,65,74,89,90,104,124,131,132,137,142,143,144,157,158,161,162,166,171,182,191,192,217,228,238

Parsley 5,6,118,140,158,178

Pasta 4,6,7,75,161,204

Peach 5,130

Peanut oil 183

Pear 6,159,160

Peas 4,63

Pecan 5,96

Peel 14,20,36,45,64,84,100,103,112,122,133,149,151,160,171,185

Penne 6,161

Pepper 3,4,5,6,7,12,19,31,58,113,119,128,130,137,143,149,161,162,163,176,183,185,191,206,210,212,215

Pesto 4,5,48,116,118

Pickle 6,163

Pie 200,219

Pineapple 3,4,6,7,36,93,164,184,216,221

Pizza 6,156

Plum 8,231

Polenta 5,6,104,119,166,167

Pomegranate 6,168

Porcini 4,65

Pork

3,4,5,6,7,17,43,81,87,105,130,135,152,168,169,171,172,177,218

Port 3,4,6,8,34,58,155,229

Potato 3,4,5,6,7,8,14,23,39,44,63,83,109,127,149,170,171,185,192,198,212,225

Prosciutto 4,7,8,83,156,212,226,227

Pulse 76,151,237

Pumpkin 6,172,173

Q

Quail 5,6,103,105,106,107,174,175

R

Rabbit 8,233

Radicchio 7,217

Red Leicester 5

Rhubarb 6,7,164,222

Rice 6,7,8,175,186,236

Ricotta 3,6,15,179

Rock salt 33,80

Rosemary 3,19

Rum 6,184

S

Saffron 6,185

Sage 5,107

Salad 3,4,5,6,7,8,9,23,24,37,38,52,55,57,59,82,86,91,92,93,96,107,109,114,124,137,148,149,153,163,178,185,186,204,206,208,217,219,220,224,229,232

Salmon 3,4,5,7,8,15,82,107,108,133,187,188,189,235

Salsa 3,5,6,7,8,33,36,95,110,112,164,190,215,216,233

Salt 3,9,10,11,13,14,15,17,19,20,21,24,25,26,27,28,29,32,33,34,35,36,37,38,41,44,45,46,48,50,52,53,57,58,59,61,62,65,66,69,70,72,74,76,77,78,83,84,85,90,91,92,94,95,96,100,101,102,106,107,108,109,112,113,114,115,117,118,119,120,125,126,127,128,129,131,132,133,134,139,141,142,144,146,151,153,154,155,156,157,158,162,163,164,165,166,169,170,171,173,174,175,176,179,182,183,185,188,190,192,197,198,199,200,201,203,206,209,210,212,214,216,217,218,221,223,225,226,227,228,229,233,234,235,237,238

Sardine 3,34

Sausage 4,5,7,54,103,111,190,191

Savory 7,191

Scallop 3,4,5,6,35,58,109,139

Sea salt 121,178

Seafood 4,60

Seaweed 4,82

Seeds 5,7,10,101,208

Shallot 5,7,117,194

Sherry 3,19,213

Sichuan pepper 27,31,215

Snapper 6,176

Sorbet 8,231

Sorrel 4,6,7,83,165,187

Soup 3,5,6,7,44,124,144,145,151,173,185,197

Spinach 3,4,6,7,13,62,145,179,196,206

Squash 4,7,90,201

Squid 7,208

Steak 3,4,5,6,7,8,19,36,53,86,98,116,133,178,188,219,221,225

Stew 4,6,60,63,178

Sugar 3,7,16,156,210

Swiss chard 78,79,109,192

Swordfish 5,7,112,213,214,215,216

T

Tabasco 17,18,28,29,37,44,70,175,204

Taco 3,7,29,201

Tahini 4,67

Taleggio 3,39

Tamari 7,218

Tapioca 3,4,16,77

Tarragon 3,5,7,44,128,188

Tea 174,206

Teriyaki 4,51

Thyme 3,7,34,187

Tomatillo 4,5,7,59,112,223

Tomato 3,4,5,6,7,8,26,32,36,49,57,74,75,100,120,136,146,153,167, 187,195,201,210,223,224,233,237

Truffle 3,4,19,65

Turkey 5,8,124,226,227

Turmeric 5,94

Turnip 3,4,27,83

V

Veal 3,5,38,114,115

Vegetable oil 120,149,210

Vegetables 3,6,8,15,22,167,228

Vinegar 3,6,26,155,169

W

Walnut 4,5,86,123

Watermelon 8,233

Wine 5,6,129,178

Worcestershire sauce 17,55,93,94,96,98,233

Z

Zest 87,92,141

Conclusion

Thank you again for downloading this book!

I hope you enjoyed reading about my book!

If you enjoyed this book, please take the time to share your thoughts and post a review on Amazon. It'd be greatly appreciated!

Write me an honest review about the book – I truly value your opinion and thoughts and I will incorporate them into my next book, which is already underway.

Thank you!

If you have any questions, **feel free to contact at:** *author@thymerecipes.com*

Linda Crawford

thymerecipes.com

Made in United States
North Haven, CT
16 January 2025